Violence in Early Islam

Violence in Early Islam

Religious Narratives, the Arab Conquests and the Canonization of Jihad

Marco Demichelis

I.B.TAURIS
LONDON • NEW YORK • OXFORD • NEW DELHI • SYDNEY

I.B. TAURIS
Bloomsbury Publishing Plc
50 Bedford Square, London, WC1B 3DP, UK
1385 Broadway, New York, NY 10018, USA
29 Earlsfort Terrace, Dublin 2, Ireland

BLOOMSBURY, I.B. TAURIS and the I.B. Tauris logo are trademarks of
Bloomsbury Publishing Plc

First published in Great Britain 2021
This paperback edition published 2022

Series design by Adriana Brioso
Cover image: Citadel of Aleppo, Syria. (© dmitriymoroz/Getty Images)

A catalogue record for this book is available from the British Library.

A catalog record for this book is available from the Library of Congress.

ISBN: HB: 978-0-7556-3799-7
PB: 978-0-7556-3803-1
ePDF: 978-0-7556-3800-0
ePUB: 978-0-7556-3801-7

Typeset by Integra Software Services Pvt. Ltd.

To Enea *(my son)*

Contents

Preface viii
Acknowledgements xii

Introduction 1

Part 1
1 The Arabs outside Arabia and before Islām 15
2 *Ghazawāt* and *Futūḥ* 41
3 The religious factor: When did an Islamic identity emerge? 67
4 Can we still consider the *Futūḥ* Islamic? 93

Part 2
5 Qur'ān, otherness and Jihād 111
6 The Qur'ān and militant violence in chronology 127
7 The evolutionary process of belligerency and the canonization of *Jihād* in early Islām 151

Conclusions 167

Notes 171
Bibliography 216
Appendix 239
Index 240
Index of Qur'anic Passages 252

Preface

Deradicalizing Jihād

A few years ago, El Sayed M.A. Amin published an essay entitled 'Reclaiming Jihad. A Qur'anic Critique of Terrorism' (2014) in which he underlined the incoherence existing between *Jihād* and *Ḥirābah*. More explicitly, the author focused his attention on verse 60 of the sūrah *al-'Anfāl*: 'Prepare against them whatever forces you [believers] can muster, including warhorses, to frighten off [these] enemies of God and of yours, and warn others unknown to you but know God. Whatever you give in God's cause will be repaid to you in full, and you will not be wronged', and the connotation that *turḥibūna* (to frighten off) and *quwwah* (power/strength) assumed over the centuries: from al-Ṭabarī, Ibn Khatīr and al-Rāzī up to contemporary authors such as Muṣṭafā Zayd (d. 1978) and S. Quṭb (d. 1966), stressing the evolutionary hermeneutical attitude towards an important topic for inter-religious debate.

It is important to emphasize that Sayed Amin, who underlined the works of contemporary authors such as 'Abd al-Raḥmān Spīndārī, M. Mutawallī al-Sha'rāwī (d. 1998), Yūsuf al-Qaraḍāwī etc., argues that those who claimed that 'Terrorism is part of Islām and whoever denies it automatically becomes an unbeliever' assume a decontextualizing procedure, both in relation to the meaning that these terms have had over the centuries, and in reference to today's situation, '*kharijitely*' supposing a black-and-white radical vision as bringing fragmentation and sectarianism to the entire Islamic *Ummah*.

However, to discuss why an Egyptian scholar has felt the need to write on this topic is a clear, rhetorical and rather naïve question, but also closely linked to the Islamophobic attitude promoted in the past few decades in the West, and to the over-fundamentalist Wahhābī-inspired approach, which arose in the late twentieth century in the Arab-Islamic world.

Political-economic and ideological-religious ends stand behind this over-violent contemporary Islamic narrative and remained at the margin of this publication. On the contrary, the first and the second part of this book highlight the historical and hermeneutical reasons why the Islamic narrative, framed since the eighth century, on the canonization of *Jihād*, needs to be amply reconsidered in relation to how the conceptualization of the *Just War* is differently identified in a more multidisciplinary and methodological approach based on the humanities.

Sayed Amin probably felt the need to write an academic work that could reach the entire 'world' in clarifying the huge disconnection between *Jihād* and Terrorism, as between Islām and *Ḥirābah*; my intention, on the other hand, is to focus on a "deradicalizing" historical and hermeneutical approach to the relationship between *Jihād* and Just/Holy War in showing up the non-existence of a concept of belligerent sainthood in the seventh century as well as of a just Muslim warrior from the beginning of the Arab conquering campaigns in the same period.

The ongoing common '*adage*' that Islām and inter-religious violence have been reciprocally engaged since the beginning of its history as well as in its formative thought is something on which it is important to reflect with a solid foundation, in particular today, when the ideology of the 'Clash of Civilisations', the over-religious revanchism in the United States and in the Middle East, and the huge increase of Islamic Terrorism (from the 1980s onwards) have had an impact on the life of the world and the 'West' as well.

A wise approach would require clarification of the contemporary reasons for the first suicide attạcks on buses by Ḥamās against Israeli civilians in 1993 to the most recent ones in Madrid, London, Paris, Barcelona etc. and in the entire Islamic world, which have increased hugely, causing thousands of casualties, 90 per cent of whom, it is important to recall, are Muslims.

The advent of an ideology of 'Global Jihadism' should be concretely considered more in relation to the debate on the importance that Orientalism and Colonialism had in the nineteenth century as well as in the new contemporary Occidentalist narratives during the Cold War, than in relation to the early Arab conquering *ghazawāt* (raids) of the first century.

However, these historical narratives on the relationship between Islām and Violence against non-Muslims have been completely reshaped in the age of social media, showing the 'fake' idea that everything that is attributable to Islām is violence, or, worse, that this religion has been historically cruel to religious otherness ever since the beginning of its existence.

I expect to find this trivial reasoning in magazines, in right-wing newspapers, in social network groups, in the populist speeches of politicians, even in pseudo-academics' books; what is harder to consider is the 'incredible lightness of the doubt' which emerges, on the contrary, in prominent works by academic scholars who continue to assume that Islām existed from the death of Prophet Muḥammad (632), that the Qur'ān was completely assembled a few decades later and that the famous conquests were already Arab-Islamic and imbued with a religious conceptualization of *Jihād* as Holy/Just War.

This narrative not only presents countless historical and methodological errors, but today has been exploited by Islamophobic and racist positions, generating the common idea that Islām and an inter-religious *Convivencia* have always been impossible.

Replying through mutual awareness, 'deradicalizing Jihād' infers the need to go back to the origin of the meaning of this term, its early adoption in warfare, but also outside it, the earliest written texts of reference, and its relationship with the formative age of an Arab-Islamic identity.

The most important aspect to consider is the relationship in the Late Ancient era between the previous holders of power: the Byzantines and the Sasanians with the new ones, the Arabs who, like the Germanic populations close to the Western Roman Empire's border, were already known and enlisted in the imperial armies and partially Romanized and Hellenized (the Germans, not the Army).

As Robert G. Hoyland assumes in the Introduction of *In God's Path. The Arab Conquests and the Creation of an Islamic Empire*, the fact that the Arabs' domination of

Syria, Mesopotamia and Egypt was astonishing is clearly related more to the 'nomads'' capabilities in warfare (like the Mongols, the Huns and many others) and the speed of their conquests than, I suggest, to the previous complex conception of the sanctity of war in a new form of religiosity, the prophetic phase of which ended only two years before the start of those pillage and raids which rapidly transformed themselves in a permanent conquest.

This logical assumption, based on the impossibility of arguing about the existence of a new religion few years after the death of its Prophet, can similarly be shared with earlier Abrahamic religious traditions, but it is also related to a new inner religious consciousness emerging in a scenario dominated by Arab politics and in a geography where Islām, like the early Islamic believers, remained a minority for at least two and a half centuries after Muḥammad's death.

Considering that the first phase of conquest ended in the East in 751, the official date of the battle of Ṭalās, and in the West in 732, the official date of the Battle of Poitiers/Tours, and that the last attempt to conquer Constantinople was in 715–717, it is evident that the Arab conquests have to be considered differently, starting from the assumption that *Jihād* was probably the expression of a more ascetic-warlike praxis in existence after the creation of the borders of the 'Islamic' empire.

It is historically evident that independently of the narrative on religious violence, Jesus's prophetic message is far from being automatically contemplated as the beginning of the Christian era, even though for historiographic reasons, the birth of Mary's son was officially adopted as symptomatic of a new age. The council of Jerusalem (*c.* 50 AD), a pre-ecumenical council which established Jewish circumcision as not compulsory for Jesus's followers, obviously opened up the future religion to universalism, as well as to an aspect of evident distinction from Judaism but, at the same time, it cannot be established as having already identified a paradigmatic aspect of the new Christian religiosity (Sanders E.P., 1987).

In parallel, the first identification of Judaism with the designation of those characteristics that make the people of Judea 'Judeans' is from the Maccabean historical phase (in the second to first centuries BCE), many centuries after the Exodus and the Jewish conquest of Canaan; afterwards, being Judeans, like being Hellenized, assumed a much wider conceptualization and distinction (Shaye J.D. Cohen, 1999).

A similar methodological approach for Islām is necessary to erase the banal idea that the Arab conquests were already Islamic, as they were based on an 'offensive' *Jihād* or, worse, on an inner Islamic violence against otherness, innate in the process of its formation.

It is clear that a first historiographic problem is connected with the same early Islamic narrative which emerged in the works of Ibn Isḥāq (*c.* d. 761/767), Abū Mikhnaf (d. 774), H. ibn al-Kalbī (d. 819), al-Wāqidi (d. 823), Ibn Sa'd (d. 845) and al-Balādhurī (d. 892) up to al-Ṭabarī (d. 923) who were the first to partially support the existence of an Islamic religious identity after Muḥammad's death. However, as F. Donner, R. Hoyland, S. Judd, M. Bonner and Th. Sizgorich have emphasized more recently, the early Islamic chronicles played a significant role in shaping a first Islamic narrative on the religious identity of the early Arab conquerors.

This book, on the contrary, starts from the assumption that Syria, Mesopotamia and Egypt were conquered by a plural Arab group with an inner complexity and a multifaced historical awareness in which chronicles, archaeological-numismatic data, architecture and the identity of the creed emerged as still unable to recognize a clear new religious consciousness.

We probably have to wait 140 years (after the Prophet's death) to consider an Islamic moral attitude to war as well as the production of the first texts on the subject: the famous *Kitāb al-Jihād, Kitāb al-Siyar* and *Kitāb al-Maghāzī*. In parallel, we have to wait the same period of time before there is a geographical border between the Islamic political empire and the Byzantine Christian one (Calasso/Lancioni, 2017).

This study begins by deconstructing all the historical contextualizing attitudes in the formative age of Islām: nobody denies that today the exploitation of the concept of *Jihād* has taken on a political as well as an ideological proportion, assuming that global violence with a religious Islamic basis has become dangerously dominant in the media as well as in different Muslim countries. However, it is also equally important to consider that the early conceptualization of *Jihād* and *Jihadism* today really has limited religious and historical aspects in common, as do the early caliphates (Umayyad and 'Abbāsid) with the recent fake of Daesh/Isis.

It should be clear that this is an *extravaganza* of clichés. However, the word 'Deradicalizing', which has become very popular in the last few years in relation to the 'securitarian' approach towards a young European-Arab radicalized generation, needs to be adopted today to try to detach and save an important Islamic religious and theological concept, *Jihād*, from the trivialness that it has gained in a contemporary hegemonic and sectarian *scenario*.

If Sayed Amin clarifies that the Islamic revelation is completely dissociated from any kind of Terrorism, the contemporary connotation of offensive *Jihadism* as a form of *Jihād* also needs to be eradicated from its historical Islamic tradition and from Quranic hermeneutics. On the contrary, Jihadism needs to be assumed as part of a "modernist-Occidentalist" narrative which emerged after the cultural influence of the combined effect of Orientalism and Colonialism. Unfortunately, the great importance of European Colonialism until the end of the Second World War, the end of the Cold War and of the ideological superpowers in the following decades is at the basis of the new narrative psychosis which has affected different cultural areas, not only the Islamic one.

It is therefore clear that 'Deradicalizing Jihād' is connected not only with the attempt to emphasize a re-appropriation by the Muslim majority of their own religious and historical consciousness, but with preserving the plurality of thought within Islām as well as in relation to religious otherness.

Acknowledgements

This academic project was directly related to my Marie Curie (IF 2016), I worked on it from June 2017 until the end of 2019 as Marie Curie Research Fellow at the Institute for Culture and Society at the University of Navarra. This university offered me a training session with the evident intention to prepare a competitive Individual Fellowship which was submitted in September 2016. For this reason, I first wish to thank Prof. Montserrat Herrero and Santi Aurell for their total support, suggestions and advice in highlighting the academic interest in this project. In parallel, I need to thank the entire ICS administrative staff and the University of Navarra International Project staff, but in particular Javier Irigoyen Barrio, Cristina Garcia Fresca-Frias, Leyre Ovalle, Helena Baigorri and Vanessa Munoz.

I would also like to express my gratitude to the University Library and my colleagues of the Religion and Civil Society group of research, in particular David Thunder, Juan Pablo Dominguez and Rafael Garcia Perez.

The research actions to make this monograph a concrete outcome have been possible only through two phases of investigation attended in 2017 and 2018—the former to the Institute of Oriental Studies at the University of Bamberg in Germany, and the latter, at the Faculty of Religious Studies of the Catholic University of Lyon, in France. During both, the possibility to reflect and to face with Prof. Patrick Franke, Prof. Michel Younes and Prof. Ali Mostfa has been particularly important to better frame the project re-elaboration.

Last, but not least, I need to thank prof. Emeritus Fred Donner who with incredible dedication has read my entire work giving important advices to ameliorate the structure, its receptivity and the works' quality.

Introduction

For a different understanding of religious 'violence' in early Islamic History

History and the state of the art

Literature on Islām and inter-religious violence is a major interdisciplinary topic which has been analysed in the last two centuries. Its impact has been deep in re-framing a new apocalyptic visio over the past few decades and in particular after 9/11.[1] Similar powerful titles (see note 1) developed the 'common' generalized idea that 'Religions are the main cause of world violence', 'Religions produce terrorism' and that Abrahamic creeds are usually fundamentalist. This is a theory that has held a strong position since the post-Enlightenment and the Positivist thought of Ernest Renan[2] in the nineteenth century, and more recently in the works by René Girard and Mark Juergensmeyer.[3] If Renan had been thought of as an anti-clerical positivist already imbued in the French ideology of '*républicainisme*', the latter pair have been considered post-religious and post-secular.

Islām has been hugely targeted in symbolically being the major threat to World and Western security; however, this trivializing narrative needs to be framed within historical events which have affected Europe since Modernity and Middle Eastern geography in the contemporary period.

Vehemence against a different religious community, due to the fragmentation of the Catholic Church, has played a significant role in shaping, on the European-Western side, national identities which, for political theorists and kingdoms, were based on the principles of *una religio, in uno regno* (one religion, in one realm) or *cuius regio, eius religio* (whose realm, his religion). This concept arose with the Peace of Augsburg in 1555 which ended the first German religious conflict between Catholics and Protestants, continuing in the following century until the Peace of Westphalia of 1648 which ended the Thirty Years' War (1618–1648). The idea that a nation belongs to a unique *ethnos* with a definite geography, a specific language and one clearly predominant religion, represents a strategic cultural repository from which to select a narrative and traditions that allow nationalism in a clearly Euro-centric discourse.[4] However, the European conceptualization of the Modern state over a historical phase of four centuries, from the Renaissance and Humanism to the Ages of Revolutions (1775–1917), was imposed on the entire world through a 'Modernist'[5] outlook during Colonialism (1798–1962), emphasizing a massive and rapid changeover which had an impact on non-Western cultural areas all over the world in different ways, from China to Japan and from the Middle East to Sub-Saharan Africa. Religious violence in the Islamic world and its inter-religious dimension have had an increasing impact in recent centuries, partially due to the geographical plurality of regions that from the Levant to the Indian subcontinent were not concretely affected by previous 'national' and 'nationalist' discourses.[6] The assumptions that Islam expanded through aggressive conquering campaigns and that the Qur'ān is a violent revelation find a vast literature of reference over the centuries from the Eastern-Western European Medieval Age to Modernity,[7] equally affecting the figure of Prophet Muḥammad and the subsequent Muslim Caliphs and Sultans.

However, over the last fifty years, the historical comprehension of the first century of Islām and the process of canonization of the Qur'ān have been deconstructed and analysed in a more interdisciplinary way, imposing an ongoing new understanding which, step by step, is modifying the historical awareness of the Islamic formative age.

Different sources – archaeological, numismatic, historical, anthropological, religious-hermeneutical – have been developed and combined to bring early Islamic history towards new insights.

Since the 1970s, historians and experts in Islamic and Qur'anic Studies such as John Wansbrough, Patricia Crone, Uri Rubin, G.R. Hawting, H. Kennedy, Irfan Shahid, M. Lecker, M.J. Kister, Fred Donner and Robert Hoyland[8] have contributed, sometimes with excessive audacity, to showing a new imagery of early Islamic history, reformulating it more within a more inclusive monotheistic *milieu* than clearly identifying a new religion (*Islām*) from the beginning.

In recent decades, the advent of Islām has started to be described not only as coinciding with the Arab campaigns of conquest which, in a century, brought a huge geographical area under the Caliphates' rulership, but as a formative phase in which the Islamic identity was also put in parallel with different aspects. The fairly 'common' question 'How could the Arabs of the Peninsula have conquered this extended empire in such a short time?', which has usually had an answer related to an early Islamic warfaring attitude (*jihād*), finds a very convincing reply in R. Hoyland's *In God's Path*:

> The Arabs' victories were certainly stunning, and their progress was much faster than that of settled powers like the Romans, but it is comparable with armies comprising a high proportion of nomads.[9]

This is historically clear, univocally considering nomadic populations such as the Mongols of Genghis Khan, the Turk-Mongol hordes of Timur, Attila's Huns and the Hephthalite. It is also significant to highlight that if the aforenamed had tremendous conquering capabilities, usually they had more limited ones in preserving effective state control. For this historical reason, it is important to make a major distinction between the Believers conquests and the concrete and internal development of the new form of religiosity with Abrahamic roots which Islām became.

The linguistic-hermeneutical coexistence and comprehension of the *Futūḥ* and *Ghazawāt* with the meaning of *Qitāl* is already slightly problematic in relation to the Qur'ān's narrative: the Islamic revelation does not effectively predict or approve any kind of campaigns of conquest outside the Arabian Peninsula. On the contrary, it took on an accommodating and favourable position on the Byzantine side against the Persians-Sasanians (Q. 30: 2-7)[10] in the last Roman-Persian war (602–628), while the limited description of local raids can still be understood in the anthropological Arab cultural *milieu* based on *Ghazawāt* praxis, even though the term *Ghazwa* appears only once in the entire revelation.[11] It is completely different to assume that these conquests were already rooted in the early conceptualization of *Jihād*, which is the focus of **the first part of this book.**

As already stated in the Preface, can we think about a Christian religion after Jesus's ascension? Or do we need to wait until the early understanding of how the Christians differentiated themselves from Judaism? Can we talk about Islām immediately after Prophet Muḥammad's death in 632? Or do we need to wait until some clear differences emerged between this new form of religiosity and the previous Abrahamic traditions?

This is the main reason why we cannot talk about 'Islamic conquests' from the beginning; we probably have to wait until 'Abd al-Malik ibn Marwān (d. 705) to start identifying the leading political rulers of this extended empire as the Caliphs of a new religious community 'in progress'.[12]

The first half of the eighth century is a historical phase in which the Arab conquests were already coming to an end, as was the first Arab empire in history, the Umayyad (661–750). In parallel, contemplating the conquest of Syria, Palestine, Egypt, Mesopotamia and the Iranian plateau including cities such as Damascus, Antioch, Jerusalem, Alexandria, Edessa, Ctesiphon, Susa, Ecbatana, Ray (Raghes), the most urbanized and culturally dynamic regions of late antiquity (634–705), has to be considered differently from the conquests of more rural geographical areas in western North Africa, or as Sogdiana, Khwārazm, Khorāsān, Margiana, Zamindawar etc. (693–751). In other words, the former conquests (634–654) were by rural Arabs who were reaching a more urbanized and culturally religious complex geography, still unable to share an 'Islamic' identity; the latter, on the contrary, were performed in new rural geographical areas when the awareness of being a believer was clearly stronger, as was the resistance to Arab assimilation by the local populations.[13]

Contrary to what historiography has always done by adopting paradigmatic dates to distinguish different periods, historical transitions are usually not so catastrophic, but need time to be absorbed and understood.

This is also clear in relation to 'oral transmission' and 'religious revelations' which for many reasons – historical, linguistic, geographical and logical – do not follow the common 'collection of traditions' that are usually attributed to them.

The 'Abbāsid Islamic narrative on the *Futūḥ* as well as on the canonization of the Qur'ān by the third *Khalīfa ar-Rāshidūn*, 'Uthman ibn 'Affan (d. 656), cannot be considered as a real fact: he was said to have collected the early *Muṣḥaf* (today's meaning: collection) from seven or nine versions and formed three or four copies which were sent to the cities of Damascus, Baṣra and Kūfā, while one probably remained in Medina. Even if this were true, a few copies of God's revelation cannot be considered as able to create a new religious tradition and doctrine, in particular in a new geography.[14]

The words adopted to define the dual scientific approach that has affected academia in recent decades considering the studies on the early Islamic centuries reflects on Fred Donner's definition of '*revisionism*' and '*reformism*': the first highlights an innovative academic approach that added to those previously used and underscored, emphasized an outcome that usually goes beyond the concrete investigative result; the second, on the contrary, gives clearer attention to what can be verified using the same interdisciplinary methodological approach, but without any kind of excessive revisionist attitude.[15]

This duality does not aim to favour an internal clash showing a clear preference; both are necessary and the former usually puts forward an interesting theory which is partially confirmed by the latter; however, clear differences persist in identifying *reformists* as more engaged in preserving a less revolutionary historical attitude, while the *revisionists* are often more likely to innovate without real support from the sources, but with a greater capability of insight.

Albrecht Noth's *Quellenkritische Studien zu Themen, Formen und Tendenzen frühislamischer Geschichtsüberlieferung*, published in 1970,[16] played an important role, even though it was not translated into English until many years after the German original, because for the first time he considered a textual critical analysis of 'Islamic conquests' and the first Muslim century using studies of the Hebrew Bible and the Christian Gospels. Günter Lüling in *Über den Ur-Koran* (Erlangen, 1974) assumed, like many other Western scholars, that the Qur'ān was not only the word of God, but more drastically the elaboration of Muḥammad's own life and thought and tried to understand it in the context of the standard Islamic biography, the *Sīra an-Nabawiyya*. Lüling's work was deeply criticized for its unfounded and arbitrary thesis, such as that the Prophet was at first a Christian; however, it was his methodological approach more than his theoretical outcomes that persisted, being adopted to implement future investigation into Early Islamic History.

A stronger and clear revisionist formulation emerged in particular after the publication of John Wansbrough's *Quranic Studies* and Patricia Crone-Michael Cook's *Hagarism: The Making of the Islamic World*. The former supports the idea that the Quranic text became a definitive canon of scripture only a couple of centuries after Muḥammad's death, in the early ninth century, in the 'Abbāsid era and certainly outside the Arabian Peninsula, the Qur'ān, for the SOAS' professor, emerged in a sectarian milieu of interconfessional debate among different forms of monotheism.

This idea about the sectarian interconfessional milieu has gained increasing support with Western historiography of the Middle East, in particular in the writings of Fred

M. Donner and Robert G. Hoyland.[17] In other words, in the first century, Islām was not yet Islām, but a more comprehensive and inclusive monotheistic creed with a praxis and doctrine that were still uncertain. In parallel, the Qur'ān has a revelation finally framed in the early 'Abbasid era remained problematic concerning different aspects that cannot analyzed in this work.

The latter theory, on the contrary, is framed by Crone-Cook's revisionism which on some occasions emerges as a little too surprising, in particular concerning the idea that after the eviction of the Jews by the Byzantines, in particular from Edessa, many of them joined Muḥammad's forces to conquer Jerusalem and the Holy Land, with the Prophet still alive and supporting the Arab campaigns. This theoretical line found further confirmation in Stephen J. Shoemaker's *The Death of a Prophet*[18] and *The Apocalypse of Empire* in which theoretical positions are, however, deeply rooted in apocalyptic-messianic texts and traditions such as the *Doctrina Iacobi nuper Baptizati* (634 CE) or *the Secrets of Rabbi Shim'ōn b. Yoḥai.*

> Since Muhammad was a bellicose prophet who had preached *jihād*, it is possible that the conquered peoples of Palestine and the Near East merely assumed that he was leading the *jihād* that subdued their territory and brought it under the dominion of his religious movement.

To consider apocalyptic-messianic texts as part of possibly credible historical sources poses a problem of trust, as F. Donner himself argues: 'Il est d'ailleurs important de se rappeler, qu'en réalité, la plupart de ces textes judaïques et chrétiens ne disent pas que les 'Sarrasins' croyaient en un Messie; ils recourent plutôt aux images apocalyptiques et messianiques pour expliquer la signification de l'émergence des musulmans.'[19]

> (It is also important to remember that in reality most of these Judaic and Christian texts do not say that the "Saracens" believed in a Messiah; rather they argue to apocalyptic and messianic images to explain the meaning of the Muslims emersion.)

These early apocalyptic theories are also historically related to Emperor Heraclius's anti-Judaic stance after their insurrection in Palestine against the Byzantines during the Sasanian invasion of the Roman territories in the first phase of the war between Constantinople and Ctesiphon (602–628).[20]

Regardless of some indefensible historical theories, the '*revisionist*' works and debates have revitalized the study of early Islām and *Hagarism* remains an important essay for its multilingual methodological approach; at the same time, '*reformist*' scholars were following Peter Brown's *The World of Late Antiquity* (1971), developing a broadened perspective, reformulating the historical age of Late Antiquity and the use of archaeological and numismatic sources, for the possibility of a better understanding of the early Islamic age.

Coins, Arabic papyrology and new archaeological findings closely connected with Byzantine or Sasanian studies have started in recent decades to re-shape the historical comprehension of the seventh century, reformulating the understanding of this crucial period with a more solid basis, in particular regarding their dual relationship with Arab clans and confederations.[21]

However, in this case too, some studies have favoured deeply revisionist theories which have developed fairly imaginative premises, like Volker Popp's[22] idea that the Byzantine defeat was a Sasanian post-627–628 counteroffensive[23] led by Christian Nestorians due to local and rural anti-Constantinople discontent.

Yehuda Nevo's hypothesis is also very intrepid.

> There were no Islamic conquests into Syria; Byzantium had already abandoned its Eastern provinces and Arab tribes began to move in. The Arabs at that time (corresponding in the traditional narrative to the Rashidi and early Umayyad periods) were largely pagans, not Muslims. Islamic descriptions of pagan life derive from cult practices in the Negev, not Ḥijāẓ. The elites of the new Arab populations in Syria, still clients of Byzantium, adopted an indeterminate form of monotheism that had its basis in Judeo-Christian trends in Syria, not Arabia. Muḥammad is not a historical figure, nor are any of the early caliphs.[24]

Muʿāwiya Ibn Abī Sufyān was effectively the first caliph, having won an intra-Arab struggle, to form a unified 'national' leadership. Still, Muʿāwiya's concrete propensity to Islām is doubtful while the first verifiable physical references to Muḥammad do not occur until the reign of ʿAbd al-Malik (685–705) and the fighting of the second *Fitna*. Even if it is true that the second righted guided caliph attested his faith in the Prophet's figure, it is harder to say in which specific qualities, political and religious, guaranteed his confidence.

Notwithstanding, neither case is based on solid interdisciplinary roots because they do not consider the historical background of proto-Islamic-Christian contradistinctions and the complexity of the inter-tribal relationship of the Arab clans; however, some intuitions should be reconsidered in relation to new evidence.

Many revisionist theories have the merit of having developed a concrete interdisciplinary analysis of this 'obscure' historical period; however, the large amount of recently added information usually needs a certain period of 'incubation' and a very broad analytical capacity able to appease and rationalize the plurality of this interdisciplinary understanding. This capability relates all singular historical events in connection with a literary understanding of them, a better comprehension of the Qur'ān, a geographical and sociological ability to distinguish urban from rural areas and an aptitude to read events through a broad analytical *spectrum*.

For these reasons, the state of the art in which this work is deeply rooted, without emphasizing the list of primary sources which appear in the Bibliography, is based on the critical studies and articles by authors such as Fred M. Donner and Robert Hoyland,[25] but also Stephen J. Shoemaker and Chase F. Robinson,[26] Lawrence I. Conrad[27] and Alfred-Louis De Prémare,[28] Irfan Shahid (Kawar),[29] Ella Landau-Tasseron,[30] Khalil ʿAthamina,[31] Walter E. Kaegi[32] and Thomas Sizgorich,[33] only to name some of the most quoted on the early proto-Islamic historical background.

After this level of analysis, the **second part** will tackle the famous 'verses of the Sword' (2: 190–195, 217; 9: 5, 36–39; 22: 39–41 etc.) but also selected passages on the Qur'anic definition of Otherness, specifically religion-otherness (2: 142–150; 5: 48, 62: 9–11 etc.). This hermeneutical analysis will be put into relation with Qur'anic historical chronology, or, better, in reference to what is currently supposed as being the canonization and collection of this revelation. Early *Sabab/Asbāb an-Nuzūl*, the *Sīra an-Nabawiyya*, the early collections of *aḥādīth* and *al-Muwaṭṭā'* by the Imām Mālik (d. 795) which certainly played a significant role in conjunction with the early *Fiqh Akhbar* version.[34] Nevertheless, some peculiar aspects of the Qur'ān's inter-religious violence will be considered: the greater hostility in the last, chronologically recognized, Qur'anic sūwar, specifically the ninth and the fifth; Wansbrough's debate in connection with archaeological discoveries as well as Nevo's 'Towards a prehistory of Islam';[35] and the Ṣan'ā' Quranic Palimsest.[36]

If, on the archaeological side, there have been difficulties in discovering complete Islamic *Shahādah* (with the part which includes the figure of Prophet Muḥammad) until the last decade of the seventh century, in parallel, there are contemporary poets like Ash-Shammākh adh-Dhubyānī (d. 656) or Abū Dhu'ayb Khuwaylid ibn Khālid (*c.* d. 649) who did not mention the impact of new 'religious Islamic' topics or concepts during the last part of their life even though they fought during the conquering campaigns.[37]

As Fred Donner argues in *Narratives of Islamic Origins*, the circumstantial evidence of the incorrectness of Wansbrough's main thesis is similarly contingent to that adopted by the SOAS professor about the framing of the Qur'ān, which clearly needed a longer period of time to be concretize. However, considering early Islamic inter-religious violence, historical events can be helpful in considering when, where and how the Qur'anic's *Jihād* had an impact on early Islamic history and on which analytical frame we can fix it: this is the core of this study.

The historical evidence that the regimentation of war and its moral and ethical Islamic rules appeared in texts such as the *Kitāb al-Jihād* by A. Ibn al-Mubārak[38] (d. 797), the *Kitāb al-Siyar al-Ṣaghīr* by Muḥammad ibn al-Ḥasan al-Shaybānī[39] (d. 803 or 805), the *Kitāb al-Siyar* by Abū Isḥāq al-Fazārī (d. 802)[40] or particular books of Ḥadīth Collections such as in *al-Muwaṭṭā* by the Imām Mālik (d. 795),[41] in the second half of the eighth century, during the early 'Abbāsid period; it seems, at least indicatively, that we need to wait until the end of the early Arab conquests and the fall of the Umayyad dynasty to contemplate the literary emergence of the Hegemonic *topoi* theme, like the early Islamic religious identification of *Jihād*, which can hardly be linked to a 'normal' bellicose attitude, but is something different.

The correspondence between the emergence of the above-mentioned works with the later more violent Qur'anic *sūras* and the early *Ḥadīth* Collections, comprehensive of short *Kitāb al-Jihād* sections, is, at least, concurrent or slightly earlier; in parallel, in the Umayyad period, the internal fight of the *taḥāluf* (Arab confederation) was narrated in detail through a poetic pre-Islamic *Hijā'* that is dissociated from the early eighth-century topos of *Jihād*, in which the ascetic-monastic theme (*zuhd*) emerged more clearly.[42]

Finally, we also need to assume a new and different updated viewpoint in considering the influence that the Arab Christian confederations of Syria, Palestine, Jazīra and North Arabia played in framing not only the early Believers' Christological understanding, highlighted by the uncanonical Gospel passages found in the Qur'ān, but by their Christian attitude to war in battling against the Persians and their Arab *foederati* forces since the fifth century.[43]

The **conclusions** of this work do not intend to make an incredible leap in time of twelve centuries to accentuate the methodological detractors, but they will reflect on the historical parallelism between the Western and Eastern Roman empire decadence, the end of the Ancient age and the increasing role played by the *Foederati* forces inside-outside the Roman Limes.

At the same time, the cliché which depicts Islām and Muhammad as inextricably rooted in a form of religious violence is an ideological posture which has nothing to do with scientific investigation.

Although some Qur'anic verses are violent, their contextualisation recalibrates their intensity. Simultaneously, the Prophetic phase (622–632) even considering some "battles", from Badr to Ḥunayn, fades if compared with the Roman-Persian wars, and their religious narratives in the same century. Finally, if the Qur'an, in comparison with the Gospels is verbally more violent; the final act, the conquest of Mecca: the polytheist city that rejected the Prophet's initial message, was peacefully captured without any bloodshed. The Mecca's conquests emphasizes the assumption that finally, any kind of political or religious contrast can be accommodated through diplomacy, is prominently reassuring and clearly antithetical to any form of radical fundamentalism.

1. Methodological approach and unresolved questions.

'Interdisciplinarity' is probably one of the most abused words in academia: leaving irony aside, this book is an attempt to take it as a base at different levels.

The analysis, first, second parts and conclusions will be based on the intersection of sources: historical (Islamic and otherwise), religious (Islamic and otherwise), epigraphic etc., for a crosscheck on different origins to investigate the historical period from the sixth century of late antiquity in the Levant, with particular attention to the Arab Christians until the end of the Umayyad caliphate (750 CE).

The archaeological and numismatic investigative path will validate the historical chronicles from the side of the conquerors as well as of the vanquished. In addition, an anthropological and geographical analysis will be associated in a rural-urban debate in trying to understand the reasons why, for example, *al-Jābiyah*, the capital of the Banū Ghassān *foederati* Byzantine forces, remained the capital of the Banū Umayyad governorate of Syria for at least twenty years after the conquest of the region by 'Umār ibn al-Khaṭṭāb and until Abū Sufyān's son became Caliph in 660 CE.[44]

Another investigative path will consider historical-chronicle literature and its analytical *spectrum* of the seventy years following the Prophet's death (632 CE), the intra-clan Arab confederations' relationship and its inter-religious perspective: Arab-Christian to be precise.

If Fred Donner's *Muhammad and the Believers. At the Origins of Islam*, like H. Kennedy's and Robert Hoyland's essays and articles,[45] underlines more than once the level of religious plurality of the first Arab conquerors and of the early proto-Islamic community, it is plausible to highlight that a preponderant majority of local inhabitants, Arabs and otherwise, were still unable to comprehend the religious sensitivity of the new conquerors, as the latters in considering their beliefs in contrast or continuity from the other Abrahamic faiths.[46]

Other distinctions need to be considered with reference to the *Ridda* wars and the battle of Mu'tah (629 CE), neither of which is mentioned in the Qur'ān, together with the expedition to Tabūk (631 CE) which, on the contrary, is indirectly quoted in the tradition of the *Asbāb an-Nuzūl* in connection with different verses (2: 262; 9: 38, 42–47, 49, 65, 74, 102–103, 106; 17: 76; 32: 16).[47] The distinction of the Qur'anic violence against Meccan polytheists, Jews and Christians, is related to their status and the historical circumstances which will emerge in the analysis of the first and second parts.

The methodological crosschecking of the investigation will affect the first part in identifying the level of violence of the Arab conquering campaigns which followed the Prophet's death. The same method will be adopted in considering the religious awareness of the early conquerors and of those who started to fight each other (the first and second *fitna*) in the early community of 'believers'. However, these two topics need to be inserted in a broader discourse which reflects on the influence exerted by the Arab-Christian confederations of the north, the role that was played on the Byzantine-Sasanian side, and their effective religiosity, in an interdisciplinary analysis between Late Antiquity and Early Islamic age. The sources adopted can be distinguished into different categories:

1. The historical ones, on the Islamic and non-Islamic side, Byzantines and Arab Christians, will be linked to the belligerent attitude and the level of correlated narratives.[48]
2. The archaeological and numismatic sources, as well as those on the style of early Islamic Architecture, will be used to prove the early Islamic identity or its absence.[49]
3. The anthropological and inter-religious sources of the late antique-early Islamic period will have a specific focus on political allies and the confederate system.
4. Last but not least, the Early Islamic literary narrative, *Ḥadīth* collections and pietistic-mystic-war-related literature (*zuhd*) will be put in relation with specific attention to the influence of the Monastic Christian Arab background.

Many questions remain unanswered on the religious status of the early Arab conquerors: in the Islamic chronicles by Ṭabarī and Balādhurī, for example, Mu'āwiya ibn Abī Sufyān is identified as the ruler who fought against the *Ahl al-Bayt* during the first *Fitna*. However, very limited information is reported about who gave military help to the Banū Umayya in backing their attempt as well as showing their rights in the succession to power.

Archaeological and numismatic sources and early Umayyad architecture observed the rise of a preliminary Islamic identity, with the discovery of a complete *Shahādah*: لَا إِلَٰهَ إِلَّا ٱللهُ مُحَمَّدٌ رَسُولُ ٱللهِ (There is no God but God and Muḥammad is his Prophet) which are dated around the caliphate of 'Abd al-Malik ibn Marwān (685–705 CE) and the second *fitna* (680–692 CE); but what was the impact of this long military confrontation on the early community in shaping its religious identity?

The military clash with Constantinople and the attempt to conquer it during the Umayyad age, at least a couple of times (674, 715–717 CE) will bring a sort of *status quo* in the third and fourth decades of the eighth century with the creation of a fortified border (*thughūr*): how will this process have an impact on the Umayyads, a couple of decades before their annihilation by the 'Abbāsids and who will continue to play a significant military function against the Byzantines?

Finally, contrary to standard thought which stressed an early Islamic influence on Byzantium through the Iconoclastic debate, it would be important to consider the opposite as well, in particular in relation to the role played by the Arab-Christian confederations of the north of the Peninsula.[50]

This interdisciplinary methodological approach will be enriched by the impact of the Qur'ān's 'canonization' process as the framing of an early Islamic religious juridical awareness on warfare and inter-religious confrontation. The extensive works of A. Neuwirth, N. Sinai, G. Said Reynolds etc., without considering Wansbrough's main thesis, clarify that if 'Uthmān Ibn 'Affān played a role in the 'setting up' process, this was not concluded before the beginning of the age of *Fitnas*, as it continued in the following century, until, probably, the early 'Abbāsid one.[51]

The complexity of the debate on the compilation of the Qur'ān clearly lies outside the scope of this book; however, the debate on the 'Sword verses' is particularly connected with the real meaning that the word roots such as *Ḥrb, Qtl, Ḍrb, Khṣm* and *Jhd* assumed in the text, the 'possible' historical context, and their adoption in the decades of the conquering campaigns.

The main question which remains unsolved reflects on the intersection of the analytical plans: if early Arab believers were unable to strictly identify themselves as members of a new religion, can the campaigns already be classified as religious?

Secondly, as Thomas Sizgorich, Paul L. Heck and Ch. Décobert have already hypothesized, the early recognition of a *mujāhid* with something different from a normal *ghāzī* suitable for a *ghazwa* (an expedition, incursion) the *mujāhid* would probably require a different interpretation of this ascetic-belligerent attitude.

Is *jihād* therefore something associated with a deeper hermeneutical interpretation of the Qur'anic text, linked with previous knowledge and understanding of Christian Oriental monasticism?[52]

If the Arab conquests and the early proto-Islamic century were more inter-religious than the 'classical' narrative has portrayed and the first conceptualization of *jihād* was historically quite dissimilar from its later canonization as 'holy/sacred war', the contemporary narrative on it would need to take a different perspective.

Part One

1

The Arabs outside Arabia and before Islām

The complexity in framing the 'middle ground' between historical periods is not due to the absence of actors, facts or causes, but, on the contrary, due to the abundance of the interdisciplinary historiography in considering the huge number of reasons which shape consequences and the subsequent events. In other words, if the Arab-Believers conquering campaigns of the seventh century were able to annihilate the Sasanian empire and to confine the Byzantine one within a Greek-Aegean world, this is dissociated from the 'Islamic narrative' which would like to show a Muslim warfaring force that was already extraordinarily strong, conventionally connected with a sacred conceptualization of *Jihād*.[1]

On the contrary, just as Constantine the Great (d. 337) before the battle of the Milvian Bridge (312 AD) was far from being a Christian, the Arab conquests which started in the third decade of the seventh century were far from being 'Islamic'. This assumption will be established in the following two chapters in an attempt to dismantle the simplistic contemporary idea that *Islām* has easily been associated with violence from the beginning of its history.

However, to prove the above assumption, making it credible and accurate, it would be important to start from the Arabs, as generally considered and their integration/non-integration in the extended geography between the two most significant empires of the late ancient age, northern Arabian Peninsula included. The interest will focus more on the Byzantine-Arabs' side than on the Persian-Sasanian one, for one main reason: Byzantium outlived and interacted clearly more with the early Arab Umayyad caliphate (661–750) with Damascus as its capital than with the 'Abbāsid one (750–1258), which arose as culturally immersed more in an Eastern Persian dimension than in a Christian-Syrian one.[2]

The problematic debate about the Arabs and Byzantium in the sixth century and before the beginning of the conquering campaigns had been already summarized in M. Whittow's article: 'Rome and the Jafnides: Writing the History of a 6th century tribal dynasty' and in reviewing Irfan Shahid's (alias Irfan Kawar) first volume, *Byzantium and the Arabs in the Sixth Century* (1995). Without entering the debate, it is clear that if Fred Donner and Robert G. Hoyland have been able to reconsider the 'Narratives of Islamic Origins' from the Islamic/non-Islamic point of view,[3] the same has been done in relation to the real historical and religious impact that the Jafnid branch of the Banū Ghassān Confederation played in the last century before the advent of the Umayyad dynasty.

The more emphatic pro-Arab analysis by Irfan Shahid, better supported by Syriac-Arab sources – John of Ephesus, Michael the Syrian, the *Chronicle to 1234,* but also the Chronicle of Seert (Siirt in Hoyland, 1997), Agapius of Manbij or Hierapolis (d. 942) etc. – is contested by the 6th contemporary post-Procopian Greek historians such as Aghatias Scholasticus,[4] and Theophylact Simocatta in his *Historiae*, who, on the contrary, are more critical of the role of the *Foederati* in the later Ancient age.

To anticipate one of the main aspects of this section, it is evident that during the sixth century, the rise of a new Arab-Christianized and partially assimilated rural élite is not only the hypothesis of a contemporary pro-Arab author of Palestinian origin:[5] artistic and epigraphic sources such as decorative architecture buildings, churches and monasteries have been considered an expression of an evolutionary perspective, even though, without reaching the level of the Nabateans or, afterwards, of the Umayyad dynasty.[6]

As Pierre Louis-Gatier shows, the Jafnides' Greek epigraphic sources clarified that the name of Arethas (al-Ḥārith) Ibn Jabalah (529–569) appeared in Qaṣr al-Ḥayr ibn Gharbī, eighty kilometres south-west of Palmyra (Syria) as well as that of Arethas ibn al-Ḥārith which appeared in a mosaic in the village of Nitl, in the Mādabā region (Jordan).

A few kilometres north of Nitl and fifteen kilometres south of ʿAmmān, in a place called Tall al-ʿUmayrī, a Byzantine mosaic shows on its base in Greek (here in French): '[…] Seigneur Jésus-Christ, Dieu de Saint Serge, protège le *magnificentissimus* comte Almoundaros. […]', probably al-Mundhir ibn al-Ḥārith (569–581).

> (Lord Jesus Christ, God of Saint Sergius, protects the magnificentissimus count Almoundaros.)

However, not all the names that appeared in the inscriptions can be clearly attributed to historical figures that emerged in the Chronicles: the case of Arethas ibn al-Ḥārith is emblematic.[7] The main difficulties in understanding the complexity of the relationships between the different branches of an Arab confederation, like the clans of Mecca with those of Medina, as well as the Banū Lakhm[8] with others, are the same which tried to clarify the solidity of the relationship between Constantinople and its *Foederati* system.

1. Byzantium and the *Foederati* system. From the fourth to the sixth century, a brief historical excursus.

The historical evidence of the role played by Arab confederations in the long conflict between the Byzantines and the Sasanians, as well as their importance during the sixth century, is problematically related not only to the different identities of the *Chronicle*'s author,[9] but to the concrete relationship that Constantinople and Ctesiphon assumed in preserving the control of the south-eastern/western parts of their empires.

The Byzantine foreign policy regarding the Arab confederations, like the Western Roman Empire in relation to the Germans, historically had the same consequences: just as Germanic populations entered and fragmented the Italian, Iberian peninsulas and Gaul, reaching the North African coast and extinguishing *de facto* the western portion of the Empire, different Arab confederations, from the end of the fourth century, gave greater attention to raids (*ghazawāt*) in Palestine, Syria and Sawād, emigrating to the rural areas of the less populated regions between the two empires.

In parallel, if the Romanization of the Germans symptomatically emerged considering historical protagonists such as Flavius Stilicho (359–408), a Vandal and high-ranking general, as well as the *Dux* and *Patricius* of Gothic or Scythian-origin Flavius Aetius, who blocked Attila's Huns at the *Catalaunian Plains* (451) with a Roman-Germanized army, it can therefore be easy to assume that a similar procedure and attitude were adopted by Constantinople on the Arab side.

Without taking a detrimental approach to Procopius and post-Procopian Greek historians, as well as an Arab-Syriac apologetic appraisal, the historical evidence is that the Byzantines needed to defend the eastern-southern desertic *limes* against Mundhir ibn al-Nuʿmān (503–554), the *malik* of the Banū Lakhm confederation.[10]

This requirement probably emerged not during the Anastasian war of 502–506, but in the subsequent reigns of Justin I (526–532) and Justinian (541–562).

The historical possibility that the Jafnid branch of the Ghassān confederation substituted, on the Roman side, the role played by the Arab confederation of Banū Kinda is an option which takes us too far from a concrete understanding of this chapter.

However, it is clear that in the sixth century the Byzantine and Sasanian empires were playing a local-global war-game in trying to weaken each other at different levels, using embassies, the impact of religions and their heretical infiltration in a far-distant geography: from Mesopotamia to the southern Red Sea area, including the Aksum empire and the Ḥimyarite kingdom.[11]

Nonnosus's embassy to the Kinda, in considering the few lines that have remained of it, is quite clear:

> Nam avus ab Anastario Imp. (491–518) as Aretham (Al-Hareth, Ambri f. Saracenorum Chindenorum principem) missus est, ut pacis foedera componeret. Pater vero Nonnosi sub Justino Imp. (518–527) ad Almundarum, ac postea ad nepotem Arethae Caisum, Chindenorum et Maadenorum prefectum, venit legatus. Denique Nonnosus a Justiniano ad eundem Caisum, cui persuaderet ut ad imperatorem se conferret, tum vero ad Auxumatarum regem Elesbaam et ad Homeritas prefectus est. Apud Caisum nihil videtur profecisse, quandoquidem Abramae tandem, denuo ad Caisum misso, contigit ut Saracenum istum ad Justinianum adduceret.[12]

> (In fact, his grandfather was sent from the Emperor Anastasius I (491–518) to Aretha (Al-Hareth, chief of the Arabs of Kinda) to make a peace's treaties. Nonnosus' father, indeed, was sent under the Emperor Justin (518–527) as Ambassador/Legatus to Almundarum, and afterwards to the grandson of Arethae, Caisum, military chief of Kinda and Midian.
>
> Lastly, Nonnosus is sent as a military 'prefectum' by the Emperor Justinian (527–565) to the same Caisum, who would like to persuade him in meeting with the Emperor, but then is (sent as prefectum also) to the monarch Elesbaan of the Axumites and to Himyar. With Caisum anyway, (Nonnosus) does not seem to have made progress, until finally, to Abramae, for the second time sent to Caisum, happened that this Saracenum (Caisum) was sent to Justinian.)

The failure of the Syriac-Arab ambassador to bring the Kinda on to the Byzantine side notwithstanding clarifies Nonnosus's family inheritance in being diplomatically linked to the Byzantines for at least three generations. As explained by Constantin Zuckerman, the *foederati* were usually part of a larger scheme in which their role was particularly active-agile in relation to both the military forces and the diplomats related to them.[13]

M. Lecker's article '*Kinda on the eve of Islam and during the Ridda*'[14] also elucidates the increasing importance of the religious factor.

The Kinda's partial conversion to Judaism probably boosted the support they gave to the Sasanians in re-conquering South Arabia against Abraha's pro-Byzantine successors, who conquered it in the first half of the sixth century.

If confirmed, this event frames the possibility not only for an Arab branch confederation of emigrating *au rebours* (south-north direction, of the Arabian Peninsula, but also the opposite), but of depicting a complex kind of political-religious relationship between the two empires of the north and their *foederati* Arab forces.[15]

Irfan Shahid's *rise and fall of the Salīḥ* identified this clan (the *Salīḥ*) after the Tanūkhids as another one which played a military role on the side of Constantinople. The evolutionary relationship between Byzantium and these Arab clans was narratively built up in the Arab-Islamic and Greek sources, with a clear policy of consecutiveness, where, for some obscure reasons – political, economic or religious – these previous *foederati* potentates were dismissed and replaced by a new one, with their last *malik* exiled far away, usually to the south of Italy.[16]

This kind of relationship is also confirmed by Joshua the Stylite, in his *chronicle*, when in describing the Roman *foederati* in the fifth century, he called them Th'alabites, probably a clan (Banū Tha'labat) that was part of the Ghassān confederation.[17]

However, without Byzantine sources on all those Arab clans and confederation, there would have also been very limited information on recognizing any kind of concrete role that the same played in relation with Constantinople.

Procopius in his *History of the Wars* (trans. Dewing, 1.17.45), John Malalas (trans. Jeffreys, p. 434, 445) and Menander the Guardsman (trans. Blockley, fr. 6.1, 9.1) usually called them the *Saracens* of the Persians just as the Jafnids are those of the Romans, while the Syriac historians like Joshua the Stylite, John of Ephesus (d. *c.* 588) and Evagrius Scholasticus (d. 594) defined them the *Ṭayyāyē* of the Persians and of the Romans: this was probably the original Aramaic term to define the nomadic Arabs.[18]

More evidence appears in stressing the role of the *Foederati* Arabs during the intense Roman-Persian warfaring phase of the sixth century, when the presence of local rural kingdoms clarified their integration in the hierarchical imperial system.

Jābiyah and *al-Ḥīra*, slightly more than Mecca and Medina, were their pre-urban Arab areas.[19]

It is no coincidence that Simeon of Beth Arsham's visit, in 524 AD to the Ghassān, defined the place as 'the camp of Jabala, king of the Ghassānids'.[20] Clear sources emphasized that the first *phylarch* of the Byzantines with a clear anti-Naṣride[21] role was al-Ḥārith V Ibn Jabalah (528–569), even though it is still doubtful whether his father, Jabalah IV ibn al-Ḥārith (518–528), had already formed an alliance with the Romans.[22]

Mundhir, holding the position of king, ruled alone over all the Saracens in Persia, and he was always able to make his inroad with the whole army wherever he wished in the Roman domain. Neither any commander of Roman troops, whom they call *duces*, nor any leader of the Saracens allied with the Romans, who are called *phylarchs*, was strong enough with his men to array himself against Mundhir, for the troops stationed in the different districts were not a match [individually] in battle for the enemy. For this reason, the emperor Justinian [527–565] put in command of as many clans as possible Harith, the son of Jabala, who ruled over the Saracens of Arabia, and bestowed upon him the dignity of king (*basileus*), a thing which among the Romans had never been done before.

(Procopius 1.17)[23]

Conversely, Procopius in his *History* also mentioned Abū Karib ibn Jabalah, the brother of al-Ḥārith V Ibn Jabalah,[24] who was chosen as *phylarch* of the *Palaestina Tertia* or *Salutaris*, the southernmost part of the region.

This [the Arabian] coast immediately beyond the boundaries of Palestine is held by Saracens, who have been settled from of old in the Palm Grove. These groves are in the interior, extending over a great tract of land, and there absolutely nothing else grows except palm trees. The emperor Justinian [527–65] had received these palm groves as a present from Abikarib, the ruler of the Saracens there, and he was appointed by the emperor phylarch over the Saracens in Palestine. And he guarded the land from plunder constantly, for both to the barbarians over whom he ruled and no less to the enemy Abikarib always seemed a man to be feared and an exceptionally energetic fellow.

(Procopius 1. 19. 8–16)[25]

Abū Karib suppressed the Samaritan revolt of the 529 AD and his territory extended geographically as far as the gulf of 'Aqabah.

On the opposite side, a fragment of Malchus underlines that in the fifth century the Persians still had in Amorkesus, probably the Arab Imru' al-Qays of the tribe of Nomalius, someone who received a sort of honour, but who nevertheless tried to become *phylarch* on the Romans' side as well.[26] Unfortunately, there is as little information on al-Ḥīra as there is on Jābiyah.

One of the main problems on the Lakhm and on the Ghassān side, as their reciprocal leading branch, is the use of the same name and *laqab* for entire generations. Imru' al Qays, al-Mundhir, al-Nu'mān, like Jafnah, Jabalah, al-Ḥārith were adopted from generation to generation in the main sources without marking them with numbers (the numbers were added later), as usually adopted by more important kingdoms.

Theophylact of Simocatta's *History*, in describing Chosroes's time (531–579), underlines how many different nations in the southern part of the empire were native to Arabia and were previously Roman allies: the solidity of these alliances had always been uncertain; it was not until the sixth century that their solidity started to be confirmed.[27]

The history of the Arabs on the Persian side is dominated by the figure of al-Mudhir III ibn Nuʿmān (503–554), an Arab polytheist with the ability to make incursions in the Roman territories, directly conducting raids, seizing booty and taking prisoners.

There is historical evidence that Justinian's promotion of al-Ḥārith V ibn Jabalah as *phylarch* in 528–529 is directly linked to the Naṣride's plundering activities and al-Mudhir's raids in the Roman territory.

Al-Ḥārith's initial defeat in the battle of Callinicum (531) was amply reported by Procopius (*History*, I, 17. 46–47) who accused him of having abandoned the Byzantines, causing their defeat, while John Malalas, whose *Chronographia* is usually more reliable, argues that some Arabs indeed fled, but not Ḥārith V ibn Jabalah and his forces.[28] However, Procopius's accusation emerged as without any solid bases; I. Shahīd argues that the Byzantine general Belisarius was dismissed, while al-Ḥārith V remained in charge.[29] A peace agreement which ended this phase of war is thought to have been signed in 532.

In the following decades, reciprocal raids would have affected the entire area.

Justinian's military reorganization and centralization process, with an increased Byzantine presence in defending the oriental territories – from the Armenian region in the north to the Palmyrene desert areas of the south – was not particularly appreciated by the Jafnid *foederati*, who were very sceptical about the urban concentration of power, in particular when the local Roman Duces treated them as 'inferior' forces of defence.[30]

On the one hand, al-Ḥārith V was endowed with great authority over all the Arab *foederati* of the *Phoenice*, *Syria* and *Euphratensis* and probably of the northern part of the *Arabia deserta*, while Abū Karib had authority over *Palestina*, *Arabia Tertia* and *Ḥijāz*, but many doubts remained in particular concerning the last one.[31]

Al-Ṭabarī in his *Ta'rīkh* argues that when Khālid ibn al-Walīd signed a final alliance with Dūmat al-Jandal, in 633, he found in front of him Arab Christian people of the Bahrā', Kalb, Ghassān (as generally understood), even Tanūkh: in other words, it is clear that at that time, the middle northern Arabian area was a predominantly Arab-Christian territory.[32]

Justinian's administrative and military system in the third decade of the sixth century probably integrated the two main provincial *phylarchs* along with the Dux and the civil governor in looking for stronger collaboration; nevertheless, the possibility of Roman military chiefs leading Arab *foederati* units could be considered a hazard. The debate, on this aspect, remained open as did that between Macdonald and Grouchevoy on when the *phylarch*'s role also became an administrative one, with the possibility, for example, of imposing local taxes.[33]

A new phase of war between Constantinople and Ctesiphon started in 540, which caused a new one between al-Ḥārith V (d. 569) and al-Mundhir III Ibn al-Nuʿmān (d. 554) as well.

However, after 545, even though the Romans and Persians had reached a truce, the Arab *foederati* continued to fight each other: Procopius reports[34] that al-Mundhir III captured and killed one of the sons of al-Ḥārith V, and the Jafnids were very close to capturing two of the Naṣride chief.

This epic juxtaposition, nevertheless, ended in 554 when al-Mundhir III started a new raid into Roman territory, devastating it, but encountering al-Ḥārith in battle, and he was killed in the Syrian territory of Chalcis.

Michael the Syrian's *Chronicle* also reports that a son of al-Ḥārith V, named Jabalah, was killed in the same battle.[35]

In the following decades, the military confrontation between the two eminent *Foederati* forces continued; the reciprocal deterioration of the relationship between the Jafnids and Byzantium, as between the Naṣrids and the Sasanian, nevertheless needs to be further investigated in parallel with the *bellum geste*, as well as the religious and imperial perception of Otherness.

2. Byzantium, Sasanians and the non-Chalcedonian Christian Arabs: the perception of otherness

The famous peace treaty of 561 AD between Constantinople and Ctesiphon exalted the Jafnids' role on the Byzantine side, so that I. Shahid gives al-Ḥārith V the Roman title of *Patrikios*, even before the diplomatic agreement.

In 563, Arethas (al-Ḥārith V) paid a highly successful visit to Constantinople making a great impression and obtaining everything he wanted from the emperor.[36]

The treaty included a commercial clause which highlights:

> It is agreed that Saracen and all other barbarian merchants of either state shall not travel by strange roads but shall go by Nisibis and Daras and shall not cross into foreign territory without official permission. But if they dare anything contrary to the agreement (that is to say, if they engage in tax-dodging, so-called), they shall be hunted down by the officers of the frontier and handed over for punishment together with the merchandise which they are carrying, whether Assyrian or Roman.[37]

This gave the Ghassānid and Lakhmid confederations as well as Arab merchants and the caravans of Ḥijāz huge power with a safe trade route, called the *incense route* of the north.

This economic aspect, to which we will return later, became particularly important in shaping economic relations between the northern Arab confederations of Arabia with those of the southern regions.

More than the Orientalist imagery of incense and spices, Gene L. Heck reports that agricultural products, wine made from dates and grapes, jewellery, usually made in Medina like the gold produced in the Fadak and Khaybar oases by Jewish clans, blacksmithing, leather making, textiles and perfumes, increased the reciprocal knowledge and relationship of Arab clans, not only encouraging trade activities but also shaping a more cultural *milieu*.[38]

The Arab Romanization process during the Justinian phase affected more the Ghassān ruling clan, the Jafnids, but probably also reached many others such as Balī, Judhām, the Syrian branch of Lakhm: 'Āmila, Kalb, Taghlib, Iyād etc.

A significant element of the role played by Byzantium in bringing the Arabs on to their side was the process of Christianization: al-Ḥīra was becoming an important centre of eastern Christianity, even though the ruling family of the Banū Naṣr was still polytheist as al-Nu'mān III ibn al-Mundhir's (d. *c.* 602) late conversion (*c.* 594) seems to emphasize.

> If the Barbarians have become inmates of Christ and abandoned gold and silver and all they possessed, and if women have persevered heroically in their contests for Christ's sake, how much more should we abandon our wretched hovels and opulent residences and be with Christ in the fair mansions prepared for us in our father's house.[39]

On the contrary, as the above sentence shows, again referring to the martyrs of Najrān, the northern Arab confederations on the Roman as well as on the Persian side were active in highlighting an international Christian-Miaphysite pietistic strength in martyrdom, not only in relation to the historical events which occurred outside the Roman world, but in considering the impact that they had on the different geographies of the late ancient age, as in the following centuries in the proto-Islamic period.

The Lives of Eastern Saints is a hagiographic collection, probably written in the 570s by John of Ephesus, in which the fragmentation of the Miaphysite church in Persia is fought by Simeon of Bēth Arshām, during his missionary life, by converting many Bardaisan, Marcionites, Manicheans, but also Zoroastrians, Nestorians and Saracens of al-Ḥīra.[40]

The same work mentions the prominent role played by the Arab-Roman leader al-Mundhir III, son of al-Ḥārith Jabalah V who was a strong supporter of the Miaphysite church among the Northern Arabs.

The main problem is that as long as the Empire was ruled by Justinian and his pro-Monophysite wife, Theodora, the emperor's religious efforts in the fight against non-Chalcedonians was moderately limited to words. On the contrary, the increasingly religious role played by al-Ḥārith V and his son al-Mundhir III in building churches and monasteries among Arabs, and in assuming a reconciliatory position in the ongoing fragmentation between the Chalcedonian and the non-Chalcedonian churches, was equally promoted by al-Mundhir III, in trying to preserve a sort of unitary northern Arab front.

Michael the Syrian's *Chronique* underlines the role played by a certain Jafnah, a member of the leading clan, in trying to reconcile the Patriarch Damian of Alexandria (d. 605) with that of Antioch, Peter of Callinicum (581–591), inviting both to a meeting at the Church/monastery of St Sergius of Jābiyah in 587.[41]

The growing involvement of Jafnids in religious-Christological debates resembles, on a smaller scale, that of the Byzantine emperors in Constantinople. It is therefore important to highlight how an assimilationist policy was *in actu*, on the religious side as well as on an educational-linguistic one. The great majority of the Arab-Roman inscriptions discovered in recent decades by archaeological excavations are in Greek, with rare cases in Syriac, while the translation or the adoption of the Syriac liturgical language in proto-Arabic is also attested by different sources.[42] Michael the Syrian also reported that al-Ḥārith V was capable of expressing himself in Greek and Syriac, as he attended theological debates during encounters between Chalcedonian and non-Chalcedonian religious and political figures.[43]

There was certainly among the Jafnids, more than among the other Arab clans affiliated with the Ghassānid, an increasingly close connection with Constantinople,

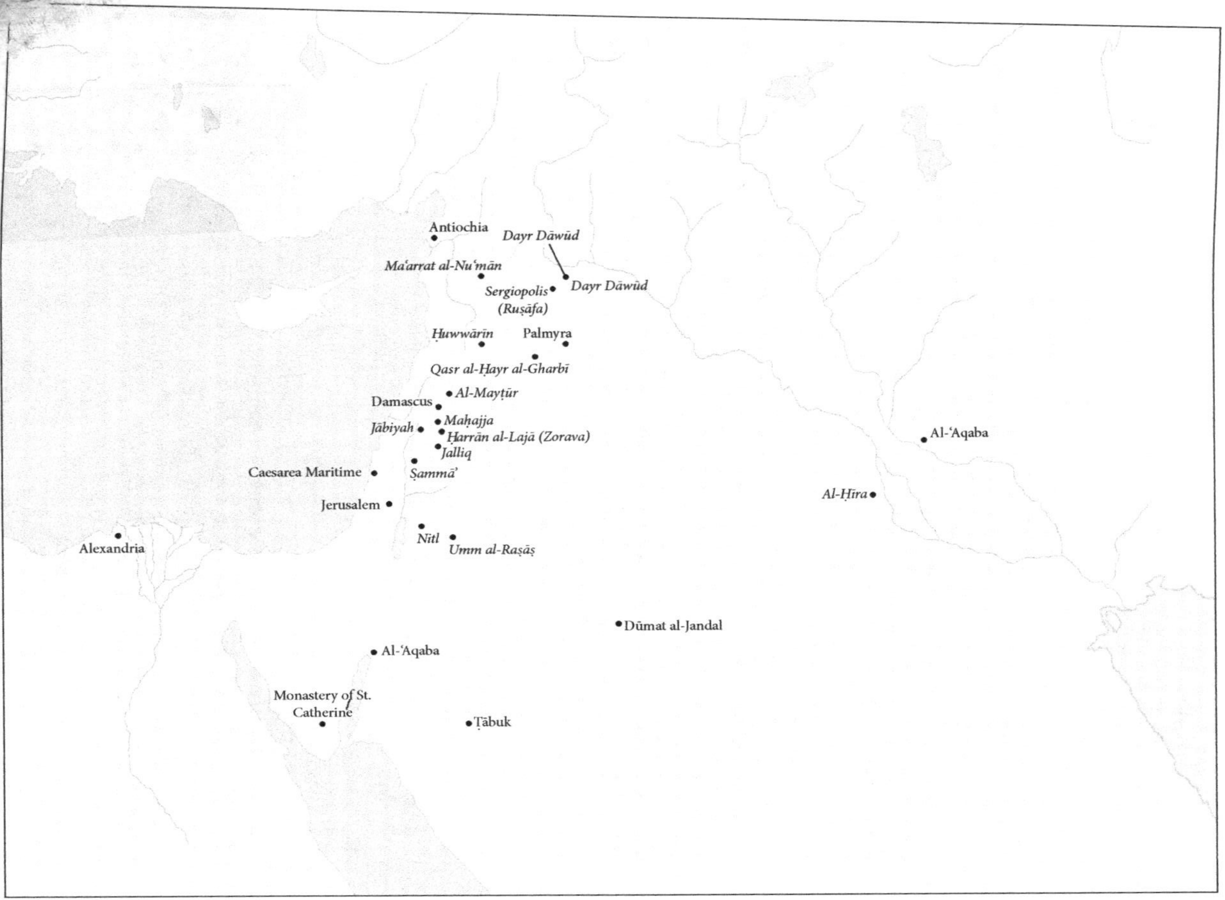
Antiochia
Dayr Dāwūd
Ma'arrat al-Nu'mān
Sergiopolis
(Ruṣāfa)
Dayr Dāwūd
Ḥuwwārīn
Palmyra
Qasr al-Ḥayr al-Gharbī
Al-Mayṭūr
Damascus
Maḥajja
Jābiyah
Ḥarrān al-Lajā (Zorava)
Jalliq
Caesarea Maritime
Ṣammā'
Jerusalem
Al-Ḥīra
Al-'Aqaba
Alexandria
Nītl
Umm al-Raṣāṣ
Dūmat al-Jandal
Al-'Aqaba
Monastery of St.
Catherine
Ṭābuk

which will also be attested by early Islamic sources, but that must not make us consider the entire pro-Byzantine Arab partnership as equally affiliated. The foundation of churches and monasteries in different locations was not only decisive in showing their power as well as their deep Christian religiosity (even though non-Chalcedonians) and geographical influence but was also clearly indicative of proselytism.[44]

The location of some of these monasteries is known in Jābiya, near Yathrib, in Ḥarrān al-Lajā, Najrān, Jalliq, Ḥuwwārīn, Sammā', Ma'arrat al-Nu'mān, Maḥajja, in al-Mayṭūr near Damascus, as well at Nitl in Jordan (Shahid 1996, 10–11; Shahid 2002, 29, 149–156; Piccirillo 2003, 267–284; Shahid 2003, 285). They also founded some nunneries, for example, in Jābiyah and probably in Jalliq (Dayr Kiswa). The complexes of Qaṣr al-Ḥayr al-Gharbī (monastery of Haliorama) and at Umm al-Raṣāṣ should probably be connected with the foundation of the Ghassānid monastery (Shahid 2002, 184, 188–189, 206–211; Shahid 2003, 287; Key Fowden 2004, 568). By founding the monasteries, the Jafnids were continuing the tradition which went back to the times before the arrival of the Ghassānids in Byzantine territory. For instance, the rulers of Salīḥ (the Ḍajā'ima dynasty) are credited with the construction of Dayr Dāwūd located between Seriane (Isriye) and Sergiopolis (Ruṣāfa) (Shahid 1989a, 473).[45]

The level of Christian assimilation for the Jafnids was so important that St Sergius was their military saint and martyr as well as their patron saint, although they also venerated St Julian, St George, John the Baptist and probably Elias.

St Sergius's martyrdom, which was very emblematic for its brutality (they put sandals on him which had long spikes on the inside, and he was forced to run nine miles in front of the ducal chariot along the *Strata Diocletiana*), is also associated with the Jafnids' affection for him. Brought to Reṣāfa when he was offered a last chance to repent, on his refusal, St Sergius was taken outside the walls and beheaded.[46] Reṣāfa (Sergiopolis in the Roman era) was populated by nomads, traders and pilgrims, thanks to its geographical location as a fortified station on the *Strata Diocletiana*. In parallel, St Sergius's *passio* is related to the suffering of the people who for different reasons need to walk for their work, such as emigrants or merchants.

Al-Mundhir III's building, dedicated to St Sergius, 20 metres in length and 17 metres in width, is located where it is supposed that the Saint was martyred and was probably not initially adopted as a church.

The interpretation that it was a sort of audience hall or a place to celebrate the victories against enemies cannot be proven. Dianne Van de Zande considers it a *Ḥarām:* a safe place for people who need to find protection, but also a place, I add, adopted as a Saint's *reliquiarium*, bringing them from the main Church of Reṣāfa, outside the walls, on the feast day of St Sergius, in *tishrīn*. Independently of the real purpose of al-Mundhir's religious building, the Jafnids' Christianization and assimilation are without any doubt very emblematic among the Arabs of Syria and Palestine.

Nevertheless and independently of their Romanization and zeal for Christianity, with the death of Justinian and the advent of the subsequent emperors – Justin II (565–578), Tiberius II (578–582) and Maurice (582–602) – the relationships with the Ghassānids' leading authority started to turn sour for political and religious reasons.

The Jafnids' assimilation with Constantinople was not symptomatic of complete submission, in particular referring to inter-Arab political and economic reasons. In

567, a raid by the Ghassānid was carried out against the Jewish oasis of Khaybar as reported by Islamic sources and Ḥarrān's inscription,[47] without any kind of direct Byzantine military support. With the death of al-Ḥārith V, his son al-Mundhir III, a pious Christian like his father, but an even greater general, after new victories against the Lakhm, asked to Constantinople for more gold and soldiers: in other words, an ulterior step up in the Byzantine military and political hierarchy.

The Emperor Justin, encouraged by the Chalcedonians' anti-Monophysite sentiments, tried to organize a plot to kill him, which failed bringing the Jafnids to a 'pause of reflection' concerning their alliance with Byzantium.

Under the reign of Tiberius II, in the last year of Justin's official reign, al-Mundhir III continued to successfully increase his military victories, capturing al-Ḥīra in 575, as well as showing all his pietistic religious affiliation to Christian miaphysism as a special reason behind his triumphs (an aspect on which we reflect later).[48]

In the following year, al-Mundhir III would probably have been invited a couple of times to Constantinople to obtain further honours such as titles. However, Tiberius's campaigns of 580 against the Persians, led by the Chalcedonian and future emperor Maurice, gave al-Mundhir's detractors the possibility of declaring him a traitor, in particular due to the *Strategikon*'s failure (Maurice, the future emperor) compared to the Jafnids' victories.[49] Al-Mundhir III was betrayed by the Chalcedonian patriarch of Antioch and the imperial curator, a certain Magnus, whom the Jafnids' *phylarch* trusted: arrested and taken to Constantinople, he remained there for some years until the emperor's death (582).

The Jafnids' revolt against Byzantium brought looting and damage, the siege of Bostra,[50] as well as some local military defeats for the Romans' limited forces. The advent of Maurice (682–602) as Byzantine emperor, after Tiberius, was not to provoke a clear improvement between the Jafnids and the Romans; on the contrary, al-Mundhir III was exiled to Sicily, while al-Nuʿmān VI ibn al-Mundhir (reign 581–583, d. unknown), his son, was probably pushed to espouse the Chalcedonian side in exchange for his father's exile, as well as a prominent new leading military role in the army, but he refused.

However, on this last aspect the sources are unclear: Michael the Syrian does not clarify this passage,[51] while the chronicle of Seert asserts that Maurice 'dismantled long standing relations with the Ghassānid Arabs and attempted to force the conversion of their leaders to Chalcedonianism pursuing a policy of rural missionary work, which was especially successful in the Caucasus',[52] but clearly failed on the Jafnids' side.

In 586, a couple of Arab *phylarchs* fought in the Byzantine victory of Solachon, but little information is added on the Jafnids.

The dissolution of the Jafnids' role on the eastern and southern Byzantine frontiers, the possible release of al-Mundhir III on Maurice's death (602), and the existence of another Arab Ghassānid branch able to substitute them during this emperor's reign still remain obscure,[53] as well as their possible restoration during the age of Heraclius (610–641).[54] W. Kaegi insists:

> The rebellion of the Ghassanids, who had been Byzantine federated allies, after Maurice's very imprudent arrest and exile of their phylarch al-Mundhir in 581 and

> the termination of their subsidies, and the slaying of Nuʿmān III b. al-Mundhir, King of the Lakhmids, in 602, somehow with the connivance if not explicitly on the orders of Chosroes II, had demonstrated the perils of antagonizing hitherto friendly Arab tribal groupings while they had given Arabs relatively recent examples of the perfidy of rulers of empires and additional reason to be wary of their intentions. It was important for Byzantium to retain the friendship of at least some of the tribes. But those events had taken place more than a half-century earlier, and their memory would have existed for some Arabs (perhaps Arabs both inside and outside the Byzantine Empire) and for some Byzantine officials at various levels of authority and rank. Only Monophysite histories mentioned the rebellion of al-Mundhir; court histories such as Theophylact's omitted that embarrassing subject, even though knowledge of it might have helped Heraclius and his advisers make more intelligent decisions.[55]

It is probable that the crumbling of the late ancient empire's relationship with their Arab *foederati*, on both sides, is directly related to their subsequent inability to stop every kind of *ghazawāt* which affected Palestine, Syria and Mesopotamia at the end of the last Roman-Persian war in 628. However, the problematic aspect of the inner conflict between the Byzantines and the Jafnids, as between Khosraw II and the Naṣride al-Nuʿmān III ibn al-Mundhir, who was incarcerated and killed in 602, remained unclear even if linked to political-religious reasons: for the former, the longstanding conflict between Chalcedonians and non-Chalcedonians, specifically with the Arab Monophysites, for the latter, the conversion of the Lakhmides' main ruler to Nestorian Christianity.

While the leading Ghassānid clan made raids against the Byzantines in the 580s as a local insurrection against Constantinople's behaviour, the Naṣride-Lakhmides, on the Persians' side, ended their alliance in relation to historical events which affected both the end of the sixth century and the beginning of the seventh century.

The conversion of Nuʿmān III ibn al-Mundhir, and also of his sons Ḥasan and al-Nuʿmān IV ibn al-Mundhir, who were baptized in the fourth year of Chosroes II (590–591) and shortly killed afterwards by order of the same Shah, is described differently depending on the source.

In the Chronicle of Seert, Nuʿmān III converted after being freed from a demon, even though it is unclear who performed the exorcism: Simeon bin Jabir, the bishop of al-Ḥīra called Sabrishoʿ, the bishop of Lashom or a monk named Ishoʾzkha. He became probably a Nestorian.[56] The dating, however, is problematic: if Nuʿmān III and his sons converted in the fourth year of Chosroes II's kingdom, we are around 593–594 and not in 602 which moreover is the year which coincided with their murder by the same Persian Shah.

The *Patrologia Orientalis* (PO) is quite paradigmatic in showing something particularly significant:

The interpretation of this passage is also important in relation to the article by Ph. Wood and Greg Fisher which stressed the attention on al-Ṭabarī as a possible more explanatory source in emphasizing the conflict between the Sasanian Shahanshah and the Naṣride ruler in comparing it with Maurice's final conflict with the Jafnids. However, the parallel is jarring: the inner religious conflict in the Byzantine empire between Chalcedonians and non-Chalcedonian churches is historically established independently of the role that the Jafnids played, while in the Chronicle of Seert,

Nu'mān III is shown to be a supporter, with his eldest son Ḥasan, of Chosroes II against Vistāhm (d. 596 or 600).

> Il regnait (Nu'mān III) sur tous les Arabes qui se trouvaient dans les deux empires des Perses et des Grecs. Si l'un ou l'autre de ces deux rois, qui étaient alors en paix, lui demandait appui, celui-ci s'empressait de lui venir en aide. Son fils agit pareillement.[57]
>
> (He reigned (Nu'mān III) over all the Arabs who were in the two empires of the Persians and the Greeks. If either of these two kings, who were then at peace, would have asked him for support, he would come to help them. His son acts the same.)

Moreover, it is also proven that before conversion to Christianity, the Naṣride needed to ask permission from the Shahanshah. The conversion to Nestorianism of an Arab ruler in a geography such as al-Ḥīra already deeply affected by Christianity is also logical.[58] On the contrary, the dissolution of the Sasanian empire was already more visible than the Byzantine one: the internal rebellions against the centralized Persian power, Bahrām Chobin on the one hand (589–591) and Vistāhm on the other (594, 595), are symptomatic that the plural souls of the empire – the Parthian, the Armenian, Ṭabaristān and Jilān – were imploding with rebellions that could be very significant.[59]

It is possible, in relation to a more precise dating, that the conversion of the Naṣride chief and his offspring took place probably eight to ten years before 602; afterwards, Nu'mān III reigned over all the Arabs on the Persian side, but probably also had better relations with the Romans, when Chosroes II himself, during the uprising of Bahrām (590), pushed the Shah under the protection of Byzantium and its Arab *foederati*, including Nu'mān III who probably played a role.

Nevertheless, in this case, if conversion to Christianity seems clearly disconnected from the Shah's order to kill him, the real reason why this paradigmatic event took place in 602 is still unclear.

A possible interpretation which brings us directly to the battle of Dhi Qār (*c.* 609) is completely dissociated from the poet 'Adī ibn Zayd's narrative against Nu'mān III's decision to imprison him, and reflects on the last phase of the Sasanian-Byzantine war which broke out at the beginning of the seventh century.

It would be logical nonsense to consider the 'common' accusation against Nu'mān of not having helped Chosroes II against Bahrām,[60] when a few years later Nu'mān III's son Ḥasan militarily helped the Shah against Vistāhm, as reported in the PO.[61]

A different hypothesis, on the contrary, would be that when Phocas overthrew Maurice in 602, the emperor who helped Chosroes II to regain power against Bahrām, the Naṣride did not accept being involved in a new war against Constantinople when the Shah ordered it, with the beginning of the last Roman-Persian war (602–628).

As reported by I. Shahid, at the beginning of the last Sasanian-Byzantine war, the geography involved was northern Mesopotamia, Armenia and Anatolia, all areas where Arab *foederati* were not really in charge, following a second phase when Syria and Palestine were conquered and sacked (613–614).[62] The fact that historical sources report the presence of Arab forces fighting for Rome and Persia in their last confrontation but without identifying their names probably stressed the inability of Constantinople and Ctesiphon to preserve any sort of alliance with their previous *foederati* of the sixth century.[63]

The subsequent Islamic narrative on Dhī Qār's battle emphasized a clear connection between Nu'mān III's murder and a local insurrection against the Persians, as reported by al-Ṭabarī, Mas'ūdī and Ḥamzah al-Iṣfahānī.[64] However, the stories which are attributed to the rise and fall of the Naṣride resemble those of other important figures of clans at different autocratic courts: if we consider the Fall of the Barmakīds, in the ninth century, even bearing in mind their different role in the 'Abbāsid palaces of Baghdād, it is not described very differently by al-Ṭabarī.[65]

The battle of Dhi Qār, probably between 604 and 611, clearly shows the Arab confederations' ability to raid Persian territory and to defeat a Sasanid-Arab *foederati* army.

Fred Donner's interpretation of the rebellious tribesmen of Banū Bakr ibn Wā'il's confederation, who raided the southern Sassanian territory at different times before the definitive Arab conquests in the 630s, emphasizes how the Arab anti-Persian forces which won the battle were probably members of different clans such as Banū Shaybān ibn Tha'laba, Banū Dhuhl ibn Tha'laba, Banū Qays ibn Tha'laba etc., some of which were probably, as reported by Lecker, also part of the Ghassān confederation and that we will find again in the famous 'pact' of Medina, although as Jewish.[66] In his article, Donner argues how the Banū Bakr ibn Wā'il were partly still pagan and partly already Christians, in particular the Banū Bakrī. They played an important role in spreading Christian Miaphysism and Monophysism throughout the Peninsula:

> The bishop and the religious chief of the Monophysite Christians of Najrān in Muḥammad's days was a Bakr b. Wā'il.[67] This suggests that some part of Bakr was deeply enough Christianised such as to 'export' men, learned in the faith, to other areas. The conquest accounts notify us that Christians formed a significant part of the B. 'Ijl b. Lujaym, and we know that the 'Ijlī chief Abjar b. Jābir was a Christian at the time of Islam's appearance and remained a Christian until his death in al-Kūfa in the A.D. 660's.[68] There also appear to have been Christian communities with churches among the B. Ḥanīfa in al-Yamāma, and B. Yashkur of al-Yamāma may also have had Christian converts. As for the clans of B. Shaybān, it is known that a Christian of B. al-Muḥallim kept his faith until after the coming of Islām, while the famous chieftain Bistām b. Qays of the B. Hammām b. Murra was a Christian. Hence it seems that Christianity had established a foothold, at least, in these two aristocratic clans of B. Shaybān.[69]

Without adopting the position that the Arab struggle against the Persians was in support of Byzantium, which cannot be considered due to the absence of concrete sources, and that this proto-Islamic uprising was already related to an Islamicized romantic-narrative stressed by the Chronicles of the ninth century,[70] the anti-Sassanians' alignment as sentiments of the Banū Shaybān and Bakrī does not seem to be rooted in specific reasons, unless they are related to the classical up-down relationship between the Arabs and the Persians in the region. On the contrary, some of them, after Dhi

Qār, signed an agreement of reconciliation with the Persians, while others such as Bishr 'al-Salīl' ibn Qays of the Banū Hammām ibn Murra's clan (of the Banū Shaybān) supported the female prophetess Sajāh, during the *Ridda* wars.[71]

It is therefore evident that a much more religious connection between the battle of Dhi Qār and the subsequent proto-Islamic conquest needs to be excluded, with some clans of the Bakr ibn Wā'il confederation on Khālid ibn al-Walīd's side in the early conquering campaigns.

The possibility of finding clear connections between the different actors before and during the Arab conquering campaigns in the 630s remains difficult, in particular due to the great complexity of the Arab confederation system.

The only clear assumption that can be maintained is that the Arab confederations on both sides were going through a fragmentary phase: the difficulty of Sassanians and Byzantines in finding a new leading authority, such as the Jafnids and Naṣrides had been in the sixth century, is evident; the Chronicles are unable to report names until Jabalah ibn al-Aiham (d. *c.* 645), which Islamic sources defined as the last king of the Ghassānid, in a clear simplistic way.

In parallel, their Christian Miaphysite, Monophysite and Nestorian faith is important in defining their level of urbanization and also of Romanization. As for the Jafnids and Naṣrides, the level of Christian narrative in reporting Saints' miracles and being local *mecenates* in building churches, monasteries, populating the rural areas of Syria, Palestine and northern and southern Arabia with Christian communities is something that is not only related to later Islamic sources,[72] but reported by the Byzantine ones.[73]

A final postulation reflects on the difficult relationship between the Greek urban élite, to whom the Byzantine historians such as Procopius, Theophylact Simocatta, Agathias etc. certainly belonged, and the Arab *foederati*. If the Jafnids were probably an élite of an élite, completely Christianized (even though non-Chalcedonians) and Hellenized, who revolted against Constantinople only on a few limited occasions, as did the Naṣride, on the Sassanian side, different clans of the aforementioned confederation were still strongly addicted to raids and pillage, not only against their enemies but, as the battle of Dhi Qār highlights, as a form of retaliation and revenge.

This practice must not be considered as excessively violent, but as quite normal: when, during the first part of the last Roman-Persian war, Ctesiphon was winning, many Jews and Christians slayed each other, in particular in Jerusalem.[74]

The Saracens' raids were not considered abnormal, but on the contrary, and even if their religiosity was usually questioned by Byzantine Greeks as a clear form of detrimental superiority, non-Chalcedonian sources emphasize the Jafnids' great religiosity, the miraculous conversions of monks and their building of monasteries.[75]

3. The Ghassān and the Ḥijāz

The above analysis has tried to identify the importance of the Arab confederations' relationship with the late ancient potentates of the region, the role that they played in the sixth century and their cultural *milieu* in a context between assimilation and independence. The Jafnids and the Naṣrides were the élite of a confederation which had important relations in the Arabian Peninsula, from its southernmost part to the Ḥijāz. One of the significant differences between the northern confederation and the Ḥijāzī inter-tribal affiliations was that if Jafnids and Naṣrides obtained political-military authority as *primus inter pares* from an external actor – the Byzantine emperor and the Sassanid Shah – making them *foederati*, the connections between the less urbanized clans of the same northern confederations and the others in southern Arabia still remained deeply related to the traditional customs based on marriage policy, adoption, *nisba* and more generally *al-Īlāf*.[76]

The exchange of brides between clans could symbolize alliances of different kinds such as mutual co-operation; however, this practice was more common when an alliance was already signed, to cement something in place or had been recently approved, than to start a new one without a previous agreement.[77]

As reported by Ibn Ḥabīb (d. 859), it is possible that in pre-Islamic times, the Quraysh confederation did not give their women in marriage to members who were not of the same coalition; at the same time, it is also possible that women were given to members of renowned clients to stress the hierarchical level of the ally; however, all these were unwritten laws, but a custom which could change depending on specific cases.[78]

In relation to the changeover that had impacted the north at the end of the sixth century and the beginning of the seventh century, Byzantines and Sassanid had revolutionarily modified their stronger alliances with the Jafnids and Naṣrides without being able to substitute them. Conversely, if these clans were returned to anonymity, like those who tried to replace them, the confederation of the Ghassān and Lakhmide certainly did not disappear together with the clan directly or indirectly allied with both of them.

It seems evident that the pro-Byzantine confederation still played a significant role on the northern Mediterranean side of the Peninsula, not only in controlling and receiving *akhbār* (information) from local clans, but also in sharing common goals with some of them.

Looking at Muḥammad's family, it is easy to ascertain that his grandfather 'Abd al-Muṭṭalib was the son of a woman of the Banū Khazraj, the clan which in Medina was trying to obtain a greater role against the Aws and their Jewish allies.

M. Lecker argues that the Ghassanid confederation presence at the second 'Abaqa meeting (622) in suppor of the defence agreement with the *Muhājirūn*, was directly linked to the Khazraj leading authority in Medina and their anti-Jewish position, reached after the battle of Bu'ath (*c.* 617).

At least three branches of the Khazraj seem linked with the Ghassān: the Banū l-Ḥārith ibn al-Khawraj, the Banū Zurayq and the Banū al-Najjār. Referring to the first clan, they had members who lived in the Shām and in Medina during the pre-Islamic age, as well as after the arrival of Muḥammad; two of them, Abū l-Dardā' and his uncle Subay' Ibn Qays, probably attended the 'Aqabah meeting as *Naqīb* (people that investigate and whom you can trust).[79]

The most interesting aspect, however, is related to the Banū al-Najjār:

> Here we find a case of immigration in the opposite direction: among the Najjār there was a family from Ghassān, more precisely the Banū l-Muḥarriq (or

> al-Ḥārith al- Muḥarriq). This connection with Ghassān is significant because of Muḥammad's family relations with the Najjār: his grandfather's mother Salmā bint 'Amr was one of them. Incidentally, Salmā was a relative of Sawda (again from the Banū Najjār on the mother's side) whom Muḥammad married several months after the *hijra* in a move meant to strengthen his link with the Najjār, and through them with the Khazraj as a whole.[80]

In considering the articles by Lecker and S. Arjomand on a similar subject,[81] it seems that the proto-Islamic capacity in the Ḥijāz to build up a new confederated and religiously plural community was not only directly involved in forming a huge coalition against the enemies of Mecca, at least in this geographical area, as the Ghassān were a tribal and not a religious alliance, the coexistence between Jews, Christians and polytheists was, at the beginning, still possible.

The general peace and security stipulated by the creation of a first *Ummah* through the Pact of Medina (*c.* 623) eliminated the legitimacy of violence of the politically autonomous Arabian tribal society. Conversely, it did not eradicate fighting in the case of the clans which did not sign it and started in being enlisted as enemies of the believers (*mu'minīn*).

The inclusion of three Ghassānid clans in the early agreement with Muḥammad, one of them Jewish (Banū Tha'laba) is a significant aspect to be considered in trying to better comprehend the historical events and complexity of the alliances in the pre-Islamic age.[82]

However, to argue that Muḥammad was backed by the Ghassānids and by their Byzantine overlords seems slightly unnecessary.

If it is probably historically true that the early believers were more affiliated in supporting the Byzantines against the Sassanids during the ongoing war, as the Qur'ān itself seems to suggest in 30: 2-7,[83] 'the Ghassānid cause would have been served by the destabilisation of Medina and the replacement of the Jews, longtime allies of the Sassanians, with a political entity friendly with Byzantium. One must bear in mind that several years earlier, the Jews had played an active role in the Sassanian takeover of most of the Byzantine territories including Palestine.'[84]

This seems quite antithetic with respect to the previous sentence which reflects the religious plurality of the Ghassānid confederation, in stressing that it was a political and not a religious one.

On this last aspect, the Jafnids, when enlisted as *foederati*, played a very significant role in suppressing the revolts by Jews and Samaritans in the sixth century from 529 AD onwards. It is therefore clear that there were important differences in being directly involved as *foederati* and *phylarch* for Ctesiphon and Constantinople in the north and being part of a complex confederation in the southernmost regions where Jews, Christians or believers or polytheists seems to have been the only true factor of religious distinction.

It is historically evident that Islām would have emphasized that 'no Muslim is allowed to be allied with an infidel'; however, until the creation of a concrete new Islamic religious identity, the pre-Islamic alliances between Quraysh and their converted allies or part of those who emigrated to Medina remained in force.

If the battles between Muḥammad and the Quraysh were effectively fought, his peaceful conquest of Mecca in 630, more than a military one, is a clear request for political submission to the Prophet as a new ruler,[85] with the destruction of the deities of the Ka'ba as a religious step towards Abrahamic monotheism.

It is not a coincidence that the term *fitna* has been historically adopted in stressing a phase of strife in which previous alliances were annihilated.

Another important 'story' which directly associates the Prophet's family with the Ghassānids reflects a narrative related to Hāshim ibn 'Abd al-Manāf (d. *c.* 497), the great-grandfather of Muḥammad who, as reported by al-Ṭabarī, from a source of Ibn al-Kalbī, states that the Quraysh, at that time, were stricken by dearth and drought and that they started to travel regularly to Palestine to buy flour, about twice a year.

'Abd Manāf's sons were four: Hāshim, 'Abd Shams, the eldest, al-Muṭṭalib, the youngest, their mother being 'Ātikah bt. Murrah al-Sulamiyyah, while Nawfal's mother was Wāgidah. They jointly inherited their father's authority and were called 'those who make mighty' (*al-mujabbirūn*).

Al-Ṭabarī reports that they were the first of the Quraysh to obtain immunity which allowed them to travel far and wide from the sacred precincts of Mecca. Hāshim obtained a treaty for them with the Greek rulers of Syria and with the Ghassān; 'Abd Shams obtained a treaty for them with the Great Negus, as a result of which they travelled regularly to Abyssinia; Nawfal obtained a treaty for them with the Persian emperors as a result of which they travelled regularly to Iraq and Persia; and al-Muṭṭalib obtained a treaty with the kings of Ḥimyar, as a result of which they travelled regularly to Yemen (this is a clear narrative allowed to emphasize that the Quraysh as the Banū Hāshim were already capable to trade and travel all around the close Middle Eastern World).[86]

It is therefore possible that before the *Hijra*, the Banū Hāshim and their progeny were well known by the Ghassānid confederation of the north, and that independently of their religion were allowed to bring caravans and exercise trade as the peace treaty of 561 had already identified. The economic *spectrum*, in other words, made the Ḥijāz, previously federated in the Ghassānid confederation, related to the organized caravans led by the Quraysh. The religious plurality of the proto-Islamic phase, including Muḥammad's prophetic phase, highlights how a concrete and strong religious identity was still absent both from the believers of Medina, and from the Jews on the side of the Ghassān; on the contrary, the Jafnids, like the other Arab Christian confederations of the north, were already imbued with a clearer and more complex Christological identity.

4. The religious status of war and the Jafnids

The 'canonization' of *Jihād* in Islām is a peculiar aspect which evolved following the early recognition of the main differences between Islām, Judaism and Christianity in parallel with a clearer distinction between *ghazawāt* and a belligerent standpoint where actions are assimilated into a militarized form of religious ascetism.[87]

The effort to distinguish the former from the latter in a historical phase in which Arab raids and pillage were common practice is an important element in focusing on the relationship between revelation and violence, but in the first place between the Arab conquering campaigns and religious fighting.

In the fourth and fifth centuries, Nilus of Sinai, a monk from Alexandria, and Ammonius, a disciple of St John Chrysostom and a supporter of the Bishop Cyril, describe the raids of the Arabs in the Sinai Peninsula as barbaric attacks against pilgrims' caravans and isolated monks as a very normal practice, almost religiously accepted by a stoic and brave faith. Ammonius, in his *Relatio*, is more precise about it, reporting how 'a multitude of Saracens suddenly fell upon us because the one who was in possession of the phylarchy had died. All of those whom they found in the surrounding dwellings, they killed, but those whom they did not find escaped to the stronghold as soon as they heard the uproar'.[88]

Independently of the possible fabrication of the text, there was a historicized perception of the Saracens, as authors of raids against which others were enlisted in defence of the more densely populated, urbanized and economically productive territories. It is evident that these raids were not usually able to reach fortified towns due to the absence of the necessary technical equipment to penetrate solid walls; however, it is also true that in limited cases, some quṣūr had been already sacked after a longer siege. The Jafnids and Naṣrid, even though they were famous for their cavalry forces, had also carried out a number of sieges in the sixth century.[89]

Nevertheless, what emerges as most important for this study is the impact that Romanization and Christianization had in relation to the Ghassānid victory celebrations and their belligerent attitude, in particular during the sixth century.

The Arab *foederati* of Byzantium in late antiquity – Tanūkhids, Salīḥids and Ghassānids – had been peninsular Arabs before they were integrated into Roman military forces. After the change in their status, their victory celebrations – like many other aspects of their social life – were strongly influenced by those of an empire in which such celebrations reflected the imperial ideology.[90]

The best attested celebrations of Arab *foederati* are clearly linked with the Jafnids, even if some stories are related to the previous centuries as well.[91] What emerges as significant is an *Imitatio Imperii* that generally took place in relation to both the secular and the religious spheres.

The reign of al-Ḥārith V ibn Jabalah (d. 569) coincided with that of the Emperor Justinian during which a belligerent attitude invested the entire empire with celebrations as the maximum expression of community participation, with public rejoicing in a sort of *gaudia publica* through military parades, the building of arches of triumph and religious commemorations.

These peculiar attitudes were clearly adopted by the Jafnids after their important victories of Daras (530 AD), when their cavalries in Belisarius's army were able to defeat Mundhir III Naṣrids forces, but more specifically after the battle of Chalcis (554 AD) when the victory, like the killing of Mundhir, was also celebrated as a divine sign. The abundant sources, all contemporary and authentic, relate to three different traditions – Greek, Syriac and Arabic – and are complementary to the *Vita* of St Simeon the Younger, the *Chronicle* of Michael the Syrian who probably quoted earlier documents such as pre-Islamic poetry by authors such as 'Alqamah al-Faḥl.[92]

The battle of Chalcis is probably the most important for this study in stressing the Christian identity of the Jafnids in fighting as believers.[93] The assimilation with Byzantium, including how the empire conducted its military campaigns and their victory celebrations, is particularly important in stressing it as one of the factors of influence that the Jafnids had deployed to the Ghassānids more in general and in the proto-Islamic age more specifically.

The *profectio bellica* is described by one of the main pre-Islamic poets and panegyrists of the Jafnids and Naṣrid, al-Nābighah al-Dhubyānī, who in one of his odes described the Ghassānid king leading his chivalry coming out from al-Jābiyah and emphasized the 'shod' *mun'ala* of the horses in preparation of the campaign.[94] However, al-Nābighah can only be partially considered as a trustworthy source, due to the fact that he also served as the main poet to al-Ḥīra, as the main panegyrist at the Naṣrid court of al-Mundhir III ibn al-Nu'mān (505–554), al-Mundhir IV ibn al-Mundhir (574–580) and al-Numān III ibn al-Mundhir (580–602).

In the liturgy of war, al-Nābighah emphasizes that the battle was fought for two days; the Jafnids customarily invoked their patron saint Sergius, and two figures from the Bible, Job and Jesus, but also St Simeon the Younger, who was still living as a stylite on his column, not far from the scene of the battle, on *Mons Admirabilis*, near Antioch.

The Jafnids firmly believed that the extended aid of the Saints during the battle decided its outcome in their favour, a clear narrative that we will find in the early Islamic religious interpretation of their conquering campaigns.[95]

The impact of the Naṣrid's chivalry in the battle was described by the Greek source of la *Vita* of Simeon Stylite, as was the response of the Jafnids led by al-Ḥārith V riding his horse *al-Jawn* and holding two swords, *Mikhdam* and *Rasūb*: a clear Arab and Bedouin custom of giving nicknames to horses and swords is reported in an ode by 'Alqama al-Faḥl.[96]

The victory and the celebrations of the martyrs, including the first born of al-Ḥārith, Jabalah (d. 554), who was probably buried in a *martyrium* at Chalcis, were performed through a thanksgiving celebration in the church of Jābiyah where the same martyrs were celebrated; in parallel a jamboree in a more Arab style was held with a parade of horses and warriors like the celebration of the wedding between Princess Halimah and one of the most distinguished fighters, as suggested by previous tradition.

Most important was the recitation of poetry in the *rajaz* metre, the short one related to the memories of battles in pre-Islamic Arabia. The religious impact on Arabic poetry can easily be recognized in the following *murū'ah*, which remained quite unfamiliar in considering pre-Islamic composition:

Theirs is a liberal nature that God gave
To no men else, their virtues never fail.
Their home the Holy Land: their faith upright:
They hope to prosper if good deeds avail.
Zoned in fair wise and delicately shod,
They keep the Feast of Palms, when maidens pale,
Whose scarlet silken robes on trestles hang,
Greet them with odorous boughs and bid them hail.
Long lapped in ease tho' bred to war, their limbs
Green shouldered vestments, white-sleeved, richly veil.[97]

The above elegy, more than a religious ode to their victory, seems a stylish example of their elegant dress in which the green of their robes resembles that adopted by the Prophet Muḥammad and by those who usually represented him dressed in this colour.

The following victories, in this case, led by the son of al-Ḥārith, al-Mundhir III (569–581), were also described with an increasing Christian religious understanding.

The military campaign which ended with the battle of 'Ayn Ubāgh (570 AD), like the role played by al-Mundhir III, is ecclesiastically presented as '*et auxiliatus est Dominus Mundaro, et devicit Qabus et crux triumphavit*', the cross triumphed not only in relation with the fact that, probably, the victory coincided with the Day of Ascension in the liturgical calendar, but that Syriac ecclesiastical sources emphasized the clear consciousness of the Jafnids in fighting against pagan Arabs, as the Naṣrid still seems to be.[98]

However, if we consider the pre-Islamic poetry about the same historical event, the odes to the Jafnids and the lamenting of the Naṣrid women are clearly not imbued with religious Christian references; this suggests that still in the second half of the 6th, the link between religious affiliation and epic-bellicose events was probably only partially evident.[99] The Bedouin *topoi* remained predominantly elegiac and independent of the Romanization-Christianization process; on the military side, one of the main reasons why the Byzantines enlisted the Jafnids as *foederati*, recognizing their role as *phylarch,* was for their skill on horseback in making the Roman Army look more lightweight and unreliable; pre-Islamic poetry exalted the Ghassānids' ability in warfare as horsemen, suggesting us why they were signed up for this Imperial partnership.[100]

The conquest of al-Ḥīra in 575 AD was finally considered an astonishing victory which John of Ephesus described as: 'And he was extolled by all men. The two powers [Persia and Byzantium] also regarded with astonishment and admiration his spiritedness and courage and the victories he had achieved.'

The campaign of the Jafnids is presented as a retaliation for the penetration by the Naṣrides into Byzantine territory. It also seems that the Roman *foederati* infiltrated the enemy's land, moving during the night or trying to maintain their secret intention as long as they could.

In his analysis, Irfan Shahid stressed that this army was a Christian one and a just one, like the 'Just War' waged against the actions by the Lakhmids against the Christians of the Roman Empire with the prophetic certainty that their historical enemies would have suffered a bitter defeat.[101]

However, a definitive passage able to express that the Jafnids' last wars were already enriched by a religious Christian narrative remains quite certain due to the fact that Mundhir III was an excellent 'Christian'.[102]

In fact, when he conquered al-Ḥīrah, he destroyed the city except the Christian buildings, preserving all the Nestorian and Monophysite churches and monasteries:

> Itaque omnes vehementer profecti ad Hirta pervenerunt et in id silentio inciderunt, cum incolae eius valde inordinati silerent et tranquilli essent. Et exercitum totum

> qui in eo adfuit trucidaverunt et perdiderunt; et oppidum totum ecclesiis exceptis surruit et incendit tabernaculum suo in medio eius statuto, et in dies quinque consedit. Et Tayaye omnes quos comprehenderat comprehendit et vinxit.[103]
>
> (Therefore, all those who had left came quickly to Hira and in silence they attacked it, while its inhabitants were idle and quiet. They slaughtered and destroyed all the military forces that were in the city, the whole city destroyed except for the churches, and set fire to the (polytheistic) sanctuary located in the middle of the city, and in five days they encamped. And the Tayaye, all who found, won and took prisoners.)

This is also emblematic of al-Mundhir III's attempt to show their 'religious' superiority, referring to the Naṣrids who still remained pagan, in displaying his piety, but also in preserving only Christian edifices in the enemy capital. Moreover, this destruction finds evident similarities with that performed by Muḥammad's followers after their peaceful entrance into Mecca (630), against the polytheists' divinities in the Ka'bah.

The return journey from the Orient is a triumphant ride enriched by booty, the prisoners of war previously captured by the Lakhmids and new ones from al-Ḥīrah itself, in addition to the munificent endowments for the construction of new monasteries and churches.

> The munificence of Mundhir toward the churches and monasteries on his return to Oriens clinches the fact of his involvement in Christianity throughout his campaign. In fact, it was the fifth time that John of Ephesus presents Mundhir as a soldier fighting for the cause of Christianity. It is well that the references are gathered together in this connection: (1) his Christian sentiments are reflected even before the reconciliation with Justinianus when he expresses his chagrin and grief, as a Christian, over the devastation of Roman territory by the godless Lakhmids in 573; (2) it is also reflected in his letter to Justinianus; (3) in his address to his army before the campaign against al-Ḥīra; and (4) in his sparing the churches of al-Ḥīra the destruction he inflicted on the other parts of the city. The victory that Mundhir scored by his capture of al-Ḥīra impressed not only the two powers and the Arabs of the Peninsula but also the inhabitants of al-Ḥīra itself, who were the most involved. The famous Christian poet of al-Ḥīra 'Adī ibn-Zayd, who was a member of the house of Ayyub-the diplomats in the service of the Lakhmids – composed a poem in which he referred to the fall of al-Ḥīra.[104]

Irfan Shahid highlights the religious aspects, which are clearly confirmed by epigraphic sources more than by literary ones, in particular in relation to *topoi* of the poetic Bedouin style in which frivolous arguments, even in the Islamic age, continued to be more appreciated.[105]

It is important to consider indeed that on the Jafnids' side, the impact of Byzantine narratives, for example those related to finding the 'True Cross',[106] and more generally the Romans' canonization of the Sacredness of the War against a pagan enemy, was an aspect of which the Jafnid élite were quite aware in the sixth century.[107]

As Th. Sizgorich over-emphasizes in his critical study on sacred Christian violence in late antiquity, we need to wait until the Emperor Theodosius (d. 395) in the late fourth century to consider the narrative of the Roman-Byzantine emperor as the main actor in stressing Christianity's triumph over paganism. The religious vision of authors such as St Ambrose in stressing the emperor's mission in defending Christianity as well as becoming its main representative and ruler, also coercing their non-Christian subjects towards the true faith,[108] is emblematic of an increasing 'politicization' of the Christian attacks against Jews and pagans, in particular by ascetics, zealous and violent warriors.

Procopius, in the sixth century, detailed the classic manifestation of Justinian's authority and compassion, as a builder of churches and monasteries in conjunction with his attempt to forcefully drive the abandonment of the old gods to preserve Christian Orthodoxy: the sword and the cross became inseparable symbols in a *koine* of aggressive monotheism which coexisted with the pietism of monks.[109]

It is therefore evident that Justinian's military relations with the Jafnids were already based on a reciprocal comprehension of a bellicose attitude based on Christian religiosity, monastic pietism and a peculiar Christological interpretation in which their disagreement could be accommodated by the belief of Justinian's wife (Theodora) in Miaphysism and in al-Ḥārith V's military victories and defence of the eastern territories from their enemies.

From the fourth century, monks and religious figures such as Cyril of Alexandria (d. 444), John Chrysostom (d. 407) and the archetypical Christian monk Antony, as shaped by the narrative imagination of Athanasius bishop of Alexandria (d. 373), formed their own communities and brought Christianity to the most Hellenistic city in Egypt, emblematically transposed in fighting Arianism, Manicheans and Magians.[110]

In the following centuries, Chalcedonian and non-Chalcedonian monasticism played an important task in stressing the connection between early Christians martyrs and the place where they were supposedly martyred through the presence of monasteries, churches or even only ascetic figures. The hagiographic literature in Greek and in Syriac formed a narrative of zealous holiness which shaped a common feeling of being part of a community, in particular in rural areas where the spectrum of Christological contrasts was of little importance, in comparison with the sacredness of the monks' behavioural attitude.

J. Goehring argues that monastic communities of ascetics usually included the presence of believers with an opposing view on Christ's doctrine who tried to preserve unity, sometimes being accused of bringing heresy to society.[111]

The importance of the Christian-Monastic tradition and the lives of Saints and Martyrs in rural areas in which Arab confederations had established their domains played a significant role in the religious conversion of this nation as well as in their engagement with an active apostolate among them.

On the death of al-Mundhir III (554 AD), as related in the *Life of Symeon the Stylite the Younger*, the defeat and the murder of the Naṣride ruler is described as the prophetic victory of the suffering saint as a protagonist against a tyrannical ruler, the Arab pagan. The lives of saints, directly involved in the Arab conversions, the importance of Aḥūdemmeh's mission in the Jazīra, as described in the sixth century, and the description of the baptism of al-Nuʿmān III (*c.* 594 AD) after the Naṣride had been defeated on several occasions by the Byzantine Christian counterparts, highlighted a close connection between being a soldier of Christ and achieving military victory at the same time.

A militant form of pietism linked with a narrative of miraculous holiness which brings to the fore figures such as St Sergius, Īshō'yabh, Aḥūdemmeh, Jacob Baradeus etc. permeates a great sense of manifest destiny and belonging to a different life after conversion to Christianity.

> The bands of Christian Tayyaye attached to the Romans, having been attacked by insanity, heard about this man's holiness, and sent their king, whose name was al-Ḥārith bar Jabala, with their magnates to him, so that God might visit them through him. And Ḥārith took gold with him with offerings to give the saint of God would visit them through his prayers. But the whole affair was revealed to Jacob by God, and when they crossed the Euphrates to come to his monastery, the saint appeared to Ḥārith in his monastic robe at full morning and said to Ḥārith: O Barbarian, why did you doubt the gift of God? Return to your land and your magnates and release the man from Sinai whom someone is detaining in your camp and you will be delivered immediately from distress: for it is thanks to him that you have been afflicted. Henceforth Satan will not be permitted by the Lord to work destruction among you, until you enter the camp. Take your money with you, for we do not want to possess anything apart from God. At this open vision, Ḥārith and his magnates marvelled. He went back to his camp and found that from the hour that the blessed one said to him 'the devil shall not work any destruction in your camp', from the very hour, on that very day, they were cured. And they asked and enquired around the whole camp until they found a certain man bound in a tent. And he released him and sent him to Sinai and slew the man who had bound him in his tent with the edge of his sword. And day by day, Ḥārith yearned to see the saint.[112]

This excerpt is emblematically similar to the one which described the conversion of the Naṣrid al-Nuʿmān III: his possession by the demon or Satan, the intervention of one or more monks and bishops in trying to preserve a more ecumenical merit, the miracle and the evil spirit's departure from al-Nuʿmān III's body are very representative of a sort of praxis which stressed a common narrative.[113]

It is historically apparent that the Jafnids played a role in developing the anti-Chalcedonian church, both in establishing and founding churches and monasteries, then in a long series of victorious military campaigns on the side of the Byzantine as well as independently against their 'classic' enemies: the Naṣrid.[114]

From al-Ḥārith V ibn Jabalah (528–569), who was followed by al-Mundhir III ibn al-Ḥārith (569–581) to al-Nuʿmān VI ibn al-Mundhir (581–582, d. unknown), the Jafnids became increasingly powerful and religiously capable of shaping a Christian identity that could take on a paradigmatic equidistant position of being an Arab, but a Romanized Arab as well.

The more active anti-Chalcedonian position taken up by Tiberius and Maurice, the exiling of al-Mundhir III and al-Nuʿmān VI, and the eradication of the Jafnids as the most important patrons of the Arab *foederati*, clearly weakened the Byzantine defence on the eastern and southern borders as the first phase of the last Roman-Persian (602–628) war clearly highlighted.

However, the sanctified violence of a monotheistic faith and support from God, Jesus and the saints in defeating the enemy continued to be given great consideration in the last decades of Byzantium, as was also probable on the side of their Arab *foederati*. The Melkite bishop of Alexandria, Eutychios, in depicting the Emperor Heraclius's belligerent attitude against the Persians, describes him with violence and as having religious suppport:

> I believe in our lord Jesus the Messiah, that he will aid me against the Persian people, and he will protect me from the Shah and his companions [...] and whenever the emperor encountered a Persian man, or woman or child on the road, he would have decapitated them. [...] the city was conquered, and every man, woman and child were killed. And the bellies of the pregnant women were slit open, and the foetuses was taken from them and they were smashed on rocks. And the emperor Heraclius said: 'I am the one whom the prophet David foretold when he said in Psalm 136, Blessed shall be he who takes your babies and shames them on the rock![115]

The saints' and patrons' help, nevertheless, does not automatically frame the war as 'holy' as well, but only as 'just'. On the Jafnids' side, the war was just because the reasons for waging it were just, but intercession by the saints remained a characteristic which did not mean canonization at juridical level. The Jafnids' main rulers, starting from al-Ḥārith ibn Jabalah, are portrayed as fair military and religious chiefs in waging a just war against their enemies and Christ's enemies, in particular Arab pagans. In other words, war is appropriate because the Christian ruler is fair-minded in making it; however, unlike the Islamic canonization of just war in the eighth century, we have no sources which, with reference to the sixth century, are able to frame the sacralization of war for the Arab *Foederati* at a juridical level. On the contrary, the sacralization of war by the Byzantine Christians was already considered a common praxis at theological level,[116] but without a clear understanding of its impact on the Arab *foederati*. The patrons' request for intercession, like the religious celebrations after victory, is an important facet that shows an increasing affiliation by the Jafnids between religion and war: war is just because the Arab Christian forces are fighting for the right cause, but not because their actions in war are more moral than those of the other enemies. If the moralization of their actions is still absent, the adoption of the saints' lives and their faith and absolute trust in God, but also their suffering for martyrdom, were already prominent features that, at least, the Jafnids were able to amalgamate with a more Bedouin inclination for raids and pillage.[117]

2

Ghazawāt and *Futūḥ*

While the Byzantines and the Sasanians were fighting their last war (602–628) with the enlistment of their reciprocal Arab *foederati*, the Ḥijāz was taking a 'revolutionary' step which was to completely change the geography of late antiquity.

Muḥammad's early policy, still in the Meccan phase, was to convince his co-religionaries that his personal need for contemplation came to him (after 610) by an inspired (*waḥy, awḥā*) revelation, whose words remained graven in his mind without being forgotten. However, only an inter-clan Quraysh minority recognized Muḥammad's experience as properly inspired: part of them were members of his clan, the Banū Hāshim, while some were of the Banū Taym, of the Umayya and Asad. It is possible that the elitism in the Quraysh inner structure did not allow an orphan, as Muḥammad was, to try and assume a more important role in the confederation, specifically when he adopted a clear anti-polytheist stance. After the 'natural' death of his wife Khadīja and of his uncle Abū Ṭālib in 619, the personal attacks became more frequent and the need to find protection necessary.

The previous persecution by the Quraysh of the early believers of the lower classes, as reported in the *Sīra an-Nabawiyya*,[1] allowed a small *Hijra* by part of the community under the protection of the Christian Emperor of Axum. The Meccans were probably terrified that those believers had been sent there to find protection but also to try to convince the Emperor to invade Ḥijāz, as the Negus Ella Asbeha had already done in Yemen, at the beginning of the sixth century. This purpose which does not clearly emerge from the biography of the Prophet emphasized the geographical connection between Ḥijāz and the inclusive *milieu* of the late antique world as R. Hoyland, Th. Sizgorich and F. Donner[2] stressed, which from the southern part of the Peninsula, via Adulis, the most important Red Sea commercial harbour of the Abyssinians, reached Egypt on one side and the *Palestinia Tertia* on the other, to Gaza, *Caesarea Maritime* and the most important cities of the north of Syria and Jazīra.

The above option seems to be confirmed by the fact that the Quraysh sent 'Abdullah ibn Abū Rabī'a, but above all 'Amr ibn al-'Āṣ, the future 'Believer' commander and conqueror of Palestine and Egypt, son of one of the main Meccan opponents to the Prophet, to the Negus, to try to convince him to send the 'emigrants' back to Mecca (in relation to the Islamic Narrative).

Another *akhbār* (report) not directly included in the *Sīra*, but reported by early Islamic historians such as Ibn 'Abd al-Ḥakam (d. 871), argues that when 'Amr told the Negus that the 'emigrants' considered Jesus, the son of Mary, as reported in the Qur'ān (4: 171): 'We say about him that which our Prophet brought, saying he is the servant of God and His apostle and His spirit and His word which he cast into Mary the blessed virgin', the Abyssinian Emperor replied: 'By God, Jesus, Son of Mary, does not exceed what you have said by the length of this stick' provoking a fracture in the Christian African community and an uprising against him, but 'The Negus won his battle with God's help and Zubayr came back with the good tidings'.[3] 'Amr ibn al-'Āṣ in this case assumed a clearly malevolent attitude, as in the Classical *Sīra*,[4] in trying to convince the Negus to adopt an anti-Islamic position; however, to admit that in 614, the Islamic narrative on Jesus, son of Mary, was already clear and well known is part of the narrative itself.

It is therefore evident that 'Amr ibn al-'Āṣ, who became a 'believer' only shortly before the conquest of Mecca, was a refined politician sent to Axum to test the real political-military intention of the Negus.

Another *akhbār*, reported by Ibn 'Abd al-Ḥakam,[5] argues: 'After the battle of the Ditch, 'Amr proposed to some Qurayshites that they should go to the Negus, because Muḥammad continued to grow in strength, and life would be better under the Negus than under him. […] It occurred to 'Amr ibn al-'Āṣ that it would be advantageous for the Quraysh to have him killed. So, he asked the Negus to do this, after having offered him his presents. But the Negus became angry and said, "You demand the extradition of the messenger of a man who is visited by the Great Namus who used to come to Moses? […] You would do better to obey him and to follow him, for he and his followers will no doubt get the better of their adversaries, just as Moses overcame Pharaoh and his army."'

The following 'story', written by an Egyptian historian, and also reported afterwards by al-Ṭabarī, is used to show the reasons why 'Amr ibn al-'Āṣ converted to Islām; moreover, this narrative is particularly interesting as it focuses on different interpretative readings:

1. The historical fear of the Quraysh about a possible Aksumite invasion: both stories emphasized what is also stated in the Qur'ān, in the *Sūrah al-Fīl* (105), as symptomatically related to historical events which took place eighty years earlier and that created a clear sense of anxiety in the Meccan community. This aspect underscores an awareness of impotence against the major actors of late antiquity and this 'narrative' frames Aksum as a clear supporter of the new Prophetic *visio*, as will be emphasized with the figure of Heraclius, who, like the Negus, would have liked to have become a Muslim but encountered huge internal opposition.[6]
2. The inner fragmentation of the 'community' between those who followed the Prophet from the beginning and those who opposed him, 'converting' afterwards. The existence of a historical narrative which tried to make these early opponents and unbelievers more 'believers' than reality, as well as Ibn 'Abd al-Ḥakam's story on 'Amr ibn al-'Āṣ (and the main source for al-Ṭabarī), highlights the difficulties in shaping a coherent history of early Islām capable of being convincing for the following generations.[7]

3. The increasing importance of the former unbelievers in the conquering campaigns after the Prophet's death (632), and in leading and ruling them, became one of the most important aspects of attrition in the early community. Khālid ibn al-Walīd, who opposed the Prophet probably until 628–629, became the most important general of the early conquests (then being nicknamed *sayf Allah al-Maslūl*), but he was dismissed by 'Umār ibn al-Khaṭṭāb for envy and strategic reasons, as reported by Kh. 'Athamina.[8] The second rightly guided caliph was unable to repeat the above attempt with 'Amr ibn al-'Āṣ who, in practice, conquered Egypt without his permission, intelligently and strategically arguing that the conquests of Palestine and Syria could have not been maintained against Byzantium, if the Arabs had not been successful in conquering Egypt as well.[9] The historical relationships and alliances between 'Amr ibn al-'Āṣ and the Banū Umayya started before the Prophet's death and continued during the following phase.

All the above facets stressed not only the Arab Ḥijazī's inability to raid the north if internally fragmented, but that the early 'believers' and main military rulers remained 'unbelievers' until a few years before the conquest of Mecca and were rapidly enlisted as commanders-in-chief to the great discontent of the early *muhājirūn* and *anṣār*.[10]

The *Sīra* reflects on the above conflict when, after the bloody battle of Ḥunayn (630, after the conquest of Mecca) against the Banū Hawāzin, Thaqīf, Qays, Jusham etc. The *Anṣār* were particularly mad with the Prophet: 'the apostle had distributed these gifts among Quraysh and the Bedouin tribes, and the *Anṣār* got nothing, these tribes of *Anṣār* took the matter to heart and talked a great deal about it, until one of them said, "By God, the apostle has met his own people". [...] He said (an Anṣār), "Had you so wished you could have said and you would have spoken the truth and have been believed – you came to us discredited and we believed you, deserted and we helped you; a fugitive and we took you in; poor and we comforted you."'[11]

The Prophet replied to them: 'Are you disturbed in mind because of the good things of this life by which I win over a people that they may become Muslim while I entrust you in your Islām? Are you not satisfied that men should take away flocks and herds while you take back with you the apostle of God? By Him in whose hand is the soul of Muḥammad, but for the migration I should be one of the Anṣār myself. If all men went one way and the Anṣār another, I should take the way of the Anṣār. The People wept until the tears ran down their beards as they said: 'We are satisfied with the Apostle of God as our lot and portion.'[12]

This discourse reconciled the souls of the believers, at least for a while.

1. The battle of *Mu'tah*, Ṭābuk's mission and the *Ridda* agreements

The first military confrontation between the northern Christian Arabs and an expedition of Medinan 'believers' probably occurred in September 629, close to the village of Mu'tah, twelve kilometres south of al-Karak (today in Jordan).

The reasons for this expedition remain uncertain in the sources; moreover, the information about the three front-runners that Muḥammad decided to send to the north can help us try to better decipher the possible purpose.

Zayd ibn Ḥāritha, Ja'far ibn Abī Ṭālib and the poet 'Abd Allāh ibn Rawāḥā[13] were the leading figures of the mission and all of them died during the battle; however, there was also Khalīd ibn al-Walīd, who was not made the main military authority, probably for a couple of reasons: his very recent acceptance of Muḥammad's preaching and probably the fact that this was not a real military operation.

Zayd ibn Ḥāritha, the first-in-command, was a member of the 'Udhra branch of the Banū Kalb, a historically deeply Christianized clan from northern Arabia and the Najd area. Kidnapped when he was young, enslaved in Mecca, he was purchased by Khadījah and freed by Muḥammad on the day of his marriage and later adopted by the Prophet.

However, before being a 'General' in the fight against Mecca, Zayd is historically recognized as an eminent strategist, close to Muḥammad and completely trustworthy.[14] At the same time, and unlike Ja'far ibn Abī Ṭālib, Zayd was not a Banū Hāshim, the clan of the Prophet. This aspect, independently of millenarian and apocalyptic overtures on Zayd,[15] highlights how Muḥammad wanted to put a member of his clan, a cousin and older brother of 'Alī ibn Abū Ṭālib, as second-in-command.

Ja'far was also an emigrant to Abyssinia where he lived with his wife for twelve years. After that, according to some dubious Islamic traditions, he travelled to spread Islām abroad, as far as the Xingjiang region of China, before returning to Arabia. However, it is evident that Ja'far had acquired a more cosmopolitan status for having lived overseas for a lengthy period of time.

Finally, the poet 'Abd Allāh ibn Rawāḥā ibn Tha'alabah was an eminent member of the Banū Khazraj about whom we have little information; however, it is quite evident that all three figures emerged as having particularly connections with northern Arab clans and confederations: Zayd ibn Ḥāritha as a Kalbite, who after being freed by the Prophet, was able to restore a relationship with his family again, even though he continued to reside in Mecca and subsequently in Medina.

Ja'far ibn Abī Ṭālib, who lived under Christian Axumite protection for a long period of time, was probably one of the best experts on the Christian *milieu* on the other side of the Red Sea, but also of northern Arab confederations. Finally, as reported by M. Lecker in his article 'Were the Ghassānids and the Byzantines behind Muḥammad's Hijra?',[16] the Banū Tha'alabah, even though were majorly Jewish, it was a clan part of the Ghassānid confederation.

Therefore, unlike the usual Islamic narrative, the expedition's possible goal was not a military but a diplomatic one, starting to enlarge the coalition of clans in support of Muḥammad's cause, still against the Meccans whose city had not yet been reconquered.

The status and the expertise of the three commanders-in-chief, in particular on clan affiliation and their skills and knowledge, suggest that the Prophet's real intention was logically linked with finding an agreement that could bring huge political and religious support before moving against his hometown.

However, the size of the expedition, and, on the contrary, the need to defend themselves in case of attack in a geographical area 360 kilometres north of Tabūk and 550 kilometres north-west of Dūmāt ibn Jandal, stressed the possibility that a mission with peaceful intentions could have reached a different outcome.

This hypothesis is clearly difficult to prove; however, it seems possible, also because the military expeditions which were to take place after the conquest of Mecca and Ṭā'if and directed toward Tabūk or Dūmāt ibn Jandal were never geographically very far from Ḥijāz. It seems probable indeed that the expertise of Zayd ibn Ḥāritha, Ja'far as the 'Abd of 'Abd Allah ibn Rawāḥā could have been useful in a diplomatic encounter with the clans of Tabūk and Dūmāt ibn Jandal, for example, but to penetrate so far north, where probably part of the Balī, Kalb and Ghassān tribes did not recognize their clan affiliation, was a hazard.[17]

Another inexplicable aspect of the defeat of Mu'tah, as suggested by F. Donner's analysis, is the non-involvement of 'Amr ibn al-'Āṣ, whose mother was a Balī,[18] which again stressed the lack of clarity about this mission.

However, the Mu'tah raid, on which Byzantine sources do not add any significant aspects,[19] historically emphasized how, before the re-conquest of Mecca, independently of the real nature of this operation, the Prophet's prestige and, in this case, military power were insufficient to be a concrete threat to security for the empires of late antiquity.

It is evident that the Arabs who supported Muḥammad were not numerically sufficient or already politically persuasive in convincing part of the northern Arab confederations to support him.

On the contrary, something changed after the conquest of Mecca and the battle of Ḥunayn, in parallel with the submission of all the clans located geographically around Ṭā'if.

The expedition to Ṭabūk assumed a different perspective after Ḥunayn (630), even though, as highlighted by the Qur'ān itself (9: 41-42, 92), the Prophet's co-religionaries were not unanimous in obeying Muḥammad's orders. In this case again, the Islamic sources are not very clear about the concrete 'believers'' intentions, and the attribution to Emperor Heraclius of the aim of organizing an expedition against Medina resembles more of a rumour than something more tangible.[20]

Conversely, an important aspect to consider in this case is the fragmentation of the community in reacting to the Prophet's intention to send this mission to the north. Some of them, usually called *munāfiqūn*, found some excuses not to be enlisted in it, so much so as to define the raid: *ghazawāt al-'usra*, a raid of hardship. The great difference between Mu'tah and Ṭabūk was the outcome: Muḥammad reached an agreement with the Arab clans of the region, probably the Banū Qudhā'a sending Khālid ibn al-Walīd to Dūmat al-Jandal to seek an agreement with Ukaydir ibn 'Abd al-Malik al-Kindī, the leading Christian Arab authority of this oasis, with whom the 'believers' also reached a deal.[21]

The Islamic 'narrative' stressed that all the missions sent in the last phase of the Prophet's life were already Islamic and always reached an agreement as well as the submission and the payment of the *jizya*. This narrative, however, has little basis in relation to the subsequent *Ridda* disagreements, after Muḥammad's death.

As F. Donner, L. Conrad and R. Hoyland emphasized in their respective analyses on early Islamic historical traditions on the conquering campaigns, the purpose was to show how this phase had already started before the death of the Prophet, to highlight the divine inspirational enforcement in making his message universal and an expression of clear divine will.[22]

However, the early historical sources which started to develop this kind of 'political-religious' understanding of the Arab conquests were written from the second half of the eighth century onwards: Abū Mikhnaf's (d. 774) *Futūḥ al-ʿIrāq* and *Futūḥ al-Shām*, in parallel with Ibn Isḥāq's (d. *c.* 767) biography of the Prophet, played a significant role in giving an early Islamic hegemonic *topos*, inspiring the following generation of historians: Hishām ibn al-Kalbī (d. 819), al-Azdī al-Baṣrī (d. *c.* 825), al-Wāqidī (d. *c.* 823), Ibn Hishām (d. 835), Ibn Saʿd (d. 845) up to al-Balādhurī (d. 892) and al-Ṭabarī (d. 923).[23] This *topos*, moreover, cannot find concrete historical, archaeological or religious confirmation concerning tangible evidence of the existence of an Islamic identity which had already emerged in both the Prophetic and post-Prophetic phases. On the contrary, the 'narrative' of the Islamic Conquests is often contradicted by the same in relation to different historical events, as the Mu'tah, Ṭabūk and the *Ridda* wars underlined.

As previously stated, the battle of Mu'tah took place because the Medinan mission penetrated deep into Jordanian territory controlled by different Arab confederations; the Islamic reasons behind the expedition of Ṭabūk did not find any confirmation; on the contrary, the same sources admit that Heraclius was in Syria and did not really intend to organize a mission to the north of Arabia. Finally, the raid which reached Dūmat al-Jandal led by Khālid ibn al-Walīd obtained an agreement that the same sources defined as no longer considered after Muḥammad's death in 632, one year later.

All these incongruities, if they are certainly related on the one hand to the Arab confederations' historical 'liquid' society referred to, on the other, it ascertained the vagueness of the kind of 'agreements' (*al-Īlāf*) independently of their real existence.[24]

In the Qur'ān, *Sūrah* 106 recites: 'He did this [referring to God's will] to make the Quraysh feel secure, secure in their winter and summer journeys. So, let them worship the Lord of this House: who provides them with food to ward off hunger, safety to ward off fear.'

These 'historical' Meccan verses attributed to God's will probably refer to the Byzantine-Sassanian treaty of 561 AD in relation to the caravans that the Quraysh confederation were allowed to organize twice a year. However, the solidity of this pact was guaranteed in the second half of the sixth century by the mutual undertaking of the Jafnids–Naṣrids not to attack these trade journeys, recognizing them as completely different from a *ghazwa*, a pillage raid.[25]

This is an important passage that did not happen in the case of Mu'tah.

The historical confirmation related to Mu'tah, Ṭabūk and Dūmat al-Jandal is doubted by other *akhbār* linked to the same historians of the early Islamic age.

In his *Mecca and the Tribes of Arabia*, M.J. Kister reports, for example, that a tribal leader of the Banū Kalb, Ubayy ibn Sālim al-Kalbī, after the Meccans had realized that they lacked the necessary funds to complete building the Ka'ba, came to the Quraysh and asked them to help them financially to build it.[26] As reported by G.R.D King, the existence of paintings that seemed to portray 'Īsā ibn Maryam and his mother confirmed a kind of Arab Christian role in building this monotheistic religious temple.[27] As stated by al-Jawwās ibn al-Qaʿṭal and reported in the *Jamhara* of ibn al-Kalbī: the right side of the House which you cover with curtains belongs to us – an inheritance left by Ubayy ibn Sālim al-Kalbī.[28]

The Banū Kalb, who were the main political authorities in the oasis of Dūmat al-Jandal, would have continued to be closely linked with the Meccans in the pre-Islamic age and in the following early Islamic period, in particular considering their alliance with the Umayyads.

In other words, thanks to the genealogical reconstruction of Ibn al-Kalbī, that certainly stressed the importance of the clan he belonged to, he could be identified as one of those who, already Christianized, was not unaware of the events which were taking place in the Ḥijāz, as well as already being linked with the Banū Umayya before Muʿāwiya ibn Abī Sufyān strengthened their reciprocal relationship when he became the governor of Syria.[29]

More than the *Maghāzī* narrative which stressed the existence of a world not yet *in actu*, the *Ridda* wars also have to be reconsidered in relation to a clearer understanding of this brief phase.

The *Ridda* is probably an expression of the recognized independence that every Arab clan would like to preserve, far from a centralized attempt of control made by Medina and Mecca after the Prophet's political victory. This is an aspect that clearly emerged in the inner fragmentation and sectarianism in the age of the *Khulafāʾ al-Rāshidūn* (632–661).

The religious interpretation of this term which already identified the *Ridda* as a form of apostasy should be reconsidered in preferring the more secular interpretation of 'abandonment, withdrawal from a previous agreement'. The Islamic narrative on it emphasized the existence of the rise of new Prophetic figures, male and female, that would like to assume a parithetic stance to Muḥammad, being recognized equal to him.[30]

However, Shoufani's analysis generally identified them as already part of the 'Islamic' conquering campaigns, denying, moreover, that all of them had already recognized the Prophet and Islām as a new form of religiosity.[31]

The Islamic sources stressed the recognition of the *Ridda* religious wars as rooted in the analysis emerging from the *Kitāb al-Ridda* of al-Wāqidī (d. 823) which, as Ella Landau-Tasseron tries to determine, was probably one of the first written sources on the topic;[32] however, even this theoretical approach moves from the assumption that after the Prophet's death (632), Islām was a clear doctrine, which could easily be distinguished from others, but this is doubtful.

On the contrary, the subsequent fragmentation of the Arab alliances which followed Muḥammad's death started to divide the 'Believers' from the beginning, from the reunion of the *Saqīfah*.

Before the first *Fitna* (656–661), the wars which unified the different Arab confederations had its backbone in the Ḥijāzī alliance between Medina, Mecca and Ṭā'if with an increasing role played by the Quraysh élite.

After them, there were those on whom the respect of agreements signed with the Prophet was imposed, under the leading figure of Abū Bakr and the military skills of Khālid ibn al-Walīd: Banū Aslam, Ghifār, Sulaym, Ka'b ibn 'Amr, Juhayna, part of the Ṭayyi', Tamīm, Asad, Ghaṭafān, all from Najd. Inversely, the great majority of the northern Ḥijāzī and Syrian tribes, who probably had not signed any kind of *Ḥilf*, the Banū Kalb, Bali, 'Udhra, Quḍā'a, all of them mostly Christian, did not intervene.[33]

As F. Donner timidly suggests: 'But the conquests also developed from the events of the Ridda in a more integral way. For it was the firm subjugation of the nomadic warrior tribesmen of Arabia by the Islamic state that put into the hands of the new ruling élite the means to undertake an expansionist movement of unparalleled proportions.'[34] In other words, the submission to a Ḥijāzī élite had to be counterbalanced by the promise of something attractive and, anthropologically, only one thing had been able to emphasize this unitarian purpose: a promise of enrichment.

2. The Arab conquests in non-Islamic sources and the heresy of the Saracens

The non-Islamic sources described the 'Saracens'' conquest of the 630s in a very interesting way; contrary to the later Islamic ones which, starting from the second half of the eighth century, were to stress a very common and homogeneous understanding, the former, for the role played by the Arab *foederati*, are more authentically linked to the authors' elitarian role and to the idiomatic language adopted.[35]

Sophronius, Patriarch of Jerusalem, for example, the most important religious figure of the holy city who wrote in Greek and was fully part of a Byzantine élite, reproached them as being 'the wild barbarous Saracens who are filled with every diabolical savagery' and continued:

> the godless Saracens entered the holy city of Christ our Lord, Jerusalem, with the permission of God and in punishment for our negligence, which is considerable, and immediately proceed in haste to the place which is called the Capitol. They took with them men, some by force, others by their own will, in order to clean that place and to build that cursed thing, intended for their prayer and which they called a mosque.[36]

However, the author of this passage is historically confirmed as having died (*c.* 619 or 634, Jerusalem was peacefully occupied in 638) before the Arab conquering campaigns, which raises doubts as to who the bishop of Jerusalem is really referring to. At the same time, the German archaeologist Herbert Busse confirmed that the early 'mosque' was located in the eastern atrium of the Church of the Holy Sepulchre, so, inside the Christian religious building.[37]

Another interesting quotation by the Jerusalem patriarch again reveals the disdain with which he considered those 'Saracens':

> a strong and vigorous sceptre to break the pride of all the barbarians, and especially of the Saracens who, on account of our sins, have now risen up against us unexpectedly and ravage all with cruel and feral design, with impious and godless audacity. More than ever, therefore, we entreat your Holiness to make urgent petitions to Christ so that he, receiving these favourably from you, may quickly quell their mad insolence and deliver these vile creatures, as before, to be the footstool of our God-given emperors.[38]

This quotation is particularly interesting because it emphasized the same behavioural attitude of which Procopius accused the Jafnids, previously described. Sophronius asserts that those Saracens had to return being the footstools of our God-given emperors as the Arab *foederati* forces had been before these conquests. It is evident that the Patriarch of Jerusalem is quite unaware of the diversity and complexity of the Arab confederation system and he assumed that this is another raid of the region.[39]

It is evident that the early perception of the Believers conquests is religiously attributed to God's wrath due to the great fragmentation of the Christian community; moreover, the violence and the insecurity due to this new situation also partially addressed the fear that these Believers would become allies of the Jews, more than the Saracens, about whom there are no sources that described their religious affiliation as the spiritual enemy of Christianity.[40]

Anastasius of Sinai (d. *c.* 701), in a dialogue with a Jew, argued:

> Do not say that we Christians are today afflicted and enslaved. This is the greatest thing, that though persecuted and fought by so many, our faith stands and does not cease, nor is our empire abolished, nor are our churches closed. But amid the peoples who dominate and persecute us, we have churches, we erect crosses, found churches and engage in sacrifices.[41]

The inter-religious debate at the beginning of the eighth century was particularly rich as it was rooted in an inner conflict that on the one hand highlighted the long dispute on the Christological interpretation of the scriptures, as well as the political-religious attempt to reunite the community in appeasing Chalcedonian–anti-Chalcedonian positions, while, on the other, overstressed the ongoing conflict between Christianity and Judaism which not only affected the Arabian Peninsula in the previous century, but emphasized the existence of the different anti-Jewish policies of Constantinople.[42]

In relation to the first aspect, Heraclius's impact (610–641) in attempting to solve the schism between the Eastern Orthodox Chalcedonian Church and the monophysite non-Chalcedonian one is shown by the theological compromise based on monoenergism: Christ is the incarnate *Logos* of God with two natures, divine and human, but a sole energy, keeping in this case a monophysite sensibility. The position, accepted in Rome, Constantinople, Antioch and Alexandria, was rejected by the Syriac Orthodox Church and by Sophronius of Jerusalem, who more than other religious figures attributed the 'Saracens" conquest as connected to the 'sinner' statuses of the Christian believers and churches.[43]

Byzantine anti-Judaism, on the contrary, which historically emerged from the epoch of Theodosious I (d. 395) continued in the following centuries, increasing the accusations against the Jews of having helped the Saracens conquer the Roman lands of Syria and Palestine.

The famous *Doctrina Jacobi*, to which we will return later, was able to link a certain historical event, the killing by the Arabs of the Byzantine *candidatus* in *Caesarea Maritima* with the anti-Christian sentiments of the majority of the Jews, Samaritans or not, who lived under Constantinople's rule.[44]

Independently, this source is also one of the first, with that in Syriac by Thomas the Presbyter (d. *c.* 640) which attributes to Muḥammad a sort of connection with Prophecy, even though it attributes him with an anti-Christ posture; on the other hand, anti-Jewish literature like the *Trophies of Damascus*,[45] that assumed a different 'narrative' which is supported by the same Islamic sources on it,[46] argued that Christians still predominated in the city, their churches had not been harmed and the city walls remained intact. The author of this text argues that Arabs had long constituted a substantial proportion of the region's population and the Ghassānids, the Byzantine empire's Arab allies, had based themselves in nearby Jābiyah, exerting much influence in the province.

The city also enjoyed a cosmopolitan reputation, like the composition of the audience: 'a crowd of Hellenes, many Saracens, some Samaritans, a community of Jews and an assembly of Christians' was in no way unusual.[47] This seems to reflect F. Donner's 'believers' theory' about early Islām.

The more we move away from the few years needed to conquer Palestine, Syria, Mesopotamia and Egypt, the deeper the Christian analysis of a theological Islamic conceptualization of Christianity becomes. Absent in Maximus the Confessor (d. 662), it appears in written sources attributed to the priest, monk and abbot of St Catherine's monastery Anastasius Sinaita, a Greek author who in his *Hodegos*, the Greek original text of the latin *Viae Dux*: 'A guide along the right path', firstly analyzed the early Saracens' understanding of Christ/'Īsā ibn Maryam.

'Before any discussion, we must first anathematise all the false notions which our adversaries might entertain about us. Thus, when we wish to debate with the Arabs, we first anathematise whoever says two gods, or whoever says that God has carnally begotten a son, or whoever worships as god any created thing at all, in heaven or on earth.'[48] This passage seems quite close to some Quranic verses. However, as S. Griffith writes:

> In chapter ten he says explicitly that the Arabs put forward these ideas when they hear the statement of Christian doctrines. Given the congruence of these Arab ideas with the criticism of Christian doctrines found in the Qur'ān, it makes most sense to conclude that Anastasius is in fact reflecting the teaching of the Qur'ān when he mentions what the Arabs say about Christian doctrines. And it is pertinent that he mentions these Arab ideas in a work directed against the Monophysites, because the Qur'ān's criticism of Christianity makes most sense as criticisms when one recalls the likelihood that they were initially directed against the Monophysite expression of the Christian creed.[49]

This theological parenthesis is to stress and briefly anticipate that some Christological parts of the Qur'ān had already reached a monastery such as St Catherine, a unique place of culture in the Sinai Peninsula, but also the whole of Egypt; Anastasius's beliefs that these new Arab conquerors had some heretical ideas about 'Īsā ibn Maryam could be appropriate in considering proto-Islām as a kind of Christian heresy, as John of Damascus (d. 749) will clearly show afterwards.[50] This is an interesting aspect that we can find in parallel in the Syriac sources of Jacob of Edessa (d. 708).

In some of his letters and canonical legislation, Jacob of Edessa argues about the increasing reciprocal understanding between Christians and 'believers' on religious matters, stipulating that one does not need to be rebaptized Christian if one has become a Muslim and later wants to go back and profess Christianity; in parallel, a woman who is married to a Muslim man can continue to receive the holy eucharist even if afterwards she converts to Islām.[51] In addition, the same author, writing to John the Stylite (of Litarab, d. *c.* 737–738), reports:

> The Muslims too, although they do not know nor wish to say that this true Messiah, who came and is acknowledged by the Christians, is God and the son of God, they nevertheless confess firmly that he is the true Messiah who was to come and who was foretold by the prophets; on this they have no dispute with us [...] They say to all at all times that Jesus son of Mary is in truth the Messiah and they call him the word of God, as do the holy scriptures. They also add, in their ignorance, that he is the spirit of God, for they are not able to distinguish between word and spirit, just as they do not assent to call the Messiah, God or son of God.[52]

S. Griffith clearly emphasizes how the last sentence of the above quotation highlights that Jacob of Edessa certainly knew the Qur'anic verse: 'People of the Book, do not go to excess in your religion, and do not say anything about God, if not the truth: the Messiah, Jesus, son of Mary, was nothing more than a messenger of God, His word directed to Mary and a spirit from Him' (4:171).

The West Syrian sources on the Arab conquests stressed the violence used against the Christian monks around Mardin: one of the victims, a certain Simon, was the brother of Thomas the priest, whose Chronicle is probably the main source of this historical event. However, al-Balādhurī argues that the fortress of the city was conquered by the forces of 'Iyāḍ ibn Ghanm (d. 641); Thomas the Presbyter (d. *c.* 640) who reported this bloody fact died the same year. Considering the proximity of these historical events, some doubts emerged. However Thomas's Chronicle made a first explicit allusion to Muḥammad in a non-Islamic source, nicknaming the troops as the Arabs of Muḥammad,[53] as well as reporting some belligerent events which correspond to the conquering campaigns.[54] This chronicle also reports on raids in poor villages of Palestine where Christians, Jews and Samaritans were killed while the entire region was plundered: this methodology was very common to the Bedouin lifestyle.

Another important Syriac source that gives interesting information about the Arab conquests and the subsequent historical events is that attributed to Sabeos, the Bishop of Bragatunis, whose chronicle went up to the 660s and the first *Fitna*.[55] The most interesting aspect is that this pseudo-Sabeos's analysis seems particularly enriched by historical passages that cannot be observed in other previous sources. His analysis, for example, stressed the support of the Jews of Edessa for the Arabs who conquered Palestine and Syria; however, when they tried to rebuild the Temple of Solomon in Jerusalem, they did not receive permission from the new Arab rulers.[56]

Pseudo-Sabeos is one of the first to recognize Muḥammad's monotheistic *visio* as closely related to an Abrahamic background. However, he also recognized that his capability of trying to unify the Arabs was strongly related to a political dimension.[57]

At the same time, the attraction of Muḥammad's Arabs' for the southern regions of the Byzantine empire, in particular the Holy Land, is militarily confirmed by the strategy adopted in trying to isolate and conquer it after having already defeated the main Roman army (after the battle of Yarmuk in 636). Sabeos reports information about the battle of Dāthin (*c.* 634) near Gaza, which is usually more described as a raid,[58] when the huge expedition followed the caravan trail, crossing the River Jordan not far from Jericho. On the contrary, Sabeos's information about the battle of Yarmuk is non-existent, unlike later Islamic sources,[59] but also other non-Muslim sources.[60]

The importance of Sabeos's information is also related to the first *Fitna*, which involved at least four parties: that of ʿAlī ibn Abū Ṭālib which settled on the eastern side, Muʿāwiya in Syria and Palestine, one in Egypt and the last, related to the Arabs of Ashkelon, which as suggested by R. Hoyland could refer to ʿĀʾisha's supporters. 'Those in Egypt and Arabia united and killed their king (ʿUthmān), pillaged the royal treasures and established another king (ʿAlī)', which fits what we know from Muslim writers of the coalition between the Egyptians and the Medinese.[61]

It is possible that the proximity of these historical events, from the murder of ʿUthmān ibn ʿAffān to the Battle of the Camel and that of Ṣiffin (657), did not make it possible to properly understand a complicated phase of inter-clanic relationship; moreover, it is evident that after the rulership of ʿUmar ibn al-Khaṭṭāb, pseudo-Sabeos increasingly refers to Muʿāwiya as the political figure of reference in the region. The construction of a first naval force and the attempt to conquer Constantinople from the sea is not confirmed by other sources;[62] on the contrary, Dionysius of Tel Mahre, Theophilus of Edessa and Theophanes the Confessor argued differently about the Syrian governor's real intentions. The target was not the Byzantine capital, but Cyprus: there were different expeditions and battles, some Arab and some Roman victories and Emperor Constantine was directly involved, but in the end the island was occupied by the Saracen forces.[63]

It is clear that non-Islamic sources highlight a plurality of approaches to the Arab conquering campaigns that, on the one hand, can emerge as quite confusing and, on the other hand, can make the analysis complex and enriching.

The methodological approach furthermore must consider political and religious narratives as directly linked to every author's personal bond with Constantinople, Emperor Heraclius as the political leader and the Christological positions assumed in the first decades of the seventh century.

It is evident how Greek sources, linked to a Byzantine-Romanized religious élite such as John Moschus, Sophronius of Jerusalem and later John of Damascus, are more oriented towards considering the Saracens' invasion as a form of pervasive raids (*ghazawāt*), made by 'heretic barbarians'. The confusing Christological approach of early Islām to ʿĪsā ibn Maryam will not only be confirmed by John of Damascus, but as reported by R. Hoyland, 'until 775, no Christian text will adopt the term of Muslim to define the Arabs'.[64]

In relation to violence by the Arabs, on the contrary, Greek, Syrian and Armenian sources are able to give some limited information about belligerent events: in John Moschus and Sophronius of Jerusalem, they are rare; while in Thomas the Presbyter and Sabeos, they are more extensively reported.

However, as we move away from the years of the conquests (634–656), the information becomes more religiously oriented to trying to define the Arabs' devotionism. In parallel with this first phase, which we can find until the end of the seventh century, information praising the newcomers can be found in Gabriel of Qartmin (d. *c.* 648), Benjamin I Patriarch of Alexandria (d. 665), a Maronite Chronicle, Jacob of Edessa (d. 708) etc.

It is therefore evident that Nestorians and Monophysites had a better consideration of the new rulers in relation to the religious freedom which ensued and compared to the previous Byzantine and Sasanian domination. Isho'yahb III of Adiabene (d. 659) argued: 'As for the Arabs, to whom God has at this time given rule (*shūlṭānā*, prob. *sulṭān*) over the world, you know well how they act towards us. Not only do they not oppose Christianity, but they praise our faith, honour the priests and saints of our Lord, and give aid to the churches and monasteries.'[65]

John bar Penkaye (d. 687) notes, for example, that 'the Christian religion and its members were respected, before calling them, (God) had prepared them beforehand to hold Christians in honour; thus, they also had a special commandment from God concerning our monastic station, that they should hold it in honour'.

No attempts were made by the Arabs to force conversion: 'Their robber bands went annually to distant parts and to the islands, bringing back captives from all the peoples under the heavens. Of each person they required only tribute, allowing him to remain in whatever faith he wished.'

And on Mu'āwiya's rule, he reports: 'Justice flourished in his time and there was great peace in the regions under his control; he allowed everyone to live as they wanted' and he later adds that crops were bountiful and trade doubled. In fact, his only criticism was the lack of persecution: 'There was no distinction between pagan and Christian', he laments, 'the faithful was not known from a Jew.'[66]

However, as reported by Bar Hebraeus in *Chronicle Ecclesiastica*, the ability to obtain favours from a new ruler was not so easy because inter-confessional policies were directly related to a plurality of factors.[67]

In his analysis, Penkaye is also able to give us information about the second *Fitna* which he defined as a sort of revolt, led by al-Mukhtār al-Thaqafī (d. 687), and partly carried out by slaves, prisoners of war and freemen. However, the Christian witness argues that behind this uprising, there was also certainly a religious-political reason which reflects al-Mukhtār's support for 'Abd Allāh ibn al-Zubayr, the champion of the house of God. John, contrary to Islamic sources, argues that 'we have here a rebellion of men wrenched from their homelands and forced into a life of servitude in the strange environment of the Arab garrison towns, and who have now seized the opportunity afforded them by Mukhtār to rebel against their masters'.[68]

The apocalyptic's description of the second *Fitna* – 'for here is a people against a people and a kingdom against a kingdom; here are famines, earthquakes and plagues, only one thing is missing for us: the advent of the Deceiver'[69] – is more respectful of Messianic Christian beliefs than any kind of concrete religious proto-Islamic interpretation, also because John Bar Penkaye, unlike other Chroniclers, highlights as the last datable event the death of al-Mukhtār in 687, before the end of the second *Fitna*, which, on the contrary, would have continued until 691.[70]

Until the end of the second *Fitna*, the non-Islamic sources are unable to give us a deeper comprehension of Islām and of religious men's understanding of the Arabs; in parallel, the Latin chronicle by Arculf, who probably visited Jerusalem in 683, reports 'that famous place where once stood the magnificently constructed Temple, near the eastern wall, the Saracens now frequent a rectangular house of prayer which they have built in a crude manner, constructing it from raised planks and large beams over some remains of ruins. This house can, as it is said, accommodate at least 3000 people'.[71]

This quotation which confirmed the presence of a preliminary mosque in the area occupied today by the al-Aqṣā stressed the attention of the existence of a prayer location already differentiated from Synagogues and Churches; the debate on the architectural connection with religiosity in this historical phase needs a wider debate which will be presented shortly.

F. Donner, however, in *Visions of the Early Islamic Expansion: Between the Heroic and the Horrific*, on the plurality of the 'narratives' involved, described it: 'the Islamic conquests are roundly denounced as having not only some evil side-effects, like all wars, but as being somehow different because their goal was alleged to be the fanatical, repressive, and destructive subjection of non-Muslims',[72] which is what, on the contrary, is absent from the non-Islamic sources.

There are few excerpts, as already mentioned, which report the violence of battles with the Byzantines and raids made against villages and monasteries performed by the 'barbarian' Saracens; on the contrary, there is no clear proof that this specific intensity of violence was made for political or religious reasons.

It is historically clear that every process of expansion cannot be dissociated from a considerable level of violence and there were certainly military episodes and instances of gratuitous violence against military but also non-combatant forces. However, it has also been reported how the Caliph Abū Bakr, in dispatching his armies to Syria, ordered that women, children, monks and fruit trees or crops were to be spared, and that when the armies of the Believers were welcomed to a city, they should make a pact guaranteeing that they would be ruled over according to their laws and practices.[73]

If, on the one hand, this is indicative of an early political-military intention to make raids capable of becoming a sort of permanent occupation, on the other hand, the preservation of a social, economic and religious *status quo*, in a similar *milieu*, is equally confirmed.

Dionysius of Tel Mahre reports how the caliph 'Abd al-Malik ibn Marwān (d. 705) appointed a capable Christian of Edessa, Athanasius Bar Gumoye, to serve as a guardian for 'Abd al-Malik's brother 'Abd al-Azīz ibn Marwān (d. 705), still a child, when he was appointed governor of Egypt. Athanasius effectively ruled the country until 'Abd al-Azīz reached the age of majority and his family continued to hold an important position in the administration in the following decades.[74]

Jacob of Edessa (d. 708) finally argues that in dire need a deacon may serve soldiers on a military campaign, and if compelled by the Arabs, a monk or a priest may participate in battle, though he faces suspension if he kills someone.[75] Jacob seems willing to be lenient in matters that 'do no harm'. A priest may donate the blessing of the Saints to Muslims or pagans and may teach the children of Muslims, Harranians and Jews.[76]

With regard to the first aspect, this introduces the following section. The presence of Arab Christian soldiers in the early 'Believers' army, before and after the Arab conquering campaigns, is confirmed here by Jacob of Edessa.

3. Old Élites – new élites in dialogue. Why did Muʿāwiya ibn Abī Sufyān (d. 680) live in Jābiyah for two decades?

In approaching the heart of this historical analysis – the existence of an early conceptualization of the holiness of war in Islām during the conquering campaigns in relation to religious otherness – it is important to introduce a dual approach: the former reflects on the understanding of religious plurality in the early communities of seventh-century 'Believers'; the latter, on the concrete religious-political identity of the conquerors and their approach to the previous Byzantine and Sassanian cultural *milieu*.

The central meaning of *otherness* in this historical phase assumes a theoretical interest in considering it through an inclusive-exclusive perspective. The other, as reported by Harry Munt, can be perceived as being *either like me*, or *not like me* in a black-and-white understanding. Approaching the grey, the other can also be *either who is too much like me* or *who would like to be like me* (the assimilationist perspective) and it is in this specific case that F. Donner's 'Believers' were probably developing an identitarian path in the seventh century. The problem is alterity and similarity, but at the same time, the problem is how much I know about myself, my religion and how much I know about the Others' religions and religiosity, in particular when a conquest leads me to start living in a different geographical area.[77]

Since the beginning of European studies on early Islām, the perception is that at least until the end of the second *Fitna*, the early community did not have a real confessional identity in relation to the Other's faith, orthopraxis, dogmas etc.[78] Donner highlights that being a 'Believer' was not an expression of a personal confessional identity, but a shared belief in a monotheistic understanding of God as the creator and judge of the world, as well as the conviction that there will be a Day of Judgement.[79] All the debate on the expectation of the arrival of the Davidic Messiah, that Jesus was the Messiah and that his status was peculiar in relation with a debate with Christians, became religiously relevant in a second phase, probably after 692 when, for political-religious reasons, the early inner *ḥunafā'* needed to take a decisive step in this direction.[80]

Until the end of the prophetic phase, when Muḥammad played an important role in the early community, his attempt to delegitimate the Bedouin lifestyle and reject kinship-clan identities as a basis of the community is emphasized in the Quranic message, as well as by the actions of the Prophet. The children of Israel, the Christian followers of Jesus and the early Believers of Muḥammad defined themselves as part of a community based on confessional inclusiveness, also allowing previous unbelievers and polytheists joining it.[81]

As Uri Rubin clearly highlights, the pre-Islamic conceptualization of *Ḥanīfiyya* is poetically reported by figures such as Umayya ibn Abī l-Ṣalt of Ṭā'if, Abū Qays Ṣirma ibn Abī Anas, the Prophet's enemy Abū 'Āmir 'Abd 'Amr ibn Ṣayfī of the Banū Aws of Medina, who already practised *tarahhub*: wearing a mantle and searching concealment, as Christian monks did, but without necessarily being Christians.[82]

Gil's related study reports that Muḥammad's verbal dispute with 'Amr ibn Ṣayfī was probably based on a different understating of being *Ḥanīf*, opening a debate on it and bringing this early conflict more on to the political than the religious scene.[83] Ibn Sa'd, in reporting this story, argued that 'Amr ibn Ṣayfī was prominently considered more eager to observe *Ḥanīfiyya* than anyone else in Medina, identifying it as the religion of Abraham.[84]

Another *Ḥanīf* important to mention was 'Uthmān ibn Maẓ'ūn of the Banū Jumaḥ, who was probably an ascetic monotheist even before encountering Muḥammad. Like early 'Believers', his ascetic attitude was problematically considered by Abū Bakr and 'Umar ibn al-Khaṭṭāb, who never liked him for his pietistic immoderation, even though, in relation to the second *Khalīfa al-Rāshidūn*, there was probably also a more personal problem, because his wife, Zaynab, was 'Uthmān's sister.

Ibn Sa'd, in his *Ṭabaqāt al-Kabīr*, reports how once 'Uthmān asked the Prophet how he could suppress his carnal passions more, as he was considering making a vow of chastity, even castration. Muḥammad honestly replied: 'You already fast the entire day and pray during the night, however, your eyes and your body have some rights on you, so, pray and sleep, fast and break your fast.'[85] He stressed a more moderate position, as later reported in the Qur'ān 16: 78 and 30: 21.

It is important here to consider the plurality of the early 'Believers' in evaluating their spiritual feelings, as well as those who were diametrically related to the influence that the Arab Abrahamic faith was having in a geography which was increasingly affected by their influence.

As the very first verse of the Qur'ān emphasizes: 'Read! In the name of your Lord who created: He created man from a clinging form. Read! Your Lord is the most Bountiful One who taught by the pen who taught man what he did not know' (96: 1-5), the community was inclusive to make this learning approach as open as possible.

The Prophet's wavering in naming a successor has been differently interpreted in the contemporary period. His unexpected death and the inability to find a successor so as not to exacerbate inner conflicts in the community after the 'admission' of Quraysh and of Ṭā'if make the decision of the *Shūrā* under the Saqīfa more complicated.[86]

The debate and initial conflict during the consultation between *Anṣār*, *Muhājirūn* and Quraysh increased when Abū Bakr assumed a pro-Quraysh position, repudiating *Anṣār*'s claim to succession and rejecting religious criteria as a basis for eligibility to rule.[87]

From the beginning of the post-prophetic phase, Abū Bakr acted to preserve the unity of the *Umma* as a political entity, in a historical phase in which the huge majority of Arab clans had a limited knowledge about a new form of religiosity, just as they had about the different meanings of being *Ḥanīf*.

The first and the second *al-Khulafā' al-Rāshidūn* (632–644), under whom the majority of the conquering campaigns in the Near East took place, tried to preserve political unity in projecting it towards an ongoing status of war and conquest that most of the Arabs not in command perceived as an updated version of *ghazawāt*.[88] Proto-Islām had not had nearly enough time to eradicate the clan's existing policies and political alliance system based on the *Jāhilī* concept of *al-Bayt, Sharaf* and *Siyāda*.

It is evident that under the *Saqīfa*, Abū Bakr and 'Umar ibn al-Khaṭṭāb probably emphasized the element of noble origin in trying to prove that the *Anṣār*'s claim to succession was unfounded, as well as to create a more unitary front in considering the Quraysh and their more 'cosmopolitan' Arabs' relationship in making an inclusive political agreement.[89] Contrary to a religious 'meritocratic' step, the *Muhājirūn* were able to follow a path that was still pre-Islamic, in assuring alliances and unity.

Unlike the debate which followed R. Hoyland's publication, *In God's Path*, it is evident from my point of view that the 'Believers'' attitude was far from being religious (Bism-Allah interlocution was already part of the Hanifiyya's form of reverence without a clear and specific divinity of reference) and from being 'national' as we can try to understand this term's meaning in the seventh century.[90] Reconsidering the Arab-Byzantine's *foederati* approach, Jafnid and Naṣrid clans were to the Ghassānid and Lakhmid confederation as the Quraysh were to the Ḥijāzī region.

In parallel, as the battle of Mu'tah shows, there could never have been a military victory against the Byzantines and the Sassanians without a unitary front of the majority of the Arab confederations of the Ḥijāz, Najd and probably the northern Arabian region (Ṭābuk, Dumat al-Jandal); in addition, as the *Ridda* wars emphasized, the fragmentation of the Arabs in relation to the emergence of different figures who attributed 'prophetic' abilities to themselves was already in vogue.

U. Rubin's analysis of the meaning of *Ḥanīfiyya*, and its inclusive-exclusive aspects in the Medinan phase, with the rise of Musaylima ibn Ḥabīb, Sajāḥ bint al-Ḥārith ibn Suwayd b. ʿUqfān and Ṭulayḥa ibn Khūwaylid ibn Nawfal al-Asadī as 'religious' figures, stressed a risky destructive outcome which cannot bypass pre-Islamic *Jāhilī*'s policies for something still unclear and divisive.[91]

In trying to answer the question of who the Arab 'Believers' and non-Believers were, the Islamic sources clearly did not excessively stress the presence of clans whose Islamic affiliation was still in doubt. However, it is also historically and geographically true that during the early campaigns in 634 and before the battle of Yarmuk (*c.* 636) and Qādisiyya, the 'Believers' had to cross areas where the most important Arab tribes were the Balī in Balqā, the southern region of 'Ammān, Transjordan and Palestine; Judhām and Lakhm in the same area, but on the eastern side; the Kalb in the Palmyrene; and the Ghassān, generally understood, in the Ḥawrān (southern Damascus); while finally Tanūkh and Bahrā' lived in the Jazīra.

Members of these Arab Christian clans are mentioned on the 'Believers'' side during the battle of Yarmuk and during the Iraqi campaign: al-Qa'qā' ibn 'Amr (Tamīm), Diḥya ibn Khalīfa (Kalb), Jarīr ibn 'Abdullāh (Bajīla), Maṭar ibn Fiḍḍa (Qays ibn Tha'laba), al-Mundhir ibn Ḥassān ibn Ḍirar (Ḍabba), Jabala ibn al-Ayham (Ghassān)[92] etc.

However, as reported by F. Donner, it is probable that the Arab Christian participation in the Syrian and Iraqi campaigns was on both sides.[93] The Islamic narrative on Jabala ibn al-Ayham is quite confusing about his real affiliation: Ibn 'Asākir, Ṭabarī and Balādhuri, probably using Azdī al-Baṣrī, argued that the chief of the Ghassān started the battle on the side of the Romans, but, afterwards, we find him on the side of the Anṣār: 'you are our brethren and the sons of our fathers', which remains quite obscure, also because the same sources identified him as leaving Syria with the Byzantines after the Arab occupation of the entire region.[94] In considering the case of Jabala and the battle of Yarmuk, it could also be possible that he started on the side of the Romans, when the huge Byzantine army was directed towards Damascus and then Jābiyah,[95] but afterwards, aware of the clan's relationship with different Anṣār, changed coalition.

Finally, reflecting on the Islamic narrative about the disagreement between Jabala ibn al-Aiham and 'Umar ibn al-Khaṭṭāb, which has the goal of showing that from the beginning the *Jizya* was imposed on non-Muslims, the possibility that this was really concrete is quite limited.

The payment of the *Jizya*, as a tax imposed on non-Muslims not directly related to providing services for the new rulers, is certainly associated with the establishment of a structured empire and with the local governatorate capable of knowing their respective population. The information at our disposal stressed how a first census was probably attempted by the Umayyad caliph Mu'āwiya ibn Abū Sufyan for Egypt and done by 'Amr ibn al-'Āṣ around 658, while we need to wait until 'Abd al-Malik ibn Marwān for one in Syria, probably around 685. Despite this, the non-Islamic sources argued that there was no census in Egypt until 692, at the end of the second *Fitna*.[96]

It would have been quite improbable to impose taxation without a previous comprehension of the numbers of male inhabitants, peasants, traders and their religious affiliation; on this topic the Islamic sources emerged as quite dubious because all of them, even though with a different emphasis, highlighted an un-historically rapid level of conversion to a sort of Islām and which does not reflect the information emerging from other sources.

However, one of the most important passages in considering the relationship between the old élite system and the increasing presence of a new one is related to the peaceful affiliation among them as a significant feature which could preserve the *status quo* during a civil war in the community of the 'Believers' themselves.

The context of the first *Fitna*, which broke out with the killing of the third Rightful Caliph 'Uthmān ibn 'Affān (d. 656) in Medina, more than emphasizing the unity of the 'Believers' emphasized their fragmentation. The over-rapid expansion process of the Arabs boosted the inner conflict in relation to political, economic and social reasons: the raids were reaching poorer geographical areas on the Iranian plateau as well as in North Africa and the pillage was no longer very satisfactory; at the same time, the excessively distant presence of the clan of origin and of the family fostered internal incomprehensions between ruling figures and part of the soldiers. At the same time, 'Umar ibn al-Khaṭṭāb (d. 644) had imposed that only unproductive agricultural land, without an owner, could become property of the soldiers, opposing every kind of pre-Islamic pillage habit and increasing conflict for the appropriation of land.

In parallel, the Quraysh élite continued to increase their political and economic power, being able to own important properties without even being part of the conquering campaigns: this was the case of Ṭalḥa Ibn 'Ubayd Allāh and az-Zubayr ibn al-'Awwām.

Finally, the possibility of controlling the military expeditions and the generals who led new raids outside Mesopotamia to the east and in North Africa, to the west, increased the level of insecurity and instability. It is no coincidence that the majority of the insurrections against the central government in the early Islamic age came from the borderlands.[97]

The relations between the most important figures of the 'Believers' were becoming even more conflictual, in particular during 'Umar ibn al-Khaṭṭāb's strong caliphate: his difficult relationship with Khālid ibn al-Walīd and 'Amr ibn al-'Āṣ is known.[98] This also continued during the reign of 'Uthmān, who was accused of a lack of piety and clan nepotism.

Contrary to the unitarian Islamic *topos*, the decades which followed the conquests saw great political-religious continuity in Iraq, Syria and Palestine in the urban as well as in the more rural areas: the former more populated by the former Byzantine–Sassanid élite; the latter, by the new Arab conquerors. The urban élite negotiated to preserve the *status quo* from the beginning through their religious leaders, as the example of Sophronius of Jerusalem's letters clarified; in the countryside, new *aḥlāf*, between the clans, updated the inter-Arab relationships in making new strategies and alliances.[99]

As A. Papaconstantinou argued:

> Faith-defined communities are seen by many as a hallmark of Islamic society. Yet to what extent is this system co-terminous with Muslim rule, as has usually been assumed? When one analyses the first decades of Islam, it is difficult to find a trace of it. This is not simply an argumentum ex silentio: there is also positive evidence that points to a different social situation.[100]

Reflecting on this, it is important to outline how in the absence of a new centralized government, like Constantinople and Ctesiphon earlier, and until Damascus, the religious authorities in the cities and in the countryside became the new one: monastery's abbots, monks and priests became the newcomers' figures of reference.

The increasing power of canon law to cover marriage, property and inheritance among the clergy as for the laity has usually been understood by M.G. Morony as a sign that, in the absence of the old imperial empire, the religious communities were improving their own legal systems in enlarging their specific sectors of competences.

At the same time, the administration in Syria, Palestine, Iraq and Egypt, when updated, remained in Christian hands. This is not only the case of the famous Chalcedonian Manṣūr ibn Sarjūn, the grandfather of John of Damascus, who participated in the negotiations for the capitulation of the main town in Syria and then became the head of Mu'āwiya's tax administration. This position was held later by his son and grandson until the death of 'Abd al-Malik and it is also the case of the Nestorian Banū 'Ibād, Arabs of al-Ḥīra who were employed by the first Umayyad caliph as tax collectors for the Muslims, but they were also allowed to keep a legal system based on church districts in which the local priest served as a judge in accordance with the civil authorities.[101]

It is evident that the large number of Christian communities in Iraq was allowed by the Umayyad themselves to use local religious authorities to keep an administrative and juridical system which, at this time, was very necessary.[102] One of the most interesting aspects, reported by A. Papaconstantinou in relation to the early *dhimmi*,[103] concerns the Jacobites, who reached an agreement with Muʿāwiya to pay a tribute in exchange for protection against the persecution of the Melkites.

> The passage carries several important implications. Firstly, that this protection, and the price that went with it was only afforded on an *ad hoc* basis, after negotiation and well after the conquest; secondly that the Maronites were neither protected nor had to pay anything; and thirdly, that the Chalcedonians were at that time in a position to persecute the Jacobites, to the point that the latter needed state protection.[104]

However, A. Papaconstantinou's article is quite confusing for the adoption of unprecise Christian terms; the first historically recognized Maronites' patriarch was elected around 685 when Muʿāwiya was no longer in power; nevertheless, this subject is particularly interesting to introduce the question: Why did Muʿāwiya ibn Abī Sufyān (d. 680) live in Jābiyah for two decades?

It is historically reported that Muʿāwiya, who became governor of Syria around 639 as chosen by ʿUmar ibn al-Khaṭṭāb, resided in Jābiyah, the capital of the Ghassānid confederation for at least twenty years, before being proclaimed caliph in Jerusalem, a highly symbolic town for the whole of Christianity, but also for the 'Believers', before reaching Damascus.[105]

Ibn ʿAsākir in his *Taʾrīkh Madīnat Dimashq* clearly affirms how Hishām ibn al-Kalbī also argued that the Arab Christians of the Ghassānid confederation, who did not follow the Byzantine forces outside Syria, rapidly converted to Islām and took part in the battle of Ṣiffīn (657) and Marj Rāhiṭ (684), becoming jurists, poets, generals and governors.

The famous Ḥassān ibn Mālik ibn Baḥdal al-Kalbī (d. *c.* 688–89) became the most important ally of the Umayyad during the historical period of the *Fitnas*.[106] However, with the increasing anarchic situation in Syria and Palestine, due to the internal fragmentation of the first 'Believers" community, and with the Byzantine on the other side of the Anatolian border, it is difficult to think that many Christian Arabs converted to such an unrepresentative new religion as well as one which was so unclearly different from Christianity.[107]

This assumption is indirectly confirmed by the conversion process to Islām in different geographical areas of the Arabian Peninsula at the end of the historical *al-Khulafāʾ al-Rāshidūn* period. As Harry Munt clarifies in reporting some excerpts from letters, written by the Iraqi Catholicos Isho'yahb III to Rev-Ardashir in Fars (probably in the decade 649–659) for failing to halt the conversion of increasing numbers of Omani Christians (Mazūnāyē in Syriac) to Islām, it would make it difficult to think that more deeply Christianized areas such as Syria and Palestine were already Islamicized in the same period as, on the contrary, Islamic sources clearly emphasized.[108]

However, the comparison between the Islamization of Arabia in the seventh century with the Christianization of the Arabs along the Byzantine borders in the fourth to sixth centuries looks more problematic, considering that the leading élite of the Naṣride did not convert until the end of the sixth century. As reported in Munt's article in relation to the possible reasons why the *Mazūnāyē* abandoned their faith,

Isho'yahb III argued that the *Mazūnāyē* themselves said that it was not because the *Ṭayyāyē* forced them to abandon their faith, but because they obliged them to give up half of their possessions to keep their faith.[109] This would have been an Arab Christian narrative adopted to slightly disempower their responsibility for future conversion to Islām.

The importance of considering the Banū Umayya's matrimonial policy after they were integrated in the 'Believers" community is important to understand their future political strategy.

It is evident that the Islamic narratives on them are quite problematic, in particular for the 'Abbāsids' subsequent attempt to discredit them; moreover, as Tayeb el-Hibri stressed, Ṭabarī's historical interpretation of 'Uthmān ibn 'Affān's murder remained unclear.

The turbulence of 'Alī's reign is not very respectful of the personal expression of Muḥammad's cousin that 'the best servant of God is one who is an '*Imām 'ādil'*, which means reflecting on the ability to balance the moral and political obligations between family and state consideration'.[110]

Proto-Shī'a's utopic understanding that the leading 'Believers" figure must be a member of the Prophet's clan and the best at the same time, an *Imām,* while the proto-Sunnite reply highlighted how, after the caliphate of 'Umar ibn al-Khaṭṭāb, the main difficulties were absorbed by the technical-bureaucratic complications in ruling an empire with increasing management-political problems is emblematic of the issues that the situation revealed.

It is evident that a fraction of the early 'Believers" community, independently of their personal and direct affiliation with the Banū Hāshim, needed a prolonged 'Prophetic' phase to better consider Muḥammad's teachings, to better try and absorb them, and to better comprehend the political options.

On the other hand, the Banū Umayya who, with the exception of 'Uthmān ibn 'Affān and few more, had recently accepted the Prophet as a significant political and religious figure and who had significant clan-economic contacts in and outside the entire Peninsula were already able to impose their authority a few decades after the Prophet's death, becoming deeply influential within the early 'Believers" community.

At the same time, 'Uthmān ibn 'Affān, who had married two of the Prophet's daughters, had a limited engagement with Muḥammad's clan because both Ruqayyah (d. 624), with whom he had emigrated to Abyssinia for a while, and Umm Kulthūm (d.630) died before the Prophet and without giving a male heir: 'Abdallāh ibn 'Uthmān, Ruqayyah's son, died two years after his birth.

The fact that Umm Kulthūm married 'Uthmān the same year Ruqayyah died is indicative of the Prophet's interest in preserving the tie with one of the few Umayyads who followed him.[111] The presence of other Umayyads, such as Khālid ibn Sa'īd and Abū Ḥudhayfah ibn 'Utbah ibn Rabī 'ah, who did not enjoy the same 'marriage' treatment, clearly stressed who was preferred by the Prophet.

Muḥammad used 'Uthmān ibn 'Affān politically to negotiate the peaceful entrance to Mecca to arrange a pilgrimage (628); his diplomatic ties played a significant role in signing the treaty of Ḥudaybiyyah in which the Meccans, like the majority of the Arab confederations of Arabia, started to recognize the 'Believers' of Medina.[112]

Finally, the detail that 'Uthmān's maternal grandmother was a sister of Muḥammad's father, and that Abū Sufyān's grandfather was also a brother of 'Abd al-Muṭṭalib, highlighted how at a family level 'Believers and Meccan polytheists' were as interconnected as a spider's web.

Conversely, it is also true that with the Prophet's death (632), as with that of his wife, Umm Kulthūm, two years earlier, 'Uthmām's matrimonial policy was addressed to implementing the relationship with the Quraysh and with the Christianized Arab clans of the north:

1. Fākhitah bint Ghazwān,
2. Umm al-Banīn bint Uyaynāh of the Banū Fazāra (a branch of the Najdī Ghaṭafān),
3. Fāṭima bint al-Walīd, the daughter of Khalīd ibn al-Walīd, the famous generals of the conquering campaigns and member of the Banū Makhzūm, a Quraysh tribe,
4. Umm 'Amr Umm Najm bint Jundūb of the Banū Jundūb clan, which was a branch of the Banū Jadīla,[113] a Christian clan related to the Ghassānid confederation,[114]
5. Ramlah bint Shaybah, of the Quraysh clan of Banū 'Abd-Shams,
6. Nā'ila bint al-Furāfiṣa, a Christian woman of the Banū Kalb, one of the most important Christian clans of the Ghassānid confederation. It is reported that when 'Uthmān was killed (656), Muʿāwiya ibn Abū Sufyān asked to marry her twice: the first time she refused; but the second time, she replied with a letter containing two front teeth which she had deliberately broken, stressing that she was no longer beautiful and Muʿāwiya should not ask her again.[115] However, as reported by M.J. Kister, Nā'ila's father, Al-Furāfiṣa b. al-Aḥwaṣ b. 'Amr b. Tha'laba b. al-Ḥārith b. Ḥiṣn b. Ḍamḍam b. 'Adiyy b. Jandal, obtained the heritage of the goldsmiths' work of the Fadak Oasis.[116]

This brief geneaological excursus has the purpose of showing how the third *Khalīfa al-Rāshidūn* was already oriented, after the death of the Prophet's daughters, to strengthening the political connections with the Quraysh, the most important of them, 'Abd Shams and Makhzūm, and the Banū Kalb, the most important clan of the Ghassānid confederation in the north of Arabia.

This was the same policy that Muʿāwiya adopted after having reached Syria and Palestine as well as after having been chosen by 'Umar as Governor of the latter.

Muʿāwiya (d. 680) married Maysūm bint Baḥdal, the daughter of Baḥdal ibn Unayf ibn al-Kalbī, the chief of the Banū Kalb whose members played a significant military role in the Umayyad army, passing from the Sufyānid to the Marwanid phase and making a prominent contribution during the entire second *Fitna* and afterwards.

A grandson of Baḥdal ibn Unayf ibn al-Kalbī and nephew of Maysūm, Ḥassān ibn Mālik (d. 688/89) became the Umayyad governor of Palestine and Jordan during the rule of Muʿāwiya and Yazīd, remaining an eminent member of the court afterwards.

However, Muʿāwiya also married Fākhitah bint Qaraẓah ibn 'Abd Manāf, a Quraysh woman, and Nā'ila bint 'Umārah al-Kalbī, the daughter of a paternal uncle of his first wife, another Kalbite woman, but he probably divorced her very quickly.[117]

It was evident that Jābiyah was, more than other villages, the most secure place for a new governor who was increasingly driving his clan affiliation with those

Christian Arabs who had already inherited an increasingly significant role in the region. Considering the 'racial' differences, the Umayyad were not the Byzantines, but Arabs like the Banū Kalb; at the same time, the latter would have played a significant function for the new dynasty of Damascus, not as *foederati*, but even better: the closer relationship reached through a matrimonial policy that the Umayyad decided to pursue was maximized when the Umayyad became caliphs in 661.

The information on Yazīd ibn Muʿāwiya (d. 683) is quite fragmentary to portray a clear continuity. However, as reported, the first-born of the Caliph grew up in the Kalbite clan and in the Umayyad one, marrying a Kalbite woman at first, the mother of his son Muʿāwiya II, while Khālid ibn Yazīd's mother was Umm Khālid bint Abī Hāshim of the 'Abd al-Shams clan.[118]

The outbreak of the second *Fitna* shows the greater difficulties in keeping the Umayyad-Kalbite alliance.

With the death of Yazīd I (683) and of Muʿāwiya II (684), the only male son borne by a Kalbite woman and the absence of a Sufyānid candidate, many clans of north Arabia, such as the Qays, started to support Ibn al-Zubayr as *amīr al-mu'minīn*, whose forces occupied Egypt, imposing a local Zubayrid governor (684).[119]

The worsening situation pushed the Quḍā'a branch of the Kalbite confederation to elect another non-Kalbite son of Yazīd I, Khālid ibn Yazīd, as *amīr al-mu'minīn*; but his tender age, the Zubayrid's increasing support in Syria, as well as the al-Mukhtār millenarian movement in Iraq emphasized the search for a valid candidate outside the Sufyānid branch.

As reported by different sources, in 683, the tribes of Quḍā'a, Kinda and Ghassān held a *shūrā* in Jābiyah and, after intense discussion, the alliance with Marwān ibn al-Ḥakam was proclaimed by Ḥassān ibn Mālik ibn Baḥdal, the chief of the Kalbites.[120]

At the same time the armies that took part in the second *Fitna* and fought the battles of Ḥarrah (683) and Marj Rāhiṭ (684) were mostly made up of Arab Christian clans, in particular on the Umayyad side, but also with some exceptions on the pro-Zubayrid forces: P. Crone reports that the Judhām of Palestine did not accept submitting to a son of a Kalbite woman, as Yazīd I was.[121]

It is also true that Marwān ibn al-Ḥakam had already married another Kalbite woman, Layla bint Zabbān ibn al-Aṣbagh al-Kalbī, even though 'Abd al-Malik ibn Marwān (d. 705) was the son of a previous Qurayshite wife, ʿĀʾisha bint Muʿāwiya ibn al-Mughīra.[122]

As a usual praxis, before every expedition which brought the Umayyad army towards a new military confrontation, the 'meeting point' was in Jābiyah, the old Ghassānid capital.

At the battle of Marj Rāhiṭ (684), Kalbite, Ghassānide and Tanūkhid forces were mostly present and in the following years, some of the most important generals of Marwān ibn al-Ḥakam and 'Abd al-Malik were Ḥumayd ibn Ḥurayth ibn Baḥdal al-Kalbī (d. 693) and Sufyān ibn al-'Abrad al-Kalbī (d. 701) who secured Iraq for the Umayyad dominion against the enemies.[123]

The first,[124] a cousin of the caliph Yazīd I and Ḥassān ibn Mālik ibn Baḥdal al-Kalbī (d. 688–9), governor of Palestine and Jordan, commanded the Kalbite in the battle of

Khāzir (686) against pro-'Alid forces, while the second, Sufyān ibn al-'Abrad al-Kalbī, as reported by A. Borrut, was involved in the military operations against 'Amr ibn Sa'īd ibn al-'Aṣ al-Ashdaq in 688/89 and successfully led the siege of Damascus where the latter had sought refuge.

At the same time, Sufyān ibn al-'Abrad al-Kalbī became even more famous for having supported the Iraqi governor al-Ḥajjāj ibn Yūsuf (d. 714) against the Azraqī Khārijītes in Mesopotamia, finally having instrumentally defeated Abd al-Raḥmān ibn al-Ash'ath (d. 704) at Dayr al-Jamājim and at Maskin in 702–703.

Considering his engagement in the Umayyad cause, Sufyān ibn al-'Abrad al-Kalbī was an outstanding military figure whose bravery was celebrated by poets while H. Kennedy defined him the first example of a '*quwwād*': a professional military commander.[125]

The above analysis seems to emphasize how until the end of the second *fitna* (692), prominent Kalbite figures, directly linked to Baḥdal ibn Unayf al-Kalbī (d. *c.* 650) assumed military and political roles in the early Umayyad caliphate. It is difficult to argue until when they remained Christians, as if they probably converted to the preliminary 'believers" creed when 'Abd al-Malik's definitive victory, at the end of the second *Fitna*, underlined the rise of the Marwānid as the concrete leading authority of a more cohesive empire. This is only a logical hypothesis.

However, their loyalty, unlike the tempestuous relationship between the Jafnids and the Byzantine, was never questioned independently of their religious affiliation, like that of many Ghassānids, Thanūkhids, Bakr, Taghlib[126] and other originally Christian Arab clans which continued to fight on the Umayyad side. At the same time, it is also significant to report how some Arab Christian clans, such as the Banū Judhām of Palestine, supported Ibn al-Zubayr against the Umayyad, being defeated in the battle of Khāzir (686) by the Kalbite army.

The Kalbite-Umayyad (Marwānid) alliance continued under 'Abd al-Malik ibn Marwān (d. 705), then under his brother, 'Abd al-Azīz ibn Marwān (d. 705), who became the Egyptian governor.

J. Mabra's analysis stressed a Kalbī lineage on 'Abd al-Azīz Marwānid's side, as he was the son of Laylā bint Zabān ibn al-Aṣbagh ibn 'Amr ibn Tha'laba who hailed from the Banū 'Adī ibn Janāb clan of Dūmat al-Jandal.

It is historically evident then that if Mu'āwiya-Sufyānid's branch was mostly linked with the Syrian Kalbite branch, the Marwānid also had important allies in the northern Arabian Kalbite branch too. The forefather of this alliance seems to be 'Abd al-Raḥman ibn 'Awf, the 'Believers" conqueror of Dūmat al-Jandal and Tumāḍir bint al-Aṣbagh ibn 'Amr, the daughter of al-Aṣbagh ibn 'Amr, the city's ruler. In this case as well, the Islamic narrative stressed an immediate conversion to Islām; 'Abd al-Raḥman ibn 'Awf was put in charge of the Kalb's *ṣadaqa*, while Imru' l-Qays, Tumāḍir's brother, is reported as having worked directly for the Prophet.[127]

However, various other sources attested that pre-Islamic Christianity persisted in Dūmat until at least the middle of the Umayyad age, in particular due to its importance for Christian pilgrimages: it was a centre of passage to reach Jerusalem, for the Arab-Christians coming from Najrān and the Peninsula.[128]

Nevertheless, it is historically evident that without considering the ongoing presence of the previous urban Byzantine administration, in the fifty years after the conquest of

Syria, Palestine, Jazīra and Mesopotamia, the Arab Christian clans, and the Kalbite confederation more specifically, played a hegemonic role not unlike that played by the Jafnids and Naṣrid in late Antiquity.

It is historically clear that if an early conceptualization of the just war should be considered an option in the Arab confederations' belligerent attitude, the same should be recognized as being part the Arab Christian forces' background. As already stated, the Arab Christians had produced a religious interpretation of militantism in relation to their level of Romanization and Christianization; at the same time, it is probable that until Dūmat al-Jandal, the northern Arab geography was quite Christianized as the sources above have clarified.

It is important to emphasize that *Ghazawāt* and warfare were considered from different perspectives on the Arab and Byzantine sides, and if fighting for God and Christ, on the religious side, was given great consideration, there was also certainly a more secular and prosaic attitude linked to prestige and pillage.

Nevertheless, it is highly credible that until the elaboration of an early pietistic and personal belligerent attitude as a preliminary praxis which probably emerged in the second *Fitna* and during the struggle against the Khawārij, the '*jihād*', as it will begin to be considered in the eighth century, was completely dissociated from the conquests and more personally interpreted by the Arab Christian side of the Kalbite, Bakr, Balī, Ghassān etc. than on the 'Believers" one.

3

The religious factor: When did an Islamic identity emerge?

1. From Abrahamic traditions to a new religion: A methodological approach

After having considered historical evidence in showing the complexity of the passage in the sixth and seventh centuries between the former state system and the new proto-Islamic one, it is important here to frame a plural methodological approach in trying to decipher whether the Islamic conceptualization of 'Just War' could already have existed in the seventh century, following Muḥammad's death, or was far from being identified as Islamic.

To make it credible, it is obvious that the most relevant question we need to consider is from when we can contemplate the existence of Islām as a new *credo* able to distinguish itself from Judaism and Christianity, and, more specifically, to outline the peculiarity of Abrahamic continuity in contrast with religious otherness.

The ancient Greek definition of Religion identified it with the term *threskeia/threskos*: 'who is afraid of God', while the more concrete Latin-Roman term of *Religio* corresponds more to the execution of a praxis, a rite, something that needs to be repeated; finally, Cicero in *De Inventione* argued that a religion is 'all about the care and veneration of a superior being whose nature we define as divine'.[1]

In *Das Christentum,* H. Kung outlines how *ethos* and *mores* are closely connected around a 'Revelation' in every Abrahamic religion and around the paradigmatic figure which makes this word of God accessible.

Following it, the historical process of 'Revelation' begins through a first hermeneutical–theological approach which starts from the interpretation by those who were closely in touch with the 'Revelation' or with the paradigmatic figure who was inspired by it.

Can Christianity exist without Christ, or Islām without Muḥammad? Were both of them, independently of their status, aware that they were in the act of creating a new religion? Probably not.[2]

Christ or 'Isā ibn Maryam was a paradigmatic Jewish figure who was not recognized as Messiah by his religious community for political and religious reasons. However, as the *Qumrān* written sources stressed, the proto-Christian *humus* of the encounter between Judaism and those who attributed to Christ the role of Messiah is already indicated in the praxis of the Essenes' pre-Christ community where 'Isā is never mentioned.

In parallel, the pre-Islamic poetry of Ḥijāz, which in the years that followed the *Hijra* sometimes praises the figure of the Prophet and at other times ignores him, reflects the elegiac approach of a Bedouin Arab style which emphasizes the *humus* for every kind of subsequent 'Revelation'.[3]

Hishām ibn al-Kalbī in his *Kitāb al-Aṣnām*, one century and a half after the Prophet's death, depicts the same *humus* from which the monotheistic *visio* of Muḥammad would have emerged both in reference to polytheism and to the Abrahamic roots which have been already stated, in reflecting on the *Ḥanifiyyah*, the concept of which however is not mentioned by Hishām.[4]

The relevance of this analysis frames a plural methodological approach in which historical, archaeological and religious sources will be used to try to answer the main question of this section's title. Considering the former, the most significant aspect is the possibility of distinguishing the historical differences between the first and the second *fitna* as paradigmatically linked to the early appearance of something more connected with a new 'religious' identity. The huge difference between the 'civil strife' which followed 'Uthmān ibn 'Affān's murder, and the long war that broke out after the *bay'ah* was granted to Yazīd I, in continuity with his father's caliphate, is not symptomatically different, unless in relation to the narrative that this second struggle brought out due to the 'Islamic'–non-Islamic narratives.

This feature is connected with the religious, literary and archaeological sources at our disposal and the necessary interpretation that different specialists have made. The emergence of an early new religious identity, to which we will return in the part devoted to the Qur'ān, should be included in the space of not only historical sources, but the geographical–epigraphic ones which emphasized the recognition of the early differences between Islām and the previous Abrahamic faiths, Judaism and Christianity.

Conversely, if the 'Islamic narrative' elaborated by the 'Abbāsid stressed from the beginning the idea that Islām already existed after Muḥammad's death and that this aspect already had a huge influence on the *Ahl al-Kitāb*, it would be important to start by re-framing a different awareness based on the impact that Judaism and Christianity had on the Islamic formative age on historical, archaeological and religious levels.[5]

2. The relevance of the first and second *Fitna*

The great historical difference between the first and the second *Fitna* shows that the Umayyad restoration in the core of the early Arab empire – Syria and Palestine, Egypt and Mesopotamia, Arabia and Iran – would have encouraged a new imperial policy in which Islām would appear as a new and important aspect of identity.

The caliphate of 'Abd al-Malik (d. 705) is emblematic of this purpose. The military victory of this Umayyad caliph against his enemies, 'Abd Allāh ibn al-Zubayr (d. 692) and all those who supported him, was transformed into the victory against those who denigrated the Umayyad as not being 'believers'.[6]

If the first *Fitna* is emblematically linked to rulership legitimacy but broke out due to the great political carelessness linked to the third Khalīfa's assassination in

656,[7] the second one stressed more deeply the legitimacy of the clan, the Umayyad who historically accepted Muḥammad's message only before the Prophet could be recognized as a new ruler of Ḥijāz. The fragmentation of the 'believers'' community during the debate which broke out in the first *Fitna* is more historically connected with clan and personal aversion among the early *Ṣaḥāba* than with the concrete understanding of Islām as a religion.[8] Indeed, since the political rivalries that motivated this confrontation remained current, the internal strife within the community provoked an inner division which was partially recomposed with 'Abd al-Malik's victory, then erupted again with the 'Abbāsid revolution (747–750) and the ongoing 'Alid attempts to reconcile Caliphate and Imamate.

However, if the narrative on the first *Fitna* usually remained based on sources two–three centuries old, the second civil war which broke out when Yazīd I was caliph (680–683) produced more traces in the eighth-century analysis.[9] It is evident that the 'Alid were more interested in collecting, creating and circulating a memory about the first and the second *Fitna* in the clear attempt to support their political claims and to justify their resistance against the Umayyad, who are usually presented as a tyrannical rulership which incoherently assumed the position of spiritual and political leadership that was legitimately of the *Ahl al-Bayt*.[10]

This discordance is the outcome of an inner 'Believers'' production of traditions and narratives that reflect the huge inner fragmentation of the early *Umma*, as the article by Moshe Sharon demonstrates; in parallel, the Umayyad developed a narrative of their own, emphasizing how the heirs of 'Abd al-Shams were the real *Ahl al-Bayt*.

> 'Abdallah b. 'Alī (the uncle of the first 'Abbāssid Caliph) sent the leaders of the people of Syria to *amīr al-mu'minīn* Abū al-'Abbās and when they presented themselves to him, he said to them: 'O people of Syria, what caused you to side with the Umayyads against Banū Hāshim when the latter are the *ahl al-bayt* of the Messenger of Allah, and they are more than anybody else, the most suitable of all the people for this matter. The Syrians swore to Allah, that there is no God but he, that they had no knowledge whatsoever that the Messenger of Allah had any family nor any *ahl-bayt* except Banū Umayyah, until you (namely, the 'Abbāssids) took over. Abū al-Abbās – so the tradition concludes – smiled out of surprise at the ignorance of the Syrians.'[11]

The debate on the legitimacy of the *Ahl al-Bayt* is particularly important in stressing how, until the second *Fitna*, a religious awareness dissociated from the Arab clan inheritance was far from being unconsidered. The Abrahamic tradition of the House of David as it emerged in the Old and New Testaments was probably inspiring for the Caliph 'Abd al-Malik in stressing a new narrative to identify the Umayyad as much a part of the *Ahl al-Bayt* as the Banū Hāshim.

Considering Quraysh clan genealogy, there was certainly a closer family connection between the Banū Umayya and the Banū Hāshim, than between the latter and the Banū 'Adī and the Banū Taym, the clan of the second and the first *Khulāfa al-Rāshidūn* respectively.[12] However, it is also evident that Hāshim and 'Abbās could strongly attribute to themselves a family status that the Umayya could not; this excursus, contrary to the Quranic message, emphasized the importance of the clan 'Narrative' opposing a 'believers" unity, *de facto*, which did not exist in the first centuries after the Prophet's death.

In parallel with this non-religious aspect there is another one which historically reflects on the second *Fitna* and that is relevant for our analysis.

This Ḥadīth appeared in the *Kitāb al-Sunan* by Abū Dāwūd al-Sijistānī and it appears to have been reported by the Prophet's wife, Umm Salama:

> It was narrated from Mu'ādh bin Hishām (he said): My father narrated to me, from Qatādah, from Ṣāliḥ Abī Al-Khalīl, from a companion of his, from Umm Salama, the wife of the Prophet, that the Prophet said: 'There will be a dispute following the death of a *Khalīfah,* and a man from al-Madīnah will go out, fleeing to Makkah. Some of the people of Makkah will come to him and will bring him out against his will, and they will pledge allegiance to him between the Corner (Black Stone) and the *Maqām.* An army will be sent against him from Ash- Shām, which will be swallowed up by the earth in Al-Baidā', between Makkah and Al-Madīnah. When the people see that, the devoted worshipers from Ash-Shām and the best people from Al-'Irāq will come to him and pledge allegiance to him. Then there will arise a man from the Quraish whose maternal uncles are from Kalb, who will send an army against him and he will prevail over them. That (defeated army) will be the force of Kalb. The real loser will be the one who is not present when the wealth of Kalb is divided. He (the Mahdī) will divide the wealth and rule the people in accordance with the *Sunna* of their Prophet. Islām will become established on earth and he will remain for seven years, then he will die, and the Muslims will offer the funeral prayer for *him.* Abū Dāwud said: Some of them narrated from Hishām: Nine years. And some said: Seven years.'[13]

This tradition, which historically reflects the second *Fitna*, identified az-Zubayr ibn al-Awwām as the Medinan Qurashī who, the son of a famous companion of the Prophet, refused to pledge alliance to Yazīd I as caliph after the death of Mu'āwiya ibn Abī Sufyān (680).

> An army will be sent against him from Ash- Shām, which will be swallowed up by the earth in Al-Baidā', between Makkah and Al-Madīnah: *wa-yub 'athu ilayhi ba'thun min ahl al-Shām fa-yukhsafu bihim bi'l-Baydā bayna Mecca wa' l-Madīna.*

This historical passage is probably related to events which followed the death of Ḥusayn ibn 'Alī (d. 680). No mention is made about killing the Prophet's nephew, while the most interesting aspect reflects the understanding of *al-Baydā* (or *al-Kashf bi l-Baydā*) which is attributed to a desertic depression between Medina and Mecca where the army of a Sufyānī was to be annihilated by the reappearance of the Mahdī.

This part of the Ḥadīth, contrary to Attema and Madelung's opinion of it, is probably a *collage* with a significant eschatological apocalyptic base but which needed a historical scenario.[14]

If the latter is the second *Fitna*, the eschatological interpretation does not reflect concrete historical events attributable to the second conflict which affected the community of the 'Believers'. Madelung argues that the first military mission which 'swallowed up' was that led by Muslim ibn ʿUqba al-Murrī (d. 683) and al-Ḥuṣạyn ibn Numayr al-Sakūnī (d. 686), but both Umayyad generals were victorious in the battle of Ḥarrah (683) and they probably would have been able to conquer Mecca if Yazīd I had not died in Damascus, making the decision to return to Shām.[15] In other words, the Ḥadīth narration of the historical events does not properly respect the concrete actions from the beginning; at the same time, the emphasis on the Apocalyptic-Messianic *scenario* is un-historically represented from the opening مَّ يَنْشَأُ رَجُلٌ مِنْ قُرَيْشٍ أَخْوَالُهُ كَلْبٌ فَيَبْعَثُ إِلَيْهِمْ بَعْثًا فَيَظْهَرُونَ عَلَيْهِمْ وَذَلِكَ بَعْثُ كَلْبٍوَ

> (Then there will arise a man of Quraysh whose maternal uncles belong to Kalb and send against them an expeditionary force which will be overcome by them, and that is the military expedition of Kalb.)

If it is possible that the maternal uncles could be identified as Ḥassān ibn Mālik (d. 688/89) in referring to Yazīd I whose mother, the famous Maysūm, was the Kalbite wife of Muʿāwiya; nevertheless, the meaning of the term أَخْوَالُهُ remains obscure in relation to the real relationship of this Quraysh: the fact that this term could be also translated by brothers or uncles without specifying the side makes it more difficult to identify the real protagonist.

There is also another suitable option in referring to the caliph 'Abd al-Malik, whose father Marwān married a Kalbite woman, Layla bint Zabān ibn al-Aṣbagh al-Kalbī, who certainly also had a large family.

The following passages, as supported by Madelung, emphasized Zubayrid propaganda, which tried to forecast historical events: 'Islām will become established on earth and he will remain for seven years, then he will die, and the Muslims will offer the funeral prayer for *him*. Abū Dāwud said: Some of them narrated from Hishām: Nine years. And some said: Seven years.'

'Abd Allāh ibn al-Zubayr started being an alternative caliph for nine years between 683 and 692, after the death of Yazīd.[16] However, as reported by Michael Cook, if the first expedition remains probably related to the caliphate of Yazīd I, the second one reflects on a following period, before the battle of Marj Rāhiṭ (684), when the Umayyad were close to succumbing and which links it with a different protagonist.[17]

Mehdy Shaddel also tried to justify that the first expedition was not a military one but attributed to ten noblemen led by al-Nuʿmān ibn Bashīr al-Ansārī (d. 684) and ʿAbd Allāh ibn ʿIḍāh al-Ashʿarī who failed in trying to reconcile the community after al-Ḥusayn ibn 'Alī's assassination in Kerbalā'.[18]

F. Donner argues that Yazīd I, before the Kalbite expedition led by Muslim ibn ʿUqba al-Murrī and al-Ḥuṣạyn ibn Numayr al-Sakūnī, sent Ibn al-Zubayr's brother, 'Amr, to stop him, but he was killed, incarcerated and defeated, by his same brother.

In this case, the above tradition could find more historical feedback, even though 'Amr ibn al-Zubayr is a phantom in the Islamic sources without a real concrete existence.[19]

It is possible that this 'weak' tradition has been elaborated through a *collage* which reflects two different historical phases.

The most important aspect for our study is that the Zubayrids, who elaborated it, considered the Kalbite not only as unbelievers and part of an anti-Islamic coalition led by the Umayyad, but as deeply involved against the Messianic figure who will finally impose the *Sunna* and the Prophet's message.

The different levels of 'Narratives' here are fascinating because they not only confirm the strong connection between Umayyad and Kalb, but highlight their un-Islamic nature (without saying whether they were still Christians), and their enmity towards Mecca and Medina which was sufficient to fight the *Mahdī* in an already apocalyptic *scenario*.

It is understandable that the reaction in stressing the Messianic intervention in identifying the true 'Believers' from the false ones was linked to belonging to specific clans as historical *believer* figures rather than to others. The depiction of Yazīd I as not morally suitable to be an *'amīr al-Mu'minīn* is in continuity with the accusation attributed to 'Uthmān ibn 'Affān before his assassination. 'Abd al-Malik's attempt to shape a more 'identitarian' version of religiosity, after the end of the second *Fitna*, is emblematically related to a new imperial policy which wanted to limit the ongoing fragmentation. It is not circumstantial that during his caliphate as well as during the fight against Ibn al-Zubayr's, the early complete *Shahādah* which includes Muḥammad as the envoy of God started to appear.[20]

The first anti-Trinitarian debates, as a principal point of distinction between Islām and Christianity, also emerged in the following decades.[21]

'Abd al-Malik's reforms at the end of the second *Fitna* stressed the central fact that whatever identity Islām had had before this paradigmatic event, the absence of great sophistication did not allow such a clear distinction in an Abrahamic *milieu*, while it was not until 'Abd al-Malik's caliphate that early differences were shown, in particular concerning the understanding of the Christian identification of Jesus.[22]

As J.E. Brockopp argues in stressing Steven C. Judd's analysis of 'early Umayyad Piety', the attention to authors such as Abū 'Amr al-Sha'bī (d. *c.* 721–727), 'Ubaydallāh al-Zuhrī (d. *c.* 670–678), 'Abdallāh ibn 'Awn al-Arṭubān (d. *c.* 768), al-Awzā'ī (d. 774) and Sufyān al-Thawrī (d. 778) cannot properly show the existence of an 'Umayyad scholarly community'.[23]

More than a pietistic approach, Judd's work highlighted the above authors' search for traditions; they were playing an increasingly significant role at the Damascus court as diplomats, *muḥaddithūn*, as well as fighting against the first Qadarites' early theological assumptions in the first half of the eighth century.

It is quite evident that independently of the Marwānid caliphs' position, these early Muslim intellectuals were trying to shape a new religious base rooted in early Qur'ān documentary evidence and *ḥadīth* collections, trying to collect together Muḥammad's companions' scriptural and mnemonic legacy.[24]

Before 'Abd al-Malik's caliphate, the space for the emergence of an 'Islamic' *intelligentsia* was limited due to the ongoing inner conflict in the attempt to accuse the adversaries, more than trying to be inclusive.

The same diplomatic inconclusiveness between al-Mukhtār al-Thaqafī (d. 687) in supporting Muḥammad ibn al-Ḥanifiyya (d. 700) but also in trying to share an alliance with Ibn al-Zubayr, who refused, is emblematic in showing that a political-clan sectarianism, more than a religious one, was still in action.

The cruelty of the fights, the Prophet's companions killing one another in the first and in the second *fitna*, the partial destruction of Medina in the battle of Ḥarrah and Mecca afterwards, the behavioural attitude of some Khawārijite branches such as the *Azāriqa* are all examples that the accusations against an Umayyad ruler as well as those against Damascus' enemies were part of a slanderous narrative in which the early Islamic traditions were clearly involved.

Dramatically, it is with the end of the period of the Prophet's companions that the 'Believers' began to discover an independent new religious approach which cannot, in any case, deny the growing political-clan fracture which arose during the first and second *fitna*.

Nevertheless, until the end of the second civil conflict, the Christian Kalbite as well as 'Abd al-Malik's Damascus administration pushed the Umayyad to dominate the 'Believers'' community: the Arab-Greek administrative personnel were probably worried about losing their prerogatives; their being Christian would have not changed after 'Abd al-Malik's victory; the Kalbite confederation, like other Arab Christian clans, was directly involved in the military operations and their victorious outcome would probably have pushed them to a more concrete Islamic conversion in the eighth century.[25]

'Abd al-Malik's military victory in the second *fitna* permitted him to later frame an ideological position which fortified a new 'Islamic' understanding, in the attempt to save what remained of the Prophet's original message.

The Umayyad, who were usually denigrated for having accepted Muḥammad only at the end of the prophetic phase, were not able to strengthen the 'original' *visio* of the Prophet, who would have liked to limit tribal kinship to validate an intra-believer one, but to shape a new centralized political-religious line based on their legitimacy as the heirs of Muḥammad's message and the *Khalīfa* for God's will.

3. The archaeological-numismatic sources on early Islām

The importance of epigraphic sources in showing the emergence of a new belief is a major aspect for identifying the *credo* in a new religiosity that could emerge from an Abrahamic milieu.

The existence of a 'belligerent' attitude, attributable to Islām, cannot be framed before identifying for whom this fighting was done, independently of whether it was for God, a Saint or a Prophet.

It would be hard to consider the holiness-sacredness of war in Islām if the name of Prophet Muḥammad is not properly mentioned until seventy years after his death (632), without any archaeological-numismatic sources mentioning him,[26] as well as a limited number of non-Islamic historiographic ones.[27]

As I am neither an archaeologist nor a numismatist, the analysis below is univocally based on academic works resulting from field research and which focus on early Islamic coins, religious and non-religious buildings, tombstones and graffiti.

All these artefacts, buildings and relics are symptomatically related to the Caliphs' concrete power and sovereignty in imposing their will, in developing a personal artistic style as well as reflecting their religious affiliation.

1. Clive Foss in his famous study entitled 'A Syrian Coinage of Muʿāwiya' argued that during the first Umayyad caliphate, probably around 668–670, a first census and new taxation system was introduced, updating the Byzantine system but also trying to improve it.[28] Until this census, Christian peasants probably did not pay taxes, because they were unknown to the Treasury after a stormy historical period which started from the last Roman-Persian war (602–628) and continued with the Arab conquests (634–656). However, taxation requires money and money needs coinage; it is feasible that at the time, as reported by S. Heidemann,

> In the first decades after the Islamic conquest until the onset of Umayyad rule, the region of Syria and northern Mesopotamia remained in regard to its monetary organisation mainly a dependent Byzantine province. Copper coins were provided from Constantinople until 655–8. On the basis of the gold hoards, only a diminishing number of post-Heraclius *solidi* can be observed. On logical grounds, it might be assumed that the treasury in Constantinople was able to draw (through unknown intermediaries) gold from the Arab-occupied, former Byzantine territories in exchange for imperial copper coins in order to balance the trade. Perhaps with the rise of Umayyad rule in Syria, imitation of Byzantine copper coins occurred. It can be regarded as an indication of a shortage of copper coins. We do not know exactly what measures were applied, but they led step-by-step to a monetary independence of Syria and northern Mesopotamia from the Byzantine money supply. The demand for small change was met by a multitude of mints. At first, they produced mere imitations, but their iconography and their inscriptions more and more abandon the Byzantine models. Finally, 'Abd al-Malik's reforms – beginning with silver and gold around 72/691-2 – separated both currencies through the introduction of an indigenous Islamic coin type.[29]

The circulating Byzantine coins were dated, and their sequence ends in 658; it is unlikely that all the subsequent imitative currencies were adopted for more than thirty years, until 'Abd al-Malik's later coinage reform (693–695) which was also to introduce Islamic epigraphic sentences, such as a complete *Shahādah* for the first time.

Strictly speaking, since they are undated, they could be as early as the beginning of 'Abd al-Malik's reign in 685. But there is, however, a gap of some thirty years, including the entire reign of Muʿāwiya, in which no new coinage was minted.

It would seem logical to assume that at least some of the bilingual series should be attributed to him, but Michael Bates, in his abundant writings,[30] has attempted to compress all these into the few years before 693. Since his articles were published, however, much new material has appeared and been studied, and an appreciation of the great complexity of the imitative, derivative and bilingual series has taken root.

As a result, his 'short' chronology now finds few followers, though nothing substantial has replaced it. The famous *Nessana papyri* seem to highlight how until 674–677, no taxes were paid but the *Rizq*, an equal number of units of wheat and oil, was a form of transaction, paid in advance for a period of two months. This report seems to stress how until the 670s, no regular taxes were collected as a part of a uniform and centralized fiscal system, or at least for an area around Gaza and the southern part of Palestine.[31]

At the same time, the *rizq* seems to have been given not to tax officials, but directly to individual representatives of the Arab tribes, as a lump sum requisition.[32] However, an excerpt from the Maronite Chronicle, in giving information about Muʿāwiya's caliphate, emphasized (AG 971):

> 'Many Arabs gathered at Jerusalem and made Muʿāwiya king and he went up and sat down on Golgotha and prayed there. He went to Gethsemane and went down to the tomb of the blessed Mary and prayed in it. In those days when the Arabs were gathered there with Muʿāwiya, there was an earthquake; much of Jericho fell, as well as many nearby churches and monasteries.' – 'In July of the same year the emirs and many Arabs gathered and gave their allegiance to Muʿāwiya. Then an order went out that he should be proclaimed king in all the villages and cities of his dominion and that they should make acclamations and invocations to him. He also minted gold and silver, but it was not accepted because it had no cross on it. Furthermore, Muʿāwiya did not wear a crown like other kings in the world. He placed his throne in Damascus and refused to go to the seat of Muḥammad.'[33]

The earthquake reported by Michael the Syrian and Theophanes the Confessor was in 658 and the enthronement of Muʿāwiya in Jerusalem is emblematically related to the first *Fitna* when after Siffīn, the Umayyad champion received the *Bay'ah* from the majority of the post-Byzantine authorities, Christian Arab clans and 'Believers' of Syria and Palestine.[34]

The official date of this report can be considered between 658 and 661, when after the killing of ʿAlī ibn Abū Ṭālib, Muʿāwiya was officially recognized as Caliph.

If the veracity of the quotation in relation to the Earthquake and the enthronement is confirmed by different sources, those related to Muʿāwiya's coinage remain obscure both for political and for numismatic reasons: it would be quite illogical to ask for huge political and military support, organizing such a 'Christian' ceremonial,[35] and afterwards try to modify the currency on a specific identitarian religious aspect in a region populated by Christians.

In parallel, the *Nessana papyri* emphasized the lack of coins in circulation, to the extent of having to consider the *rizq* in rural areas. In spite of this, it is true that *Nessana papyri* probably referred to the end of Muʿāwiya's caliphate (674–677).

The allusion in the Maronite Chronicle to the raid organized by the Umayyad caliph against Byzantium and Constantinople began with the fight to control Cyprus in the 650s, and continued with different expeditions led by Yazīd ibn Muʿāwiya and Abū Ayyūb al-Anṣārī (d. 674) in 668–669, with a second one in 674–678. Those raids probably played a significant role in the attempt to hoard cash, loot Byzantine territories, even if none reached the target in conquering Constantinople.[36]

Independently of the possibility that Muʿāwiya tried to adopt a Byzantine style of currency without the Cross, this policy would have not been implemented until ʿAbd al-Malik's caliphate, in the 690s when, for the first time, the currency adopted showed Islamic script emphasizing Muḥammad's role.[37] However, the first coins which reported a complete *Shahādah* probably came from Ibn al-Zubayr's side, on a Persian style of mint, from the Zubayrid governor of Bīshāpūr ʿAbd al-Malik ibn ʿAbd Allāh.[38]

This summary aims to emphasize how, regardless of the historical veracity of Muʿāwiya's attempt to propose a different and less identifiable religious coin during his caliphate, until the end of the second *Fitna*, the Umayyad dynasty would not have had the strength or the intention to impose an Islamic coin with a clear accent on Prophet Muḥammad.

2. The chronicles on the existence of early Islamic religious buildings and non-religious ones, the conversion of churches to mosques, the importance of Jerusalem in the imperial Umayyad narrative before, but also after ʿAbd al-Malik's caliphate, are important aspects on which to reflect in connection with early Islamic identity. If there are serious problems in identifying where ʿUmar ibn al-Khaṭṭāb prayed after his triumphal entry into Jerusalem around 637–638, the information on Muʿāwiya is more feasible as A. Marsham as already rectified in his article.

If it is possible that the *Bayʿah* received by the Umayyad champion came from different actors and in different phases – from the Syrian Army, from the governor of Egypt ʿAmr ibn al-ʿĀs and after ʿAlī's killing, from his son Ḥasan – the 'year of unity' as the final celebrations of the beginning of the Umayyad caliphate were emphasized in Jerusalem around 661–662.[39] In parallel, the Maronite Chronicle confirmed how in 659–660, many nomads reached Jerusalem and made Muʿāwiya king as reported above (no. 339), following a sort of peregrination around the most important Christian religious sites of the city.

The attraction of the early 'Believers' for churches and Christian religious buildings is confirmed not only by S. Bashear and M. Guidetti in deconstructing the Paradigm of the partition, referring to the famous St Johannes church in Damascus, but by the fact that several churches were safeguarded and used after the seventh-century conquests (as is the case of the Edessa Church to the reconstruction of which Muʿāwiya contributed);[40] the contiguity of the preservation of Christian buildings like the construction of early Mosques is probably a better explanation.[41]

This *adage* would like to confirm an ongoing progress in the 'Believers – Islamic' religious identity which after early difficulties moved towards a more solid independence; however, sharing a church as a *locus orationis* in the seventh century, like the life of early 'Muslims', in a space that was largely ruled by Christian religiousness finds confirmation in sources.[42]

> Indeed Muslims strove for establishing new holy places (see, for instance, the development of the tombs of the companions at *Muʿtah* in the 9th century) and

holy dates (the most important one being the *hajj*), but, also given the minority status of Muslims in the area, this process took some time to consolidate.[43]

As Bashear described, the early 'Believers" attraction for churches is preponderantly linked to *locus orationis* dedicated to Jesus Christ and the Virgin Mary, the two most venerated Christian protagonists of the Qur'ān, while this practice of attending prayers in the churches began to disappear around the middle of the eighth century, when the presence of a huge network of mosques was probably already emerging in the region.[44] Finally, it seems clear that independently of the sources, the presence of an early and single 'mosque' in Jerusalem, until the construction of the *Qubbah al-Ṣakhra*, highlights the importance of this holy city for all the 'Believers'.[45]

At the same time, the architectural influence of the *martyria* typology erected around something, such as a rock, a cenotaph or a place of veneration, was probably emblematic in the construction of the Dome of the Rock during the caliphate of 'Abd al-Malik.

The rock of the Kathisma Church, the place where Mary had rested on her journey to Bethlehem, in relation to the plan and the rock around which it was built should be seen as one of the possible sources of inspiration for the Dome of the Rock, built in Jerusalem in 692.[46] The Kathisma Church was likely a Christian site venerated by early Muslims because of its connection with Mary and Jesus: the Qur'ān narrates Jesus's birth and the site was probably selected by early Muslims in place of an 'Islamic nativity shrine intended to honour 'Īsā and Maryam through a commemoration of the former's birth'.[47]

It seems that the site's attraction diminished around the eleventh century and started to be abandoned; however, while the Christians generally focused attention on Bethlehem as the main place to concentrate the narrative of the nativity, the Muslims identified the sacred space of the *Ḥaram al-Sharīf* as the 'Cradle of Jesus'.[48]

It is evident that, at least for the first century, in particular in Syria, Palestine, Iraq and Egypt, the possibility of praying in churches remained a common practice; at the same time as Bashear's article clarified and Tor Andrae only supposed, the *Qibla*, the direction of the prayer, was not clearly and uniquely oriented towards Mecca, but probably also towards Jerusalem.

> As for prayer in churches, the present inquiry has proved beyond doubt that such was not an uncommon practice all over the area and throughout the first and early second centuries. However, the material reviewed above does not address the crucial question of where 'Umar, Mu'āwiya, 'Amr b. al-'Āṣ and other prominent companions and successors directed such prayer. [...] Added to the important discovery of the *two-qibla* mosque of Be'er Orah, our findings may give a certain support to Tor Andrae's suggestion of an early eastern *qibla*. However, we feel that, as far as the first century is concerned, one cannot speak of "one original *qibla* of Islām, but rather of several currents in the search for one. It is also plausible to suggest that this search was eventually decided *after* Islām acquired a central sanctuary, prayer places, and religious concepts and institutions of its own.[49]

The discovery is not unique: there are traditions which referred to early *ṣaḥāba* of the Prophet which argued about the eastern-facing *Qibla* in the mosque of 'Amr ibn al-'Āṣ in Fusṭaṭ, as well as of other mosques built in the Umayyad period. It is emblematic that until the end of the Umayyad's caliphate, Jerusalem was increasingly considered as a holy place paritetically in competition for political and religious reasons with Mecca and Medina.[50] The importance of these aspects also needs to be related to the non-religious palaces of *Qaṣr Hishām* or *Qaṣr al-Mshattā*, which are clearly affected by the decorative points of Byzantine-Persian influence.

3. Tombstones and graffiti are the last category of archaeological finds on which to attempt a reflection concerning the preliminary 'Islamic' – 'Believers" identity and that constitute the skeleton of the analysis concerning the canonization of a 'Holy/Sacred War' during the conquering phase.

Evident doubts concerning it emerged in particular because early Umayyad armies were still enlisting Arab Christian soldiers.

A recently published article: 'An early Christian Arabic Graffito mentioning 'Yazīd the King',[51] argues that this *graffito* discovered close to *Qaṣr Burqu'*, northeast of Jordan, near the ruins of an Umayyad desert castle, was designed by an Arab Christian, who, wanting to leave trace of himself, carved a rock with the cross and the verse: *† dkr ʾl-ʾlh* (first line), *yzydw ʾl-mlk* (second line).

The close presence of an old Roman and Umayyad fortress suggests that the author was a military man who attested his personal *bay'ah* to the main authority of his age. The main problem is that the only Yazīd in pre-Islamic Arabic sources belongs to the Ghassān and his name was Yazīd ibn al-'Aswad: he was a descendant of Ka'b ibn 'Amr ibn al-Muzayqiyā', but not a *Phylarch* and certainly not a King.[52]

In parallel, Yazīd ibn Qays al-Ḥujrid, mentioned by Nonnosus (the Arab diplomatic figure at the service of Constantinople in the sixth century), could be a different option, but geographically illogical: why would an Arab Christian from central Arabia reaching the north of Jordan, or passing through it, carve a graffito which emphasized his personal alliance to a figure living hundreds of kilometres to the south?

The same problem would emerge in referring to Yazīd ibn Kabasat, who was probably an authoritative figure of the Kindah, but again in this case, the missing reason is inherent to the *graffito* legacy, which, on the contrary, is all the more convincing if we refer to Yazīd ibn Muʿāwiya (d. 683), whose mother was the famous Maysūm of the Banū Kalb. He himself married two Ghassānid princesses, including, but this is more speculation than historical fact, Umm Ramla, the daughter of Jabala ibn al-'Ayham.

Non-Islamic sources stressed, as the Byzantine-Arab *Chronicle of 741* underlines:

> When he died, the son Yazīd took his place for 3 years; [He was] a most pleasant man and deemed highly agreeable by all the peoples subject to his rule. He never, as is the wont of men, sought glory for himself because of his royal rank, but lived as a citizen along with all the common people. Few or no victories were achieved in his times in the armies sent forth by him.[53]

At the same time, the Islamic sources argue about Yazīd and his father's intense relationship with figures of the pre-Islamic Christian élite as well as the Arab Christian poets, Sarjūn ibn Manṣūr al-Rūmī al-Naṣrānī and al-Akhtāb, Ghiyāt al-Taghlibī (d. 710); the idea that both were infamous Caliphs who usually drank with Christian friends is amplified so that Sarjūn also convinced Yazīd to send 'Ubaydallah ibn Ziyād as Iraqi governor, putting the 'black' Christian secretary behind the murder of the Prophet's grandson: an un-historical position.[54]

The association of the above factors, Yazīd's family ties and the presence of important Christian figures in the Umayyad seventh century, logically attributes this *Graffito* to an Arab Christian soldier who wanted to emphasize his oath of allegiance to Yazīd ibn Mu'āwiya. However, if Donner, quoting John bar Penkaye, highlights how a sizable component of the Umayyad Syrian Army was Arab Christian, in particular from the Banū Kalb, this graffito is very important as concrete proof that this assumption can start to be given more consideration from a historical point of view.

The geographical evidence that this *graffito* has been found close to an Umayyad desert *qaṣr* means that this epigraph was very likely carved by a Christian soldier in the Umayyad army.

In parallel, the use of the term *Malik* again belongs to a tradition of Christian Arabic inscriptions known from the pre-Islamic period, in considering the Byzantine style of attributing authority to local Arab chiefs as phylarchs in the sixth century.

At the same time, the anonymous Maronite chronicle reporting information about Mu'āwiya's enthronement in Jerusalem argues that 'many Arabs gathered in the Holy town to make Him king' while Ḥnanisho' the exegete (d. 700) still described 'Abd al-Malik as 'King of the Arabs'.[55]

The importance of this epigraphic source in proving the presence of Christian Arab soldiers, monophysites or not, in the Syrian Umayyad army, is particularly important in the analysis of the early Islamic conceptualization of *Jihād* and how it was not yet canonized in the second half of the seventh century.

In 1932, the Egyptian scholar Hassān el-Ḥawāry discovered a tombstone among many, dated 71 AH (691) from Aswān cemetery in which the epitaph refers to an Arab woman, 'Abbāsa, daughter of Jurayj, son of Sanad, attested to be part of the *ahl al-Islām* and for the first time there appeared a clear *Shahāda*: *allā ilāha illā llāhu, waḥdahū lā sharīka lahū wa-anna, muḥammadan 'abduhū wa-rasūluhū ṣalla llāhu 'alayhī wa-sallama*: 'there is no deity except God, He alone, He has no partner, and that Muḥammad is His Servant and His Messenger'.

If the *ahl al-Islām*, reference has been considered particularly suspected for this period by R. Hoyland in "The content and context of early Arabic inscriptions" (1997, page 87, note 65), the importance of this inscription is highlighted not only by one of the first complete Islamic professions of faith, but also by the phrase *lā sharīka lahū* – 'He has no partner' – which is usually interpreted as distinguishing the early Muslim belief from the Christian one in the Trinity and it is also repeated in the frieze on the Dome of the Rock.

Does this important building, the construction of which is traditionally dated around 692, have to be considered one of the early Islamic religious edifices or is it still symbolically affiliated to a community of 'Believers'?

The importance of the frieze is emblematically linked to different Qur'anic suras or part of them – Q. 113; 33, v.54; 17, v.3; 64, v.1; 67, v.2; 69, v.1; 67, v.2; 33, v.54 (repetition); 4, v.169–171; 19, v.34–37; 3, v.16-17 – including some anti-trinitarian verses which can also be considered very indicative of the increasing 'Believers" understanding of the Christological complexity of 'Īsā ibn Maryam as well as the emphasis by the Qur'ān in 4:171.[56]

However, the main problem in assuming that the Dome of the Rock's inner inscriptions were anti-Christian is linked to the partial or total restoration of the internal Dome's freize in the following centuries, after its construction. Al-Ma'mūn Ibn Hārūn al-Rashīd's replacement of 'Abd al-Malik's name in the foundation inscription, for example, remained quite problematic in supporting the assumption about the anti-Christian status of the Dome.[57]

The Qur'ān itself, even considering the canonized version, still maintains an unclear awareness of the Trinity '*Thalātha*', as well as of the complexity of the Christological debate.

Verse 116 of the *Sūrah* 5 recites: 'When God says. "Jesus, son of Mary, did you say to people, Take me and my Mother as two Gods alongside God?" – '*attakhidhūnī wa 'Ummiya 'Ilāhayni min dūni Allāhi*'. However, if on the one hand, the verse can be interpreted as not referring to them as new deities but as reported in the Gospels 'in being on the right as on the left of God' (Mark 10, 35–45); on the other hand, it clearly stressed a form of trinitarism which did not find any kind of confirmation in the history of Christian sectarianism.[58]

The possibility that from the early internal Dome's frieze some verses were carved to stress the early 'Islamic Believers" different understanding of Christ is symptomatic not only of their religious identity 'in progress', emphasized in a *martyria* religious building (a Christian one, which remained unique in early Islamic architecture), but of an initial inter-religious Islam-Christian debate which historically started at the beginning of the eighth century.[59]

If 'Abd al-Malik's reign accentuated the role of the Qur'ān and of Muḥammad for the first time, this position was deeply induced by 'Abd Allah ibn al-Zubayr's evident intention to assume a more 'Islamic' alternative caliphate position as many inscriptions from Fars to Egypt clearly showed and as different scholars have also begun to interpret.[60]

The inscriptions on the Dome of the Rock and coins highlight a paradigmatic change in parallel with the new importance of Muḥammad's prophecy and prophetic role. The caliph's decision in allowing the governor of Iraq, al-Ḥajjāj, and his group of Scholars to redact the Qur'ān also needs to be put into relation with the creation of a new iconography which defined the Caliph with the new eponym of *Khalīfa Allāh*, more than as *'Amīr al-Mu'minīn*.[61]

However, there is still an unconvincing passage about this changeover, which is hard to decipher, related to the role played by Jerusalem, the place of *bayt al-maqdis*.

Ibn Shihāb al-Zuhrī reported a *Ḥadīth* which highlighted how 'no religious journey is to be undertaken except to pray in the three mosques: the sacred Mosque, my Mosque and al-'Aqṣā Mosque',[62] which was interpreted in relation to the fact that during the second *fitna*, the 'Believers' of Syria who wanted to perform the pilgrimage were obliged to give a *bay'ah* to ibn al-Zubayr.

This verse, like others, 'The Messenger of Allah said: "A man's prayer in his house is equal (in reward) to one prayer; his prayer in the mosque of the tribes is equal to twenty-five prayers; his prayer in the mosque in which Friday prayer is offered is equal to five-hundred prayers; his prayer in Aqsa Mosque is equal to fifty thousand prayers; his prayer in my mosque (Medina) is equal to fifty thousand prayers; and his prayer in the Sacred Mosque (Mecca) is equal to one hundred thousand prayers"',[63] reveals a solution for those who wanted to attend the *hajj* during this historical phase, in a way allowing the Sacred Mosque to be replaced.

However, as the Islamic traditions highlight, the religious place for pilgrimage was the al-ʾAqṣā mosque and not the Dome of the Rock, the purpose of which as a building still remains obscure.

As reported by Ya'qūbī Wahn ibn Waḍīḥ (d. 898) in his *Taʾrīkh al-Ya'qūbī*,[64] this historical event probably stressed the 'political-religious narrative' about the Dome's building which emphasized the Umayyad's primacy in all the lands conquered by the Arabs.

As supported by Nasser Rabbat's analysis of al-Wāsitī's *Faḍā'il al-Bayt al-Muqaddas*,[65] the production of traditions associated with the sanctity of Jerusalem in Islām emerged in this phase when, after 'Abd al-Malik's military victory, the political-religious sphere was partially dissociated: Damascus and Jerusalem, the political and the religious capitals of a global empire which crowned and enthroned a new political-religious pact were emphasized by al-Wāsitī's narrative about the precious objects kept inside the Dome of the Rock at that time: the horns of Abraham's ram, the Crown of Kisra (Chosroes) and *Durra al-Yatīma*'s pearl.

Independently of their real existence and their presence in the Dome of the Rock, the horns are related to the first Abrahamic pact with God, a religious symbol which before the Ark of Covenant stressed the *Ḥanīfiyya*, the early monotheistic treaty of which the Arabs, as the heirs of Ishmael, were custodians.

The Crown and the pearl, on the contrary, are symbolic objects which suggest a secular majesty and their presence is partially confirmed by the inner Dome's mosaic representations above the ambulatory around the central Dome.[66]

However, the short distance from the only attested mosque of Jerusalem, which was probably enlarged by the same caliph 'Abd al-Malik and finished by his son, al-Walīd, stressed the religious-political awareness of an early Umayyad architecture which probably, at the beginning and univocally referred to as the Dome of the Rock, was not used as a mosque or a prayer room.[67]

According to this hypothesis, if the internal *Miḥrāb* was probably built in the tenth–eleventh century, the Dome was constructed for other reasons, possibly political or funerary ones, but this is only a speculation.

Finally, if the external building still has a Christian identity, the inner one and its decorations are victoriously linked to the Umayyad dynasty as a distinctive place in which political messages are intersected with an imperial narrative. The inner *graffiti* which showed the status of Christ, if carved during 'Abd al-Malik's caliphate, can also fulfil the important early Islamic awareness about 'Īsā ibn Maryam; if not, they can probably be attributed to a later period, such as during Al-Ma'mūn, the Ikhshīdīyūn or Fāṭimīd dynasty, who for political-military reasons had more motives to carve particularly anti-trinitarian verses.[68]

4. Apocalypticism, pietism and *Jihād*: A counterargument.

If in the last decade, academic works have offered different interpretations of early Islamic history, there is one, more closely linked to an eschatological-apocalyptic *visio*, which attributes an important connection with *jihād*, as warfare on behalf of God and God's community.[69]

At the beginning of the twentieth century, Paul Casanova, in *Mohammed et la Fin du Monde*, had already highlighted the apocalyptic comprehension of the Islamic prophet not only as the last one but, following Aloys Sprenger's earlier work, approached the wider questions between two rather extreme positions: either Muḥammad was a charlatan who initially used threats of impending doom to frighten the Meccans into following him, only to change course when this failed (Sprenger), or when Muḥammad died before the Hour's arrival, his original teachings on the subject were, 'if not falsified, at least concealed with the greatest care' by Abū Bakr, 'Uthmān and others (Casanova).[70]

This last approach has not been considered for many decades and, at the same time, has been criticized; however, more recently it has been appreciated and highlighted by some scholars such as P. Crone, D. Cook[71] and Stephen J. Shoemaker in stressing that Muḥammad's death was probably antedated as some sources, apocalyptic and otherwise, have emphasized, in the clear attempt to maintain that the Islamic armies were still led by the Prophet in their campaigns of conquest against the Persians and the Byzantines.[72]

This hypothesis would certainly emphasize the apocalyptic-messianic roots of Islām.

Conversely, many doubts remain.

Donner in one of his articles argued: 'Cette thèse de l'absence de conception messianique dans le Coran est confortée par l'absence totale d'autres termes renvoyant à des idées messianiques ou mentionnant un personage messianique. Il nous semble donc périlleux de considérer qu'il existait un messianisme islamique originel comme l'ont fait Crone et Cook.'[73]

> (This thesis concerning the absence of a messianic conception in the Koran is reinforced by the total absence of other terms referring to messianic ideas or mentioning a messianic personage. It therefore seems perilous for us to consider that there was an original Islamic messianism as Crone and Cook have done.)

At the same time, Shoemaker also admits: 'Thus, while F. Donner is certainly correct to note that the early Islamic sources do not reveal any clear belief in a coming messianic figure, as both he and Suliman Bashear rightly conclude, the Jewish members of the early community of the Believers undoubtedly would have interpreted Muhammad's eschatological message according to their own messianic expectations.'[74]

Contrary to the synoptic Gospels in which the emphasis on the destruction of the Jewish Temple is highlighted in Matthew (24, 1–51), Mark (13, 1–37) and Luke (21,

5–36) with a clear apocalyptic accent,[75] it is important to reflect on the absence of similar verses in the Qur'ān.

Those attributed to the Roman victory over the Persian empire (30, 2–7), a military success definitively obtained in 628, were probably elaborated *post-eventum*, even contemplating the speculation of al-Tirmidhī (d. 892).[76]

Shoemaker's conjecture[77] is hypothetical: if Nöldeke Th. and Bell R. assumed opposite postures in interpreting **30, 2–7**, it is true that recent studies have emphasized the inter-clan relationship between northern pro-Byzantine confederations with Meccans and Medinans, who had important economic interests in Syria before its conquest.[78]

In other words, how can you elaborate an apocalyptic-conquering verse if, in parallel, your main economic outcomes are closely connected with the geography that you are planning to vanquish? On the contrary, the most recent history on the Arab conquests highlighted how, while the booty taken during the early campaigns in the rural areas was kept, the towns and the majority of the crops were not pillaged, and the economic revenues preserved.

In the absence of concrete Quranic apocalyptic verses, such as notes referring to the *Mahdī*, and in spite of the abundance of eschatological verses, it is a major logical assumption that, without negating the influence of a Jewish and Christian apocalyptic on Islām, the conquering campaigns must be dissociated from a millenarian *jihadist* attitude, which is *de facto* hard to prove.

The Qur'ān itself says:

> When our revelations are recited to them in all their clarity, the disbelievers say of the Truth that has reached them, 'this is clearly sorcery', or they say, 'He has invented it himself'. Say [Prophet], 'If I have really invented it, there is nothing you can do to save me from God. He knows best what you say amongst yourselves about it; He is sufficient as a witness between me and you; He is the most forgiving, the most merciful.' Say, 'I am nothing new among God's messengers. I do not know what will be done with me or you; I only follow what is revealed to me; I only warn plainly.'
>
> (46, 7–9)

This verse emphasized the absence of Muḥammad's personal foresight, defining him as a messenger, as one of those who were sent by God on Earth.

Another important verse which is usually adopted in the attempt to show Muḥammad as the last of the Prophets and as the Seal of Prophecy is the famous **33, 40** which recites: 'Muhammad is not the father of any one of your men; he is God's messenger and the Seal of the Prophets: God knows everything.'

This paradigmatic verse which stressed the absence of an early 'Believers" attention to apocalyptic matters argued:

> The Israelite claim that only the Children of Israel had been chosen by God necessitated the marginalisation of collateral lines, first Ishmael and his descendants, followed by Esau and his. The Christian claim that Jesus is the Son of God necessitated the marginalisation of Joseph, the man who appeared to be – but was not – Jesus' natural father. The Islamic claim that Muḥammad is the Last Prophet necessitated the marginalisation of the Prophet's sons, natural and adopted.[79]

There is a huge Abrahamic continuity and 'Umar ibn al-Khaṭṭāb's anxiety in not accepting the Prophet's death[80] was probably more logically linked to the 'political' risks in finding a solution of continuity than a possible apocalyptic reason. 'Umar's reported sentence (no. 385) from the *Tabaqāt* is quite different from that reported in the *Sīra*:

> When the Apostle was dead 'Umar got up and said: 'Some of the disaffected will allege that the Apostle is dead, but by God is not dead: He has gone to his Lord as Mūsā ibn 'Imrām went and was hidden by his people for forty days returning to them after it was said that he had died. By God, the apostle will return as Moses returned and will cut off the hands and feet of men who allege that the apostle is dead.'[81]

This last excerpt refers to Exodus 24, 18 which narrates that Moses/Mūsā, at the foot of the Horeb mountain, climbed it to reach the place where God, through a burning bush, 'spoke' to him giving the Law afterwards.

To make this parallel, when Muḥammad's inspired (*waḥī*) revelation was performed in 632, he emphasized this as quite illogical, contrary to: 'Hold fast to this book, by which God guided your messenger, and you will be guided as the Messenger of God was guided', which stressed that now what remained as being inspirational was, as for the Prophet, the Qur'ān, the revelation of God.

More urgently than an apocalyptic vision, the Prophet's death stressed a problem of succession and inheritance in a very problematic community: Mecca and Ṭā'if had been conquered less than two years earlier and other regions of the Peninsula were far from being supportive of the 'Believers'. The 'booty' problem which arose after the battle of Ḥunayn (630) against the Banū Thaqīf has already been analysed in this book, but underlines how the community, the inner one which included Medinan, Meccan and now, Ṭā'if's inhabitants, was far from being united before the Prophet's death.

Conversely, the meaning of the linguistic metaphor *khātam al-nabiyyīn* (lit. 'Seal of Prophets') is equivocal. In the first century, some Muslims took the phrase as meaning that Muḥammad confirmed the revelations sent previously to Moses and Jesus. This understanding quickly gave way to the understanding that Muḥammad brought the office of prophecy to an end. The later meaning was facilitated by the fact that prophecy is portrayed in the Qur'ān as the exclusive possession of Abraham's descendants. The office is hereditary, and it passes from father to son, albeit with occasional intervals between one prophet and the next.

From this premise, two corollaries follow: in order to be a prophet, Muḥammad must be a lineal descendant of Abraham; and in order to be the Last Prophet, he must be childless. This is why the assertion in Q. 33:40 that Muḥammad is 'the messenger of God and seal of Prophets' is preceded by the pronouncement that 'Muḥammad is not the father of any of your men'; therefore it was necessary for the Prophet to repudiate Zayd and why Zayd had to die before Muḥammad, in 629 during the battle of *Mu'tah*.[82]

This analysis does not only raise the doubt that the Prophet died without a male heir, but that Muḥammad was the last of the Prophets. If Muḥammad was the last Prophet of the Abrahamic tradition, he has to be without an heir; in this case, there is a first problem in relation with 'Īsā ibn Maryām who also did not have sons and contrary to Christian Tradition, Islamic Orthodoxy will have him replaced by a double (4, 157–158) on the cross which stressed the possible influence of a Christian Docetist awareness.

At the same time, if early Islām elaborated this understanding for apocalyptic reasons, it firstly needed to consider the *Mahdī* as an eschatological figure empowered by the return of Jesus on Earth to make him defeat the beast: the *Dajjāl*.

However, the Qur'ān is devoid of a *Mahdī* and of a Beast; this narrative on the Mahdī will probably emerge during the *Fitnas* affecting the early 'Believers' community in the second half of the seventh century and stressing a pietistic non-violent approach in early Islām.

Finally, other verses are particularly interesting in clarifying the non-existent relationship between apocalyptic and *Jihād* in this early 'Believers' community. The famous verses of **17, 1–8**, argue:

> Glory to Him who made His servant travel by night from the sacred place of worship to the furthest place of worship, whose surroundings We have blessed, to show him some of Our signs: He alone is the All Hearing, the All Seeing. (2) We also gave Moses the Scripture and made it a guide for the Children of Israel. 'Entrust yourselves to no one but Me, (3) you descendants of those We carried with Noah: he was truly a thankful servant.' (4) We declared to the Children of Israel in the Scripture, 'Twice you will spread corruption in the land and become highly arrogant.' (5) When the first of these warnings was fulfilled, We sent against you servants of Ours with great force, and they ravaged your homes. That warning was fulfilled, (6) but then We allowed you to prevail against your enemy. We increased your wealth and offspring and made you more numerous—(7) whether you do good or evil it is to your own souls—and when the second warning was fulfilled [We sent them] to shame your faces and enter the place of worship as they did the first time, and utterly destroy whatever fell into their power. (8) Your Lord may yet have mercy on you, but if you do the same again, so shall We: We have made Hell a prison for those who defy [Our warning].

The first verse of this *Sūrah* has been historically considered as related to the famous *'Isrā'* and *Mi'rāj* from the Sacred Mosque (Mecca) to the furthest place of worship (Jerusalem probably) and the relative literature has been abundant;[83] however, the other verses are, from my point of view, dissociated from the first and frame a biblical historical excursus which is completely detached from the Prophet's night journey. Even in this case, without assuming an apocalyptic understanding, the revelation seems to eschatologically advise and threaten the Sons of Israel to not reject the last warning فَإِذَا جَاءَ وَعْدُ الآخِرَةِ because, in this case, it will be problematic in not putting them into Hell.

These warnings have been differently interpreted.

The first destruction of the temple by the neo-Babylonian Nebuchadnezzar II in 587 BCE was followed by the Romans in 70 AD, however: 'but then We allowed you to prevail against your enemy. We increased your wealth and offspring and made you more numerous' is difficult to interpret, firstly because, those who were sent against the Children of Israel that ravaged their homes are also considered servants of God, while afterwards, Israel will be able to prevail against its enemies, becoming more numerous.

It is historically difficult to think about the Babylonians as servants (*'ibādā lannā*) of a monotheistic God; on the contrary, the Romans would have been Christians, but they were not at the time of Titus' campaign; in spite of this, the second warning can be considered more in relation to the complete destruction of the temple, after the Jews had entered it to oppose a last defence, as reported by Josephus Flavius in his Jewish wars.[84]

So, if the second warning is clearer and can probably be attributed to Titus' destruction of the Temple, the first is more obscure.

Considering the historical evidence described in these verses, the 'third warning' assumed a sort of eschatological recommendation which, independently of Nöldeke's chronology includes this *Sūrah* in the Meccan period, seems to refer to the Sons of Israel and their possible oath of alliance to Muḥammad as a prophet.

However, if my last sentence is highly speculative, this brief analysis has tried to highlight the prophet as a Messenger, perhaps, the last one, but not a *Kāhin*, a diviner; it is evident from my point of view how, at least initially, Muḥammad did not assume for himself any kind of skills in prediction.[85]

Religious apocalyptic narratives, on the contrary, are rooted in this 'imaginative' *visio* of the future, sometimes related to a horrific-original idea such as St Johannes's *Apocalypse*, sometimes to future historical events which will make human beings aware of the 'end of time' (Mt., 24, 4–13; 15–25; 29–31).

The fact that the Qur'ān has few associations with an apocalyptic *visio* does not mean that an early Islamic 'narrative' was not influenced by Jewish and Christian literature which, on the contrary, was highly apocalyptic.

Shoemaker's analysis of the *Doctrina Iacobi nuper Baptizati, the Apocalypse of Rabbi Shim'ōn b. Yoḥai* to which we could add the *Pseudo Ephrem's sermon on the End of Times* or *Pseudo Methodious Apocalypse* as well as Mariano's story on the monk Sergius, Baḥīrā for the Arabs, are clearly important apocalyptic sources. Conversely, it is evident that an early religious narrative in the clear attempt to frame a 'story' about the 'Islamic' origin that can also include Muḥammad's life and his prophesying existence became necessary, in particular to counterbalance Jewish and Christian narratives about the prophetic outlook of their main religious figures, Moses and Jesus.[86]

There is a poor basis for the evidence of these events, in particular if we analyse the Islamic Chronicles which were written from the second half of the eighth century.

On the contrary, the political fragmentation of the early 'Believers' community, with two *fitnas* in a few decades, as well as the presence of an impressive apocalyptic literature in the Jewish and Christian domains, produced from the first centuries after the destruction of the Temple, as well as the influence of St Johannes's Apocalypse, can be emblematically adopted to explain the last Arab conquests.

Nevertheless, in this regard, a clear distinction has to be proposed.

The Judaic and Christian apocalyptic narrative about the Arab conquests found a significant background in their religious *milieu*, based, for several centuries, on the attempt to explain historical events, generally violent and paradigmatic, in relation to a prophetic *visio*.

The excerpt from Sophronius's sermons in trying to explain the Arab conquests after Heraclius's victory against the Persians is associated with the Patriarch of Jerusalem's theological opposition to the Byzantine Emperor's *Monothelitism* in assuming that this invasion was due to the Christians' sinful attitude towards the Christological debate.[87]

However, it is hard to consider these apocalyptic reasons expressed by different religious figures as genuine because they were established on an 'ideological' comprehension of a historical fact: the Arab conquests.

On the 'Believers'' side, the fragmentation which started after the Prophet's death (632) and entered conflict following 'Uthmān's murder (656) and Ḥussein's death (680) probably boosted the influence of a Jewish and Christian apocalyptic literature on the 'Believers'.

As argued by H. Yücesoy:

> The golden age of unity, as it would be remembered and invoked in socio-political struggles of later time, was gone. From the first to the third civil war, the Muslim community witnessed the emergence of the Khārijī sect and the galvanisation and eventual mobilisation of the supporters of the family of 'Alī around a Shī'ī cause. Both of these movements sheltered extremist subsects whose influence on the social and political life in Islamic History can hardly be overestimated. [...] In the context of confessional and sectarian disputes and of political rivalry in the first Islamic century, the initial use of the concept of Mahdī appeared.[88]

P.M. Holt in 'Islamic Millenarianism' maintains that the *Mahdī* belief in Islām was first used among the proto-Shī'a as an honorific title, gradually evolving into a full-fledged eschatological and apocalyptic title.[89] However, as W. Madelung also argues, in particular referring to the attribution made to 'Abd Allāh ibn al-Zubayr (as to Muḥammad ibn al-Ḥanafiyya) during the second *fitna*, this title probably initially identified a rightly guided caliph who would have restored 'Islām' as it had been at the origin, gradually picking up an eschatological dimension.[90] Umayyad opposition used proto-messianic concepts to stress their rights in performing their violent actions: nevertheless, these attributions were not made to attain something in the afterlife, but to change the political power and dethrone the Umayyad in their contemporary life.

It would be logical to think that a more messianic and eschatological attribution to these figures, as more generally within the early 'Believers' community, began to be re-elaborated after their military defeats.[91]

C.L. Geddes's article on the Qaḥṭānide *Mahdī* focused on the production of different traditions based on geographically plural messianic prophecies which are only partially linked to the rise and fall of Empires, the restoration of an old status and an increasing eschatological stance. From the end of the seventh century, increasing uprisings against the centralized power started with a more precise identification through a pseudo-eschatological outcome which had a pietistic attitude, sometimes violent, sometimes not.[92] 'The hour will not come until a man from Qaḥṭān will come forth leading the people with his staff',[93] a prophecy which probably encouraged Ibn al-Ash'ath's uprising against the Umayyad, who identified himself with the title of al-Manṣūr and al-Qaḥṭānī in 699 without even coming from the south of Arabia.[94]

In parallel, the Umayyad caliphs in the first half of the eighth century started to attribute to themselves the title of the *Mahdī* as an expression of just ruler, in particular referring to 'Umar II.

Ibn Sa'd in his *Tabaqāt* argued: 'M. ibn 'Alī said that the Prophet is among us while the Mahdī is from the progeny of the Banū 'Abd al-Shams. We do not know him in being anyone except 'Umar ibn 'Abd al-Azīz.'[95]

Finally, after the defeat and many murders committed against the Umayyad clan by the 'Abbāsid, the legend about the Sufyānī emerged (even though we already have some traces earlier) in the second half of the eighth century, assuming a more millenarist prophetic core and stressing Baghdād's fears in considering anti-'Abbāsid revolts, in particular if linked to a Syrian origin.[96]

This brief excursus would like to highlight how this intra-clan messianic attitude probably started to mix different narratives, moving from the inner conflict emerging in the early 'Believers' community and not in relation to the Arab conquests.

The fragmentation of a unitary front after the early conquests of Syria, Palestine, Egypt and Mesopotamia intermingled with an Abrahamic eschatological and millenarian background, the clear religious awareness of which was established in the inter-clan-confederate conflict that Muḥammad was never probably able to eliminate, even during his prophetic phase.

One of the more important aspects of this inner violence which also involved the Arab Christians who were fighting on the Umayyad side was a pietistic response which in the attempt to rearrange the myth of a past unity also needed to identify an enemy, in particular a new charismatic hero to trust.

As emphasized by J. Brockopp and Steven Judd, the formation of the early Scholars, *muḥaddithūn*, and early circles, independently of the Umayyad administration, was not related to trying to produce an early Islamic historical narrative, but using Abrahamic sources, to adopt them to re-elaborate a cornerstone linked to the figure of Prophet Muḥammad.[97]

More than using the word 'Piety' in referring to Judd's work, it is evident that his analysis frames a first generation of *muḥaddithūn* and *quḍāt* in an increasingly Islamic and Arabized Umayyad administration.

Nevertheless, on a 'narrative' level, the first scholars who are usually quoted in the attempt to produce a contribution to the life of the Prophet are 'Abdallāh ibn 'Abbās (d. *c.* 688) to whom are attributed many *Ḥadīth*, 'Urwah ibn al-Zubayr (d. 713), Wahb ibn Munabbih (d. *c.* 725–737) and Ibn Isḥāq al-Zuhri (d. 768). They probably adopted Biblical stories such as Wahb ibn Munabbih's *History of King David* manuscripts or the *Kitāb al-Mubdata'*, Book of the Beginnings, to frame the first Biography of the Prophet.[98]

Accordingly, it should be difficult to emphasize a straight correlation between Apocalyptic-Messianism, *jihād* and a Qur'anic preliminary version, in imposing a new divinely order as argued by Shoemaker. 'but in the first Islamic century, *jihād* and the faith of the Believers entailed fighting to eliminate wickedness from the world and to establish the rule of their divinely ordered polity through the world'[99] and 'there can be no question that Muḥammad expected his followers to engage in *jihād in the path of God (e.g. Qur'an 4:75, 95), which amounted to militant struggle on behalf of their divinely chosen community and its religious values*'.

The main difficulties in supporting this theoretical approach are related to the complications not only in defining 'religious values' in a 'first Islamic century', something that it still was properly not or in considering the recognition of Muḥammad as God's last messenger, but in defining the 'militant pietism' of Muḥammad as a sort of ideological war against the 'unbelievers', through a clear modernist approach.[100]

The adoption and the speculation on the *Doctrina Jacobi* and the 'Keys of Paradise', for example, in assuming a belligerently conquering attitude which was not followed by a 'forced' conversion to Islām, a rapid process of Islamization and ironically the end of the world, stressed the inconsistency in highlighting the deep *Jihādist* attitude expressed in some publications.[101]

If the Qur'ān is void of millenarian and divinatory speculations, even after a more definitive canonization process, which probably occurred during the caliphate of 'Abd al-Malik, it is hard to consider all those 'Mahdist' elaborations which were truly linked to a process of redemption which had to occur just before the end of the world.[102]

It is historically plausible that the existence of early pietistic *bakkā'ūn*, penitents and weepers emerged in the phase of the early *Fitnas*, in the second half of the seventh century, as well as directly related to the intra-Believers' murderous fights due to the political succession of the caliphate.

In 657, as in 680, the internal fights between Umayyad and proto-'Alid figures occurred in a geography which remained deeply Christian, Zoroastrian and Jewish, and in which Islām was not to become the majority religion until the ninth–tenth centuries.

It would be difficult to create a *jihādi* eschatological-apocalyptic attitude, rooted in the trustworthy and absolute confidence of being the bearers of the last revelation as the followers of the last Prophet, and, after having annihilated the Persian empire and having partially conquered the Byzantine one, not to convert the entire population to Islām.

If that did not occur, it is either because the Arab conquerors were not so imbued with apocalyptic *jihadism* or were not well aware of this drastic eschatological vision as the holders of a really 'new' religious prophetic message.[103]

'History shows us well enough that this martial piety was soon realised through decades of conquests and the establishment of a new empire under the authority of the Believers and their commander (*amīr*)'[104] is a quite 'problematic' sentence in particular without considering different options: the anthropological-economic and the historical-hermeneutical ones.

The former highlights how the 'ongoing' conquering campaigns were the only way for the Umayyad administration to have economic revenues at a time when we probably need to wait until 'Abd al-Malik's caliphate, to consider the data of the first *census* that could start imposing concrete taxes, specifically on income from the countryside and agriculture-livestock.

In parallel, the ongoing conquests were not accomplished by clans that were already sedentarized but, on the contrary, the Umayyad commanders, Muḥammad bin Qāsim

(d. 715), 'Uqba ibn Nāfi'(d. 683), 'Abdallāh ibn 'Āmir (d. 678), Mūsā ibn Nuṣayr (d. 716) etc., led armies mostly made up of Arabs who were still *badawī* and *mawālī* and who continued being semi-nomads. If Hoyland's analysis leads to thinking more about the Arab identity of these conquerors[105] just as Webb and Donner lead us to think about the plurality of the 'Believers' with an increasing Islamic distinctiveness,[106] in agreement with both, the 'economic' fact needs to be increasingly associated with the historical-hermeneutic one.

One of the peculiarities of the Arab conquests was the urbanization of a huge number of people who had previously lived as Bedouins, in towns such as Kūfa, Baṣra, Moṣul, Wāsiṭ, al-Fuṣṭāṭ, Antioch, Damascus and later Baghdād, which became a capital of probably one million inhabitants in a few decades after its foundation.

Most of these cities became garrison towns, being adopted as a launching bridge for subsequent conquests; however, to maintain huge military forces in cities was not practical, as well as dangerous, even in relation to the possibility of supplying them, than for security reasons.

At the same time, the urban areas became more important for trade activities, the financial importance of which was preserved first by agricultural and livestock ones, maintained by the population who resided in the area before the 'Believers'' conquests and who continued to supply the cities; second, by an increasing circulation of currency due to the urban expansion and consumer demand, both emphasized by the ongoing conquering campaigns in the east and in the west.[107]

Conversely, the ongoing campaigns in the direction of the Iranian plateau to the east as well as North Africa and the Iberian Peninsula to the west, the updated taxation system (*kharāj* and poll tax) and the creation of a monetary system to allow the payment of soldiers' salaries were all aspects connected with campaigns which preserved the expansion of the economy in which the 'religious' apocalyptic and eschatological *afflatus* did not have effective coherence.[108]

If 80 per cent of the entire revenues in Baṣra, as in other different areas, went on military salaries and allowances, the reform of soldiers' salaries was probably implemented by the Umayyad caliphate, going from the *'aṭā'* pension system to a proper remuneration scheme, abandoning the previous one which was becoming unsustainable in the long term.

As the generation of the early conquerors passed away, the Umayyads needed to reward soldiers currently serving in its armies more than pay pensions to people whose parents and heirs had played a significant role in the early conquests.[109]

H. Kennedy argues that from the caliphate of al-Walīd I ibn 'Abd al-Malik in 715, the pension system was replaced by the salary system, paid once a year, but, perhaps, from the beginning of the 'Abbāsid age, paid once a month.

The coincidence of this reform with the important rise of the Qaysite power against the Kalbite is emblematically linked with the first Islamicizing reform phase, started by 'Abd al-Malik and continued by his son.[110]

This internal conflict between the original and 'Christian Pretorian Guard' of the Umayyads and the Qaysite was to have continued: Sulaymān ibn 'Abd al-Malik (as 'Umar II) favoured the Kalbite; Yazīd II, like Walīd II, returned to support the Qaysite; while Yazīd III, even though for only six months (744), favoured the Kalbite again. As

Ph. Kh. Hitti comments, the latter phase of the Umayyad caliphate appears to be rather the head of a particular party than the leading authority of a united empire.

In spite of this, when D. Cook concludes that these invasions were seen as an integral part of a redemptive process which occurs just before the end of the world,[111] my doubts are wholly linked with the above analysis in which much more practical and material, rather than spiritual and messianic, aspects clearly emerged.

At the same time, without denying the existence of an Abrahamic *milieu* of messianic-apocalyptic sensibility, deeply rooted in Jewish and Christian plural hermeneutical interpretations of the scriptures which, as argued by Shoemaker, permeated the birth of an Imperial Eschatology emphasizing the annihilation of their prophesying, the main historical revivalist evidence which could have affected the early 'Believers' was probably related to the second *Fitna*, starting from the killing of Ḥussein ibn 'Alī.

However, in 680, Syria, Palestine, Mesopotamia and Egypt had already been conquered.

This historical data would have stressed how in a few decades the messianic-apocalyptic influence of Judaism and Christianity on the 'Believers' could have been so radical to directly influence the 'military' narrative of the conquering campaigns, but without appearing in the Qur'ān: quite an illogical facet in particular reflecting on 'Abd al-Malik's canonization process.

This excursus also needs to be put into relation with the emerging Quranic difference between *Jihād* and *Qitāl*: the former, 'striving in God's way', is rarely associated with 'Just War'; the latter, the common word for fighting and killing, is, on the contrary, more used in the Revelation and usually with a literal interpretation.

Therefore, while the meaning of *Jihād* means a wide range of activities, from inner struggle against unbelief to religious persuasion and a specific form of active physical fighting, the meaning of *Qitāl* is univocally attributed to fighting and killing, including in this case, on the path towards God.

Therefore, if the Qur'ān used two different terms in defining something *fī sabīli llāhi*, it is possible that these terms are not synonymous. *Sūrah* 29, 69 recites: 'Who could be more wicked than the person who invents lies about God, or denies the truth when it comes to him? But we shall be sure to guide to Our ways those who strive hard for Our cause: God is with those who do good, *wa al-ladhīna jahadū fīnā la-nahidiyannahum subulanā wa inna-llah la-ma 'a al-muḥsinīm* (v. 69 only)', which stressed the clear difference between making war and striving for God, but with pietism and kindness.

4

Can we still consider the *Futūḥ* Islamic?

Many doubts emerged in considering the early Arab conquests as properly Islamic. The historical outcome of this investigation is rooted in the assumption that it takes time to frame a new religion, even when, as in this case, Islām assumes and admits being deeply indebted to an Abrahamic Jewish and Christian *milieu*. It would also be logical to presume that in relation to the early conceptualization of 'Holy-Sacred War', the process would have been similar.[1]

The first non-Islamic chronicle which argues about the presence of 30.000 (or 3000) *mutaṭawwi'ūn* (volunteers), probably enlisted to fight on the way of God, is Michael the Syrian (d. 1199) who in his *Chronicle* writes:

> La mème année, Soleiman fit préparer Maslama à marcher contre Constantinople. Il réunit deux cent mille hommes de troupes, et cinq mille bateaux qu'il remplit de troupes et de vivres. Il rassembla douze mille ouvriers, six mille chameaux, six mille ânes pour porter la nourriture des chameaux et les provisions de route des ouvriers; sur les chameaux il fit charger les armes et les instruments de siège. Il leur fit préparer des vivres pour plusieurs années, et il mit à leur tete comme général, 'Omar, fils de Hobeira. Soleiman fit ce serment: 'Je ne cesserai de combattre contre Constantinople avant d'avoir épuisé le pays des Taiyaye, ou de l'avoir prise.' Trente mille de ceux qu'on appelle *moṭṭawa'a* avancèrent avec eux.[2]
>
> (The same year, Soleiman had Maslama prepared to march against Constantinople. He gathered two hundred thousand troops, and five thousand ships, which he filled with troops and supplies. He gathered twelve thousand workers, six thousand camels, six thousand donkeys to carry the food of the camels and the road provisions of the workers; on the camels he loaded the weapons and siege instruments. He made them prepare food for several years, and he put at their head as general 'Omar, son of Hobeira ('Umar ibn Hubayra). Soleiman took this oath: 'I will not cease fighting against Constantinople until I have exhausted the land of the Tayyaye, or have taken it.' Thirty thousand of those called moṭṭawa'a (volunteer) advanced with them.)

The same information was to be reported by Bar Hebraeus (d. 1286) in his *Chronicon Ecclesiasticum*,[3] but it is absent from Theophanes the Confessor (d. 817), Agapius of Hierapolis (d. *c.* 941–42),[4] as well as from Islamic sources such as al-Ṭabarī (d. 923) and al-Ya'qūbī, while it is reported by Ibn Qutayba, 'Abdallāh ibn Muslim (d. 889).[5]

Without excessively focusing on the number of soldiers, it is important to consider that it was not until the twelfth century, in a historical phase of inter-religious crusades, that non-Islamic chronicles emphasized the presence, during the 717–718 siege of Constantinople, of an early kind of *mujahidīn*.

This *Khabar*, therefore, shows up evident difficulties if we assume that only after this second siege, or in the early 'Abbāsid age, the 'production' of apocalyptic Ḥadīth about the fall of the Byzantine capital appeared for the first time.

In his *Jāmi'*, al-Tirmidhī (d. 892) assumed that 'the Great Slaughter (*al-Malḥamah*), the conquest of Constantinople and the coming of the *Dajjāl* (the beast) will occur in a period of seven months'[6] so that 'Constantinople will be conquered with the coming of the Hour',[7] while Ibn Yazīd ibn Mājah, in his *Sunan*, reports: 'Even if there was only one day left of this world, Allah would make it last until a man from my household took possession (*ḥatta yamlika rajulun min hal baytī yamliku jabal al-Dailam wa al-Qusṭanṭiniya*) of the mountain of Dailam and Constantinople.'[8]

Various other traditions with apocalyptic messages were produced in the following centuries: the majority of them were considered weak (*Ḍa'īf*); however, the most relevant aspect to be contemplated here is the increasing association, probably after the 717–718 defeat, of an eschatological-apocalyptic *topoi*, ascribable to Constantinople as the town of the last conquest, which will be gained only through the help of a superior entity.

> The Prophet said: The flourishing state of Jerusalem will be when Yathrib is in ruins, the ruined state of Yathrib will be when the great war comes, the outbreak of the great war will be at the conquest of Constantinople and the conquest of Constantinople when the Dajjal comes forth. He (the Prophet) struck his thigh or his shoulder with his hand and said: This is as true as you are here or as you are sitting.[9]

This is quite paradigmatically and hermeneutically important in stressing that before the advent of the afterlife's kingdom in Jerusalem, the beginning of the bloody conflict against the Beast will also be linked to the conquest of Constantinople, stressing a mixture of apocalyptic-military targets, the most important of which is still missing.

It is possible indeed that if the end of the second *Fitna* (692) was an incentive for 'Abd al-Malik in framing imperial proto-Islamic thought in the attempt to better distinguish a new rising religious identity, the huge defeat of Constantinople advanced a more effective military narrative, rooted in an increasing pietistic and eschatological background.

It is psychologically evident that a monotheistic sanctified violence should emerge after an impressive defeat or a violent phase of persecutions then a huge number of military victories: this applied to the Christians, when after a long phase of harassments during the Roman age, they finally obtained, under Theodosius I (d. 395), recognition as the official religion of the empire; it also applied to the Jews, after the destruction of Solomon's Temple in 70 AD and following Bar Kokhba's revolt in 135 AD when they were no longer allowed to live in Jerusalem.

It is important to argue how, in relation to the 'Believers'' community, more than the lack of pre-Islamic narrative on an unusual conceptualization of 'Sanctified

Violence' of which the only possible overture should have been the influence of the Arab Christians *foederati*, the advent of a pietistic but also eschatological-apocalyptic awareness, attributable to 'common people's' suffering, erupted due to the internal civil wars of the second half of the seventh century.

The sorrow of the *munafiqūn* is also a very ambivalent *topos*: those that refused to be enlisted in the *Tabūk* expedition (Q. 9; 41-45, 118, but the Qur'ān does not express this in a pietistic way) when the Prophet was still alive or afterwards, those who being fearful did not try to save from certain death Ḥussein ibn 'Alī near Kerbalā are singular examples on which a 'Narrative' has been framed in the attempt to increase the 'community's' sense of belonging in a newly conquered geographical area.

According to some *akhbār*, Caliph 'Umar ibn al-Khaṭṭāb was concerned about the 'Believers' who would be dispersed among the people living in the countryside, stressing the fear about the possibility of losing their original identity: this was a very important topic which highlighted the same 'Believers' anxiety' in considering themselves as having a solid identity, in comparison with the 'conquered' people of the countryside.[10]

The Umayyad's attempt to establish a 'Believers' identity, even after the end of the second *Fitna*, through 'Abd al-Malik's new religious-Arabic policies, was not enough to develop a realistic and confident strategy capable of recognizing them as the heirs of Muḥammad's message.

The civil wars and the political dynastic complaint that was behind the internal fight between 'Believers' are the basis on which Islamic pietism was established in relation to the double influence played by Christian monasticism, in parallel with the Arab Christian clans which actively and militarily supported the Banū Umayya from the beginning.

As Th. Sizgorich, L. Conrad and Nadia Maria el-Cheick have stressed, the formation of the early history of Muḥammad's community had long been subsumed with the Quranic struggle of an armed Abrahamic whole against their enemies: the polytheists and idolaters of Meccans, the Persians and those who ruled the benighted lands beyond the Roman *Limes*.

Taking up the sword against the enemies of God was a practice shared in common by Christian Rome and the nascent Islām.[11]

The historical parallelism between Heraclius and his wars against the Persians mirrored Muḥammad's fight against the Arab confederation of the Quraysh as well as being compared with the definitive war and victory of the Romans against the Persians (628).[12]

This narrative was actively implemented in the early 'Abbāsid age in parallel with the first canonization and conceptualization of an 'Islamic' apology of violence.

A partial confirmation of this understanding emerged in the debate about the correspondence between 'Umar II ibn 'Abd al-Malik and the Byzantine Emperor Leo III the Isaurian, one of the first examples of Islam-Christian political and theological dialogue.

Independently of its forgery and probable later elaboration, the correspondence is confirmed by Byzantine sources, but not concretely by Islamic ones,[13] also because the different versions which have reached the contemporary period seem to stress an ongoing early confusion by Muslims about Jesus and Christianity, as well as the pedagogical-haughtiness of the Byzantine emperor in explaining to the caliph the most relevant Christological passages about nature as the root of Christian theology.[14]

As suggested by Hoyland R., these documents were produced in the ninth century, at the height of an intense Islamic-Christian debate and partially confirmed the final canonization of the Islamic revelation, made by Governor al-Ḥajjāj:[15] this Islamic-Christian debate already seems rooted in the main Qur'anic verses[16] that stressed the attention to Christ, Maryam, the Paraclete etc.

In other words, the narrative describing Heraclius as a prominent actor able to give legitimacy to Muḥammad's role as well as recognizing him as a true Prophet was historically counterbalanced by a 'correspondence' that was more religiously and theologically oriented and based on the Old and New Testaments, but also the Qur'ān, which highlights the main reasons why Muḥammad and Islām cannot be definitively considered trustworthy.

It is in this phase, or at least, at the beginning of it, that the just 'Islamic' belligerent praxis as a human effort on the way of God probably emerged in parallel with the first legislation on war.

1. Arab Christian influence and the early conceptualization of *Jihād*

An important distinction needs to be made between the juridical books that were to start appearing in the second half of the eighth century and in which a section on *Jihād* (generally considered as warfare)[17] emerged as a normal praxis, and the voluntary nature of fighting and living on the border of an empire which had ended its expansive phase and that was now starting to protect its frontiers.[18] However, if the finalization of borders[19] is both a significant and a descriptive facet, the construction of *'Awāṣīm – Thughūr* was more necessary with the end of the campaigns of conquest.

Geographically speaking, if on the extreme eastern-western side of this conquered land, the Hindu Kush and the Indus river became the natural frontiers of the early conquests, and the Pyrenees for al-Andalus,[20] after the Umayyad failure to defeat Constantinople in 717–718, the northern border was already established between Anatolia, the north of Syria and Armenia.

The shaping 'narrative', in developing a concrete sanctification of violence, completely absent from the pre-Islamic Ḥijāz, is an inclusive aspect which needs to resume the whole of the above analysis: *in primis*, the influence of the Christian Arab *milieu* in the 'Believers' community, as well as the difficulty, from the beginning, of finding men willing to fight, as the same Qur'ān implied in some verses (2: 216; 9: 37, 39, 83, 90).

These two aspects need to be put into relation with other significant facets: the former with the Jafnid-Ghassānid religious narrative on war and martyrdom like the pietistic monastic attitude that they emphasized through the creation of monasteries and churches; the latter, with the need to balance, as well as to encourage the defence of a frontier that with the end of the conquering campaigns needed to be properly assumed as a moral goal.

Theophylact Simocatta reports how the popular attraction to figures such as Sergius, a martyred saint, in the frontier regions separating the Byzantine and Persian empires and mostly populated by Arabs as well as *foederati* of both, is highlighted by how, for example, when the Zoroastrian Persian King Chosroes II was winning back his domain with the help of the Romans in 591, he offered this victory, and afterwards his wife's pregnancy, to the Christian saint.[21]

The sanctuary of Symeon the Stylite in Syria usually attracted members of Bedouin Arab tribes just as the cult of Sergius played a significant role in stressing the local Bishop's role, like Ahudemmeh's mission in converting Arab polytheists.[22] The impact of this cult was so important on the imagination of local Arabs that when Ahudemmeh's shrine to Sergius was burned down by Christian rivals, the Persian emperor Chosroes rebuilt it.[23]

In parallel, as M. Bonner underlines in his analysis on early *Jihād*, and the Qur'ān itself also alludes to in relation to 'Believers' who did not want to fight, the payment practice for a military substitute (*ja'ā'il*) was quite uncommon at least for the first century, even if rarely put into practice from the beginning of the conquering campaigns.

As reported, it was in Kūfa, not a geographical place close to a military border, that some jurists probably allowed it in the sense of a kind of wage: a salary to an individual who took one's place in the army.

Abū Ḥanīfa's position disapproved of the *ja'ā'il* as long as the Muslims were strong.

> If they are weak, it is all right for them to fortify one another in this manner. A man that has enough money of his own should therefore not accept such a payment but may do so if he has none. No such statement occurs in the early Ḥanafī jurists, and indeed such a position was conceivable only after the work of al-Shāfi'ī.[24]

Sarakhsī, to whom the above quotation is attributed, emphasized how until al-Shāfi'ī (d. 820), in the second half of the eighth–first half of the ninth century, the vast majority of early Islamic jurisprudence rejected this practice; 'Abd al-Razzāq al-Ṣan'ānī's (d. 827) quotation of 'Abdallāh ibn 'Umar argues that 'the man who stayed at home giving a donation to the warrior is a man who is selling his own capacity for warfare (*ghazw*). I don't know what that is'.[25]

However, as al-Shāfi'ī elaborates in the *Kitāb al-Umm*, in considering the basic purpose of *Jihād*, the defence of Islamic territories, stationing at the frontier (*thughūr*), also needs to be considered in giving the caliph the possibility to organize the seasonal military campaigns, having enough Muslims for fighting.[26]

The founder of the Shāfi'īte school was probably trying to find a solution related to the impressive decrease of the number of military forces in the 'Abbāsid armies, in particular, in comparison with the Umayyad era.

If al-Ṭabarī, in giving numbers related to the battle of Zāb (750), emphasized that God was with the Banū 'Abbās in relation to their availability of military forces, with only 20,000 against 120,000 Umayyad,[27] the early rebellions against Caliph al-Manṣūr (d. 775) stressed that probably, at that time, the army had no more than 75,000 soldiers,[28] with at least 25,000 men at the border with Byzantium which remained the most unstable frontier.[29]

This digression aims to stress that probably until the Umayyad age, the armies in the different areas of the empire were made up of Arabs and *mawālī*, directly linked to the clans and confederations which had conquered these geographical areas. For this reason, as H. Kennedy explains, there were Syrian, Iraqian, Iranian, Egyptian armies which provided forces to continue the campaigns in the eastern and western directions.[30] However, the absence of any kind of *voluntarism*, at least until the second siege of Constantinople (715–717), is highlighted by the payment process; this was an efficiency that the internal clan conflict between the different souls of the Umayyad army (Kalbite and Qaysite) revealed after the period of 'Abd al-Malik and erupted when the confrontation with the 'Abbāsid uprising became more dangerous.[31]

However, it also seems plausible that after the military success of the 'Abbāsid uprising, the caliphate army suffered from a huge lack of fighters.

Before coming to the analysis on the military-theological consistency of the early Islamic *jihād*, it is important to go back to the former Arab Christian *milieu* from which the historical canonization of *Jihād* was to emerge in the early 'Abbāsid era.

As reported by Sizgorich, the early Islamic narrative on the recognition of the Prophecy of Muḥammad, by the Christian Monk Baḥīrā, like the importance of Arab Christian ascetism in rejecting heresy and in recognizing the un-falsified message of Jesus is widely represented in early Islamic sources.

The biography of the Prophet not only reports the heroism of the Martyrs of Najrān but stressed that the Arabs there had already adopted the 'law of 'Īsā ibn Maryam'. In parallel, in arguing about the presence of early 'Believers' in Mecca, the *Sīra* underlines that some of them emigrated to Abyssinia and became Christians such as, for example, Umm Ḥabība ibn Abū Sufyān, the daughter of Abū Sufyan, the enemy of the Prophet, and afterwards one of Muḥammad's wives.

At the same time, the Monk warns Abū Ṭālib to protect and hide Muḥammad from the Jews, because if they recognized him, they would try to hurt him.[32]

As for the significant presence of Christian monks or 'real' Christian rulers, the emperor of Abyssinia, Heraclius, in the early Islamic narrative also directly formalized Muḥammad's prophetic and political role in emblematically upholding truth and veracity for early Islām (eighth century).

Al-Ṭabarī preserves late antique Christian hagiographical stories about the destruction of the Idols emphasizing a typical militant ascetism as well as 'fighters of the faith'.[33] It is as if the 'Islamic' revelation and prophecy needed Abrahamic approval, more specifically of Christianity than Judaism, because the former was also directly related to a leading political power, the Roman one.

Analogously, Christian monasticism is linked in different Islamic traditions with the idea of martyrdom (not only in *Najrān*), militant protection of the true religion and the preservation of a correct and pietistic monotheistic practice. Contrary to the Christian Orthodox-Greek scepticism about the heresy of the Ishmaelites, an important relation between Arab monasticism and early Islamic pietism brings us directly to the early canonization of *jihād*.

If the Qur'ān stressed an intermediate position about the figure of the monk (*rāhib*) between 5:82–83, which recites:

> You [Prophet] are sure to find that the most hostile to the believers are the Jews and those who associate other deities with God; you are sure to find that the closest in affection towards the believers are those who say, 'We are Christians,'

> for there are among them people devoted to learning and ascetics. These people are not given to arrogance, and when they listen to what has been sent down to the Messenger, you will see their eyes overflowing with tears because they recognise the Truth [in it].

and 9: 34–35:

> Believers, many rabbis and monks wrongfully consume people's possessions and turn people away from God's path. [Prophet], tell those who hoard gold and silver instead of giving in God's cause that they will have a grievous punishment: 35 on the Day it is heated up in Hell's Fire and used to brand their foreheads, sides, and backs, they will be told, 'This is what you hoarded up for yourselves! Now feel the pain of what you hoarded!

the early Muslim mystics in the eighth century needed to validate their actions as well as their thought in relation to those of the Christian Arab monks before them. 'Abd al-Wāḥid ibn Zayd (d. *c.* 750), the legendary figure of Wahb ibn Munabbih (d. *c.* 728), Ibrāhīm ibn Adham (d. 777), Abū Sulaymān al-Dārānī (d. 830), Abū al-Qāsim al-Junayd (d. 910) etc. eminently argue about the monks' lives, their actions as well as their piety.[34] The monks mentioned in these 'Sayings of the Fathers' are not considered for giving Christian theological advice or to emphasize the importance of a specific liturgy; on the contrary, their behaviour is far from being categorized by religious orthodoxy but imparts wisdom and dispenses praise with, in some cases, great controversies over the lost Christianity of the origin of their faith, an important 'political-religious' facet which developed the concept of *taḥrīf* (distortion, alteration).

Abū al-Hudhayl (d. 840), the famous Mu'tazilite, argues:

> I heard a Monk say that once Satan tested Jesus, peace be upon him, took him to the Temple Mount. He said to him: 'You claim that you can raise the dead. If you are honest, then ask God to turn this mountain into bread'. Jesus replied: 'One does not live by bread alone'. Again, Satan argued: 'If you are who you claim to be, jump from this place and the angels will come to carry you'. To whom Jesus replied again: 'My Lord commanded me not to put myself to test, for I do not know whether or not he will protect me.[35]

This is clearly related to the Gospel verses of Matthew 4: 1-11 and Luke 4: 1-13, even if only partially narrated.

Abū Sulaymān al- Dārānī reported:

> 'I heard a monk praying in his cell and saying: "Praise be to He who takes no comfort from those who are living and who is not distressed by those who have died"' as well as an anonymous one said: 'I asked a monk: "Give me helpful advice." He replied: "All advice comes down to one statement." I asked him: "What is that?" He replied: "Devote yourself to obeying Him and you will find that you have acquired all counsel and sermons."'[36]

Later on, there are traditions which stressed the practice of *Jihād* as performed by Monks converted to Islām and who died fighting against Byzantium, as reported by Ibn Qutayba, or the existence of Arab Christian ascetics who, travelling with a Roman Army, encountered the 'Believers' army (at the beginning of the campaigns of conquest) and apologetically exalt them after a preliminary encounter eulogizing their proto-mystic attitude: 'from a people praying all the night and remaining abstinent during the day, commanding right and forbidding wrong (*al-amr bi-l-ma'rūf wa-n-nahy 'ani-l-munkar*), monks by night and lions by day', as reported by al-Azdī al-Baṣrī.[37]

However, if the monks' militant practice can be historically associated, from the early centuries of Christianity, as a common practice with the presence of cenobitic communities since the fourth–fifth centuries of late antiquity, the military ascetic voluntarism at the frontier is more innovative and paradigmatic as well as linked to the Arab Christian *Foederati* who played the same role in the sixth century. This aspect is not considered by M. Bonner or by Th. Sizgorich in their respective analyses.

It is possible that the early Muslim community in the eighth century started to re-elaborate the events of the conquering campaigns as episodes of a larger narrative that attested God's support, their superior pious and moral attitude, the idea that Muḥammad certainly was a trustworthy prophet in antithesis with an Abrahamic world that contrary to early Muslim expectations, did not recognize them or Muḥammad himself as a Prophet.

The importance then of adopting a pietistic narrative, partially already in vogue in the Abrahamic *milieu*, partially linked to early 'Believers' after the first *Fitnas*, probably found inspiration in the Arab Christian attitude to war.

It is like a *collage* in which al-Azdī al-Baṣrī and Abū Mikhnaf (d. 774) in their respective *Fuṭūḥ al-Shām* on the one hand, and Ibn al-Mubārak and other pietistic authors on the other hand, established the formation of that military fighting voluntarism (*mutaṭawwi'a*) which, as we will see later, emerged more consistently in the early 'Abbāsid age.

If indeed, there are few sources able to report that army-voluntarism already affected the Umayyad attempt to conquer Constantinople in 717, their presence in the second half of the eighth century cannot only be more religiously motivated, but also more military-practical.

As historically supported, the existence of a *Thughūr*, before the last siege of the Byzantine capital, would be inconclusive and illogical, while in the following decades, the Arab incursions had continued until the battle of Akroinos (740) in which the Byzantines defeated the Umayyad.[38]

To attribute the construction of a frontier, in particular in relation to Byzantium, before the 'Abbāsid revolution is possible but not clearly reported by sources.

Feryal Salem's[39] identification of a figure such as Rawḥ ibn Zinbā' al- Judhāmī (d. *c.* 702–703), the Umayyad governor of Palestine and clearly related to the Arab Christian clan of the Banū Judhām, as an early version of a 'volunteer fighter' is problematic, because it is based on the simplistic idea that a clan, which in 681 rejected the oath of alliance (*Bay'ah*) to Yazīd I and his Kalbite supporters,[40] in a short time, easily conquered the confidence of the Caliphs they had previously rejected.

We are still in a historical phase in which clan affiliation, more than religious belonging, played a significant role, in particular until the end of the second *Fitna*

(692). If, in fact, Rawḥ ibn Zinbā' al-Judhāmī played an important part in trying to convince the Banū Judhām to form a new alliance with the Kalbite, until the end of the same *Fitna*, Rawḥ's clan remained consistently anti-Umayyad.[41]

On the contrary, this *akhbār* is relevant in establishing the relationship between 'belligerent voluntarism' and an Arab Christian fighter who, considering the Islamic 'narrative', was already converted to the new religion.[42]

However, at the moment, the evidence clarifies that only Ibn al-Mubārak's (d. 795) main work should be consistently considered as the first which stressed this important relationship between 'Frontier warfare' and 'personal militant ascetic behaviour'.

> Sizgorich in his work, *Violence and Belief in Late Antiquity*, emphasises martial pursuit as a form of piety in the second/eighth century. The numerous references to martial valor motivated by religious interest indicate, however, that this was not a new trend in the second/eighth century, but was, rather, a practice dating to the prophetic period soon after the advent of Islām. [...] Furthermore, assuming an early origin of martial zeal would explain the reality of Muslim expansion in the first few decades after the Prophet's death. If piety became a motivating factor only during the second/eighth century, as Sizgorich implies, it would be necessary to produce historical evidence that would explain the motivating factor that extraordinarily brought together a once tribally divided Arabian Peninsula into a force powerful enough to dominate greater Syria in a matter of decades.[43]

The above quotation continues to be a problematic argument for those who can agree about the existence of an Arab-Islamic religious identity after the death of the Prophet Muḥammad (632), as well as for those who argued that only through an aggressive religious approach would the Arabs of the Peninsula have been able to promote the conquering campaigns reaching the huge geographical dominations we know.

This idea, however, is based on the assumption that 'orality' and 'subsequent narratives' can be adopted instead of historical evidence, while, on a source level, we have to wait until the second half of the eighth century to consider early Islamic juridical books about warfare by Imām Mālik Shaybānī, al-Fazāri, Ibn al-Mubārak and Aḥmad ibn Ḥanbal.

If 165 years separate the death of Prophet Muḥammad and that of Ibn Mubārak, it is hard to think that in this period different factors did not play a more significant function in establishing an early version of ascetic *jihād* as the first concrete example of appeasement between *qitāl* and *zuhd*.

If Donner's historical intuition about the 'Believers' is based on the absence of numerous sources capable of dogmatically distinguishing proto-Islām from Christianity and Judaism, as well as on the non-appearance of archaeological findings in the same direction, R. Hoyland, in his more secular analysis, stressed the historical Bedouin's belligerent attitude as the main active strength of the campaigns of conquest.

In parallel, as Steven C. Judd and J. Brockopp have differently highlighted, we have to wait until the first half of the eighth century to consider a first generation of religious scholars, *muḥaddithūn*, who started to collect traditions in parallel with the wandering role that *qurrā'* and *quṣṣās* were playing as pietistic cenobite monks in the territories under Umayyad control.[44]

Ibn al-Mubārak, in his *Kitāb al-Jihād* as well as in the *Kitāb al-Zuhd*, stressed God's consideration about the sacredness of war in relation to the ascetic piety of an individual warrior who performed this action in the absolute awareness of his own will (*niyya*): 'Who was killed fighting for the desire to admire the face of God, you will find him in Paradise.'[45]

Unlike other texts, such as the *Kitāb al-Siyar* of Isḥāq al-Fazārī (d. 804) of whom Ibn al-Mubārak was a close friend, the *mujāhid*'s piety and ascetism are the basis of his physical strength and his isolation on the *thughūr*. Al-Mubārak's search for a form of ascetic pilgrimage, far from any urban area, is not only a polemic facet which echoes an inner reflection on the evidence that fighting on the way of God was possible at the frontier only, but a more relevant expression that: 'the fighting for the world; for the wealth; for the fame as inner personal pleasure, as well as reaching to fight sincerely in trying to get God's pleasure'[46] is not only the way to reach Paradise but is the only way of being a *mujāhid fī sabīli llāhi*.

The importance of these verses underscores the main difference between fighting for God's will and doing the same for the world or personal duties; ibn al-Mubārak's intention to include in his *Kitāb* an important *ḥadīth* about 'Abdallāh ibn al-Rawāḥa (d. 629):

> The Messenger of God sent an army in which was 'Abdallāh ibn al-Rawāḥa. The army left and 'Abdallāh remained behind to pray with the Messenger of God. After the Prophet completed his prayer he said, 'O Ibn al-Rawāḥa, are you not in the army?'. He said: 'Yes o Messenger of God. But I wanted to take part in the prayer with you. I know their location and I can catch up with them.' The prophet said: 'By the One in whose hands is my soul, if you spent all that is in the earth in charity you would not be able to recompense the value of their departure.'[47]

It is interesting to reproach a quietist although pietistic attitude of a Prophet's companion from Medina (Banū Khawrāj) and poet who was put third-in-command[48] on the expedition of Mu'tah, and who died in this (629) against the Arab *foederati* forces of Byzantium.

However, unlike F. Salem's interpretation, this *ḥadīth*, which is not considered among the most canonical, was probably included to stress how the 'departure' for a mission is sometimes more important than carrying out a common duty; this reflect not only the personal difficulties in leaving for a military expedition, as already mentioned in the Qur'ān (2: 216; 9: 37, 39, 83, 90), but in recruiting volunteers at the border in the early 'Abbāsid period.

The literature which emerges in this historical phase is defined by C. Melchert as renunciant: renouncing life's pleasures, as unsurprisingly related to an attraction for warfare in performing an ongoing life based on danger and hardship, stressing how the best fighter is he who becomes indifferent to every kind of worldly affliction.[49]

This narrative approach is emphasized by another famous *ḥadīth*: 'Every prophet has a monasticism (*rahbāniyya*). The monasticism of this community is *jihād* in the path of God'[50] is mainly attributed to a belligerent pietistic attitude which includes the whole community, the Prophet Muḥammad *in primis*, as well as all the early believers and companions.

However, the predominant Quranic term which defines and makes the meaning of fighting coexist with that of killing (*qitāl*), at least on the juridical level, underlines a new and different spectrum with *jihād*; on the contrary, at least for Ibn al-Mubārak, the active form of monasticism in Islām is closely linked to a practice of *Zuhd* as related to a human being that 'if one is willing to do a good work but then does not do it, God has a complete good work in his favour'[51]; 'Wandering monasticism was mentioned in the presence of the Prophet of God and the messenger of God said: God gave us in its place *jihād* on the path of God and the *takbīr* from every hill'.[52]

As we will see in the following part, the majority of the juridical texts that emerge in this phase and include the book of *jihād*, in their traditional collections, are not related to encouraging piety or self-sacrifice. The *Siyar* of al-Fazārī, as well as the *Kitāb al-Umm* and the *Risāla fī 'Uṣūl al-Fiqh* of al-Shāfi'ī, the *Kitāb al-Siyar* of al-Awzā'ī and *al-Mukhtaṣar* of al-Muzanī (d. 878), al-Shaybānī's *Siyar* as *Kitāb al-Aṣl* and his Ḥanafite followers, still did not adopt *jihād* as the correct word to substitute *qitāl* agaist the *ahl al-Ridda, ahl al-Baghy,* or *al-Mushrikīn,* while, in the *Muwaṭṭa',* the Imān Mālik, the *qāḍī* Ibrāhīm Ḥammād ibn Isḥāq (d. 935) and Ibn Abī Zayd al-Qayrawānī (d. *c.* 996-997) initially assume the word of *jihād* in identifying legislation on war.[53]

The legislative texts were necessary in a historical phase when the conquests were over and fighting at the frontier had to be regulated for common understanding.

Ibn al-Mubārak's main proposition, in the *Kitāb al-Jihād,* unlike the *Kitāb al-Zuhd,* is to frame a first 'doctrine' on the Islamic sacredness of War rooted in ascetic pietism, individual *niyya* and the attitude of fighting the infidel; however, as Aḥmad ibn Ḥanbal reports in attributing it to 'Abd al-Razzāq al-Ṣan'ānī and Ibn al-Mubārak: 'If one man spends the night with equals in battle while the other spends the night praying God, I think that the one who recollects God as those who recite the Qur'ān are better'.[54]

This is more disengaged from a concrete bellicose purpose, but with a flight from the masses, fleeing from the corruptive influences of the crowd; the desire for solitude in which the believer should perfect his soul in assuming a more ascetic attitude.

More than a martial valour of conquests which directly stressed the peculiarity of enrichment and booty, never named or even considered by Ibn al-Mubārak's text, the emphasis is based on the individual's merit and reward, *ajr*, independently of the kind of compensation – spiritual or material – but in relation to the inner intention of the action. Ibn al-Mubārak highlights moral conduct in war as dissociated from an increasingly juridical-case law, in arguing a sort of independence from a *Quḍāt* control.

Quite antithetically, the Imām Mālik in the *Muwaṭṭā'* argues:

> Invasion (*al-ghazw ghazwān*) is of two kinds: the invasion for which valuables are spent, the participant is willing, the commander is obeyed, and corruption is avoided, thereby this invasion is good for all. The other kind of invasion is that for which valuables are not spent, the participants are not willing to fight, the

> commander is not obeyed and corruption is not avoided, thereby it is not a reward for its doer (*fadhālika al-ghazū lā irji'u ṣāḥbuhu kafāfan*).[55]

The first obligation that a *mujāhid* needs to consider is about himself as a *volunteer*. The perfect coherence of the praxis and the intention is the basis for sincerity, but it is also very hard to reach a balanced inner steadfastness.

In other words, my community is protected because my intention is pure and not absorbed by material or narcissist goals.

The narrative related to a figure such as Ibrāhīm ibn Adham (d. 782), who was born in Balkh, far from Syria, moved to Baghdād and afterwards made a pilgrimage to the Holy Land and who died as a *ghāzī* and garrison member (*murābiṭ*) against the Rūm,[56] is again emblematically connected with an inner personal ethical intention.

The identification of this *topos* with the geographical landscape of a monastery, where in spite of preserving the knowledge, the purpose is to preserve the morality of an entire life, is completely dissociated from a conquering campaign in which the enriching target was clearly more important than the spiritual emphasis, because it was rooted in pillage.

> The *Mujāhid* is the one who fights against himself to obey God, while the *muhājir* is the one who emigrates from sins.[57]

The personal goal is preserving purity, the more practical one is to defend the community; the balance between them is in the *niyya* (the personal intention).

This is one of the main reasons why those *mutaṭawwi'ūn* were probably absent during the conquering campaigns, while, on the contrary, they will emerge in the following century when a religious pietistic elaboration will be reached to affect an early and more complex form of spirituality.

This pietistic *topos* also needs to be inserted in relation to the analysis that subsequent military reforms were to affect the 'Abbāsid empire in the first half of the ninth century.

2. *Jihād* and war, *Jihād* as testimony.

This historical aspect is important in focusing on a rationalizing narrative about belligerence and *Jihād*, as well as stressing its temporary success in different phases of Islamic history which clearly started with Ibn al-Mubārak's famous text but without finding great historical continuity.

In an attempt not to be misinterpreted, the pietistic intimist behavioural attitude of the early canonization of *Jihād* is the original and earliest concrete form of 'belligerent monasticism' which from the beginning will emerge as partially dissociated from the juridical texts produced in the same historical period, and in relation to the military reforms which affected the 'Abbāsid empire under the caliphate of al-Ma'mūn (813-833) and al-Mu'taṣim (833-842).

Considering the military essays which appear in Ibn al-Nadīm (d. 990) *Fihrist*[58] and focusing in particular on two, al-Jāḥiz's *Risāla fī Manāqib al-Turk*[59] and Khalīl Ibn al-Haythām al-Hartami's *Mukhtaṣar Sīyāsāt al-Ḥurūb*,[60] it is important to consider the concrete absence in referring to Ibn al-Mubārak's conceptualization of *Jihād*.

Both were probably written during al-Ma'mūm's rule and his political inheritance phase which deeply affected the 'Abbāsid world in the first half of the ninth century.

This was a phase when the military reforms by al-Ma'mūn (813-833) and al-Mu'taṣim (833-842) drastically changed the structure and the internal ethnic composition of the army.

In parallel, al-Mu'taṣim's military victories against the Byzantines in 837–838 with the occupation of Ancyra and Amorioum, after Bābak's Khurramites insurrection had been supported by the Byzantine Emperor Theopilos,[61] highlighted how this reorganization re-arranged the role of the *mutaṭawwi'ūn* in the army.

Until the era of al-Ma'mūn, the process of the Army's Turkization remained limited while al-Jāḥiz's analysis stressed the presence of the *Khurāsāniyya* (from the Iranian area of Khurāsān): this army was particularly faithful to the Caliph and with it he defeated the *Abnā'* of his brother al-Amīn, during the civil war (811–813).[62] Al-Jāḥiz's work highlights the role played by this *Khurāsāniyya* army: it was the cornerstone on which al-Ma'mūn built up his power and dominion, against the *Abnā'*, whose origins were probably also from Khurāsān, but that after a few decades in Baghdād were easily corrupted by power becoming a sort of pretorian guard of Amīn.[63]

As long as al-Ma'mūn was in power, the frontier with Byzantium remained a geographical place where yearly incursions (*ghazawāt*) guaranteed tribute and booty as well as the presence of the Caliph at the border portrayed the image of a ruler who fought against the empire's enemies in giving prestige to the dynasty.[64]

Ḥārūm al-Rashīd's incursion in 781 led 100,000 men to the Sea of Marmara, and his incursion of 806, when as Caliph he devastated the Byzantine territories with a huge army of 135,000 soldiers, volunteers excluded, were adopted as symptomatic of the 'Abbāsid's engagement in fighting against their historical enemies.[65]

A similar narrative also affected al-Ma'mūn's caliphate, even though the civil war with his brother, the *Miḥna* and his presumed pro-Mu'tazilite support, was negatively played out in stressing his over-liberal *visio*.

The *mutaṭawi'ūn*, therefore, did not disappear, even though al-Ṭabarī rarely mentions them. It is historically interesting that the famous chronicler did not remark on them in relation to the yearly raids promoted from the caliphate of al-Mahdī (775-785) and which continued until that of al-Mu'taṣim (842), but in relation to 'suppressing evildoers in Baghdād' after al-Ma'mūn's conquest and occupation, at the end of the civil war.[66]

Al-Mukhtaṣar, on the contrary, is a text in which the author would like to give advice to a Caliph, but without assuming a religious or utopic perspective: of the thirty different kinds of soldiers named, there is nothing which clearly refers to a sort of *mujāhid*, even though the commander, like the *rijāl rasmiyyah*, the officials, should be God-fearing and patient.[67]

The mention of the passage from an army that was still an Arab clan, led by an Arab military élite to a sort of professional *jaish*, more typical of the early 'Abbāsid age, clearly highlights the historical period to which this text refers and the main military differences with the previous Umayyad era.[68]

Correspondingly, the use of the term *shākiriyya* is stressed by Kennedy in referring to a part of the army: foot soldiers and knights on horseback, which affected in particular the *Khurāsāniyya*, and therefore were adopted only for few decades in the ninth century: this characteristic places the text, or at least what has survived of it, in a specific historical phase.[69]

The important absence of a narrative referring to religion in a treaty which is more rationally oriented to the 'organization' and 'planning' of war is probably emblematically related to the fact that a few decades after Ibn al-Mubārak's significant focus on the 'pietistic behavioural' attitude of the frontier volunteers, the reformation of the army, or the war strategies, did not give excessive consideration to this specific *afflatus*.

However, it would be erroneous not to consider the preface of the *Mukhtaṣar*, in which God is clearly named as the 'Master of war', *sayyid al-Ḥarb*, stressing obedience to Him, 'because victories came from Him alone independently of cleverness or any kind of construction, competences or numbers of forces', *li'anna al-Naṣr ya'tī minhu waḥahu, wa laysa min al-dhakā' aw al-ḥilah, walā min al-qudra wa al-arqām.*[70]

In parallel, the author's rational attitude stressed that God's intentions are often obscure and the triumph of the infidel as well as the suffering of the just and honest man remained a possibility that could not be easily understood in this world.

In his short analysis, Malik Mufti argued that contrary to contemporary texts such as *al-Farīḍah al-Ghā'ibah*, the *Mukhtaṣar* is alien from favouring a zealous activism: 'its author wrote at a time when the dialogue between champions of cosmopolitan learning and champions of orthodox practice played out at a much more sophisticated and creative level.'[71]

However, more than reflecting on a text written in the 1970s and adopted as a *manifesto* of contemporary Jihadism, considerations need to be linked to Ibn al-Mubārak and his *Kitāb al-Jihād*, an author who lived around fifty years before the author of the *Mukhtaṣar* and about whom there is no consistent trace in the same *Mukhtaṣar*.

It is therefore evident that the historical debate about the early conceptualization of *Jihād* as a peculiar aspect of war remained linked to two important ambits: the framing of a political 'Abbāsid legitimation which stressed the presence of God as supportively behind their dominations; the close relationship between pietism and ascetism with a specific form of warfare, which although Ibn al-Mubārak stressed in his *Kitāb*, remained quite isolated in relation to the other juridical texts on war.

The only important continuity of Mubārak's narrative is in a proto-Ṣūfist elaboration which, however, will rapidly abandon a bellicose attitude, as Ibn al-Mubārak himself stressed in his *Kitāb al-Zuhd*.

If Feryal Salem correctly argued that 'the *Kitāb al-Jihād* is rich in historical information and reflects how *Jihād* was used as a means to portray general elements of piety', my scepticism is related to the fact that, as early as the following century, the Islamic mystical tradition rooted in the 'historical-mythological' figure of Ḥasan al-Baṣrī (d. 728) will continue in ascetics such as Mālik Ibn Dīnār (d. 744), 'Abd Allah al-Tustarī (d. 896), al-Junayd (d. 910), 'Abd Allāh al-Tirmidhī (d. 892) etc. in no longer considering the belligerent attitude at the frontier, a concrete *spectrum* of salvation, while the narrative on a belligerent *jihād* will come back into vogue later, in the eleventh–twelfth centuries.[72]

In other words, the image of the ascetic warrior offers an important first example of *Jihād*, as the Quranic tradition showed. However, the belief that *niyya* as well as the emphasis on the martyr's death in the first 'Believers' age became a model in the following centuries is not consistent until the periods when the Islamic world was in remission or under attack (invasion by the Crusaders and Mongols, Colonialism and neo-Colonialism etc.).

As the above analysis shows, the Just War made its contribution to framing a new Islamic identity after the encounter with the Abrahamic *milieu* following the early conquests.[73]

The fact that prominent mystic figures such as Ibn al-Mubārak, Ibrāhīm ibn Adham (d. 778) or 'Utba al-Ghulām (d. 784) fought with a pietistic-ascetism spirit and some of them died against the Byzantines at the frontier clearly does not mean that the early Arab conquerors were motivated by the same afflatus, 150 years earlier.

This was also because the deep personal religious motivation of *jihād* cannot be imposed as an obligation, contrary to a more specific Qur'anic *topos*, as antithetical to any kind of *niyya*.

In parallel, Sizgorich's analysis in showing the Christian milieu, but also the Khārijite one, behind this early conceptualization, is based on a different level of evidence.[74]

If Ibn al-Mubārak as well as Abū Isḥāq al-Fazārī (d. 804) wanted to stress an *Imitatio Muhammadi* or Imitatio Muhammadi's companions, just as Christian Oriental Monasticism and Arab *Foederati* wanted to emphasize an *Imitatio Christi* or an *Imitatio Martyrs/Saints*, a religious literary genre quite popular in late antiquity, M. Ibn Ḥanbal's defence of real Islām during the *Miḥna* is a symbolic step in bringing *Jihād* out of a military geography, keeping it in a religious ascetic one.

This is also because, as reported by Abū Bakr al-Khallāl in *Ahl al-milal*[75] and by al-Jāḥiẓ in *Al-Radd 'alā al-Naṣārā*,[76] the existence in the middle of the ninth century of an Abrahamic *milieu* in which many families and clan contained Muslim and non-Muslim members was still quite normal, contextually with the presence of Jews, Christians and Magians who during the summer raids against the Byzantines still accompanied and fought in the Roman land, the enemy of Islām.[77]

Ibn Ḥanbal's reply was 'Do not seek the aid of *Mushrikūn* against other *Mushrikūn*',[78] but despite this official response, it confirmed that it was evident how among the *Ghāzī*, who fought in the Roman territory, there were fighters of different religions who took part in these incursions on the Islamic side.[79]

Both texts highlighted how during the period of Ibn Ḥanbal and al-Jāḥiẓ, it was still difficult to pick out a Christian from a Muslim on the basis of external appearance, knowledge of Islām, cultural literacy, social and power positioning as well as, partially, treatment under the law.

When Abū Bakr al-Khallāl asks Ibn Ḥanbal about the existence of Jews and Christians among Muḥammad's early *Umma*, the founder of the Ḥanbalite school replied considering this a filthy question which was not to be discussed and emblematic of the ongoing debate during the 'Golden' age of Islām.

It is interesting to underline how two different authors of the ninth century, with very dissimilar (al-Jāḥiẓ and Ibn Ḥanbal) backgrounds, were trying to impose a sort of religious boundary in starting to implement a more segregationist policy.[80]

As a conclusion of this historical part, it is evident that an early canonization of *Jihād* is an expression of a model of militant piety adopted by warriors on the frontier who assumed a deep inner ascetic isolationism, and which is easily put in parallel with the more peaceful one of different mystics. A form of *jihād* that A. Ibn Ḥanbal wanted to implement during the *Miḥna*: 'the best *Jihād* is a word of justice in front of an oppressive ruler'.[81]

The significant background of this concept is a *collage* of an Abrahamic *milieu* rooted in monasticism, ascetism and Arab militantism, previously Christian and later Islamic.

Part Two

5

Qur'ān, otherness and Jihād

Introduction. Qur'ān and militantism: Jihād, Qitāl, Siyar, Ṣabr, Ḥarb *'fī sabīli llāhi'*

The common adage that Abrahamic religions are more violent than others, as well as that Islamic 'Civilization' has become a threat for global security, stressed the idea that we are not in a phase of religious revanchism, but in one of the politicization of human beings' religiosity as well as pauperization of the religious message for political ends.[1]

However, to compare religious revelations in trying to decipher whether one is more militarily vehement than another is methodologically abstruse because it is unable to consider the 'human' factor, its hermeneutical interpretation as well as the influence that internal and external factors played in different historical periods.

Until the nineteenth century, Western scholars tended to consider the broad context provided by *Sīra* literature, emphasizing it as a historical text which stressed the Meccan and Medinan phases as facts, even though only rooted in the 'Islamic' sources.[2]

Theodor Nöldeke's *Geschichte des Qorans*, in 1860, was a milestone in the Western analysis of the Qur'ān which follows the distinction between Meccan and Medinan *sūras*, and also used new criteria of style and argument, and it remained a prominent work which was also capable of considering an important Qur'anic chronological order. R. Bell's and R. Blachère's alternative reconstructions, that partly differ from Nöldeke, have not been widely accepted in comparison with the German scholar, even though they have provided a valid substitute on some occasions.[3] On the Islamic side, we have a list of Muslim writers who have managed the most widely known chronology that through 'Aṭā via Ibn 'Abbās, a famous companion to whom the *Tanwīr al-Miqbās* is also attributed, has reached the contemporary age.

The fifteenth-century chronology version of 'Abd al-Kāfi presents many differences from the ninth century one included in al-Ya'qūbī's universal history, as well as the chronology of Meccan *sūras* in the *Kitāb al-Mabāni* (anonymous author) which is very different from the list drawn up by Muḥammad ibn Nu'mān ibn Bashīr (d. 684), as reported by the tenth-century bibliophile Ibn al-Nadīm.[4] In the contemporary period, the first printed version of the Qur'ān, the King Fu'ad edition published in Egypt in

All the Qur'anic verses have been taken from M.A.S. Abdel Haleem, *The Qur'an*, parallel Arabic Text, Oxford: Oxford University Press, 2004; however, other translations have been also considered: R. Blachère, *Le Coran*, Paris: Maisonneuve & Larose, 1999, and A. Bausani, *Il Corano*, Milano: Bur Ed., 2001.

1925, is usually considered and referred to as the standard Egyptian edition as well as offering the last version of its chronology.

During the twentieth century, the attempt to work more concretely on the correlation between *Sīra* and *Qur'ān* was put in the spotlight with increasing scepticism: the growing doubts in Western academia about the truthfulness of the Prophet's biography reached its height with John Wansbrough who, in his *Quranic Studies*, asserted that the Islamic revelation was not a stable and sacred canon until at least a couple of centuries after Prophet Muḥammad's death in 632.

In parallel, the SOAS academic argued that the Qur'ān is not the outcome of the Arab *milieu*, but of a different geography, probably Palestine and Iraq and its monotheistic heretical environment.[5]

More recently, Gerald Hawting underlined how the internal Qur'anic references to *mushrikūn*, polytheists, stressed an internal intra-monotheistic debate and polemics, while the *Sīra* literature confined the influence of Christianity and Judaism to the proto-Islamic formative age.[6]

While considering some of Hawting's thoughts more interesting than others, it is evident that the complexity of the Qur'ān is due to the difficulties in considering proper historical sources that can clarify the life and existence of Muḥammad, his prophetic and political role, as well as the intricacy of the early 'Believers" history and internal conflicts after the Prophet's death.

The possibility of dissociating for a while the Qur'anic text from the Qur'ān as revelation for the entire Muslim world, as well as considering that it was assembled and canonized over a longer period, which probably ended in the early half of the eighth century, is an option which cannot be excluded *a priori*, in particular, if we reflect on its violence and militantism.[7]

According to this last aspect, it is evident that the Qur'anic text defines and describes warfare and violence as a form of expression, including religious, adopting different terms which are unequally represented in the revelation.[8]

The term *qitāl-qatala*, (q-t-l) usually translated by 'to fight', 'to kill', appears in the revelation seventy-eight times and the most famous verses in which it is used are 2: 154, 190–194, 216; 3: 157–158, 169; 4: 74; 9: 5, 12–13, 29; 22: 39–40, 58.

The term *ḥarb*, (ḥ-r-b) which neutrally defined the term of war, occurs only six times: 2, 279; 5, 33, 64; 8, 57; 9, 107; 47, 4; while the term *jihād* (j-h-d): to strive, to struggle, the term *ṣabr* (ṣ-b-r): to have patience, and *Ghazwa* (gh-z-w): 'to make a raid, an incursion', appear thirty-five times, eighty-seven times and once, respectively.

However, as reported by A. Afsaruddin, on a couple of occasions, *jihād* and *ṣabr* coexist in the same verse, 3: 142, 'Did you think you would enter the Garden without God first proving which of you would struggle (*jahadū*) for his cause and remain steadfast (*ṣabrīna*)?', and 16:110, 'But to those who leave their homes after persecution, then strive (*jahadū*) and remain steadfast (*wa ṣabrū inna*), your Lord will be most forgiving and most merciful.'[9]

Finally, considering that the Islamic revelation is made up of 6628 verses, *fī sabīli llāhi*, usually translated: 'in the cause of Allah' – 'for the sake of Allah', occurs in the Qur'ān more than 1000 times.

All the above is only partially important unless it is contextualized in the revelation, in the struggle against unbelievers and hypocrites, as well as considered in relation to the Chronology of the Qur'ān.

In parallel, this analysis will show the great difference between the militantism level of the Meccan *sūras* and the Medinan ones which extolled a change of register, with important reasons which do not require further analysis.

A peculiarity of the Qur'ān that we also need to contemplate is the adoption of different terms that can be translated with words that are not usually so close, even considering the literary meaning: *janna*, for example, is sometimes Paradise (4:124), sometimes the Garden/s (5:12; 5:65), which reflecting on the Old Bible tradition of the Genesis is clearly indicative of two different eschatological geographies.

The term *qitāl* has usually been adopted to emphasize killing and the fighting; however, if the first cannot be figuratively interpreted, the second should and could be.

> Fight (*qātilū*) in God's cause against those who fight you (*alladhīna Yuqātilūkumma*), but do not overstep the limits (*ta'tadū*), God does not love those who overstep the limits. Kill them (*wa aqtuluhum*) whenever you encounter them and drive them out from where they drove you out, for persecution is more serious than killing (*wa al-fitnatu ashaddu min al-qatli*). Do not fight (*Yuqātilūnakum*) them at the sacred Mosque unless they fight you (*Yuqātilūnakum*) there. If they do fight you (*qātalūkum*), kill them (*fāqtulūhum*), this is what such disbelievers deserve, but if they stop, the God is most forgiving and merciful. (2:190-192)

These emblematic verses used *q-t-l* in the meaning of fighting as killing, but only the first meaning is associated with *fī sabīli llāhi*, for the sake of God, an important aspect to which we will return later.

According, moreover, to 22: 38–40:

> Prophet give good news to those who do good: God will defend the believers; God does not love the unfaithful or the ungrateful. Those who have been attacked (*'Udhina Lilladhīna Yuqātalūna Bi'annahum Ẓulimū*) are permitted to take up arms because they have been wronged – God has the power to help them – those who have been driven unjustly from their homes only for saying 'Our Lord is God'. If God did not repel some people by means of others, many monasteries, churches, synagogues and mosques, where God's name is much invoked, would have been destroyed.

These verses have usually been considered the first Medinan ones which allowed the persecuted 'believers' to defend themselves on a twofold basis: they were physically expelled from their houses by the Pagan Meccans; such a persecution was attributed to the proto-Muslims for their monotheistic belief and not for any wrongdoing on their part.[10]

Mujāhid Ibn Jabr (d.722) and Muqātil ibn Sulaymān (d. 767) interpreted the fighting as having been allowed in a defensive manner, if God had not constrained the polytheists through the agency of the Muslims, then the former would have prevailed and killed the latter. Subsequently, the monasteries (*Ṣawāmi'u*) of the monks, the churches (*Biyaʿun*) of the Christians, the synagogues (*Ṣalawātun*) of the Jews and the mosques (*Masājidu*) of the Muslims would have been destroyed.[11]

This is clearly confirmed by the *Sīra* of Ibn Isḥāq.[12]

Nevertheless, in referring to al-Ṭabarī (d. 923) and his exegetical work, the debate on the passive or active form of *qitāl* in *yuqātalūna* – *yuqātilūna* is very emblematic of the internal debate that was probably affecting the Islamic community in his time: who was the real attacker, the 'Believers' or their opponents?

This debate probably concerned the Islamic community in making and defining the obligation of warfare only as a defensive as well as a moral-righteous intention. It is a duty of the Muslims to help the oppressed, except against people with whom the Muslims have a treaty (8:72) as well as to show up the justice of their cause in contrast with the immoral conduct of the enemy.[13]

Similarly, the interpretation reflects that if God did not countercheck some people by the actions of others, the polytheists would have been capable of prevailing: a ruler who prevents his subjects from oppressing one another, as well as the trustworthy believer who prevents the abuse of someone's rights through his active religious testimony, is also an exemplary witness of this kind of God's authorization of defence against the attackers.

In other words, it is impossible to let the polytheist destroy monasteries, churches, synagogues and mosques.

This verse, 'If God did not repel some people by means of others, many monasteries, churches, synagogues and mosques, where God's name is much invoked, would have been destroyed' (22: 40), reflects the original clear ecumenical attitude of the early 'Believers' (*Baʿḍahum Bibaʿiḍin Lahuddimat Ṣawāmiʿu wa Biyaʿun wa Ṣalawātun wa Masājidu Yudhkaru fīhā Asmu Allāhi Kathīrān wa Layanṣuranna Allāhu man Yanṣuruhu 'Inna Allāha Laqawīyun 'Azīzun*) in defending the places of worship of all those who argued that 'Our Lord Is God'.[14]

The importance of this verse in defining the Others in relation to the place of worship will be analysed in the following part, showing the peculiarity of the first 'Believers' in considering 'Other Believers' of their age.

A different interpretation, or better, an undermining of the above, will start to be considered from al-Rāzī (d. 1210) and the Andalusian al-Qurṭubī (d. 1273)[15] in emphasizing the importance of defending Islām from every kind of external attackers of every origin.

The Andalusian al-Qurṭubī will introduce the element of *naskh*,[16] 'omission'-'substitution', with the clear intention of distinguishing more aggressive verses in making defence obligatory; as historically evident, al-Qurṭubī lived after the overthrow of the Las Navas de Tolosa (1212), when the Almohad were defeated by a unified Christian coalition. Al-Rāzī, in parallel, lived in a time of great clashes linked to aggressive campaigns by the Crusaders and Mongols in a large part of Islamic lands as well as placing Islām in a defensive position, the reaction of which affected the Muslim hermeneutical interpretation, specifically referring to other religious communities, their revelations and the importance of their places of worship.

The fact that *fitna is more serious than killing* (2:191), *Wa Al-Fitnatu ʿ Ashaddu Mina Al-Qatli*, is a very interesting verse in the attempt to describe the early Medinan attitude in relation to a more aggressive militant vocabulary. Al-Rāzī would have adopted the meaning of *Kufr* in defining *Fitna*,[17] just as, before him, Ṭabarī interpreted the word of *Fitna* in 2:193 with *shirk* (associationism, polytheism).

However, this second interpretation associated with *Fitna* a meaning that could not historically be attributed to it in the seventh century. *Fitna* was a form of *fasād*, corruption, that the 'Believers' had to face up to in the early decades and that would have led to the famous first fragmentation (656–661).[18] *Fitna* is worse than killing: it referred to those who stressed an impediment in being believers, the Meccans; moreover, the same would hardly have referred to a concept such as *Kufr* that is evolutionary in the same Islamic revelation as well as attributed more to the non-recognition of Muḥammad's prophetic status in Abrahamic genealogy.[19]

The 'ingratitude' which opposed *Imām* until *Kufr* and *Shirk* were reached is something that affected the Meccans only temporarily because after a phase of contrast with the Medinans, they finally accepted and 'worship, devoting themselves to God'.

'If they do fight you, kill them – this is what such disbelievers deserve, but if they stop, then God is most forgiving and merciful' (*Wa Qātilūhum Ḥattá Lā Takūna Fitnatun Wa Yakūna Ad-Dīnu Lillāh Fa'ini Antahawā Falā 'Udwāna 'Illā 'Alá Aẓ -Ẓālimīna*) clearly referred to the disbelievers who wanted to be engaged in fighting at the Sacred Mosque, which was usually forbidden, in the case the believers were directly attacked in this sacred place.

In continuity, verse 193 emphasizes fighting them until there is no more persecution. *Fitna*, in the sense that there is nobody who obstructs others in believing in God: 'If they cease hostilities, there can be no [further] hostility, except towards aggressors (*al-muttaqīn*)' which also continues to find confirmation in the following verses, 2:216–218. Nevertheless, in these last verses, God's knowledge is brought in support against the ignorance of the human beings: God knows and you do not (*wa Allāh ya'lamū wa antum lā ta'alamūna*) in arguing that 'you may dislike something although it is bad for you', as well as a fighting in the sacred month which is generally forbidden, because it is a great offence to God, but it is more offensive for Him to drive People out from the path of God, to disbelieve in Him as to prevent the access to the sacred Mosque: to expel his people is a greater offence in God's eyes.

> *Wa 'Ikhrāju 'Ahlihi Minhu 'Akbaru 'Inda Allāhi Wa Al-Fitnatu 'Akbaru Mina Al-Qatli Wa Lā Yazālūna Yuqātilūnakum Ḥattā Yaruddūkum 'An Dīnikum*

Independently of the *Asbāb al-Nuzūl*'s historicization attributable to the raid of Nakhla, led by 'Abdallah ibn Jaḥsh al-Asadī during which the Meccan driver 'Amr ibn al-Ḥaḍramī was killed two months before the battle of Badr during, probably, the last days of Rajāb, one of the sacred months of the pre-Islamic age, these verses limiting fighting back in relation to the subjects listed above are clearly focused on the self-religious-determination in believing, praying, living as 'Believers': a defensive attitude.

However, in the following verse, the revelation would also like to consider a more indefinite aspect of this 'defensive' hostility because 'They will not stop fighting you until they make you revoke your faith, if they can', which, at least, in relation to the belligerent attitude against the Meccans makes this 'war' approved by God himself in still considering the reasons listed above.

In other words, since you have tried to divert the Believer's faith, without allowing them to pray in the Sacred Temple, even expelling them (there are more historical doubts about this part), now, the Believers are allowed to fight you. The circumstance may be that some believers are doubtful of embracing the new faith, but 'if any of you revoke your faith and die as disbelievers, your deeds will come to nothing in this world and the Hereafter, and you will be inhabitants of the Fire, there to remain', which is a clear threat that makes taking a step back blameworthy: 'But those who have believed (*amnū*), emigrated (*hājarū*) and striven (*wa jāhadū*) for God's cause (*fī sabīli Allāhi*), it is they who can look forward for God's mercy: God is most forgiving and merciful' (2: 218), which is the only verse in which the root of *j-h-d* is used.

The previous verses clearly emphasize how striving for God's cause could also be considered in a 'violent' way; moreover, the adoption of this word and not *wa yuqātilu* keeps the hermeneutical interpretation more open.

It is evident that the interpretation of *j-h-d* can include the *q-t-l*, but the killing or the fighting are not automatically linked with striving on God's way.

'Those who believed and emigrated and struggled for God's cause with their possessions and persons, and those who gave refuge and help, are all allies of one another' (8: 72, 74-75), elucidating that you need to believe at first, emigrate secondly, from Mecca to Medina, but also, more generally intended, to a place where your devotion is not a risk for your life, to be able, afterwards, to struggle with your 'possessions' and 'persons' on the way of God.

The words used in the Qur'ān to identify possessions and persons, '*bi'amwālihim wa 'anfusihim*', are interesting, because the former, from *m-w-l*, categorizes properties through a material possession (gold, silver, etc.); the latter, from *n-f-s*, recognizes the body, the blood, the life, the breath, but also the soul, the psyche and the essence: a human being in its entirety, physical and spiritual, that is coherently related to believing and emigrating.

The militantism of the early 'believers' in being sacred to God needs personal steps that cannot be trivially summarized by 'Holy War', but that need to consider the Arab roots of *walā'*: loyalty to God as to the Prophet, *muruwwa:* the complex moral authority of the Arab man,[20] believing in God so much as to be willing to emigrate, or considering a more anthropological approach, to make raids as a form of belligerent combativeness.

As 8: 72, 74, 75 highlight, belief in God, emigration and striving are consequently and historically related to the *muhājirūn* who decided to abandon Mecca, to follow the Prophet as well as to those *anṣār* who helped and hosted them, but these verses are less attributable to those Meccans and Banū Thaqīf of Ṭā'if who accepted the Prophet after years in which they opposed him.

It is important to consider how the following Islamic narrative will continue to mix personal and practical facets in framing the early hegemonic theme of the conquests, as well as of the *maghāzī* as the *futūḥ*, with the ongoing *topos* of emigration-travel and the early pietistic approach.[21] Emigration and struggle in the path of God are symptomatic of the ultimate hallmark of genuine religious commitment through a virtue of steadfastness (*ṣabr*) but also giving alms and lending God a fair loan (2: 245, 57:11-18, 64:17): 'God loves those who fight in His path in ranks, as though they were a solid edifice' (61:4).

Ṣabr and *Siyar* (to march, to walk, to travel, manner of ruling other people)[22] enriched the *topos* of militantism in making it a distinctive quality of Muslims and Arabs against non-Muslims and non-Arabs, in stressing a narrative able to mix religious and ethnic assets in continuity with an old Biblical *adage*.[23]

However, as the meaning of *Ṣabr* emphasizes in parallel with some Qur'anic verses (2:246, 3:146, 9: 111), the same difficulties in fighting '*fī sabīli llāhi*' had been encountered by the Children of Israel, after Moses, as well as 'How many prophets have fought with large bands of godly men alongside them who, in the face of their suffering for God's cause, did not lose heart or weaken or surrender: God loves those who are steadfast' (3:146).

God's militantism is not something attributable to the last 'Believers' only, but to the entire people of the book:

> God has purchased the persons and possessions of the believers in return for the Garden, they fight in God's way (*yuqātilūna*); they kill and they are killed (*fayaqtulūna wa yuqtalūna*), this is a true promise given by Him in the Torah, the Gospel and the Qur'ān. Who could be more faithful to his promise than God? So be happy with the bargain you have made that is the supreme triumph. (9:111)

This militancy that the Medinan verses stressed is clearly in continuity with previous revelations. However, as suggested by N. Sinai:

> The employment of the verb *jāhada* alongside or instead of the more univocal verb *qātala*, since *jāhada*, given its semantics of exertion and committed struggle, is much more suitable than *qātala* to play the role of what one may call a virtue term- that is, a term that does not just descriptively specify a certain behaviour, such as *qātala*, but also implies that the behaviour in question is exemplary and paradigmatic. This use of *jāhada* appears to be a Quranic innovation.[24]

This is an important aspect in an Arabian Peninsula still dominated by 'basic' raids (*maghāzī*) for pillage. However, like the Islamic narrative of the conquest's highlights, the 'Islamization' of Arabic military terminology was only partial until, at least, the eighth century, when the *Siyar al-Saghīr*, the *maghāzī*, the *hijra* as well as the same Ghāzī-Caliphs assumed a clear more evident religious-ideological *spectrum*.

As R. Firestone assumed, raiding and inter-tribal aggression in central Arabia remained un-religiously oriented and not associated with any kind of conceptualization of 'Holy-Sacred war',[25] until the Qur'anic narrative adopted a pre-Islamic warlike terminology including the innovation of God's support, also a very common *topoi* in Judaism and Christianity.

Firestone himself finally has to admit that 'what began as traditional Arabian raiding forays (albeit against one's own kin) came to be considered divinely sanctioned because of historical circumstances'.[26] This was a step that needed time, because it was unclear in the Qur'anic revelation itself as well as not immediately canonized during the Arab campaigns of conquest or during the *Fitnas*.

Nevertheless, the intricate complexity of the vocabulary, the Abrahamic narrative assumed in relation to the paradigmatic changeover as well as believing in God and the emigration cannot set apart the influence played by the Arab-Christians and Jews concurrently with the Arab pride in being a warrior and a man.

The identification of the enemies of God in the Qur'ān, the Others, should be helpful in considering the evolution of militantism as the credentials of the concrete fighting target of this revelation in parallel with the Abrahamic background from which Medinan belligerency originated.

1. Who are the Others and the enemies of the 'Believers'? Pagan-Unbelievers, Hypocrites (*munafiqūn*) and the *'Ahl al-Kitāb*.

The *Umma* in the Qur'ān is a religious concept and a source of identification rather than one of identity based on racial or ethnic background and is not political in nature but firmly rooted in religion. This 'utopic' *visio*, as expressed in 3:104, 'Be a community (*ummatun*) that calls for what is good, urges what is right, and forbids what is wrong: those who do this are the successful ones', as well as in 3:110, 'Believers, you are the best community (*Ummatin*) singled out for people: you order what is right, forbid what is wrong and believe in God. If the people of the Book had also believed, it would have better for them. For although some of them do believe, most of them are lawbreakers (*al-Fāsiqūna*)', is rooted in the *millat ibrāhīm*, in antithesis, but also in continuity with Judaism and Christianity which, in the Qur'ān, erroneously assumed the privilege for themselves to possess the religious truth (2: 111–121). In the attempt to overcome this inconvenient subordination, as well as to underline the identity of the new community, verse 2:125 stressed the Abrahamic root of the sacred temple, through Abraham's son Ishmael as an expression of Muḥammad's heritage.[27]

Abraham was 'neither a Jew nor a Christian, but rather a righteous *gentile* (*ḥanīf*), one who submitted to God and not one of the Associators' (3:67) which highlights the clear proto-Islamic attempt to find its roots not only to the previous revelations, the Torah and the Gospels, but in the cornerstone of Monotheism in the figure of the first Monotheist.

However, as reported by M. Watt and R. Bell, those who opposed the Prophet and his community from the beginning of the Meccan phase vary from time to time. If the terms *Kāfir* and *Kāfirūn* are widely used in the entire Qur'ān in generally defining those who are ungrateful to God, the term *Kuffār* is adopted only in the Medinan *sūras*, while the *mushrikūn*, those who ascribe partners to God, is the general term adopted to define idolaters of all periods.[28]

It is therefore evident that from the third phase of the Meccan *sūras* – as from the Medinan ones – those who opposed Muḥammad would be finally defeated before the Prophet's death (10: 46; 13:40; 40, 77), clearly referring to the Meccans who did not recognize his role and figure.

In parallel, other historical-religious verses underline the existence of religious rituals related to pagan practices: the sacrifice of cattle (22: 30), the presence of altars and votive stones (5:3, 40) as well as the existence of sacrifices offered to other deities (2: 173; 16: 115); all of which are facets that more than stressing a direct fight underscore the need to abandon an associationist praxis which had already been previously condemned by Jews and Christians.[29]

The Meccans themselves, before Muḥammad clarified his status of *Ḥanīf*, were a village of associators, possibly close to Hubal or to some of God's partners (29: 65), that recognized a supreme *Allāh*, but with complementary associated figures which stressed a form of more evident humanization of the monotheistic deity.[30]

The Qur'ān is a complex revelation in which a historical continuity between the pre-Islamic and the 'Believers'' conceptualization of Otherness, in particular in relation to the fight and the struggle on God's way, is not easy to decipher.

The Pagan-Biblical syncretism through female figures (al-Lāt, al-'Uzzah and Manāt (53: 19-23)),[31] the inner decoration of the Ka'bah with images of a probable Ibrāhīm as an old man while performing divination by the shaking arrows,[32] and one of Jesus, son of Mary with his mother and an angel,[33] are symptomatic of an outlook still partially based on the Old and the New Testaments.

The pre-Islamic devotion for Ishmael is based on the Genesis passage of 21:8–21, in which the merits of Hagar and of her son are recognized by God himself because of his father's importance for God as well as in giving him a successful progeny. The Jewish presence in the Arabian Peninsula and the work of ecclesiastical historians were probably the 'concrete' transmitters of this Biblical *story*, data and evidence for centuries and which were widely adopted to emphasize a *mythological* narrative about Ishmael's inheritance.[34]

There is however a relevant *dilemma* in reflecting on the historicization of Otherness in the Qur'ān: the 'Unbelievers' will be finally defeated by recognizing God's power and Muḥammad's prophetic role in continuity with Judaism and Christianity. The former are the Meccans, with the concrete fighting affecting the entire Medinan phase, while the latter would have been accused of being associators, liars, untrustworthy even if defined by the epithet of people of the Book (*'Ahl al-Kitāb*).

The complexity of the Qur'anic attitude towards Others is difficult to decipher because it is linked to the evolutionary attitude of the same *story* of conflict and appeasement that emerged from the lines of the revelation.

The fight against Arab paganism is expressed in 113:1–5 as symptomatic of something ancestral: 'Say (Prophet), "I seek refuge with the Lord of Daybreak against the harm of what He has created, the harm of the night when darkness gathers, the harm of witches when they blow on knots, the harm of the envier when he envies"', which reflects a clear pre-Islamic praxis: Baiḍāwī in his *Tafsīr*, as well as the Mu'tazilite Al-Zamakhsharī, argues that women who made knots in ropes and then blew (*nafatha*) on them were performing sorcery; in the Arab world, even today, there is still a popular belief that whistling attracts the devil.

A tradition claims: 'A Jew practised an act of sorcery against the Prophet by making eleven knots in a piece of string and placing this in a well. Then, when the Prophet became ill, the two sūras of refuge (113 and 114) came down'; this is probably a fake, considering that both *sūras* are of the early Meccan period when the concrete presence of a Jew as the Prophet's servant is not attested in his *Sīra*, but reported afterwards in the *Asbāb al-Nuzūl* of al-Wāḥidī (d. 1075).[35]

At the beginning of the prophetic phase, in Mecca, the plurality of religious practices was so evident that Muḥammad's strength was univocally focused on the unity of God (*tawḥīd*), on the Prophet's own message (*risālah*) and the eschatological end (*al-'Ākhirah*).

Paganism and associationism were concomitantly attributed to the Meccans as well as the Arabs who reached the village for the annual religious celebrations and markets.[36]

The pagans and associators are also usually linked to those who commit *ẓulm* (injustice and wrongdoing, respectively in 20:111 and 6:82, with both sūras still related to the Meccan period) and are depicted as *ẓālim, ẓālimūn*: one who acts unjustly or tyrannically (7:105; 18:35, both Meccans again), *ẓalūm* (14:34; 33:72), *muẓlimūn* (36:37) etc., which is not linked to the membership of other religions but again, in an anti-Meccan dialogue, with the same polytheists.

> Noah said, 'My Lord, they have disobeyed me and followed those whose riches and children only increase their ruin; who have made a grand plan, saying, do not renounce your gods! Do not renounce Wadd, Suwa', Yaghuth, Ya'uq or Nasr! They have led many astray'. Lord, bring nothing but destruction down on the evildoers (*aẓ-Ẓālimīna 'Illā Ḍalālāan*).

The most interesting aspect of these verses is that the deities reported are concretely linked not with Noah, but with the Arab pre-Islamic polytheist *milieu*: as H. ibn al-Kalbī reported in his *Kitāb al-Aṣnām*.[37] It is clear that, in these verses, Noah is artificially adopted in assuming an anti-pagan and Meccan posture in the attempt to strength Muḥammad's message.

The same attitude was also to continue in the early Medinan phase: in 2:165–167, for example, the love for other than God is clearly condemned in an eschatological perspective which will affect all those who have not recognized the superiority of Allāh; however, verses 166–167 are also an incentive to abandon their leaders before all of them are together in the darkness.[38]

The Unbelievers are deaf, dumb and blind, they understand nothing (2:172).

Simultaneously with the ongoing narrative against the Meccans, the Medinan phase introduces a prominent new dimension of Otherness that breaks the biunivocal one: Believers versus Unbelievers, bringing other protagonists into the Qur'anic dimension in parallel with the *Hijra*, the emigration to Medina.

It is clear that some Christians as well as many Jews were already present in Mecca, but this geography did not allow the Prophet to assume a concrete position on them.

The few verses in the Meccan phase in which Jesus is named are: 43:57–61 in which the 'problem' that 'Īsā ibn Maryam was without a carnal father is only hinted at, 43:63ff., in which the fragmentation of the Christians is announced for the first time, in attacking the religious division as a terrific problem that will bring them suffering, and 42:13, in which Noah, Abraham, Moses and Jesus are designated as having said: 'Uphold the faith and do not divide into factions within it.'

Finally, in 19:27, the descriptive narrative about the absence of paternity of Jesus is reported as willed by God in a miraculous way; an infant that said to the doubters:

> I am the servant of God. He has granted me the Scripture; made me a Prophet; made me blessed wherever I may be. He commanded me to pray, to give alms as long as I live, to cherish my mother. He did not make me domineering or graceless. Peace was on me the day I was born and will be on me the day I die and the day I am raised to life again.

Jesus is depicted as a prophet, a messenger, a resurrected saint of peace: if the figure of Jesus is sketched out, Christians are absent.

Nevertheless, the increasing conflict with the People of the Book, the Jews more than the Christians whose presence in Medina was limited, is based on a double standard which is problematic because it is related to individual events which affected Muḥammad and his Medinan community in the attempt to emerge against the village's inner power that opposed him. Verses 2:104 as well as 4:44–46 make the conflict with the Jews of Medina real and tangible.

However, if the struggle with the Jews is political and religious at the same time, the one with the Christians is univocally theological, as it will continue until Muhammad's death in 632.

The above verses (2:104; 4:44–46), even considering the sketchy-ironic approach, highlight a problem of vocabulary, but also of trust: the Jews of Medina play with words to make fun of Muḥammad as reported by al-Ṭabarī and other exegetes,[39] but at the same time, they concretely emphasize the non-recognition of his religious role, stressing his lack of knowledge about the monotheistic Abrahamic tradition.[40]

Nevertheless, if in 4:44, the Jews are clearly identified and accused of distorting the meaning of revealed words, a few verses later, the People of the Book, more in general, are depicted with:

> People of the Book, believe in what We have sent down to confirm what you already have, before We wipe out [your sense of] direction, turning you back, or reject you, as we rejected those who broke the Sabbah: God's will is always done. God does not forgive the joining of partners with Him: anything less than that He forgives to whoever He will, but anyone who joins partners to God has fabricated a tremendous sin. (4: 47–48)

Nevertheless, if the target continues to be the Jews of Medina in these as in the following verses (4:51), it is evident that Qur'ān mostly and indiscriminately adopts the *'Ahl al-Kitāb* without referring to all of them, but to those that were closest to the Prophet, again the Jews.[41]

This confusion makes it more difficult to consider to whom the verses 3:75–76 are concretely ascribed, in particular because the main accusation against them remained the non-recognition of the Prophet's figure: the polytheists of Quraysh came to these Jews to ask them about their opinion regarding the Believers, and the 'People of the Book' replied that the Meccans unbelievers were more rightly guided than the Muslims (4:51); this is an evident narrative adopted to increase the growing enmity between the Medinan 'Believers' and some of the Jewish clans of the countryside.

In parallel, verse 3:199, that the *Asbāb al-Nazūl* historically placed when the Negus of Abyssinia Armah (*al-Najāshi*) died around 631, states the great respect that

Muḥammad showed for the Christian ruler: 'The hypocrites commented: "Look at this one, performing the prayer of the dead on a foreign Christian Abyssinian whom he has never seen and who does not even follow his religion". Allah exalted is He, then revealed this verse'.[42]

The number of verses in which the People of the Book are portrayed with lights and shadows in relation to the incidence of trust and unbelief, support for Prophet Muḥammad as well as envy and doubt (3:75–76) is symptomatic of the hesitant relation that the same 'Believers' had with other structured religious communities.

Even although significant verses stressed the importance of having a dialogue with them (29:46) and being open-minded in believing them (3:113–115) as well as recognizing a clear continuity between the Believers and them (22:17), other verses highlight their sectarianism (2:113) and the criticism of doctrines such as the Trinity and the Incarnation of God (4:171; 5: 73–75) even accusing the Christians of unbelief: 'Those who say, "God is the Messiah, the son of Mary, are defying the truth".'

> Say, 'If it had been the God's will, could anyone has prevented Him from destroying the Messiah, son of Mary, together with his mother and everyone else on Earth? Control of the heavens and earth and all that is between them belongs to God: he creates whatever He will. God has power over everything'. (5:17)

The effective understanding and knowledge of the 'Believers' about Judaism and Christianity and the ability to distinguish them from their own specific community are problematic because they are inconsistent with the entire revelation. If in some verses, the proto-Muslims stressed an explicit demarcation of the Qur'anic community from the People of the Book, harshly criticizing them (5: 12–19; 41: 86) and, as reported above, accusing them of wrongdoing (29: 46) and of being associationists, in particular referring to the figure of Jesus (19: 34–40; 43: 57–65), the Qur'ān fails to clearly mention the Jews of Medina or to assume an evident anti-Christian attitude; on the contrary, controversial attention is more addressed to the pagan polytheists against whom they usually invoked the support of previous revelations (6: 20, 114; 10: 94; 17: 101; 26: 197).[43]

As reported by N. Sinai, it is only in the *Sūras* which form the core of the revelation that we can find clearer references to the *al-Naṣārā* or to *al-Yahūd*; moreover, the latter are often misleading or emphasize clear difficulties in understanding the religious monotheistic complexity of late antiquity.

More than depicting clear differences with the People of the Book, the Qur'ān is unable to do so on a theological and geographical level. Referring in particular to Christianity, the Christological *visio* of the 'Believers' is clearly affected by external influence, but without a resolutive perspective.

In 4: 171, as in other verses, Jesus is Messiah, the servant of God, even though only a human being, but with the Spirit of Him within and Maryam is clearly the virgin. In 4: 157–158, even though 'Īsā is only a human being, he has to be replaced on the cross by a man similar to him, probably a docetist doctrine, and 3: 59: 'In God's eyes Jesus is just like Adam: He created him from dust, said to him, Be and he was', clarified the early 'Believers'' inability to read the difference between dust (*Turābin*) and spirit (*Rūḥ*) on which, in the following centuries, Islamic theological and philosophical thought will be able to make a concrete distinction.[44]

As reported above, the problem in distinguishing themselves from the People of the Book is also found in 22: 40 in which the monasteries (*Ṣawāmi'u*) of the monks, the churches (*Biya'un*) of the Christians, the synagogues (*Ṣalawātun*) of the Jews and the mosques (*Masājidu*) of the Muslims, at the same level, will all be destroyed in the case of victory by the polytheists.

Nevertheless, the inability to distinguish a monastery from a church, a place of abstinence, observance and fasting (ṣ-w-m), from a normal place of worship (b-y-'), that Abdeel Haleem stressed as probably being a word of Persian origin, highlights how Christianity and monasticism were not evidently considered as religiously part of the same faith (as well as Monasticism was dissociated from Christianity) by the early 'Believers' contrary to Synagogues and Mosques: even though it would have been logical that at the time of the prophetic phase, only one mosque would have existed, that of Medina.

In other words, the ability to distinguish the People of the Book from the geography of worship seemed to remain problematic at the end of the Medinan period.

If the hostility against the Jews is more evident than against the Christians (5:82), the political factor probably played a significant part; the parallelism between them is quite emblematic in trying to make two distinct communities, but without evident success.

Jews and Christians are accused of emphasizing that eschatological salvation belongs only to their own community: on the contrary the Qur'ān emphasizes that salvation cannot be based on specific religious affiliation or be guaranteed by intercession (9: 113–114) and 4: 123–124 argues:

> It will not be according to your hopes or those of the People of the Book: anyone who does wrong will be required for it and will find no one to protect or help him against God; anyone, male or female, who does good deeds and is a believer, will enter Paradise and will not be wronged by as much as the dip in a date stone.[45]

Both religions are accused of deifying a human being: Jesus and Ezra (9:30) but if for the former, 'Īsā's being a son will be recognized as a clear aspect of distinction between Islām and Christianity with the complexity previously mentioned, the reference to Ezra is probably a mistake.

Lastly, if belongers to both Judaism and Christianity are accused of misappropriation (9:34) as Muḥammad has come to free them from uncertain legal obligations (7:157),[46] the Qur'ān seems more interested in stressing where they are making mistakes, than in really fighting and condemning them: 'Who believes in God and the Last Day and acts righteously will achieve salvation' (2:62; 5:69), also because if Meccan and Medinan *sūras* remain coherent in converting and fighting polytheism, respectively, in relation to Judaism and Christianity, religious diversity has to be respected as directly to do with God's will:

> We sent to you Muḥammad, the Scripture with the truth, confirming the Scriptures that came before it, and with final authority over them: so, judge between them according to what God has sent down. Do not follow their whims, which deviate from the truth that has come to you. We have assigned a law and and a path to each of you. If God had so willed, He would have made you one community, but He wanted to test you through that which He has given you, so race to do good: you will all return to God and He will make clear the matters you differed about. (5:48)

The pact (*mithāq*) between Muḥammad and God is the third one (5:7), after that with the Jews and the Christians and if the previous ones have been violated (2: 27, 63–64, 83–84; 4: 154–162; 5: 12–14, 70–71), the submission and the exemplary obedience of this last agreement is proof of the truth.

The general Qur'anic attitude towards the People of the Book is well expressed in the exegetical comment to 4:113, in which the hypocritic behaviour of Ṭu'mah, a Muslim of the Banū Ẓafar, who stole a set of armour (*dir'*) from his neighbour, Qatādah ibn al-Nu'mān, and afterwards out of fear, deliberately left it in the house of Zayd, a Jew, elucidates the revelation's sense of justice in uncovering the real sinner:

> If it were not for the grace of God and his mercy to you, a party of them would have tried to lead you astray; they only lead themselves astray, and cannot harm you in many way, since God has sent down the Scripture and Wisdom to you, and thought you what you did not know. God's bounty to you is great indeed.

And even if all the 'Believers" community was on the side of the *munāfiq* Ṭu'mah, who swore and committed perjury on his innocence, submitting an oath of trust with the support of all his clan, the guilty party was finally discovered independently of his religious affiliation.[47]

Paraphrasing it, those who are right and act correctly have nothing to fear.

If 3: 113–115 and 3:199 clearly argued about the presence of sainthood among the People of the Book as well as, more specifically, among the Christians more than in Judaism (5: 82, 85), fighting against them is very limited.

Those who need to be fought are the unbelievers 8:15, 55–57 because 'the worst of creatures (*ad-Dawābbi*) in the sight of God are the disbelievers (*al-ladhīna Kafarū*), those with whom you made treaties but they broke them every time, so if you meet them in battle make a fearsome example of them to those who come after them, so that they make take heed', and the idolaters, *al-mushrikīn* (9:5, 36, 123).

Fighting the People of the Book, without considering the famous verse 9:29, to which we will return in the following parts, is possible by logical assumption. If, as reported above, the Christians are accused of bringing unbelief (4:171, 5: 73-75) for Christological reasons, and the Jews (7:167-171; 9:30; 17: 4-8) for great infidelity towards God and his messengers, Muḥammad included,[48] the Qur'ān is far from defining them enemies of God.

Unlike the pagan-unbelievers, the Qur'ān, in relation to the People of the Book, clarified that Allāh will be the one who will judge them, explaining the mistakes that they have made.[49]

It is important, in relation to the above historical part, to assume that the Qur'ān confirmed the Abrahamic nature of the 'Believers' and their partial understanding of the complexity of the Christian-Jewish world. Muḥammad's inspired revelation was evidently unable before and after its canonization to highlight a major distinction from the People of the Book, except in relation to a limited understanding of the Christological debate. The Qur'ān's comprehension of Jesus as Christ, as well as the Messiah or the son of God, does not seem to be so clear in the Islamic revelation as 9:30 clearly emphasizes. Consequently, if the enemies of the 'Believers' are the Meccan polytheists who, after eight years of fighting, will recognize Muḥammad's role, becoming reconciled, the People of the Book, generally considered, took an intermediate position, against whom violence was not actually conceived, if not according to specific situation.

6

The Qur'ān and militant violence in chronology

The chronology of violence in the Qur'ān and its hermeneutical understanding

The debate on the chronology of the Qur'ān from a historical perspective is a fascinating argument which has interested specialists since the beginning of the contemporary period, and today it is a prominent subject in the attempt to make a more evident parallelism between Muḥammad's life, his prophetic period and the history of the early community.[1]

The attempts by Th. Nöldeke, R. Bell and R. Blachère have already been mentioned; nevertheless, the correlation between *Sūras* and the level of violence in the Islamic revelation is a topic of clear importance to decipher the narrative behind it.

We certainly do not have to be experts to understand how the level of violence in the Qur'ān increases in the Medinan *Sūras* reaching its height in the 8th, 9th and, partially, in the 5th, which are usually recognized, the latters, as being the last in the chronology of the Revelation: for W. Muir, as well as for Grimme, the 9th is the last, while for Th. Nöldeke and the Egyptian chronology it is the penultimate one; the 5th is the last for Nöldeke and the 112th for the Egyptian chronology.[2]

Different interdisciplinary approaches to the Qur'anic chronology have been adopted in recent decades: the comparison between the Islamic revelation and the *Sīra* of the Prophet in a more historical *spectrum* has been included with a terminological and thematic one as well as with respect to the length of the Sūwar.[3]

As N. Sinai states:

> For example, references to the *munafiqūn*, or hypocrites, only appear in sūrahs with a mean verse length of above ninety-two transcriptions letters. Similarly, it is only in sūrahs with relatively long verses that we encounter injunctions to fight (*qātala*) the unbelievers, explicit calls to obey 'God and his Messenger', and sustained polemics against Jews and Christians.[4]

In parallel, as already deciphered by R. Bell, the non-unitary nature of the majority of the longer *sūwar* as well as their independent originality in relation to subjects treated, the discontinuity among them and the specific terminology adopted, underscores the complexity in following a historical track directly linked with the Prophet's life and more specifically in relation to the Medinan phase.

If in the following part, we will work on different historical-thematic passages of the *sūwar* 9 and 5, it is important here to try to better understand the concrete level of violence in the Medinan phase as linked to the 'historical events' that emerge considering the Islamic narrative of the same (622–632).

Assuming that the continuity of *Sūrah* 9 with 8 is hard to prove and that the vast majority of the specialists on Qur'anic chronology put the latter in around the 88th (Egyptian), 95th (Th. Nöldeke) and 97th (W. Muir and H. Grimme) position, this speculation will only be introduced in the following part and not considered in the analysis at present.

Simultaneously, Th. Nöldeke and the Egyptian chronology will be used to establish an order that can put the Islamic narrative on warfare in relation to the Medinan part of the Revelation dividing it into three subsections: (1) the permission to fight, (2) the war against the unbelievers and against the Jews of Medina, (3) the raids against Others after the conquest of Mecca and before the death of Prophet Muḥammad (632).

1. ***Sūrah* 2** is the longest in the entire Revelation and usually considered the first of the Medinan period; nevertheless, its inner complexity is related to a process of canonization which has been unable to elucidate the cognitive steps about the different thematic parts: for example, verses 189 and 190 are thematically distant from one another, while the continuity between 190 and 191 up to 194–195 persists in stressing one of the first instances in which the Believers' permission to defend themselves is clearly emphasized.

These verses are usually linked to 22:38–48 where the 'Believers'' defence by God as well as by themselves is clarified again. According to that, from verse 42, the Revelation starts a brief Biblical excursus, quoting Noah and Moses in stressing the Old Testament's exemplary chastisement against those cities or nations that have abused God's patience.

However, there is a huge difference between 22:38–39 and 2:190–191: in the former, God's defence of those who hope and desire (*Āmanū*) softly switches towards – 'those who have been attacked are permitted to take up arms if they have been wronged – God has the power to help them, those who have been driven unjustly from their homes only for saying: Our Lord is God'. In the latter, the initial – 'Fight in God's cause against those who fight you, but do not overstep the limits [...], Kill them wherever you encounter them and drive them out from where they drove you out, for persecution is more serious than killing' – is more vocative and impositive.

Independently of the chronology (Th. Nöldeke 107, Egyptian 103), those verses seem to highlight, for the first time, the possibility to fight back, as well as to militarily contest those who have been aggressive with the 'Believers', even though clear limits need to be imposed, in order not to overstep the same.

It is evident that if *Sūrah* 22 seems to underscore an intermediate status of the 'Believers' between freedom and obstruction, it is not a coincidence that Th. Nöldeke himself considered some verses – 1–24, 43–56, 60–65, 67–75 – as still Meccans;[5] on the contrary, the complexity of *Sūrah* 2 amply confirms that we are already in Medina.

The dissimilarity is not only linked with the strong presence of Biblical references – the protagonism of the 'Children of Israel' who are directly appealed to as if they were close to the door of the Prophet's house – but there is an inclusive-exclusive dynamic which is completely non-existent in the Meccan period: 'The Believers, the Jews, the Christians and the Sabians, all those who believe in God and the last day and do good will have their rewards with their Lord. No fear for them, nor will they grieve' (2:62). The numerous verses referring to Abraham, Moses and Jesus, who had already signed an agreement with God, stressed Muḥammad's ongoing relation with them; at the same time, the early disagreement against the People of the Book's sense of superiority in an eschatological dimension (2:111–113) stressed the Medinan geographical *spectrum*.[6]

The reiteration, in verses 216–218, about the fighting, unlike the previous ones, is historically attributed to a specific event that we have already mentioned above: the killing of 'Amr ibn 'Abd Allāh al-Ḥaḍramī, who led a caravan a few months before the battle of Badr (around 623–624) during one of the sacred months of the pre-Islamic age, and which gave Muḥammad the opportunity to reiterate the importance of fighting because '*al-fitnatu akbaru min al-Qatli*' and also 'they will not stop fighting you until they make you revoke your faith, if they can'.

Unlike the previous verses of the same *sūrah* (2:190–191) – (22:38–39), this reiteration aims to confirm the permission to fight and kill a Quraysh even during a sacred month of the pre-Islamic calendar.[7]

In this case the defensive skirmish is adapted to a more 'common' practice – the killing of a polytheist during a raid (*ghazwa*) – and is justified as a contingency of fighting against *Fitna*, as well as the efforts against those who are trying to make you revoke your faith.

It is evident how, in this first phase, God's permission to fight for defence is embedded in the Arab custom of raids: leaving the *Muhajirūns*' houses and properties in Mecca gave them the need to recover a certain well-being that the attacks against the polytheists' caravans could have guaranteed. However, if the attacks against Meccan caravans at Badr (624) are a form of refund revenge, the following clashes will assume a belligerent attitude which stressed a clear religious, political and ideological struggle.

2. After having had the permission to fight, the belligerent attitude becomes multifaceted and the believer's struggle on God's way more pervasive in religious-political life. Nöldeke and the Egyptian chronology differ greatly, generally speaking, even though a sort of continuity is preserved as far as the most violent verses are concerned.

It is clear, however, that if the Meccans are the main enemies, the People of the Book are perceived as being in an intermediate position, between respect and distrust. *Sūwar* 98, 64 and 62, albeit far from the issues of violent conflict, try to convince the unbelievers and the People of the Book that the new Revelation, the Qur'ān, is trustworthy.

However, the verses which referred to the *'Ahl al-Kitāb* and the idolaters (98:6) remained confused because if, on the one hand, they attest that those who do not believe are condemned to remain in Hell, those who believe, on the other hand (pagans and People of the Book), worshipping God alone, sincerely devoting their religion to Him and keeping up the prayer, paying the prescribed alms, will be among the best.

The eschatological dimension of *sūrah* 64 emphasized that the disbelievers should act differently to reach the eternal Paradise, while 62 is interesting in highlighting how Friday, the day of congregation (*min al-Yawmi al-Jumu'ati*), was the usual day of prayer in Medina, for those who converted and for those who remained Jews, starting the celebrations in the evening to prepare for the Sabbath (*yawm al-Sabt*).[8]

This distinction seems to clarify the breakthroughs of the new religious community in the attempt to mark some differences in the praxis from the Medinan Jews. It also wanted to legitimize their greater independence from a previous adoption of Jewish rituals. This speculation on the level of attraction to and participation in Jewish rites is emblematically linked to those that the Meccan *sūwar* defined as being able to 'make less doubtful what has been revealed to you [the Prophet]', which paraphrasing the *sūrah* (10: 94–95) is advice that God gives to Muḥammad to not deny Allāh's signs.

Following the permission to fight against the unbelievers, the verses that come afterwards are related to the *sūrah* ***al-'Anfāl*** **(8)** which, the 'Islamic narrative' historically established in relation to the battle of Badr (624), however, its length as well as the absence of *Basmala* at the beginning of the following one, the 9th, has made Orientalists express some doubts on its location. The beginning of the *sūrah* is thematically related to a practical problem: the distribution of the gains from the Battle which is such a prominent aspect that from the opening it clarified the need to obey God and his Messenger on it (8: 1–5). At the same time, the early verses seem to try to reduce the power of the *'Anfāl*'s materialistic topic in stressing that the 'true believers are those whose hearts tremble with awe when God is mentioned, whose faith increases when His revelations are recited to them, who put their trust in their Lord'.

The emphasis that God and his Angels are with the Prophet (8: 9-15) and the disbelievers are condemned to lose because fear will invade their hearts (*'Āmanū Sa'ulqī fī Qulūbi al-ladhīna Kafarū*) is over-emphasized by: 'It was not you who killed them but God [...] it was not your throw that defeated them but God's, to do the believers a favour' (8:17) in the evident attempt to limit the 'Believers'' doubts in killing and fighting unbelievers with whom there was personal reciprocal knowledge and a common clan's lineage.

Both verses 8: 26 and 30, which start with 'Remember' (*Adhkurū – Idh-Yamkuru bika*, referring to the Prophet), underscore the way in which the Believers were victimized and plotted against, stressing the anger and resentment against them: the Meccans will be punished for their disbelief, they will be the losers (8:37), but, 'if they desist their past will be forgiven, but if they persist, they have an example in the fate of those who went before' (8:38): in the *sūrah* under examination there are not, as in others, references to people previously condemned by God.

Verse 8: 39 reiterates the same message in 'fighting the unbelievers until there will be no more *Fitna* and all worship is devoted to God alone, but if they desist then God sees all that they do'.

The following verses (8: 41ff) are mixed with juridical attributions in clarifying the initial topic of the *'Anfāl*, in fighting constantly during the battle, keeping

God firmly in mind (8:45), and not to quarrel during it, because God is with the steadfast (*al-ṣābirīna*) (8:46).

However, the attack against the Believers is already attributed to the hypocrites (8:47–52) who tried to bar them from going to war: they are like the Pharaoh's people and those before them who ignored God's signs.[9] It is as though the Believers' doubts in being the aggressors needed a specific elucidation, specifically in the case of the attack on the Meccan caravan.

From verse 8:55, other topics are discussed: the technical improvement in warfare against those who are the worst creatures in the sight of God is added to the Believers' need for self-confidence because if there are twenty of them and steadfast, they will be able to overcome two hundred unbelievers while if there are one hundred of them, they will overcome one thousand. In other words, God is with them and is able to militarily empower them against their enemies. This is an assumption that finds consistency in the tradition of the Old Testament.

At the same time, new military indications are given directly to the Prophet: 'It is not right for the prophet to take captives before he has conquered the battlefield. Your people desire the transient goods of this world, but God desires the Hereafter for you' (8:67); 'Prophet, tell the captives you hold, "If God knows of any good in your hearts, He will give you something better than what has been taken from you and He will forgive you"', in assuming, for the first time, that the captives have the possibility of desisting from their evilness.

However, the most important verses for our analysis are the following: 'Those who believed and emigrated and struggled for God's cause with their possessions and persons, and those who gave refuge and help, are allies of one another', *'Inna al-Ladhīna 'Āmanū wa Hājarū wa Jāhadū bi 'amwālihim wa 'anfusihim fī sabīli Allāhi'* (8:72), which is put in relation to the fact that the 'Disbelievers support one another. If you do not do the same, there will be persecution in the land and great corruption, *Fitnatun Fī Al-' Arḍi Wa Fasādun Kabīrun*'(8:73), in which the personal struggle dynamic is material and physical at the same time for those who emigrated as well as for those who gave refuge, making a clear distinction from the people who believed but did not emigrate.

The complexity of the situation is evident: for those non-emigrants but believers who are asking for help because they are persecuted for religious reasons, you need to intervene militarily if there is no previously signed treaty with those you should attack (8:72). This last part of the *Sūrah* which is probably ascribed to the early Medinan phase due to the difficulties in finding a solution to the complexity of the relations among believers, *muhajirūn* and *anṣār*, is made even more complicated by the last verses which argue: 'And those who came to believe afterwards and emigrated and struggled alongside you (*wa Jāhadū ma'akum*), they are part of you, but relatives still have prior claim over one another in God's scripture: God has full knowledge of things' (8:75).

If al-Tustarī had interpreted those last verses with these words: 'All forms of obedience to God involve struggle with the lower self (*jihād al-nafs*). There is no struggle easier than the struggle with swords, and no struggle harder than opposing the lower self': the words of a clear mystical hermeneutic;[10] the main problem for a correct interpretation remains historical.

Independently of the 'Islamic narrative' that suggests how the last verse of this *sūrah* was abrogated by 33:6, it is hard to include it in a Chronology, at least from verses 72–75.

The evidence that this *sūrah* is directly associated with the battle of Badr is circumstantial, while the normative confusion of the last verses is indicative that the 'Believers' still had some doubts about the connection between those who emigrated in attesting their intention to follow the Prophet, and those who did not, although willing to follow the promulgated monotheism.

This lack of clarity is accentuated by the great importance that on the one hand is granted by the unification between those who emigrated with those who gave them refuge, while, on the other hand, Arab kinship remained predominant: '*wa 'Ūlū al-'Arḥāmi ba'duhum 'Awlā biba'ḍin fī Kitābi*', but relatives still have prior claim over one another in God's scripture (8:75).

Ibn Kathīr's logical analysis reflects on the fact that in the case a Medinan Believer died in battle or for other reasons, a relative, even though still a Meccan unbeliever, keeps his rights of inheritance of the Believer's property.[11]

In this *sūrah*, the permission to fight back is implemented by a more precise identification of the fighter as well as the kind of the enemy that they will encounter: the hypocrites are compared to the Pharaoh's followers, those who while seeing God's signs did not believe them. The destruction for their sin is Biblical as reported in Exodus; however, if the *munafiqūn* are drowned in relation to the previous revelation, the unbelievers, who are the worst of the creatures in the eyes of God, 'if desist and incline towards peace, you (Prophet) must also incline towards it and put your trust in God (8:61)', which seems a more conciliatory position compared to that of the hypocrites themselves.

Apart from this peculiarity, the entire *sūrah* looks quite juridical in the clear attempt to develop a technical and normative *spectrum* in a new geography. The intention seems to give strength to the new community under construction and it is possible that the constitution of Medina has already been signed, as the emphasis on the hypocrites' presence in the *Umma* itself accentuates; moreover, the verses 15, 41 and 67–75 intend normalizing important aspects in relation to the *'Anfāl*, the battle's captives, the relationship between believers and the behaviour to adopt in fighting. The entire *sūrah* is focused on fighting because, at the time, fighting is the major activity in this new community for the Medinans.[12]

Following Nöldeke's chronology, between *sūrah* 8 and the third one, there is *sūrah* **47**, which is called the *sūrah of Muḥammad* and is thematically in continuity with the previous one, 46; however, some verses are more interesting than others for our analysis.

Verses 47: 4–6 continue in being indicative of the behaviour to assume during the battle and with the captives; dissimilarly, those who die in the fighting, even if the concept of martyrdom is still not mentioned, will not be dead but already in the Garden, an early description of which emerged in verses 11–15.[13]

However, the following verses 20–21 argue:

> Those who believe ask why no sūrah, (about fighting), has been sent down. Yet when a decisive *Sūrah* that mentions fighting (*al-Qitālu*) is sent down, you can see

> the sick at heart looking at you and visibly fainting at the prospect of death, better for them would be obedience and fitting words; better for them to be true to God when the decision to fight has been made,

which stressed that some of the early believers were unwilling to fight; this is a subject which is very present in the Revelation and which is supported by the hypocrites who complained that fighting each other causes breaking the bonds of kinship, as reported in verse 47:22: 'If you turn away now, could it be that you will go on to spread corruption all over the land and break your ties of kinship?'

This verse, like 33:6, would lead to developing, in contrast with 8:75, that during the Medinan phase, the 'Believers" position in breaking the ties of clan kinship, in particular in this belligerent phase and until the conquest of Mecca, was, at least, conceptualized by the Revelation itself. This quranic verse, anyway, will remain as deeply in contrast with the historical evidence, that from the *Khulāfa al-Rāshidūn* (632–661) as well as the Umayyad and 'Abbāsid periods showed clan's strategies as always a priority over those of the community of belivers.[14]

Finally, verse 35 seems to suggest that the Medinans would like to offer peace to the unbelievers, even though they had won at Badr, establishing that God was with them; nevertheless, the reasons for this decision are unclear: it is obvious that part of the *muhajirūn* were fighting against relatives and other clan members.

The presence of an unbalanced sense of belonging in part of the Medinan verses is symptomatic as a reaction to the more bellicose militantism, even if this is usually attributed to the hypocrites' behaviour.

***Sūrah* 3** (the family of 'Imrān) is as complex as the second one: if verses 13 and 14 seem to refer to the battle of Badr, it is clear that we are in a later period; verse 3:7 reports how the Revelation is made in both clear and ambiguous verses: the former are the cornerstone of the scripture, the latter are those pursued by the perverse at heart in trying to create ambiguities and to make trouble.[15]

The need to frame an increasing sense of belonging is expressed in verses 3:19: 'True Religion, in God's eyes, is Islam (devotion to Him alone)', and in 3:28: 'The Believers should not make the disbelievers their allies rather than other believers, anyone who does such a thing will isolate himself completely from God'. Conversely, a long part of *sūrah* 3 is dedicated to the People of the Book as well as Christianity and Judaism (3:33–115). A clear distinction, however, is marked by the story narrated about 'Imrān's family which reflects the life of Maryam as miraculous from the beginning: Jesus's birth is only one of the irrational aspects that are related to her life:

> The angels said: 'Mary, God gives you news about a Word from Him, whose name will be the Messiah, Jesus, son of Mary, who will be held in honour in this world and the next, who will be one of those brought near to God.' (3:45) – 'When Jesus became aware that they still did not believe, he said, 'Who will help me in God's cause?' The disciples said, 'We will be God's helpers; we believe in God-witness our devotion to Him' (3:52),

which shapes a clear parallelism with the prophet Muḥammad and the *Anṣār*. However, the following verses (55–61), on the one hand, claimed:

> 'Jesus will take you back and raise you up to Me: I will purify you of the disbelievers. To the day of the Resurrection I will make those who followed you superior to those who disbelieved. Then you will all return to Me and I will judge between you regarding your differences' (3:55), as well as: 'We related to you Muḥammad this revelation, a decisive statement. In God's eyes Jesus is just like Adam: He created him from dust, said to Him, Be and he was. This is the truth from your Lord, so do not be one of those who doubt. If anyone disputes this with you now that you have been given this knowledge, say, "Come, let us gather our son and your sons, our women and your women, ourselves and yourselves, and let us pray earnestly and invoke God's rejection on those of us who are lying".' (3:58-61)

Those verses, like the following ones (62–100) which are Christologically important,[16] are mixed with an increasing lack of confidence in the People of the Book (3:69, 75); in parallel, there is also an early attempt to define who the Believers are: 'Say Muhammad, We [Muslims] believe in God and in what has been sent down to us and to Abraham, Ishmael, Isaac, Jacob and the Tribes (*'asbāṭ*). We believe in what has been given to Moses, Jesus and the prophets from their Lord. We do not make a distinction between any of them, it is to Him (God) that we devote ourselves' (3:84), arguing that sole devotion to God is the only religion that the Believers are willing to put into practice (3:85).

It is historically evident that after the battle of Badr, an increasing conflict with the Jewish tribes of Medina was showing its first signs; it is also palpable that the Qur'ān is again univocally addressing the Jews (3: 110-112), though using the term of People of the Book.

The same verses also allowed the Believers, for the first time, to fight against the People of the Book in case of being attacked: 'they will not do you much harm; even if they will come out to fight you (*wa yuqātilūkum*), they will soon turn tail; they will get not help; and unless they hold fast to a lifeline from God and from mankind, they are overshadowed by vulnerability wherever they are found.'

Those verses clearly referred to a specific 'story' related to the prophetic phase, probably when after the victory of Badr, the Banū Qaynuqā' were exiled from Medina;[17] the same verse continues: 'They have drawn God's wrath upon themselves. They are overshadowed by weakness, too, because they have persistently disbelieved in God's revelation and killed prophets without any rights (*wa Yaqtulūna al-'Anbiya'a bighayri Ḥaqqin*), all because of they disobedience and boundless transgression', which, again, clearly reflects on the Jews of Medina, the Christians never having killed a Prophet of the Abrahamic tradition.[18]

As has clearly emerged in other parts of the Revelation, after strong verses against a specific target, the following ones are clearly more accommodating and inclusive: 'But they are not all alike. There are some among the People of the Book who are upright, who recite God's revelations during the night, who bow down in worship' (3:113–115).

In the conclusive part of the *sūrah*, two main facets are marked in the new believers' activism against corruption: the eschatological struggle to reach the Garden (3:142) for those who showed their faith in God as well as in the Prophet, and the fight against those who defined themselves Believers but, on the contrary, acted as hypocrites (3:165–167).

It is a sort of moral lesson which through the Revelation God tried to impart to the believers and which probably referred to those who remained faithful to the Prophet during the difficult phase of the battle of ʾUḥud.[19]

Only those who want to struggle for God's cause, remaining steadfast, will enter the Garden; God will test them: '*ʾam Ḥasibtum ʾan tadkhulū al-Jannata wa lammā yaʿlami Allāhu al-ladhīna jāhadū minkum wa yaʿlama aṣ-Ṣābirīna* (142), if Muhammad died or was killed, would you revert to your old ways?' (144) which placed this part of the *sūrah* closely after the major defeat of the Medinese, at ʾUḥud, in distinguishing those who lost heart or weakened or surrendered because God loves those who are steadfast (145–147).

The hypocrites, the *munafiqūn*, are those who when it was said to them: 'Come, fight for God's cause, or at least, defend yourselves', answered: 'we would follow you if we knew how to fight. On that day they were closer to disbelief than belief' (167).

The fight against the enemies assumed a paradigmatic *spectrum*, in concretely being part of the believers' side as well as the battle of ʾUḥud becoming symptomatic in exalting the faith of those who concretely followed the Prophet, from those that out of cowardice did not.

In particular, 'Abd-Allah ibn Ubayy, the leading chief of the Banū Khazraj, decided not to join the Prophet on the battlefield, remaining in Medina, contrary to his son 'Abd Allāh, who fought at ʾUḥud and was also injured.[20]

However, the simplistic reading of the Islamic narrative only tries to hide the complexity and the difficulties in the amalgamation of an early Believers' community in which different personalities and subjectivities were trying to co-exist both in relation to 'Believers' and Jews as well as to *Muhajirūn* and *Anṣār.*

Al-Ṭabarī in his *Taʾrīkh*,[21] for example, assumed that 'Abd-Allah ibn Ubayy had the same opinion as the Prophet in not fighting an open battle against the Meccans, but he reports how some 'Believers' and *Muhajirūn*, who missed Badr and its spoils, wanted to encounter their enemies in battle for different reasons and asked Muḥammad to lead them.

Ibn Ubayy, on the contrary, argued:

> O Messenger of God stay in Medina and do not go out to meet them. By God, we have never gone out of it to meet an enemy but that they have inflicted severe losses on us; and no enemy has ever entered it but that we have inflicted severe losses on them. Leave them alone, 0 Messenger of God, and if they remain, they will be in the worst possible place; and if they enter Medina, the men will fight them face to face, and the women and boys will hurl stones at them from above; if they then withdraw, they will withdraw disappointed in their hopes, as they came,

which more than a cowardly or hypocrite stance seems a more strategic one, which will be adopted afterwards, during the Battle of the Trench.[22]

However, as reported by al-Ṭabarī again, Ibn Ubayy reached the battlefield with part of the 'Believers'' army but when saw the Meccans' number he returned to Medina: 'split off from him with a third of the army, saying, "He obeyed them by setting out and disobeyed me. By God, we do not know why we should get ourselves killed here, men".

So, he went back to Medina with those of his people of the Hypocrites and doubters who followed him'.[23]

As it had begun, ***sūrah* 3** ends with an inclusive Abrahamic *visio* (3:199–200), even though a large part of the same is emblematically devoted to an aggressive campaign against religious hypocrisy, independently of the actor involved.

The Jewish Medinan clan as well as 'Believer' hypocrites seem to be considered in almost the same way; moreover, the most relevant facet is the concrete attempt to distinguish the new community from the disrespectful consideration that Jews and hypocrites started to feel for Muḥammad and his main supporters.

It is clear that the 'Constitution of Medina' was failing and even though Badr was a military success, the involvement in a frontline clash with Mecca was provoking many doubts, so much so as to divide the core of the newly established community: *Anṣār* and *Muhajirūn*.

The impression is that we are facing an inconclusive militancy without a concrete strategy and a great internal fragmentation; the fact that the very son of Ibn Ubayy, 'Abd-Allāh ibn 'Abd-Allāh ibn Ubayy, took part in the battle of ʾUḥud in disagreement with his father is emblematic of the disunity of the Medinans. Far from any kind of religious belligerency, it is the relationship with the Prophet, the war's spoils or other unknown personal reasons that make the expectation of a confrontation concrete or not.[24]

Considering the Egyptian and Nöldeke's chronology, great differences anticipate the ***sūrah* 4**: for the former, sūrah 3 is followed by 33 and 60, for the latter, 61 and 57. Independently of any doubts, sūrah 33 has usually been considered as related to the battle of the Trench:

> God sent back the disbelievers (the Meccans) along with their rage, they gained no benefit and spared the believers from fighting. He is strong and mighty. He brought those People of the Book who supported them down from their strongholds and put panic in their hearts. Some of them you 'believers' killed and some you took captive. He passed on to you their land, their houses, their possessions and a land where you had not set foot: God has power over everything. (25–27)

The description is evidently linked to the Meccans' incapacity to enter Medina as well as the sack of the Banū Qurayẓa's property and goods, again in this case generally named People of the Book. It is therefore important to stress how until the battle of the Trench, which was resolved without a military confrontation, all the clashes with the Meccans – Badr, ʾUḥud and the last one – subsequently experienced pillage against one of the Jewish clans of Medina, usually accused of being supportive of the believers' enemies.[25]

However, as reported by al-Wāqīdī, only the last one against the Qurayẓa was recorded by Islamic chronicles as a real battle with registered deaths on the Believers' side as well.[26]

***Sūrah* 60** of the tested women was probably revealed in the phase between the treaty of Ḥudaybiyya and the conquest of Mecca (6–8 AH); moreover its significance for our analysis reflects on God's permission in being kind and just with anyone who has not fought you (*qātalūkum*) for your faith or driven you out of your homes; simultaneously, God forbids taking as allies those who have fought you for your faith, driving you out of your homes or helping others to drive you out (60:8–9). This is an important assertion which probably referred to a part of the Banū Khuzā'ah, a Meccan clan that were still idolators, that with the Banū Mudlij, a branch of the Kinānah, never engaged in the fight against the Believers; on the contrary, when they realized that after ʾUḥud, the idolaters were organizing a vast expedition to destroy Medina, they sent some knights to inform Muḥammad of the imminent peril.[27]

Considering Th. Nöldeke's chronology, only ***sūrah* 61** is able to repeat something already found in 8:72.

Verse 11 highlights how only those who will struggle (*wa tajāhidūna*) for God's cause with their possessions and persons (*bi'amwālikum wa 'anfusikum*) will be forgiven for their sins and admitted to the Garden; a parallel is traced among the followers of the Prophet and Jesus's disciples in an inter-religious conclusion.

The verses from 71 to 76 of ***sūrah* 4** emerged as particularly militant and war-oriented. The fight in God's cause, univocally assumed in the revelation with *q-t-l*, is introduced again in a historical phase in which after the battle of the Trench, the Meccans are disheartened due to the lack of success against the Medinans, while the latter feel more confident of having blocked a concrete and dangerous attempt of annihilation.

The removal of the Qurayẓa is a definitive step in the clear attempt to impose Muḥammad's view as the dominant one in the Medinan area. However:

> Why should you not fight in God's cause and for those oppressed men, women and children who cry out, 'Lord, rescue us from this town whose people are oppressors! (*al-Ladhīna Yaqūlūna Rabbanā 'Akhrijnā Min Hadhihi Al-Qaryati Aẓ-Ẓālimi 'Ahluhā*) By Your grace give us a protector and give us a helper!? The Believers fight for God's cause, while those who reject faith fight for an unjust cause,
> (*al-Ṭaghūti*)

still seems an expression of a request to force the Believers to fight against their enemies, specifically now that many requests for help seem to come from Mecca.[28]

As stated in 4:77, God first imposed on the believers not to fight but to pray, to pay the prescribed alms and only afterwards to contest the community's enemies; but even when God's command reached the *Ummah*, some of them found excuses not to become involved.

The ongoing presence of hypocrites among the Believers tried to be finally resolved by arguing about the impossibility of signing a treaty with them, because they are people you cannot trust (4:88–91), while killing a Believer, except by mistake, is a grave sin, for which the punishment is Hell (4:92–93).

Verse 4:95 is a very emblematic verse in which the previous condemnation of hypocrisy is mitigated by a clearer distinction without a permanent condemnation. Those who engage in war or support them materially and those who withhold all support from the campaigns, staying at home, are not equal for God; 'God has raised such people to a rank above those who stay at home, although He has promised all believers a good reward, those who strive (*al-mujāhidīn*) are favoured with a tremendous reward above those who stay at home'.[29]

It is quite logical that those who strive on God's way, in this case the sense is clearly related to fighting, and those who risk their lives to show their beliefs cannot be considered equal to those who stay quietly at home.

However, it is interesting how this verse did not reproach those who stay at home as hypocrites but still as believers. Verses 4:95–96 are significant in deciphering a believer's ranking due to having different behaviour in war as well as identifying the *mujāhid* as a fighter in God's way.

According to Qur'anic chronology, this is only the second verse, after 2:218, in which the semantic correlation between to struggle and to fight is hermeneutically clarified. In the previous verses of the *sūwar* 2, 8, 3, the acts of belief, emigration and struggle were not directly and semantically ascribed to a belligerent attitude, contrary to the verses which anticipate 2:218 and 4:95–96 where the literary *milieu* is more emblematically linked with militancy.

It would be important to decipher when this correlation is further considered in the attempt to better identify the concrete difference between *q-t-l* and *j-h-d* in the Qur'anic context: a topic to which we will return shortly, at the end of this chapter.[30]

The following verse, 4:97, placed the previous ones in a historical phase in which the Prophet is demanding the Meccan believers to abandon the city and to emigrate to Medina because it was probably the time to politically and numerically verify the Believers' strength.[31]

It is possible that Mecca's crisis of legitimacy started, as well as the conciliatory-provocative phase for the real believers and the unbelievers, to assume a clearer political stance in front of their own community. After the battle of the Trench, the Believers fortified themselves, while the Meccans' inner doubts about their ability to resist a sort of Medinan *embargo* started becoming clearer.

Following the Egyptian chronology, ***sūrah* 47** has to be considered after *sūrah* 4; moreover, stressing the semantic correlation previously mentioned, it is important to underline the importance of the context: verses 30–31 are far from being linked to a bellicose *spectrum*: 'We shall test you to see which of you strive (*al-mujāhidīn*) your hardest and are steadfast (*al-ṣābirīna*); we shall test the sincerity of your assertion', and even if the term *mujāhid* is adopted, the hermeneutical meaning remains peaceful and not related to any kind of violent task.

It would have been different if *mujāhidīn* had been replaced by *muqātilīn* or a term closer to aggressive militancy.

According to the above analysis, *sūrah* **59** is more focused on the Jewish clan of the Banū Naḍīr who first agreed with the Prophet in never assuming a military position against him or on his side, but after the Meccans' victory at ʾUḥud, they formed an alliance with the unbelievers.

The Islamic narrative also reports that they tried to kill the Prophet and when they were asked to leave the city of the Prophet, Medina's hypocrites demanded if they wanted to fight the Believers with their support.[32]

Nevertheless the *sūrah* is closely linked to a bellicose subject: the term *q-t-l* is mentioned once (59:14) clarifying how the adoption of terminology in the Islamic

Revelation is related to the literary hermeneutics of the same in assuming a strong correlation between Islamic historical narrative, the Prophet's life and the Qur'ān. In other words, when the Qur'anic verses are hermeneutically associated with inter-clanic conflict, the historicizing legitimization of the early Believers is widely canonized through the violence of *q-t-l*, in particular when the enemies turn against previously established rules, or against their honour (*Sharaf* and *Muruwwa*).[33] However, belligerency is usually attributed to the petty and deceptive behaviour of those who will be punished by God through the believers' military actions. On the contrary, the efforts required to be steadfast are a moral-ethical projection that only partially involved the bellicose perspective.

Both Chronologies, the Egyptian and Nöldeke's, put *sūrah* 22 after *sūrah* 47 and towards the end of the Medinan period, although before the conquest of Mecca.

The quartet of the *sūwar* 24-22-63-58 (Egyptian) and 63-24-58-22 (Nöldeke, after 59 and 33) remained quite mysteriously associated with the topic of war.

If ***sūrah* 22**, as stated above, should be inserted at the end of the Medinan phase, from verse 75 it still seems pedagogically related to a Believers' community still unable to understand: 'God chooses messengers from among the angels and from among the humans'. This is an interesting aspect but dissociated from an Abrahamic background.[34] The process of the Qur'anic canonization still remained mysteriously associated with a *collage* praxis that in some cases appears more obvious.

If ***sūwar* 24** and **58** are correlated to moral aspects and not linked with militantism, while ***sūrah* 63** on the contrary is against the Hypocrites, *Munāfiqūn*, who persist in being among the believers, the historical periodization established that the latter was probably pronounced while the Prophet was leading the raid against the Banū Muṣṭaliq, a Meccan-allied tribe who had settled on the Red Sea between Jeddah and Rābigh, around 627/6 AH.

This clan, part of the Khuzāʿah, was still allied with the Meccans; moreover, after the Medinan raid in their territories, Juwayriya bint al-Ḥārith, the daughter of the defeated chief, became the sixth wife of Prophet Muḥammad, pushing them into an alliance with the Believers as well as further limiting the hypocrites' attempts to rule in Medina.[35]

The importance of ***sūrah* 48** is prominent because of its historical topic of reference: the pact of Ḥudaybiyya.

Regarding this agreement, while widely considered a huge victory in the Qur'ān, the *Sīra*, on the contrary, does not omit to contemplate the opposition to it that emerged, in particular, from 'Umar ibn al-Khaṭṭāb.[36] Ḥudaybiyya determined the early Medinan-Meccan attempt to find an agreement: an armistice of ten years which allowed the Believers to reach Mecca, the following year, to peacefully make the pilgrimage.

This last aspect, decreeing a year's delay, was rejected by some of the most irreducible 'believers', who were already ready to fight to reach the Kaʿbah and pray inside it, independently of the blood spilt to achieve this goal.

Verses 48:15–20, moreover, stressed that to pacify the souls of its community, in particular those who followed him to Ḥudaybiyya and afterwards returned to Medina, Muḥammad promised them a pillage-raid (*ghazwa*) against the Jewish oasis of Khaybar.

This location played a significant commercial role in the north of the Peninsula, even rivalling Medina; at the same time the Jews there had taken up a position against Muḥammad, and the Prophet, after having been contested for the pact that had been signed, wanted to guarantee a generous booty for the Believers.[37]

It is possible that the raid in this case, as in many others which are reported in the Qur'ān, cannot be attributed to any sort of *Jihād* or concrete religious militantism; on the contrary the same verses argue about God's omniscience about those who support the Prophet under the tree, because He knew what was in their hearts and so He sent tranquillity down to them with a speedy triumph and with many future gains (v. 19). Those gains (*maghānima*) 'have been hastened for you. He has held back the hands of hostile people (the Jews of Khaybar) from you as a sign for the faithful and He will guide you to a straight path' (v. 20, *Wa'adakumu Allāhu Maghānima Kathīran Ta'khudhūnahā Fa'ajjala Lakum hadhihi wa kaffa 'aydiya an-Nāsi 'ankum wa litakūna 'Āyatan Lilmu'minīna wa yahdiyakum Ṣirāṭān Mustaqīmān*).

There is another important *topos* in this *sūrah* that needs to be considered and which continues in the following one, **49**, and that allows wondering about the Prophet's strategic militantism.

The need to relate to the Bedouins is a complicated topic: until the end of the Qur'anic chronology they are still accused of unbelief (9: 97–98, 101) as well as of hypocrisy (48:11, 16; 49:14–18); however, the last verses of ***sūrah* 49** emphasized the main difference between *Islām* and *Imām*, in a clear accusation against the Bedouins.

Qālati Al-'A'rābu 'Āmannā Qul Lam Tu'uminū Wa Lakin Qūlū Aslamnā Wa Lammā Yadkhuli Al-'Īmānu Fī Qulūbikum Wa 'Inna Tuṭī'ū Allaha Wa Rasūlahu Lā Yalitkum Min 'A'mālikum Shay'āan 'Inna Allāha Ghafūrun Raḥīmun, and continues: 'The True Believers are the ones who have faith in God and His Messenger and leave all doubt behind, the ones who have struggled (*wa jāhadū*) with their possessions and their persons in God's way: they are the ones who are true' (49:14–15).

The pedagogical verse stresses the unfaithful but at the same time increasing relationship between the Believers and those Bedouins who started to sign a political agreement with the Prophet and that is evidently underlined in this final Medinan phase.

The correlation between the Prophet's policies of raids (*maghāzī*) started after the *Hijra*, when the conflict with Mecca caused its enlargement in the clear attempt to form a different set of alliances to isolate the city of the *Ka'ba* in the long term.

At the same time, this policy evidently showed clear frictions in the early community in parallel with an initial unstable definition of who a Muslim-Believer was, as well as the easiness, from the beginning, of accusing the Other of being a true believer or not.

The struggle in the way of God with their possessions and their persons assumes a pedagogical position in the clear attempt to show the way, for the Bedouins, to become believers. Anachronistically, the early Islamic narrative, starting from the second half of the eighth century, was to negate and ideologically underestimate the importance as well as the impact of pro-Believer Bedouin tribes during the war against Mecca and afterwards. Nevertheless, reading between the lines, as well as reflecting on published literature, it is historically clear that increasing numbers of Arabs of the Desert supported Prophet Muḥammad in isolating Mecca and its allies first, and played a significant role in the conquests, after being reported in the ranks following the *Ridda*.[38]

Egyptian chronology argued that the last *sūrah* of the Qur'ān revealed to the Prophet was the 110, which says: 'When God's help comes and He opens up (*al-Fatḥ*) your way (Prophet), when you see people embracing God's faith in crowds(*'Afwājāan*), celebrate the praise of your Lord and ask forgiveness: He is always ready to accept repentance'; however, Nöldeke claims that the words *al-naṣr Allahi wa-l-Fatḥ* are probably attributable to the conquest of Mecca.[39]

The doubt that the same verses can be attributed after the battle of Ḥunayn, when, as also reported in Muḥammad's biography, many Thaqīf and Hawāzin of Ṭā'if decided to convert in mass,[40] is a possibility taken into consideration by al-Wāḥidī,[41] although rejected by Bukhārī and Muslim.[42]

The complexity of the debate on the historicization of ***sūrah* 110** also reflects on the last ones (9 and 5) and that probably have to be fixed between the conquest of Mecca (630/8 AH) and the Prophet's death (632/10 AH).

The 'verses of War' and *Jihād* (*sūwar* 9–5)

3. The inter-connection between *sūwar* 110, 9 and 5 must not distract us from the possibility that once 8 and 9, or better, parts of them, were a single *sūrah*, subsequently fragmented for unknown reasons.

If indeed both Chronologies place the *sūwar* in different phases of the Medinan period: 8 in verses 7–12, but also 42ff and 56 seem to reflect on events in Badr (624), while, 9, in verses 25, 38–39, 74, 81, 106–110, 118, probably referred to Ḥunayn and Tabūk (630); the last verses of 8, moreover, at least from 72 and the beginning of 9 could be considered semantically in continuity, at least for verses 1 and 2, but also for the following ones.

The main topic, which is echoed at the end of 8 as well as at the beginning of 9, reflects on the plurality of treaties signed between the Believers and the idolaters in the Medinan phase from the so-called 'Constitution of Medina' up to the pact of Ḥudaybiyya.

The fact that at the end of *sūrah* 8 there is a sort of recap about the behavioural attitude to adopt in relation to the idolaters and those who became believers after the *Hijra* stressed the existence of pacts that probably have to be considered in relation to individual transactions between the Medinese and specific clans still affiliated to the Meccans, as well as Bedouin polytheists.

However, as R. Blachère outlined, those concluding verses are more focused on better defining the Medinan believers' community, stressing the pre-Islamic rules in legislating on those who accepted the Prophet's message and role after the *Hijra* and Badr. These policies were updated at the beginning of the following *sūrah*, **the 9th**.

Nevertheless, from verse 3, the previous agreements (*'Āhadtum*) were nullified by a new proclamation that was pronounced during the *yawma al-Ḥajj al-Akhari*, perhaps the 'complete' pilgrimage performed by the Believers after entering Mecca and the victory of Ḥunayn (9 AH).

The Pilgrimage was led by Abū Bakr, but the Prophet's new message was pronounced by 'Alī who essentially argued about the concession of another four months to idolaters to move within the Believers' territory in complete safety, but after that period, 'when the forbidden months are over, wherever you encounter the idolaters, kill them, seize them, besiege them, wait for them at every lookout post' (v. 5).

Some exceptions remained however for those idolaters that 'should seek your protection', the Prophet's, then grant them and make them hear the word of God, as well as for those who had already signed a special treaty with Muḥammad, close to the Sacred Mosque (which probably refers to Ḥudaybiyya) and that will continue to be respected until the expiry of the previous agreement.[43]

Referring to this last passage, if Ibn Khatīr and Jalālayn attribute those signed treaties to Ḥudaybiyya, Ibn Abbas, on the contrary, argues about some treaties contracted after it. The lack of clarity about the schedule and the referring clans – nine months–ten years, the Banū Kinānah or others – remains.

It is plausible that the end of *sūrah* 8 and the beginning of *sūrah* 9 could be semantically linked, which is a hypothesis that is strengthened by the absence of the *Basmala*.[44]

However, the importance of this digression reflects on the famous verse 5 of the latter that without this hermeneutical contextualization can easily be de-contextualized assuming a generalized perspective; on the contrary, this *Sword verse* clearly referred to the remaining idolaters of Ḥijāz at the end of the Medinan phase.[45]

As reported by Firestone, the common idea that 9:5 abrogated any restrictions of fighting during the old four pre-Islamic sacred months continues to reflect a clear personal and geographical context: the idolaters of that time and the calendar of the same period.[46]

The idea of an indiscriminate belligerent attitude against the idolaters is limited by the fact that with some of them a pact had recently been signed at Ḥudaybiyya which, if they respected it, consequently had to be respected by the other party as well (v. 7).

From verse 13, the analysis focuses on identifying those Meccans that after the entrance of Muḥammad in his hometown remained in an unclear position. It is possible that as for the Arabs of the Desert, the Prophet's peaceful conquests of Mecca, if on the one hand, were a clear political strategy that put the Meccans in the face of a *fait accompli*, due to their weakness, on the other, they provoked a rapid acceptance of the new *status quo* on the political level.

Those verses emphasized what Ṭabarī describes in his chronicle about the conquest of Mecca:

> The People assembled in Mecca to swear allegiance to the messenger of God in Islam. As I have been informed, he sat for them on al-Ṣafā. 'Umar ibn al-Khaṭṭāb was below the messenger of God, lower than the place where he sat, administering the oath to the people. He received from them the oath of allegiance to the Messenger of God, to heed and obey God and His Messenger to the extent of their ability.[47]

However, a firm condemnation remained for those who continued to be idolaters (9: v. 23–28) with whom nothing can be shared any longer, including ties of kinship; God continued to entrust you, Believers, against your enemies, as in the battle of Ḥunayn (v. 25), when their huge numbers were not sufficient to defeat you, even if (v. 27) 'after all this, God turns in His Mercy to whoever He will'.

This probably refers to the fact that after the battle, large numbers of Thaqīf and Hawāzin decided to accept Muḥammad's role.

The verses (9: 28–35) continue to be quite chaotic semantically, but also linguistically.

If 28 forbids the *mushrikūna* from going to the sacred Mosque of Mecca, limiting *de facto* the pre-Islamic pilgrimage and its commercial function, 29, the famous *Jizya* verse, says: 'Fight (*qātilū*) those who believe not in God and the Last Day and do not forbid what God and his Messenger have forbidden, such men as practise not the religion of truth (*wa Lā Yadīnūna Dīna al-Ḥaqqī*), being of those who have given the Book (*mina lladhīna 'ūtū'l-kitāb*), until they pay the tribute out of hand and have been humbled (*ḥattā yu 'ṭū l-jizya 'an yadin wa-hum ṣāghirūn*)'.

This verse, that was paradigmatically considered in the following centuries as emblematic of the institution of *Jizya*, in relation to the Muslims, as attributed to Jews and Christians, but also Hindus, after the Islamic conquest (twelfth–thirteenth centuries) of the Indian subcontinent, continues to reflect on a normative verse that again has to be contextualized in its period of reference.

If Blachère in arguing about 9:29 is *tranchant*, simplistically quarrelling that '*Tout ce passage paraît être une addition ultérieure*'[48] (this whole passage appears to be a later addition), Abdel Haleem and Uri Rubin clarified some interesting aspects:

1. *dīna bi-* is a behavioural act of obedience to the rules, established through the Prophet by God; however, to talk about a 'religion of truth' in a historical phase in which there is still not an Islamic religion or a clear Islamic jurisprudence able to elucidate this passage is quite problematic. The same hermeneutical analysis attributed to Ibn Abbas referred this verse to the Jews and Christians of the Arabian Peninsula without assuming a clear generalization.[49]
2. *mina lladhīna 'ūtū'l-kitāb*, as argued by Abdel Haleem,[50] is a partitive expression which clarified 'those of the People of the Book who do not believe in God and the Last Judgement and do not forbid what God and His Messenger have forbidden', which confirmed the local geographical space to which this verse is attributed: we are still talking about the Jews of the Ḥijāz as well as, probably, the Christians of Najrān. At the same time, if it is evident that ordinary Jews and Christians, if believers, usually consider God and the Last Judgement part of their faith; on the contrary they are not aware about what Allah and Muḥammad have forbidden because they have never lived under Islamic rules and because, as already reported above, it will take a couple of centuries after the Prophet's death (632/10 AH) for a clear *Sharī'ah* to be contemplated. In this verse, the Qur'ān allowed for the first time fighting those People of the Book who do not believe in God etc., but above all, who do not forbid what Allah and Muḥammad have forbidden; in other words, they do not respect the initial rules that emerged from the Revelation, which is practical behaviour.
3. *ḥattā yu 'ṭū'l-jizya*, until they paid the *Jizya*, reflects the payment of a 'Poll Tax', which if it is easily identifiable two centuries later, during the time of the Prophet

it was not, due to the lack of a Treasury, as well as the people who collected taxes. The Qur'anic meaning of j-z-y was 'to reward somebody for something', paying in relation to services received, which assumes a more positive connotation. It is evident that the *Jizya* will assume the right for Jews and Christians to live under Islamic protection, preserving their religions and property, without having to join the Muslim army. This last aspect, as reported in the historical part, was only limitedly adopted during the Arab campaigns of conquest, with numerically consistent Arab Christian clans who took on a military role in the conquests as well as during the *Fitnas*, for at least eighty years after the Prophet's death. As reported by M. 'Imāra, those Jews and Christians who fought on the Believers' side in the early and later military campaigns were exempted from paying the *Jizya*, because at the beginning, this sort of tax was *badal jundiyya*, in exchange for military service.[51] Even in this case, it is historically evident that we have to wait, contrary to a banal Islamic narrative about it, a longer period of time in relation to the canonization of a state system during the Umayyad age, but after the end of the second *Fitna* (692). At that time, if the early Muslim community started to pay the *Zakat*, from which the People of the Book were exempted, the latter began to pay the *Jizya*, to continue to reside under Muslim protection as well as, if not directly, involved in the army.

4. *'an yadin* is another part of the verse on which the hermeneutical interpretation has found some difficulties. If the easiest understanding reflects the simple translation – 'by their own hand', as reported by Uri Rubin – it is evident that this exegesis is late and not linked to previous material, before the canonization of the *Jizya* in the Islamic Law.[52] As reported by al-Ṭabarī in his Chronicle,[53] when the Arab conquerors, such as Khālid ibn al-Walīd, reported that treaties had been signed with the conquered towns of Mesopotamia and asked them to pay by community and not by male, it was a sort of *ante-litteram Jizya*. However, the fact that the Qur'anic verse and the expression *'an yadin* do not appear in any except one of these treaties makes Blachère's doubts more concrete. If indeed in the reported treaties entered into by the Arab conquerors, there is no evidence referring to 9:29 of the expression *'an yadin*, it is possible that at the time of the Revelation, there was still not a clear understanding of *Jizya*. Finally, if we consider the *Muwaṭṭā'* of the Imām Mālik, produced in the second half of the eighth century, the *Jizya* is cited only once, and directly linked with the stipulation of a covenant of peace.[54]
5. *wa-hum ṣāghirūn*, the last part of the verse wants to emphasize the humbleness with which the People of the Book need to act in paying the *Jizya*. Abū Ḥayyān al-Gharnāṭī (d. 1344), as reported by Abdel Haleem, argues that 'they should stand and the recipient be sitting, or that they should not be thanked for giving *jizya*, or that the receiver should say to the giver, "Pay the *jizya*", and smack him on the back of his neck, or that someone should take hold of his beard and hit him under the jaw', which is very humiliating. However, until the time of al-Jāḥiz, in the middle of the ninth century, it seems that, at least in the urban areas, the reluctance of the Christians to pay the *Jizya* was seriously considered a problem of total disrespect towards the Islamic Caliphate,[55] which again could suggest the possibility of a later addition.

The following verses (9:30–35) continue to deride Jews and Christians in accusing them of associating human beings with God (even if until today, the accusation that Judaism made Ezra the son of God remains very mysterious), of taking Rabbis and Monks (*Aḥbārahum wa Ruhbānahum,* learned person and monk-ascetic) as lords beside God. The latter accusation will be partially upended in 5:82 and we will return to it later.

If it is evident that those last *sūwar* are more inclined to better define the Believers' early community as something different from Arabian Judaism and Christianity, regarding the internal identity, the belligerent attitude still remained projected on a defensive option, 9:36 argues:

> God decrees that there are twelve months organised in God's book on the day when He created the heavens and earth, four months of which are sacred: this is the correct calculation. Do not wrong yourselves in these months – though you may fight the idolaters at any time if they first fight you (*wa qātilū al-Mushrikīna Kāffatan Kamā Yuqātilūnakum Kaffātan*), remember that God is with those who are mindful of Him.

This translation, not always univocal,[56] emphasized how, contrary to the *Jāhiliyya* Arabian conduct, it was not possible to fight an enemy during the Sacred Months of Dhūl-Qa'dah, Dhūl-Ḥijjah, Muḥarram and Rajab, while this verse cancels *de facto* the norm.

Conversely, its most important part reflects on the fact that this permission to fight the *Mushrikūm* is valid if they start to fight first, independently of the month. This hermeneutical interpretation, established by important Muslim authors,[57] confirmed the reactionary defensive attitude of belligerency in one of the last *sūwar*, of the same Revelation.

This conceptualization seems to be in continuity with 2:194 and not in contrast, as argued by Qurṭubī, in his *Jāmi'*.[58]

If the aim of the fighting (*qātilu*) is the eradication of unbelief and polytheism (*shirk*), only those who fight you are particularly dangerous as confirmed by 9:36; as well as when the unbelievers were prone to fighting the Prophet, at the time that 2:194 was revealed, they had to be fought back, as attackers against the early Medinan community.

The following verses (9:38–42) are mainly significant because if they are in continuity with the previous ones, they show, for the first time, a synonym between *n-f-r* (*nafara*: to stand up and join a fighting army) and *j-h-d* (*jahada*: to struggle) in giving an updated understanding of the conceptualization of *jihād.*

> 'Believers, why, when it is said to you, *Up and Go forth on the way of God,* [...] If you do not go out, (God) will punish you with grievous penalty' (v. 38-39); 'Even if you do not help the Prophet, God helped him when the disbelievers drove him out: when the two of them (Muḥammad and Abū Bakr), he said to his companion, "Do not worry, God is with us", and God sent his calm down to him, aided him with forces invisibles to you, and brought down the disbelievers' plan. God's plan

> is higher: God is almighty and wise (v. 40). So, go out, no matter whether you are lightly or heavily armed and struggle in God's way with your possessions and persons' (*Anfirū Khifāfāan wa Thiqālāan wa Jāhidū bi'amwālikum wa 'anfusikum fī Sabīli Allāhi*, v. 41).

These verses, which probably referred to the expedition of Tabūk, when false information seemed to announce a Byzantine invasion of Ḥijāz,[59] form a directly meaningful correlation between the action of rising up, independently of the preparation of the military equipment, and struggling on the way of God. This association, if it clearly refers to a military expedition, confirmed the Qur'anic difficulties in enforcing the link between to fight (*q-t-l*) and to struggle (*j-h-d*).

What can be historically perceived at this time is that there were few brave men, among the old and new believers, who wanted to encounter the Byzantines in battle, including during the summer when the oppressive heat usually reached its height; moreover, the incitation to leave for the mission is directly associated with a form of *jihād*, which logically could lead to a fight.

However, it is the action and the bravery in rising up, even if militarily unprepared, even if the weather is dry, that is symptomatic of showing the Believers' struggle on the way of God, which hermeneutically confirmed the absolute confidence of the Believer in God: this complete abnegation in God's faith, which, in the above verses, is specular to that for the Prophet becomes the core of the concrete meaning of being a *mujāhid*.

In other words, it is not the fighting which makes you a *mujāhid* but your absolute trust in divine transcendence. Striving on God's way, which sometimes referred to a warlike defensive attitude (as in the case of Tabūk), is only partially associated with military militancy, but more generally in a form of personal activism that put the believers' confidence in God as the most important aspect of their personal faith.

Blind belief in God as well in the Prophet makes the difference in being a Believer or not:

> Those who were left behind were happy to stay behind when God's messenger set out; they hated the thought of striving (*yujāhidu*) in God's way with their possessions and their persons. They said to one another, 'Do not go out with this heat', [...] So Prophet, if God brings you back to a group of them, who ask you the permission to go out, say, 'You will never go out and fight an enemy with me: you chose to sit at home the first time, so remain with those who stay behind.' (9:81, 83)

Verses 86 and 88 continue, possibly referring to the Tabūk expedition, in emphasizing the difference between those who strive on God's way and those who stay behind.[60] The accusation is directed to the hypocrites but also to some desert Arabs (9:90, 97, 101) who stayed behind and were:

> the most stubborn of all people in their disbelief and hypocrisy. [...] Some of the desert Arabs consider what they give to be an imposition; they are waiting for fortune to turn against you, but fortune will turn against them. (9:98) [...] But there are also some desert Arabs who believe in God and the last Day and

consider their contributions as bringing them nearer to God and the prayers of the Messenger: they will indeed bring them nearer and God will admit them to His mercy. (9:99)

This *topos* is particularly important in relation to subduing the Arabs of the Desert, but even more, if we put the above verses in parallel with 3:110/199 'Some of the People of the Book believe in God, in what has been sent down to you and in what has been sent down to them', 5:66, 10:40 and others, in which the People of the Book are equally considered and apostrophized.

The Qur'ān seems to adopt the same method in fragmenting the community between those who are on God's way, and those who are still far away from understanding it.

It is evident that those who strive on the way of God only for monetary reasons, or who too rationally calculate costs-benefits in being a Believer to take part in an expedition, are very far from being considered a real devotee by God and his Prophet. The vast majority of the verses in the 9th *sūrah*, the penultimate one for both chronologies, referred to the still ongoing presence of hypocrisy among the believers.

Even in this case, the importance of the post-Islamic narrative is important to exegetically understand the concrete meaning of the *sūrah*, which is named *Tawbāh*: repentance.

Quite surprisingly, verse 111 assumed that the eschatological expectations for the Believers in being prepared 'to kill and being killed' are something shared with what had been written in the Torah and the Gospel, in an ongoing covenant to reinforce the idea that salvation can also come from those who died fighting on God's way.

This verse, which as reported by N. Sinai and N. Reda[61] seems in continuity with 2:246/250 or 3:146, is linked with a huge generalization; in contrast, as reported above, the 9th again stressed the attempt to form a believers' religious identity, different from that of Jews and Christians (as reported above in referring to 9:30–31/36).

However, the ensuing verses finally argue about the *Tawbāh*, the pietistic act in asking God for a form of salvation even though for idolaters and hypocrites: the 9th *Sūrah* in 84, 112–118 on the one hand dismissed the obligation for Muḥammad to do it, but on the other hand, the Prophet, as Abraham before him, did not have to be blamed for having prayed for the disbelief of their ancestors as well as for the infidelity of their companions: 'God has relented towards the Prophet, and the emigrants and helpers who followed him in the hour of adversity when some hearts almost wavered. In the end He has relented towards them; He is most kind and merciful to them' (v. 117).

The interpretation is hard to investigate: the *Asbāb al-Nuzūl*, Ibn Khatīr's *Tafsīr* and other sources[62] stressed the Prophet's prayers for his uncle Abū Ṭālib, but it would be chronologically untenable, referring to it at the end of the Medinan period; even if Muḥammad would certainly have interceded for 'Alī's father, the believers are admonished to follow the example of Abraham, to whom the same verses seem to refer.

Considering the *Sīra an-Nabawiyya*, conversely, the death of the hypocrite Ibn Ubayy is differently contemplated by the sources. Ibn Isḥāq argues that the funerary prayer for him was led by the Prophet himself, with the clear opposition of figures such as 'Umar ibn al-Khaṭṭāb;[63] at the same time, the chronicle highlights how those verses

(9:84/113ff) which prevented praying for the hypocrites' souls reached the community after the Prophet's actions for Ibn Ubayy, while others argue the contrary. The Prophet's traditions argue about the fact that Ibn Ubayy was shrouded in a Prophet's mantle,[64] as well as, in referring to the same 'story', that God, afterwards, denied, through a revelation, praying at the funeral for a hypocrite.[65]

However, it would be quite shocking to hermeneutically interpret this passage as well as to admit that Muḥammad's mercy overcame that of God, in antithesis with the same *Basmala*.

Nevertheless *sūrah* 9 ends with a relational crackdown among the believers and those hypocrites and disbelievers who, while they continued to be linked through family to *mu'minīn*, act and behave differently; verse 123, the last, is directly correlated with warlike militantism, in asking to fight (*Qātilū*) 'the disbelievers near you and let them find you standing firm', which is also strategic advice in keeping the believers' military forces not so far away from Ḥijāz. It is clear indeed that the campaigns of conquest are not semantically considered by the Islamic revelation.

The last *sūrah* that will be analysed is the **fifth**. Nöldeke's and the Egyptian chronology argue differently about it, but both admit their temporal vicinity in relation to the Prophet's future biographies: if Bukhārī, Muslim, Ṭabarī and Bayḍāwī maintain that the 9th is the last, Tirmidhī, Zamakhsharī and Shūshāwī claim, that for some of its verses, the 5th is the last of the entire Revelation.[66]

As argued by Nöldeke,[67] the verses which positioned the *sūrah* in direct relation with the Farewell Pilgrimage and Muḥammad's biography are the first, in which the Prophet decreed some rules of how God made you lawful in continuity with the People of the Book (5:4–5) but also in showing your clear and higher affiliation to justice (5:8).

Independently of this digression, it is important to focus on whether the 5th sūrah can add anything relevant to our analysis on proto-Islamic militantism and *jihād*.[68] Unlike the 9th, which independently of 9:29, seems to be more active in fighting hypocrisy and unbelievers than the People of the Book, the 5th, from verse 12, begins a Biblical examination of Judaism and Christianity, starting from the *mithāq*, the pledge, previously signed by God.

The analysis is probably one of the most inter-religious Abrahamic examples of dialogical and theological confrontation in the Qur'ān, more focused on Judaism than on Christianity and it is not very violent, but clearly accused both of them of having incorrectly interpreted their revelations. The military attack against God and His Messenger (5:33) will certainly be counterbalanced, but, apart from it, most of the *sūrah* reflects on bringing information from Biblical or apocryphal Gospel sources which intend to better clarify the relationship that the Believers need to maintain with them. However, the relationship that the Believers can assume with them is quite complicated to frame easily.

1. The women of the People of the Book can marry Believers (v. 5), but Jews and Christians cannot be considered as allies, probably understood from the military-political aspect (v. 51ff); they include those who believe in God and the Last Judgement and do good deeds (v. 69); some of them are on the right course (v. 66), but many of them do very evil things (v. 66). Finally, the famous verse 82ff.

argues that the most hostile to the Believers are the Jews, probably in relation to the increasing conflict which emerged during the Medinan period, while 'you are sure to find that the closest in affection towards the believers are those who say, 'We are Christians', for there are among them people devoted to learning and ascetics'.
2. From the juridical-theological aspect, if the food of the People of the Book is also lawful for the Believers (v. 5), the deification of Jesus is a clear attempt on the unity of God (v. 17, 116ff.), as well as the disobedience of the Children of Israel: when Cain killed Abel committing fratricide (v. 27ff). However, God sent different messengers in the attempt to redeem his nations, since if 'God had so willed, He would have made you one community, but He wanted to test you through that which He has given you, so race to do Good' (v. 48) reflects God's will in preserving their differences. In parallel, verses 42ff. clarify another important assumption that every member of a community of the People of the Book needs to be judged in relation to their revelation of reference, using their main legal framework.[69]

It is obvious that this *sūrah* amply confirmed the intention to shape a new community of Believers, showing some relevant differences from the People of the Book as well as also emphasizing clear independence of them. However, two main aspects need to be considered:

1. The aggressive attitude against the People of the Book is univocally attributed to Jews, those who resided around the Believers' territories, following the conflicts that in Medina, Khaybar etc. caused increasing enmity among them. Verses 57ff. stressed when the Jews in Medina ridiculed the Believers' prayer for standing up during their *Ṣalāt*,[70] at the same time, verse 82 harshly accused the Jews of being the most hostile of the believers, unlike the Christians.
2. The existence of good people, Jewish, Sabians and Christians who believe in God and the Last Day (v.69), is strengthened in relation to the latter, in verses 82ff. when the Qur'anic message seems to exalt those Christians who, when encountering Muḥammad or a Believer, had kind words concerning their message: the Negus of Ethiopia, the monk Baḥīrā and many Christians mentioned by al-Wāhidī (d. 1075) and Ibn Abbas: a sort of delegation of more than seventy people.[71]

The presence of Christian dignitaries at the presentation of Muḥammad in Medina, after having submitted all the unbelievers of Ḥijāz, in the last months of his life, when different delegations reached the city of the Prophet,[72] remained only hypothetical and cannot be traced in any reliable historical sources.

Nevertheless, it is important to highlight that in the mentioned *sūrah*, although the prominent religious differences are stressed as well as both Jews and Christians are accused of having failed in the covenant with God, due to their behaviour and erratic theological assumptions, the level of violence against them remained limited, compared to the 9th.

Contrary to the previous one, the 5th is important to begin a process of distinguishing the religious identity between the People of the Book, even if the inconsistencies, in particular in relation to Christianity and the dogma of the Trinity, remained evident (v. 73ff., 116ff.).

The proto-Islamic belligerent attitude continued to be either defensive or still rooted in the pre-Islamic Arab practice of raid and pillage, which was commonly adopted during the war against Mecca and during the early conquering campaigns.

7

The evolutionary process of belligerency and the canonization of *Jihād* in early Islām

The evolutionary Qur'anic narrative was not able to contextualize, during the Medinan period, the figure of a Believer fighter on the way of God, in parallel with the absence of a precise canonization of the Pillars of Islām and the '*Aqīdah*. The information included in the Revelation was not sufficient to shape a *mujāhid* or to canonize the *jihād* into something that could be precisely identified.

The lack of a sacralization of the human fighter and his sanctification in warfare clearly emerged; however, it is important to outline here the main facets that arose in the Qur'ān and that with other external characteristics were able to shape a more precise figure of the Muslim fighter in the following centuries.

1. The *mujāhid*, first of all, needs to assume a clear *shahādah*, faith in God and in Muḥammad as the figure of reference in a new community. Considering the fact that the concept of Prophecy and the identification of Muḥammad as a Prophet is not clearly stated in the Revelation,[1] as it will not clearly appear in archaeological and epigraphic sources until the 690s, the main action which testified a strong intention to follow him was the *Hijra*, the emigration from Mecca to Medina, which meant abandoning the hometown, the clan, the family etc. for their belief in something. It is evident that all the early *muhajirūn*, who emigrated from 614 (the minor Hijra) and afterwards, performed an act of faith in Muḥammad's words.
2. The *mujāhid* is he who strives and is steadfast (*Ṣabr*) on the way of God (2:45, 246, 3:146, 200; 31:31), to which we can also add: '*bi'amwālihim wa 'anfusihim*' (8:72), which clarified other important qualities of this 'fighter'. The faith in Muḥammad's words needs to be shown with concrete actions which implied help through material things, but also the human being in its entirety: the body, blood, life, breath, but also the soul, the psyche, the essence. Being a *mujāhid* is a whole.
3. In parallel, the *mujāhid* can also be a militant fighter who bases his willingness to fight and kill unbelievers and polytheists in relation to some specific qualities: the struggle on the Way of God even during warfare, because *fitna (persecution) is more serious than killing* (2:191), *wa al-fitnatu ashaddu min al-qatli*. It is also being steadfast and determined not to be like the hypocrites, who are frightened of being involved in the expedition against their enemies (8:49; 9:38); being ready

to die as well as to show little attachment to the material goods of this Earth (8:28; 9:24, 34–35), even to family members that remained polytheists.

4. A *mujāhid*, independently of the context, is one who does not exceed the limits or the bounds (2:178; 5:87–88; 21:9; 44:30; 46:20 etc.) because God does not love those who exceed, as reported in the same revelation. This quality, which clearly also includes fighting (2:190), is attributable and needs to be considered by every person who wants to be a Believer and can be attributable to a *via media*, *wasaṭ*, which is particularly appreciated: 'We have made you Believers into a just community' (2:143), literally, a 'middle Nation' which means a moderate one.[2]

It is clear that all the above qualities, as important as they are for reaching salvation, are, at the same time, important in already being indicative of having gained a Paradisiac hereafter; however, the concrete absence of any reference to the fighter's sanctification is symptomatic of the lack of an initial relationship between the fighting and killing with religious sanctity.

If fighting has been prescribed to you (2:216), and even if some of the early Believers did not uniformly welcome this invitation, according to some verses dealing with fighting the unbelievers, on some occasions and in certain conditions, it is not only deserved but required.[3]

We have already addressed the defensive attitude of fighting as well as the reasons why the belligerent attitude towards an enemy is approved; however, when the Qur'ān exalts the *mujāhid* over all the other believers, it is rarely linked to warfare.

4:95 argues that the Believers who stayed at home are not equal to those who commit themselves and their possessions in striving in God's way; on the contrary, they are higher in rank (9:20); **9:88** also repeats that 'those who believe with the Prophet striving hard with their possession and persons, are those who the best things belong to'.

The conceptualization of witness, *shahīd*, as martyrs, in the case in which they are associated with the fighting (3:156–158, 169; 4:74) are exalted for their courage, but more specifically for the fact that will not be abandoned by God in the hereafter.[4] The fear of being forgotten and having strived on the way of God without any kind of compensation are very emblematic in the Islamic revelation and in a trading society still with its roots in orality.

However, between the probable canonization process of the Qur'ān under the Umayyad caliph 'Abd al-Malik (d. 705), the narrative exaltation of the Muslim fighter as a just warrior and the establishment of a frontier of an extended empire led by Muslim caliphs, there were two civil wars (*Fitnas*), which ended in 692.

In parallel, as reported in the historical part, the Arab Christian confederations – the Banū Kalb, but also the remaining Banū Ghassān, Balī, Judhām, Lakhm, Tanūkh and Bahrā' – assumed in this period of inner conflict between Arab-Believers a prominent political-military role, making a contribution to saving and preserving the Banū Umayyad's power as well as allowing them to reconquer it, in particular during the second *Fitna* (680–692).[5]

The impact of the events summarized above on the canonization of a just-warrior among the Believers was detrimental, because these previously supposed just-Believers killed one another during the *Fitnas*.

The behaviour of the companions of the Prophet himself after the killing of 'Uthmān, and before it, considering the Prophet's succession, denotes the importance of the clan-kinship interests in assuming political power and in leading the Ḥijāz and the Arabian Peninsula after its submission to Abū Bakr (*Ridda* wars).[6]

It is evident that Ibn al-Mubārak's interpretative task of the Muslim fighter[7] can be considered very distant from the litigious and irrespective framework that the early Believers after Muḥammad's death generally showed in this historical phase.

There are important aspects in contextualizing an Islamic narrative to be considered in highlighting this sense of immoral violence that during the *Fitnas* absorbed an early Believers' community still far from understanding the meaning of *Jihād*. This is also because if striving on the way of God in warfare was something presented in the Revelation, the *Fitnas* were civil wars between the companions of the Prophet. The violent death of so many of the Prophet's companions needed a solution in the clear attempt to save the unity of the early *Ummah* and its memory.

A first facet that we can find in the *ḥadīths* of the Prophet, but not in the Qur'ān, is the Prophet's intercession for the departed believers. If the verses in the Revelation are quite unoptimistic in decreeing a Prophetic intercession with God (2:48, 123, 254–255; 4:109; 39: 43–44 etc.), al-Tirmidhī in his *Sunan* even argues that Muḥammad said that the entrance can be through the intercession of one member of his community; the same author argues about a tradition reported by Anas ibn Mālik which attests: 'my intercession is for the people who commit the major sins in my *Ummah*'.[8] Abī Dawūd in his *Sunan*, considering a tradition reported by Mu'āwiya ibn Abī Sufyan, claims: 'The Messenger of Allāh said: If you make intercession, you will be rewarded', and Muslim and Bukhārī themselves narrate, respectively, in referring to the Prophet's traditions, that 'if a group of Muslims number one hundred pray over a dead person, all of them interceding for him, their intercession will be accepted'; 'some people will be taken out of the Fire through the intercession of Muhammad, they will enter Paradise and will be called Al-*Jahannamiyin* (the Hell Fire people)'.[9]

The more liberal attitude which emerged in recognizing a canonical tradition in attempting to save Believers' souls which ended in Hell can certainly be considered in relation to the increasingly violent attitude that fragmented them after the Prophet's death. The correlation between early apocalyptic *ḥadīths* and the phase of the civil wars has been highlighted by F. Donner[10]; however, it is evident that the topic of intercession, on which early Kalām debate among Mu'tazilite and Asharites authors will erupt in the following centuries, emerged as a significant topic after the internal fight among the remaining companions of the Prophet.

A second aspect to consider is the early version of Abū Ḥanīfa's *Fiqh Akbar*. The clear attempt to mitigate the political and religious schismatic attitude of the *Fitna*, as reported by Wensinck's analysis of articles 4 and 5 which affirm, respectively, 'We disavow none of the Companions of the Apostole of Allah; nor do we adhere to any of them exclusively; We leave the question of 'Uthmān and 'Alī to Allāh; nor do we adhere to any of them exclusively',[11] seems exemplary of the paradigmatic role that those civil wars played among the Believers.

Article one goes on to argue: 'We do not consider anyone to be an infidel on account of sin; nor do we deny his faith', which can be interpreted as a reaction to the violent praxis of the Khārijites 'Azāriqa-Ḥarūriyya in considering unbelievers those who did not agree with some of their theoretical approaches (*Muḥakkima*, *lā-ḥukmā illa li-llāh*). J. Wensinck determined how this early manuscript of the *Fiqh Akbar* could be dated around the middle of the eighth century, in relation to the dogmatic questions that emerged in the articles.[12] However, it is emblematic that the absence of any reference to warfare during this historical phase of conquering campaigns as well as the *Fitnas* meant that the religious canonization of war was far from being a priority.

In spite of this, it is evident that the eighth century is prominently linked to a process of establishing the Muslim Believers as fighters on the way of God in complete respect of the religious pillars; but after the main gains of the early Arab conquering campaigns, the same struggles were diminishing their success and were geographically addressed to the farthest border of an empire that was still expanding.

The Imām Mālik, in his *Muwaṭṭā'*, a collection probably produced in the second half of the eighth century, in relation to the *Jihād* argues: the *Mujāhid* on the way of God is comparable to one believer that fasts and offers nightly prayers permanently, until he comes back;[13] the following *Ḥadīth* (974–975) continued to link the fight on the way of God with a comparative approach in relation to the most important Islamic pillars while 978 is quietly strategic: 'O you who believe. Endure and be more patient and guard your territory by stationing army units permanently at the places from where the enemy can attack you, and fear Allah, so that you may be successful.'[14]

Few traditions in the collection are more explanatory of the necessary inner status of a fighter in being a *Mujāhid*: 'Shall I tell you about the person with the best status among people? It is a man pulling the rein of his horse to fight/strive on the way of Allah (*Rajul 'Ākhidun bi-'ināni farasihi yujāhidu fī sabīl Allāh*). Shall I tell you about the person of the best status following him among people? It is a man living alone with a few sheep, praying, paying Zakāt, worshipping Allah and associating none with Him.'[15]

This is quite emblematic for two reasons: 1. the tracing of a clear connection between the inner believer's feeling of unnervingly waiting to fight and the peaceful man who lives modestly and respects the pillars of Islām; 2. On a linguistic level, the Qur'anic word for fighting, *yuqātilu*, widely used in the entire revelation, has been substituted here by *yujāhidu*, more related to the concept of striving.

Aḥmad ibn Ḥanbal in his *Musnad* referring to traditions reported by 'Abd Allāh ibn 'Umar, one of the sons of the second rightly guided caliph, in questioning the Prophet about the *Jihād*, replied that striving on the way of God is only one of the eminent actions that a Believer can fulfil, and a second one reports that whoever takes part in the 'holy war' does it to his personal profit.[16]

Wensinck's interpretation of the absence of a real comprehension of *Jihād* in some versions of the tradition reflects on the historical fact that we are after the conquering campaigns: on the contrary those who exalted it are older because they are linked to the raids of the seventh century.

This clarification is doubtful as well as distant from the idea that the Believers started to form their own personal *mujāhid* religious identity before being able to explain the Islamic pillars and their *'Aqīdah*. The same author, in analysing the *Fiqh Akhbar I*, denotes the attempt to dismantle the reasons why the community became divided, causing inner *Fitnas*.

Al-Bukhārī in his *Saḥīḥ* (book 56) reports an interesting combination of definitions of *Jihād*, in which striving on the way of God is related to an Islamic historical narrative and to religious definitions without a clear attribution.

The famous: 'O Allah's Messenger, what is the best action? He replied: To offer the prayers at the fixed time; I asked: What is next', He replied: To be good and dutiful to your parents. 'I further asked, what is next in goodness? He replied: To strive in Allah's Cause. I did not ask Allah's Messenger anymore but if I had asked him more, he would have told me more'[17] is in continuity with: 'The Prophet said: Whoever believes in Allah and His Messenger, offers prayer and fasts the month of Ramaḍān, will rightfully be granted Paradise, no matter whether he fights in Allah's Cause or remains in the land where he is born.'

The people said: 'O Allah's Messenger! Shall we preach to the people?' He said, 'Paradise has one-hundred grades which Allah has reserved for the *Mujāhidīn* who fight in His Cause, and the distance between each of two ranks is like the distance between the Heaven and the Earth. So, when you ask Allah (for something), ask for Al-Firdaus which is the best and highest part of Paradise'; 'I think the Prophet also said, 'Above it (Al-Firdaus) is the Throne of Beneficent (Allah), and from it originate the rivers of Paradise.'[18]

These *'aḥādīth* stressed how the *Mujāhid* is not a normal Believer who basically follows the pillars of Islām and to whom access to Paradise can be guaranteed, even only for his keeping to the normal Islamic praxis; striving on the God's way is a plural aspect of being a Muslim and there is a wide level of ranking, to ensure the right place for all of them.

Finally, Bukhārī grants, in continuity with the Imām Mālik, a different status to the fighters on the way of God and those who fight for the spoils or for themselves. 'A man came to the Prophet and asked: a man fights for war booty; another fights for fame and a third one fights for showing off, which of them fights in Allah's Cause?' The Prophet replied: 'Who fights for the God's word to be above all things, he is on the way of God.'[19]

The Islamic tradition, in this brief excursus, was able to determine the concrete inner qualities of the *Mujāhid* from the end of the ninth century, but also to make a clear distinction between normal warfare and the 'Just war' which unlike the former needs to respect important facets, as argued by Muslim: not to embezzle the spoils, not to be disloyal, not to mutilate the dead bodies, not to kill children.[20]

This normativity was certainly marked by a belligerent literature that from the second half of the eighth century concerned the 'Abbāsid empire and is based on various *Siyar* and related texts[21] and, in parallel, on the early narrative of the conquests, elaborating for the first time the figure of the just Muslim fighter and canonizing the attitude to assume its going into battle.

However, an important distinction persists to be better analysed: the difference between the status of the *Mujāhid* who strive on the way of God, specifically when he fights, and the general conceptualization of a belligerent attitude that as much as moral is usually based on the clear evidence of killing another human being during war.

Establishing indeed the further divergence between the canonization of the just Fighter and the just War, and the holy War as well as the holy Fighter in Islām, it should be the best way to definitively understand the final goal of this work.

For this reason, if in the *Siyar* and the *Futūḥ* literatures there is the intentional attempt to establish an early Islamic narrative rooted in the superior morality of the early companions and conquerors,[22] Ibn Mubārak's efforts at describing the Muslim *mujāhid* through an ascetic *spectrum* gave prominent importance to making him Just, if not Saintly.

Conversely, the correlation between the *Siyar* literature and Mubārak's *Kitāb al-Jihād* is the successful attempt to make the past wars and the present ones continuous through a sense of justice and spirituality that remained amalgamated. In parallel, when the Arab conquests had ended, the frontiers were solidly established and the historical enemies had been identified, the enlistment in the army remained a priority. To analyse the *Siyar* and the *mujāhid* would be important to definitively focus on the canonization process of the Just War in early Islām after having already identified above that of the *Mujāhid* in the Qur'ān.

If the above hypothesis is correct, the main difference between a just War and a War in early Islām, besides the fact of having to be considered 'defensive', is linked to the moral level of justice of the *mujāhidīn* who fought it and the rules 'of engagement' on which it is based.

Fazārī's Just war and Shaybānī's are clearly based on conduct which affects combatants against other combatants without involving civilians, women and children, contrary to the indiscriminate killing that involved some Khārijite sects at the end of the seventh and the beginning of the eighth centuries.

This conduct, which includes the prohibition of mutilation, has to be applied to every woman and child independently of their religious affiliation. The main reason, explained through a *Ḥadīth*, by al-Fazārī, is that every newborn is part of *'alā -l-fiṭra*, until their parents make them a Jew, a Christian or a Muslim.[23]

In relation to the People of the Book and as confirmation of the presence of military forces which were not part of the Believers from the beginning, al- Fazārī defined them *ahl al-'ahd* (the people of the treaty) or *ahl al-dhimma*, in the event that there was absolute certainty that they were Jews or Christians. Muranyi's article on Fazārī's *Siyar*, quoting the early generation of Umayyad Muslim juridical figures and intellectuals such as Ibn Shihāb al-Zuhrī (d. 742), and the Syrian jurist al-Awzā'ī (d. 773), argued that their enrolment in the army was recognized in the same way as that of a Believer.[24]

Even though there are different narratives that are directly attributed to the second Rightly Guided Caliphs that maintain how the People of the Book could not be involved in sharing the booty, other stories reported from the prophetic phase confirm the contrary.

It is evident that until the eighth century, the egalitarian distribution of the booty in the army could also involve *ahl al-Kitāb* soldiers who, in reference to the role played by the Kalbites in the early decades of the Umayyad caliphate, continued to keep some prerogatives in this sense.[25] This inclusive attitude still persists in al-Shaybāni's *Siyar*, in the juridical section on the help of 'rebels' who fight with Muslims against Unbelievers, when it says that the booty can be divided with them, in the case of victory.[26]

At the same time, Shaybāni's text in the evolutionary analysis of the *Siyar* literature is particularly interesting in showing the importance of respecting the religious status of the conquered as well as of those who decide to convert, even if not to Islām; it is important to consider that the house, property and family of an unbeliever, whose territory has been conquered by Muslims and who then decides to convert to Islām, have to be preserved and respected.[27]

At the same time, Shaybāni's narrative binds every agreement with the *Dhimmīs* to what was decreed by 'Umar ibn al-Khaṭṭāb or by Abū Ḥanīfa, if traditions on a specific topic are not attributed to the former.

For example, Abū Ḥanīfa, unlike other jurists, considers the poll tax of the *Dhimmī* a yearly one that cannot be accumulated as debt if it cannot be paid for some years.[28]

This text, more than focused on the moral rules in warfare, defined a preliminary legislation of the relations among the nations after the Muslims conquered a territory; in the meantime, the treatises on warfare assumed in parallel a more strategic understanding in confirming the prohibition of killing civilians but also religious figures, committing treachery and mutilation. Al-Fazārī focuses on the destruction of the enemies' property which for strategic-military reasons started as being approved, although in contrast with some traditions attributed to the first two rightly guided caliphs.[29]

Another change by Shaybāni concerns the need for non-Muslims in the Army, a significant argument previously mentioned, which seems to vanish during the golden age of the 'Abbāsid empire. This aspect that emphasized the increasingly Islamic identity of the empire must also be associated with the ample reforms which impacted the army under the Caliphs al-Ma'mūn (d. 833) and al-Mu'taṣim (d. 842):[30] the need for non-Muslims in it seems to have been abandoned and juridically disapproved.[31]

Moving on from the ninth century, the canonization of *Jihād* as a general attitude of warfare, a general obligation (*farḍ al-Jihād 'ammān*) and an individual duty,[32] needs to be linked with a general 'professionalization' of the caliphate's armies, with an increasing number of Turko-Iranian soldiers coming from Khorāsān, Sind and other far-flung regions, and soldiers who had recently converted to Islām.

In the same historical period as Shaybāni, Abū Yūsuf al-Anṣārī (d. 798) in his *Kitāb al-Kharāf*,[33] a juridical treaty on taxation, assumed a more evident approval of those who convert to Islām to keep their property and possessions.

Muslim behaviour in war against other Arab polytheists needs to be mitigated in relation to their possible intention to convert; in parallel, the Arabs who are Jews and Christians have to be considered as non-Arabs and the poll tax must be imposed on the males only; on the contrary, the Arab or non-Arab idolaters only have the choice between converting to Islām or death, because they are not liable for the poll tax.[34]

The process of structuring a civil society in the Caliphate was clearly assuming a religious identification as its prominent characteristic.

It was with al-Shāfi'ī (d. 820) that the meaning of *Jihād* was to assume the focus on warfare, as a duty for every man able to perform it,[35] adopting a comparative semantic parallelism between *Jihād*, to fight and to kill. Nevertheless, if fighting and killing are univocally identified with *q-t-l* in the Islamic Revelation,[36] al-Shāfi'ī interprets it in the context of the fight against the unbelievers:

> I shall continue to fight the unbelievers until they say: 'There is no god but God,' if they make this pronouncement, they shall be secured their blood and property, unless taken for its price, and their reward shall be given by God.[37]

The *Risāla* updates the legislation on warfare stressing the behaviour of the fighter during his duty and concerns the prohibition on killing women and children, even if they are unbelievers.[38] Alongside this, the killing of a believer by mistake has to be redeemed by the payment of the *diya* if it happens in Islamic territory, while, on the contrary, if it occurs outside the *Dār al-Islām*, personal religious redemption cannot be supported by the monetary one.[39]

The inter-connection of these two parts seems quite interesting in stressing the differences between the religious attitude and the more practical one, even though both remained subject to fighting the unbelievers (not the People of the Book), as reported in the Qur'ān itself.

Jihād is, for al-Shāfi'ī, a collective duty, even though it is the individual *mujāhid* who does it, taking on a higher status in the afterlife; in spite of this, to go into battle is not obligatory; 'Alī Ibn Abū Ṭālib did not take part in the expedition of Tabūk, as many companions did not take part in that of Ḥunayn; at the same time, the fulfilment of this duty has to be performed by a sufficient number of people so as not to put the entire community at risk.[40]

Shāfi'ī compares *jihād* with the funeral and the burial prayers: both have to be performed, but it is not obligatory for all believers to attend them, also because it may be impossible for them.[41]

Jihād is thus becoming synonymous with a professional activity of warfare in a caliphate army.

To conclude, this brief excursus has to end with al-Māwardī and his *al-Aḥkām al-Sulṭāniyya wa al-wilāyāt al-dīniyya*,[42] which in a different historical period assumed a further canonization of the relationship between *jihād* and war, even though only two aspects are directly considered: the 'Amirate of War' on the leadership of the army, and the legislation on war in relation to booty, negotiations etc.

It is evident that warfare has become an official state/Caliphate-Vizierate affair.

The army has to be considered as made up of regular fighters and volunteers; the latter are 'those from the desert areas, the Arabs and other inhabitants of the towns and villages who have left for battle in accordance with Allah's instructions, may He be exalted, to people, "Go out [to battle] light and heavy and fight with your wealth and your selves in the way of Allah" (Q. 9: 41)', and that are paid from the *Zakāt* and not from the *Fay'* as they did not receive a stipend *'aṭā'*.[43] We will return to the volunteers later.

Al-Māwardī identified the characteristics of the *mujāhidīn* in relation to the Qur'anic narrative, but also to the obligations of the leaders: the former are identified as being steadfast (8:66), not to retire and not being over-rational because this could lead to over-estimating the enemy's forces; the soldier needs to fight to support the religion of Allah, defeating his enemies, and must not be over-concentrated on the future booty as the economic reasons that make him a *mujāhid*.

> Each combatant should fulfil the trust (accorded him by Allah) regarding the booty which has come to him, and that none of them should take anything from it until it has been shared amongst all those entitled to the booty: that is, those who participated in the battle and were of assistance against the enemy, as each has a claim to it.[44]

Lastly, he should not show preferential treatment towards a relative from the *mushrikūn*, or show partiality towards a friend, when having to uphold the religion of Allah (against them), for surely Allah's right is more binding, and upholding His religion is more incumbent.[45]

If it is clear that the comparative approach with fighting during the prophetic phase is still the official basis of reference with enriching narrative examples that referred to Badr, Uḥūd, Ḥunayn etc. as well as identifying the Believers' enemies (the *mushrikūn*), the same is supplemented by the ongoing canonizing *Sunna*, which referred to the prohibition of killing women and children,[46] but also more general rules related to the 'direction of war', as performed by a state or a caliphate.

Those who denied the Islamic call, refusing it and taking up arms against it (the Islamic defensive attitude still persists, at least on paper) need to be fought; on the contrary, those who reside beyond the Turks and the Romans that we are fighting now (in the period of al-Māwardī), and are not aware of the Islamic invitation to accept the Prophet's message, cannot be fought or attacked because they are unaware of the religion of Allah.[47]

This analysis continues through the identification of the other groups against whom the Believers are allowed to perform *Jihād*: the renegates of Islām, the rebels, such as the Khāwarij and the bandits, that although born Muslims did not accept the local or central authority. The absence of the People of the Book stressed the conviction that when they had been fought back, it was always because they started the fight first.[48]

Independently of historical accuracy, the canonization of the *Jihād* in a juridical and religious *spectrum* of warfare reached a more definitive understanding with the tenth–eleventh centuries.

It is important to emphasize that we will not have a juridical moral base for warfare until the decades which fixed the borders and an updated religious geographical understanding is established, associated with the professionalization of the army.

The historical evolution of proto-Islamic conquests, which ended in the first half of the eighth century, will not only mean the need for a frontier imposed as an armed one,[49] but for a process to build up the Islamic identity in defining the conquered territories in relation to the new political rulers. However, it is important to highlight how until the ninth–tenth centuries and for Palestine and Syria until the eleventh–twelfth centuries, the majority of the 'conquered' population was not yet converted to Islām, debunking *de facto* the meanings of *Dār al-Islām* vs. *Dār al-Ḥarb*.[50] Contemporary debate on the one hand assumes[51] that the 'Prophet Muḥammad himself in performing the *Hijra*[52] came out from a space to enter another one' in a sort of fixed rigidity and antithetic to the awareness of Donner, Hoyland and Ch. Robinson on the early 'Islamic' century. Villano and Vercellin wonder about a 'narrative' of contrast but that will not emerge until the time of Ṭabarī, in recognizing *de facto* the *Dār al-Islām* vs. *Dār al-Kufr* as a clear juxtaposition and with the *Dār al-Ḥarb* not as a synonym, but as a consequence.

Nevertheless, the community of early 'believers' was probably so morally plural that to consider the *Hijra* from the beginning with such a 'strong' religious emphasis in a society that was still Bedouin, in which everyone usually emigrated for different reasons, could be a historical and conceptual hazard.

At the same time, in a Believers' community led by the Banū Umayya, who never performed the *Hijra* as described in the Islamic tradition, but clearly emigrated and conquered Syria and Palestine, the religious conceptualization of the *Hijra* would also have been absurd.

It is clear, on the contrary, that the ninth-century Islamic narrative, which wanted to emphasize the *Hijra* praxis, as well as describe Muḥammad's companions, from the beginning, as already Muslims, was more important in Islamic society.

On the contrary, the end of the Arab conquering campaigns (first half of the 8th century), as well as the establishment of the different militarized borders in Anatolia, the Khorāsān region and northern Spain, clarified a political-military need, strongly dissociated from the inter-religious, plural and still Islamic minority status which affected these geographies,[53] even though politically led by new Muslim authorities in a hierarchical Caliphate structure.

There is a clear dissociation from assuming a terminology such as *Dār al-Islām/Dār al-Ḥarb* at the end of the ninth century or the beginning of the tenth and giving them a religious meaning from a more general *arḍ al-muslimīn/arḍ al-ʿaduww* (the land of believers/the land of enemies) point of view, without a clear religious identification.

In the second half of the eighth century, the literature analysed above is still reluctant to make a religious parallelism between *Dār al-Kufr* and *Dār al-Ḥarb*; at the same time, the same literature did not properly allow fighting against the *Ahl al-Kitāb*, even if in the Prophet's biography and in the Qur'anic verses, fighting against the Jews of Medina is a well-known 'story' and, on the historic side, so are the conquering campaigns against the Christian Byzantines.

If we consider the Imām Mālik's *Kitāb al-Jihād* in the *Muwaṭṭā'*, we can encounter the persuasion of being involved in the *Jihād*, some traditions on the martyrdom and many more on booty, but nothing about Christians and Jews, that on the contrary are rarely named in the entire text, except in relation to the payment of the *jizya*.[54] In addition, if we consider Shaybānī's *Kitāb al-Siyar*, the enemies of reference are the unbelievers as well as the polytheists, but even if a *Rūm* can be ransomed, his religious affiliation is never clarified.[55]

On the contrary, the tradition that the *Sawād* region is mostly populated by *Dhimmīs* (Arabs probably) is underlined,[56] as well as the help given by the Jews of the Banū Qaynuqāʿ against the Jews of the Banū Qurayza.[57]

This last aspect, in addition to 'If a Dhimmī took part in the fighting on the side of the Muslims at their request (of the Muslims), do you think that he would entitled to a share of the spoil? No, but he would be entitled to compensation',[58] emerged as particularly significant in establishing that probably, even at the end of the eighth century, the impossibility of defining the *dhimmīs* as unbelievers or polytheists was not only associated with what emerged in the Qur'ān, on both the positive and the negative side, but also that some of them were still fighting in the ʿAbbāsid army.

This emblematic step was to be confirmed by al-Shāfiʿī's *Risāla*, in dividing mankind, before the advent of Muḥammad, into two groups: the *Ahl al-Kitāb*, whose revelations had been mixed with forgeries and misbelief, and those who did not believe in God and created something that God did not permit.[59]

It is paradigmatic how early Islamic jurisprudence, even after having decreed the existence of a border when the Arab conquering campaigns began to fail, attributed to the first huge defeats by Carolingians and Byzantines (the second siege of Constantinople in 717 AD, but also the battle of Akronion in 740 AD), had some problems in defining the Believers' enemy.

The consolidation of a frontier became a political-strategic need on which many authors have already spent time[60] and on which a new 'narrative' was shaped in close connection with the creation of a nearly Islamic religious identity.

However, the early *Siyar* literature continued to abide by the Qur'anic division between *believers* and *unbelievers/polytheists*, making ongoing frontier wars against the Byzantine empire evidently Christian, but without saying so.

The establishment of a frontier, in fact, like the increasing number of *mutaṭawwi'ūn* who performed their personal *hijra* at the *thughūr*, did not eliminate the presence of *dhimmīs* in the 'Abbāsid empire who, paying the *jizya* or not, continued to be protected in relation to what the law decreed about them. The great distinction that was made in the eighth century between the *mutaṭawwi'ūn* and the normal soldiers (*ghāzī, murābiṭūn, jundī, 'askarī*) clearly reflects on the original conceptualization about the meaning of *jihād*, as well as on the evolutionary status of the Army.[61]

If with the *Siyar* and *Maghāzī* literature, the process of standardization of the meaning of war with *jihād* reached a paradigmatic changeover, in spite of the Qur'anic terms of *q-t-l* and *ḥ-r-b*, there are still some sources that were able to mark this difference, to show how the original *mujāhid* differently interpreted his engagement in warfare from a stipendary soldier.

The *Chronicle of 1234* is a non-Islamic source that identified the existence of a small group of volunteers (around 3000) in the last Umayyad campaign to conquer Constantinople in 715–717[62] led by Maslama ibn 'Abd al-Malik (d. 738) during the caliphate of Sulaymān ibn 'Abd al-Malik (d. 717). The same information is confirmed in the Chronicle of Michael the Syrian,[63] and in the *Chronographie* of Gregory Bar Hebraeus, who, like the former, numbered those who fought without being in the official army at 30000, as already reported.[64]

If this last number cannot be confirmed in earlier sources, the *Chronicle of 1234*, which seems to be quite close to Theophilus of Edessa's one, argues that those 3000 volunteers were all Arabs, but unemployed and without belongings, in the sense that they were not paid by the army or by financial sponsors of the same.

Theophilus and the *Chronicle of 1234* claim that the army was supported by many Arab financiers 'who had provided mounts for the troops on the basis of hire or sale in the hope of being recompensed from the booty to be got out of the imperial city'. The last are those who without assuming a warfaring posture, as argued in the Qur'ān, concretely supported with their 'possessions' the expedition and the army.

On the Islamic side, the sources which argued about Constantinople's siege are not so consistent about the composition of the army and cannot give us a more clear understanding of these 3000 volunteers.[65] However, al-Ṭabarī, very close to the 715–717 expedition against Constantinople, writes about the presence of volunteers in the conquest of Jurjān and Ṭabaristān,[66] as well as the existence of those *mutaṭawwi'ūna* groups during the campaign of 'Ubaydallāh ibn Abī Bakrah in Sijistān around 698–699.

This military expedition is historically recorded as a disaster as Ṭabarī and Balādhurī emphasized; at a time close to the defeat, Ibn Abī Bakrah called for 'People of Islam! Those of you who wish for martyrdom, come to me! A few of the volunteers followed him, and some of the horsemen in the army and some of the more dedicated. They fought until all, but a few were cut down'.[67]

If it is only hypothetical to assume that those 3000 *mutaṭawwiʿūn* were the early *mujāhidīn* who fought against the Byzantine, establishing the primary values of a real fighter on the way of God, this parallelism is possible.[68]

The term *mutaṭawwiʿa* is Qur'anic, but quite rare in the Islamic revelation: it appears only three times: 3:158 (*man taṭawwaʿ*); 3:184 (*faman taṭawwaʿ*); 9:79 (*Al-Ladhīna Yalmizūna al-Muṭṭawwiʿīna mina al-Muʿminīna fī aṣ- Ṣadaqāti* [...]).

In parallel, its use cannot be considered as directly associated with warfare, contrary to what C.E. Bosworth argued in the *Encyclopaedia of Islam*, but more generally to those believers who gave (all things and their time, efforts) gratuitously without claiming anything in return.

It was al-Samʿānī in the *Kitāb al-Ansāb* who defined those early volunteers as 'a group who devote themselves to *ghazw* and *jihād,* station themselves in *ribāṭs* along the frontier *(thughūr)* and who go beyond the call of duty *(taṭawwaʿū)* in *ghazw* and undertake this last in the lands of unbelief when it is not incumbent upon them nor is an obvious institution in their land'.[69]

Nevertheless, the parallelism between *mujāhid* and *mutaṭawwiʿa* cannot easily be assumed from the beginning, even though P. Crone's hypothesis that those volunteers, without pay or rations, could be non-Arab *mawālī* seems quite doubtful.

Crone's narrative assumed that those volunteers personally wanted to fight in the army to switch from being 'tax-payers' to 'tax-recipients'. Conversely, this option seems greatly in contrast with a distant *topos*, already rooted in the Qur'ān, in which a part of the Believers of the age to fight, Arabs or not, were not so greatly committed to being enlisted in the army, but found a military substitute (*jaʿāʾil*) for themselves and their male sons.[70]

This practice, already in use since the early Umayyad age, was probably adopted in the fighting against the Khārijites, but in particular with the end of the second *Fitna* and the reorganization of the army under Caliph ʿAbd al-Malik (d. 705).[71] All those substitutes would not have assumed the status of volunteers, but regular forces of the army. It is chronologically evident that only after ʿAbd al-Malik's victory against the centrifugal forces of the early community, in parallel with a clearer canonization of the Qur'ān, the *mutaṭawwiʿūna* emerged as the concrete personification of those who fought on the way of God in battle and afterwards enlisted at the frontier in defence of *Dār al-Islām*.

A last aspect has to be discussed in relation to this excursus on the origin of the 'fighter/the one who militarily strives on the way of God'. As reported by Sizgorich, the life of the predecessors can be of inspiration concurrently with the need to establish for the first time a Believer capable of sharing and developing an ethical stance based on piety and military effort.

The existence of *volunteers* as linked to the military campaigns after the end of the second *Fitna* also needs to consider the amalgamation of the previous Arab Christian clans in the Umayyad army (Ghassān and Kalbite, in particular), bringing their previous religious identification of the just war.

This step, clearly hard to prove due to the absence of sources that could confirm it directly, is based on the logical stage which has emerged in different interdisciplinary works,[72] to which significant passages from different primary sources correspond.[73]

If Irfan Shahid, in *Byzantium and the Arabs in the Sixth century*, has been able to frame the history but also the Christian religiosity of the Arab confederation of the Levant,[74] it is plausible that the non-urbanized *humus* of the geographic regions, which extended from *Dūmat al-Jandal*, the Sawād, to the Jazīra (upper Mesopotamia), Palestine and Syria included, was based on an Arab non-Chalcedonian Christianity established by monasteries, local religious communities: a coenobitic *spectrum* as we have already seen in the first part.

The hermeneutical passage from the Arab Christian narrative based on the saints' lives, higher morality and ascetism remained impressed in the Islamic narrative, regarding the link between monasticism and *jihād*.

The *Ribāṭ* became an updated geography in which to establish a personal *hijra*, as the figure of a volunteer of *jihād*.

If we identified the figure as Rawḥ ibn Zinbā' al-Judhāmī (d. *c.* 702–703), Umayyad governor of Palestine (from the Arab Christian clan of the Banū Judhām), as an early version of a 'volunteer fighter', we also need to assume the 'believers" adoption of a belligerent attitude which originally came from an Arab Christian *milieu*.[75]

The trivial belief of the easiness and rapid conversion to something that we can call Islām by members of Arab Christian clans in the second half of the seventh century has already been considered as problematic in relation to the absence of a more concrete understanding of what those 'Believers' believed.

However, which qualities made the *mujāhid* like the *mutaṭawwi'a*, just warriors?

- As for the *Imitatio Christi*, the *mujāhid* expresses an *Imitation Muḥammadi* through a *Hijra* which took him far from where he was born, for personal and coherent reasons of choice, without any assurance in relation to his life, property and family. The *mujāhid*, in this case, states an absolute confidence in God and his transcendence.[76]
- The main difference of the *Siyar* literature in comparison with Ibn al-Mubārak's identification of *Jihād* is the reflection on the importance of the *niyya* (personal inner intention) and the state (*ḥāl*) of the believer, without mentioning a divine reward (*ajr*). In other words, and unlike stipendiary soldiers, the rhetorical emphasis on the lack of concentration on the divine *ajr* does not need to be considered because God's rewards are from God and Allah only.[77] In the end, our final and sincere intention may be known by God only. No religious figure must have the control over the inner behaviour of a genuine *mujāhid*.
- The *mutaṭawwi'a* fighters are those who avoid corruption, share all they have with their companions as well as fighting without misbehaviour because through their actions they try to purify their hearts.[78]
- The *mujāhid* has no fear of poverty because he is confident that all his needs will be provided by God himself.[79] This was unlike soldiers enlisted through an *'aṭā'*,

which clearly coincided with the Qur'anic meaning of *taṭawwiʿa*, independently of the military context.
- Making God the one who decrees the end of the *mujāhid*'s life, which is clearly different from seeking martyrdom, because it is linked more closely to the ascetic manifestation of piety (*Sawāb* in *Taqwā*): showing again full confidence in God's plan for him.[80]

The above qualities are imbued with ascetic piety, full confidence in God, personal intention and rejection of materialism: all these qualities are very close to every monastic order.

'Every community has its monasticism, and the monasticism of my community is *jihād* in the path of God', but also: 'Roving monasticism was mentioned in front of the Prophet: The Prophet said: God gave us in its stead *jihād* on his path and *takbīr* on every hill'.[81]

The evidence of the impact of Christian monasticism on Islām as more generally understood is a vast subject; however, it is therefore important to emphasize how the personal qualities of the *mujāhid* are very close to those of the monk: 'A traditionalist said: "I prescribed for you that you should be strong in God, for he is the head of everything, and I prescribed for your *jihād,* for it is the monasticism of Islam. I prescribe for you silence except speaking truthfully, and you shall vanquish Satan by the means of it."'[82]

It would be trivial not to also consider the early Islamic narrative against Christian monasticism, which from the Qur'ān verse (9:31, 34) accused those people of religions of making innovations and inventing aspects which were not included in the scripture.[83] In parallel, the Islamic revelation itself in 5:82–83 argues that the closest to the believers are the Christians, and among them the devoted learners and ascetics (*Ruhbānāan wa 'Annahum*).

The hermeneutical task is clearly problematic, also because one of the two terms used in 9:31–34 to define the Christian monks is the same (*Ruhbānahum*/*ar-Ruhbāni*) as the one adopted in 5:82.

The semantic context on the contrary is clearly different: in the *Sūrah al-Tawbah*, the rabbis and the monks are accused of establishing polytheists' practices as well as consuming people's possessions, antithetically to the narrative which imagined them as poor and far from materialism.

In the *Sūrah al-Māʾidah*, on the contrary, they are exalted as being without pride, pietistic like witnesses of the 'Believers'' revelation. This is clearly in continuity with the Islamic *topos*, related to Christian figures such as the Monk Baḥīrā, Waraqa ibn Nawfal, the Negus of Abyssinia and even Emperor Heraclius.

Antithetically to Feryal Salem's position against Sizgorich Th. as well as Ofer Livne-Kafri's analogies between Christian monasticism, early Islamic ascetism, the *zuhd* and Ibn al-Mubārak's attitude to warfare, the theoretical connection would be more difficult without Irfan Shahid's works on Arab-Christianization since the fourth century.[84]

Arab Christian confederations, which played a significant role as *Foederati* for Byzantium and the Sasanid empires for at least a couple of centuries, are the paradigmatic actors in which the coincidence of a Christianization process, the establishment of a church-monastic Arab non-Chalcedonian *apparatus* is still today archaeologically and epigraphically evident,[85] in parallel with the creation of a religious war-based narrative linked to figures such as St Sergius, Cosmas and Damian as well as St Simeon the Younger and St Julian, who were usually prayed to for military victories and honoured after it was obtained.[86]

At the same time, it would also be important to think that Ibn al-Mubārak's renunciant tradition[87] cannot be univocally associated with a belligerent *jihād* attitude but, as already emerged from the beginning of the eighth century, in the early Islamic mystical tradition, from Ḥasan al-Baṣrī (d. 728) onwards.[88]

In considering Ibn al-Mubārak in his entirety, we cannot distinguish his *jihād* from his *zuhd*, not making these two terms synonymous, but taking them as inherently linked to each other because *jihād* without *zuhd* could easily be considered as an effort without the spiritual goals obtained through purity, while a *zuhd* without *jihād* would mean that you have already reached God's truth (*ḥaqq*).

If Ibn al-Mubārak grew up in a merchant *humus*, his personal efforts in developing his renunciant theology were certainly harder due to the intrinsic materiality of his cultural background. Nevertheless, the peculiarity of Ibn al-Mubārak's *jihād* and *zuhd*, as already shown by M. Bonner, is also emblematically different from the *Siyar* and *Maghāzī*, because it is more univocally focused on the quality of the *mujāhid*,[89] who needs, as a primary aspect, to be righteous and abandoned to God.

Conclusions

The cliché which depicts Islām and its Prophet's life as inextricably rooted in a form of religious violence is an ideological posture which has nothing to do with scientific investigation.

Although some Qur'anic verses are violent, their contextualisation recalibrates their intensity. Simultaneously, the Prophetic phase (622–632) even considering some 'battles', from Badr to Ḥunayn, fades if compared with the Roman-Persian wars, and their religious narratives in the same century.

Muḥammad's main enemies were the Arab Meccan polytheists, but unlike the sack of Troy by Achea, or that of Jerusalem by the Christian crusaders in 1099, the Prophet peacefully entered his hometown without bloodshed.

Concurrently, Ibn al-Mubārak's *Kitāb al-Jihād,* seems to describe in great detail how many early Arab unbelievers, after their conversion to Islām, automatically showed their over-zealous attitude as *mujāhdīn,*[1] in exalting their faith in the Prophet as well as in the new religion.

The case of 'Amr ibn al-'Āṣ and his brother Hishām (who died at Yarmuk) is emblematic in showing how faith can change your previous life decisions. Ibn al-Mubārak is particularly centred on re-framing some stories without avoiding criticism of the Umayyad and some of its figures: 'Abd al-'Azīz ibn Marwān (d. 705) or 'Abdallāh ibn 'Abd al-Malik (d. 750), accusing both of them of not trusting God.[2]

Nevertheless, this narrative, in the attempt to categorise the early 'Believers' as already being Muslims, as well as ethically and morally superior to any other correligionaries or enemies, is a common *topos* that will be abundantly adopted in the first 'Abbāsid period in depicting the behaviour of the Prophet's early companions.

This peculiarity highlights a 'utopian' vision clearly antithetic to the *Fitnas* and the inter-clanic conflict which emerged after the Prophet's death; in parallel, the presence of a just Muslim warrior that existed from the beginning will continue to hold a significant attraction for many centuries of Islamic history, until contemporary historical events recalibrated the relationship between military victory and a moral fighting standard (*jihadism*).[3]

This conclusion would like to resume the main aspects that emerged in this study in the clear tentative to give the possibility to reflect on the sacralization of violence in early Islām. However, all the following details are indebted to the preliminary assumption that the 'creation' of a new religion, a new faith and *credo* is not immediate, but gradual independently from the means of communication adopted by the early disciples and followers. The orality of a message can help the speeding up expansion of the new doctrine, but afterwards are the written words that are able to fix the new message and the differences from the previous ones.

According to it, the idea that the Arab confederations conquest of Mesopotamia, Syria, Palestine and Egypt was directly linked to the early canonization of war within Islām, which gave to the Muslims armies an unbeatable incentive to defeat the Byzantines and Sasanias empires, it is a narrative rooted on a historical *topos* framed in the early 'Abbasid age.[4]

The main reasons connected with this theoretical framework are two-dimensional and related to historical and religious-Quranic purposes. The former is linked to overthrowing late antiquity in relation to the early Islamic age, the second, to the canonization's process of a new religious revelation that until the first half of the eight century was still confused as a Christian heresy.[5]

The historical approach, as reported in the Introduction, needs to consider in parallel the end of the Western Roman empire (476 DC) as quite exemplary to the empowering of those *foederati* forces which played an increasing military task since the fifth century: the Arab confederations. As the Germans romanization process, started since the second century DC, impacting on its western side, in particular after the emigrating pressure of new populations coming from the *steppe*; the population of the Arab peninsula, emigrated in the north direction as the contrary since Antiquity, but only in the seventh century, for a short time, was able to coordinate a conquest that annihiliated the Sasanians and conquered Syria, Palestine and Egypt.

As for the western Roman empire were the romanized "barbarians" and their generals who preserved for at least a couple of centuries Rome's western borders, framing, afterwards, the early Roman-Barbarians new kingdoms of late antiquity: the Ostrogoths in Italy, the Vandans in North Africa, the Visigoths in the Iberian Peninsula, the Burgundians and the Franks etc.[6] Not so differently, were the Arab Christianized confederation of the North of Arabia who preserved the eastern Roman Empire borders in the fight against its historical enemy: the Persian empire, who in parallel used other Arab confederations to fight back. Only, afterwards, the most powerful confederation of the Arabian Peninsula, the Quraysh, were capable to organize northern conquering campaigns, in which the Romanized and Christianized Arab role was central for the winning actions, but also for the immediate following leading-organizative order. This historical phase, anyway, until the end of the seventh century, was particularly difficult in the tentative to preserve the unity of the early conquests that in considering the area of Mesopotamia, Syria, Palestine and Egypt was performed in less than a decade.

This phase of huge anarchy was only partially calmed down by the creation of an empire deeply indebted to the previous administrative system and a clan-confederative structure of alliance that intermixed loyalties, matrimonial policies without the imposition of religious innovations. In a territorial land in which Chistological debates, the fight among the Calcedonian-anti-Calcedoniant front played a significant role, even at the etnic level, the break-in of a new already structured religion would have not allow the conquerors to dominate the new lands, but only to lose them in few decades. Contrariwise, it would have been the opposite.

This was unambiguously and only possible because the conquerors were never truly perceived as a schismatic threat, on the contrary, the majority of the non-Calcedonian sources emphasized their welcome in having decreed the end of the Byzantine autocratic orthodoxy, while on the side of Constantinople, the Saracens conquest, it would have overstressed millenarian and apocalyptic scenarios.[7]

This cognitive resume is able to open, moreover, the gates of the religious early Islamic narrative which in the eight century started to framework the religious story, step by step in the setting of a new faith with an Abrahamic origin.

The empowering of the religious conquest *topos* became quite natural to rise the superiority of a faith that defeated the Christian byzantine, the same that century before with Theodosious I the Great, adopted the Crux and the Saint's flags to spread the canonization of war for their victories against paganism.

However, as the analysis on the Qur'ān of the second part clearly highlights, the adoption of a bellicose afflatus needs to be concretely and majorly directed towards the Meccan polytheists than any other religions. The *Ahl al-Kitāb*'s identification in the Islamic revelation remains, until today, dubious,[8] in relation to better understand the concrete Jewish and Christians faith and praxis in the Arabian Peninsula.

The historical aspects that are important to summarize here below in support of this framework are the following:

1. The byzantine Christian canonization of war and the influence played by the Arab Christian confederation in the Arabian Peninsula.
2. The above view finds confirmation in the Umayyad matrimonial policy which favoured the Banū Kalb confederation since 'Uthmān Ibn 'Affān's latest strategy.
3. The framing of war (as a religious action and activity) in the early Islamic age started in the 'Abbasid one, while the army under the Umayyad dynasty was still linked to clan and genealogical alliances.
4. Early *Jihād* has nothing to do with warlike activity but with a personal inner actitude of the singular volunteer in going to war as in patrolling the frontier.

The Qur'ān's analysis is in continuity with the above resume. Wondering on its level of violence, the parallelization of the meaning of *Jihād* with that of a specific warlike action is very limited in comparison with the more common identification of the bellicole violence (*qitāl*); at the same time, the few verses in which this correlation is clear, are indicative of the fight against paganism and polytheism. Independently from the fact that there are Christians and Jewish who act unfairly, this don't authomatically allow Muḥammad's believers in fighting against them.

In parallel, the "Believers" 's accusation to Jewish and Christians in being associationists (29:46; 5:12–19) is complicated, because if the Jewish are not, in relation to their strict monotheism, the Qur'anic understanding of the figure of Christ and its Christology is complex and not easy to determine in relation to its own analysis.

According to it, the correlation between the violence expressed in the Islamic revelation with the peaceful medinese attitude in conquering Mecca (as reported by the same Islamic story), emblematically highlight the difference between narrative and praxis.

To conclude, it is important to highlight as Ibn al-Mubārak's moral praxis in patrolling the frontier with Byzantium as well as his ethical approach in dedicate part of his life at the service and defense of its own religious community is impeccable. Unfortunately, the trivialization of Mubārak message, as of that of the Qur'ān on it, has never played favorably to the non-Muslims' and Muslims understanding on the correlation between *Jihād* and belligerency in their own history.

Notes

Introduction

1 Jonathan Fine, *Political Violence in Judaism, Christianity and Islam: From Holy War to Modern Terror*, New York: Rowman & Littlefield, 2015; J. Harold Hellens, *The Destructive Power of Religion: Violence in Judaism, Christianity and Islam*, Westport, CT: Praeger, 2007; R.J. Hoffmann, *The Just War and Jihad: Violence in Judaism, Christianity and Islam*, Amherst, NY: Prometheus Book, 2006; Berger Alan, *Trilogue and Terror: Judaism, Christianity and Islam after 9/11*, Eugene, OR: Cascade Books, 2012; Bat Ye'or, *Islam and Dhimmitude. Where Civilizations Collide*, Hackensack: Fairleigh Dickinson Press, 2001; Andrew Bostom, *The Legacy of Islamic Anti-semitism: From Sacred Text to Solemn History*, Amherst, NY: Prometheus Books, 2008; *The Legacy of Jihad*, Amherst, NY: Prometheus Books, 2005.

2 Ernest Renan, *Averroès et l'Averroïsme*, Paris: Calmann Lévy Editeur, 1882; *Etudes d'Histoire Religieuse*, Paris: Michel Lévy Frères Ed., 1863; *Histoire des Origines du Christianisme*, Paris: Michel Levy Ed., 1863–1883; *L'Islamisme et la Science*, Conférence faite à la Sorbonne le 29 mars 1883, Paris: Michel Lévy Ed., 1883.

3 René Girard, *Battling the End: Conversations with Benoît Chantre*, East Lansing: Michigan State University Press, 2010; Mark Juergensmeyer, *The New Cold War? Religious Nationalism Confronts the Secular State*, Berkeley: University of California Press, 1993; *Global Rebellion: Religious Challenges to the Secular State, from Christian Militias to al-Qaeda*, Berkeley: University of California Press, 2009; S. Cowdell, C. Fleming, J. Hodge and C. Osborn (eds), *Does Religion Cause Violence? Multidisciplinary Perspectives on Violence and Religion in the Modern World*, New York: Bloomsbury Academic, 2018.

4 Anderson Benedict, *Imagined Communities: Reflections on the Origins and Spread of Nationalism*, London: Verso, 1991, p. 7; Philip Barker, *Religious Nationalism in Modern Europe. If God Be for Us*, London: Routledge, 2008, pp. 22–3.

5 By 'Modernist' the author means the adoption and updating of words, concepts and meanings from one historical and geographical background to another, which for cultural reasons show some incompatibilities, for example: the concept of Nation and Nationalism in the Islamic world. In parallel, the use of 'Modernist-Modernism' terminology also assumes the imposition of a new socio-political or socio-religious understanding of the world from a hegemonic cultural point of view to a subjugated one. State, Nationalism, democracy, religious nationalism etc., which were politically, religiously and culturally abstruse before the nineteenth century for the Islamic world, have been imposed as common values without having given to the subjugated colonized actors the necessary time to digest them, contrary to what had taken place in Europea since the fifteenth century.

6 The Safavid dynasty (1501–1736), on the contrary, shows a peculiarity in re-shaping a new Persian-Twelver Shīʿa identity, which permeated and remained the entrenched

foundation of contemporary Iran. Andrew J. Newman, *Safavid Iran. Rebirth of a Persian Empire*, London: I.B. Tauris, 2006.

7 Sophronios, *Christian Sermons*, trans. Kaegi W., 'Initial Byzantine Reactions to the Arab Conquests', *Church History*, 38 1969, pp. 139–49; John of Damascus, *John of Damascus on Islam: The Heresy of the Ishmaelites*, trans. D. Sahas, Leiden: Brill, 1972; Theophanes, *The Chronicle of Theophanes the Confessor*, trans. Cyril Mango and Roger Scott, Oxford: Clarendon Press, 1997; Sydney H. Griffith, 'The Arabic account of 'Abd al-Masīh an-Najrānī al-Ghassānī', *Le Museon*, 98, 1985, pp. 331–74; S. Brock, 'Syriac Views of Emergent Islam', in G.H.A. Juynboll, Carbondale (ed.), *Studies in the First Century Islamic Society*, 1982, pp. 9–21; R. Hoyland, *Seeing Islam as Others Saw It. A Survey and Evaluation of Christian, Jewish and Zoroastrian writings on Early Islam*, Princeton, NJ: Darwin Press, 1997, pp. 53–255; John V. Tolan, *Saracens. Islam in the Medieval European Imagination*, New York: Columbia University Press, 2002, pp. 40ff.

8 Wansbrough, John, *Quranic Studies: Sources and Methods of Scriptural Interpretation*, Oxford: Oxford University Press, 1977; Patricia Crone, Martin Hinds, *God's Caliph. Religious Authority in the First Centuries of Islam*, Cambridge: Cambridge University Press, 1986; Patricia Crone and Michael Cook, *Hagarism. The Making of the Islamic World*, Cambridge: Cambridge University Press, 1977; Rubin, Uri, *Muhammad the Prophet and Arabia*, London: Routledge, 2011; Rubin, Uri, 'Al-Ṣamad and the High God. An Interpretation of Sura CXII', *Der Islam*, 61/2 (1984), pp. 197–217; Rubin, Uri, 'Quran and Tafsir. The Case of 'an yadin'', *Der Islam*, 70 (1993), pp. 133–44; Hugh Kennedy, *The Great Arab Conquests*, London: Phoenix Paperback, 2007; Irfan Shahid, *Byzantium and the Arabs in the VI centuries*, Vols. 2, Washington: Dumbarton Oaks, 1995–2009; Lecker M., 'Were the Ghassānids and the Byzantine behind Muḥammad's Hijra?', in Denis Genequand and Christian J. Robin (eds), *Les Jafnides. Des Rois Arabes au service de Byzance*, Paris: Editions de Boccard, 2015, pp. 277–94; Donner Fred, *Narratives of Islamic Origins: The Beginning of Islamic Historical Writing*, Princeton, NJ: Darwin Press, 1998; Donner, Fred, *Muhammad and the Believers. At the Origin of Islam*, tr. Italian, *Maometto e le origini dell'Islam*, Torino: Giulio Einaudi Editore, 2011; Hoyland, *Seeing Islam as Others Saw It*; Hoyland, Robert, *In God's Path. The Arab Conquests and the Creation of an Islamic Empire*, Oxford: Oxford University Press, 2015.

9 Hoyland, R., *In God's path. The Arab conquests and the Creation of an Islamic Empire*, p. 3.

10 Tommaso Tesei, '"The Romans Will Win!" Q. 30: 2-7 in Light of the 7th C. Political Eschatology', *Der Islam*, 95/1 (2018), pp. 1–29.

11 Elsaid M. Badawi and M. Abdel Haleem, *Arabic-English Dictionary of Qur'anic usage*, Leiden: Brill, 2008, p. 665.

12 Fuess A. and Hartung Jan-Peter, *Court Cultures in the Muslim World. Seventh to Nineteenth Century*, London: SOAS/Routledge Studies on the Middle East, 2011, pp. 21–90.

13 C.E. Bosworth, 'Ubaidallah ibn Abi Bakra and the Army destruction in Zabulistan (79/698)', *Der Islam*, 1 (1973), pp. 268–83.

14 Nöldeke Th., Schwally Fr., Bergsträßer G. and Preztl O., *The History of the Qur'an*, ed. and trans. Wolfgang H. Behn, Leiden: Brill, 2013, pp. 209ff; Nöldeke, Th., *The Qur'an: An Introductory Essay*, ed. N.A. Newman, Haytfield: Interdisciplinary Biblical Research Institute, 1992; Neuwirth A., Sinai N. and Marx M., *The Qur'an in Context. Historical and Literary Investigations into the Qur'anic Milieu*, Leiden: Brill, 2011,

pp. 255–60, 281ff., 407ff.; Donner Fred, *Narratives of Islamic Origins: The Beginning of Islamic Historical Writing*, pp. 35ff., 174ff.

15 Fred M. Donner, 'The Study of Islam's Origins since W. Montgomery Watt's Publications', 23 November 2015, University of Edinburgh, pp. 1–33.

16 The essay in its second edition was subsequently translated into English by Michael Bonner, with the title *The Early Islamic Historical Tradition*, Albrecht Noth and Lawrence I. Conrad, Princeton, NJ: Darwin Press, 1994.

17 Fred Donner, *The Early Islamic Conquests*, Princeton, NJ: Princeton University Press, 1981, pp. 251ff.; *Muhammad and the Believers. At the Origin of Islam*, pp. 214ff.; 'The Formation of the Islamic State', *JAOS*, 106/2 (1986), pp. 283–96; 'Centralized Authority and Military Autonomy in the Early Islamic Conquests', in Averil Cameron (ed.), *The Byzantine and Early Islamic Near East*, Princeton, NJ: Darwin Press, 1995; Hoyland, *Seeing Islam as Others Saw It.*, pp. 53ff.; 'New Documentary Texts and the Early Islamic State', *BSOAS*, 69/3 (2006), pp. 395–416; 'Epigraphy and the Emergence of Arab Identity', in Aa. Vv. (ed.), *From al-Andalus to Khurasan. Documents from the Medieval Muslim World*, Leiden: Brill, 2007, pp. 220–42.

18 Stephen J. Shoemaker, *The Death of a Prophet. The End of Muhammad's Life and the Beginnings of Islam*, Philadelphia: University of Pennsylvania Press, 2012, pp. 18ff.; *The Apocalypse of Empire. Imperial Eschatology in Late Antiquity and Early Islam*, Philadelphia: University of Pennsylvania Press, 2018.

19 Fred Donner, 'La question du Messianisme dans l'Islam primitive', in *Mahdisme et millénarisme en Islam*, Revue des Mondes Musulmans et de la Méditerranée, Aix en Provence: Edisud ed., 2000, pp. 24–5; Hayrettin Yucevoy, *Messianic Beliefs & Imperial Politics in Medieval Islam*, Columbia: South Carolina University Press, 2009, pp. 18–35.

20 Eutychius, *Das Annalenwerk des Eutychios von Alexandrien*, ed. and trans. M. Breydy, Louvain: 1985, pp. 471–2, Sebeos (attrib), Histoire d'Héraclius par l'évêque Sebéos, trans. F. Macler (Paris, 1904); Hoyland, *Seeing Islam as Others Saw It*, pp. 540ff.; Chase F. Robinson, *Empires and Elites after the Muslim Conquests*, London: Cambridge University Press, 2000, pp. 23, 41, 56–7.

21 Peter Pentz, *The Invisible Conquest. The Ontogenesis of Sixth and Seventh Century Syria*, Copenhagen: The National Museum of Denmark, 1992; Fred M. Donner, 'Visions of the Early Islamic Expansion: From the Heroic to the Horrific', in Nadia El-Cheick, Shaun O'Sullivan (eds), *Byzantium in Early Islamic Syria*, Beirut: American University of Beirut and Balamand: University of Balamand, 2011, pp. 9–29; Jeremy Johns, 'Archaeology and the History of Early Islam: The First Seventy Years', *Jesho*, 46/4 (2003), pp. 411–36; Jere L. Bacharach, Sherif Anwar, 'Early Versions of the Shahāda: A Tombstone from Aswan of 71 A.H., the Dome of the Rock and Contemporary Coinage', *Der Islam*, 89/2 (2012), pp. 60–9; Irfan Kawar, 'The Arabs in the Peace Treaty of A.D. 561', *Arabica*, 3/2 (1956), pp. 181–213; Irfan Shahid, 'Arab Christianity before the Rise of Islam', in *Christianity. A History of the Middle East*, ed. Habib Badr, Middle East Council of Churches, Studies & Research Programme, 200.

22 Volker Popp, 'Die Frühe Islamgeschichte nach inschriftlichen und numismaticschen Zeugnisses', in Karl-Heinz Ohling, Gerd-R. Puin (eds), *Die dunklen Anfänge. Neue Forschungen zur Entstehung und frühen Geschichte des Islam*, Berlin: Schiler, 2005, pp. 16–123.

23 After Heraclius's victorious campaigns against the Sasanian-Persians, Paravaneh Pourshariati, *Decline and Fall of the Sasanian Empire. The Sasanian-Parthian Confederacy and the Arab Conquest of Iran*, London: I.B. Tauris, 2008, pp. 161ff.

24 Yehuda Nevo, Judith Koren, *Crossroads to Islam. The Origins of the Arab Region and the Arab State*, Amherst, NY: Prometheus Books, 2003.
25 Robert Hoyland, *Muslims and Others in Early Islamic Society*, Aldershot: Ashgate Variorum, 2004; 'The Early Christian Writings of Muhammad: An Appraisal', in Harald Motzki (ed.), *Muhammad. The Issue of the Sources*, Leiden: Brill, 2004, pp. 276–97; 'New Documentary Texts and the Early Islamic State', pp. 395–416.
26 Chase F. Robinson, *Empires and Elites after the Muslim Conquests*, Cambridge: Cambridge University Press, 2000.
27 Lawrence I. Conrad, John Haldon, *The Byzantine and Early Islamic Near East*, Princeton, NJ: Darwin Press, 2004, Vol. VI.
28 Alfred Louis de Prémare, *Les Fondations de l'Islam*, Paris: Editions du Seuil, 2002.
29 Irfan Shahid (Kawar), 'Procopious and the Ghassanids', *JAOS*, 77/2 (1957), pp. 79–87; 'Arethas, son of Jabalah', *JAOS*, 75/5 (1955), pp. 206–16; 'The Last Days of Salīḥ', *Arabica*, 5/2 (1958), pp. 145–58.
30 Ella Landau-Tasseron, 'The Status of Allies in Pre-Islamic and Early Islamic Arabian Society', *Islamic Law and Society*,13/1 (2006), pp. 6–32.
31 Khalil 'Athamina, 'The Pre-Islamic Roots of the Early Muslim Caliphate: The Emergence of Abū Bakr', *Der Islam*, 76 (1999), pp. 1–32; 'A'rāb and Muhājirūn in the Environment of Amṣār', *Studia Islamica*, 66 (1987), pp. 5–25.
32 Walter E. Kaegi, *Byzantium and the Early Islamic Conquests*, Cambridge: Cambridge University Press, 1992.
33 Thomas Sizgorich, *Violence and Beliefs in Late Antiquity*, Philadelphia: University of Pennsylvania Press, 2009.
34 Al-Wāḥidī, *Asbāb an-Nuzūl*, trans. M. Guezzou, Amman: Royal Aal-Bayt Institute of Islamic Thought, 2008; Ibn Isḥāq, *Sirāt Rasūl Allah*, trans. A. Guillaume, Oxford: Oxford University Press, 1955; Muhammad Abdel Haleem, *Understanding the Qur'an*, London: I.B. Tauris, 1999; Mālik ibn Anas, *al-Muwaṭṭā*, ed. Bashār 'Awwād Ma'rūf, Beirut: Dār al-Gharb al-Islāmī, 1997, Vols. 2, trans. R. Tottoli, Torino: Einaudi 2011; A.J. Wensinck, *The Muslim Creed*, New York: Barnes & Noble, 1932.
35 Y. Nevo and J. Koren, 'Towards a Prehistory of Islam', *JSAI*, 17 (1994), pp. 108–41.
36 Asma Hilali, *The Sanaa Palimpsest. The Transmission of the Qur'an in the First Centuries A.H.*, Oxford: Oxford University Press, 2017.
37 This is probably possible because even if they became aware of the existence of this new monotheistic message, probably formally embracing this form of religiosity, their Bedouin lifestyle did not immediately change in the following decades; on the contrary, the campaigns which they continued in more rural regions allowed their pre-Islamic traditions to live on, Sezgin F., *Geschichte des arabischen Schrifttums*, Leiden: Brill, 1975, p. 239; C.A. Nallino, *La Letteratura Araba, agli inizi all'epoca della dinastia Umayyade*, Roma: Instituto per l'Oriente, 1948, pp. 48–9.
38 Abdallāh Ibn al-Mubārak, *Kitāb al-Jihād*, ed. Nazīh Ḥammād, Beirut: Dār al-Nūr, Yuṭlabu min Mu'assasat al-Risālah, 1971.
39 Muḥammad ibn Al-ḥasan al-Shaybānī, *Kitāb al-Siyat al-Ṣaghīr*, trans. Majid Khadduri, Baltimore, MD: Johns Hopkins University, 1966.
40 Abū Isḥāq al-Fazārī, *Kitāb al-Siyar*, ed. Fārūk Ḥamād, Beirut: 1987.
41 Anas ibn Malik, *Al-Muwatta'*, ed. Y. Ibn al-Laithī, Beirut: Dār al-Kutub al-'Ilmiyyah, 2005, chapter 21.
42 Sezgin F., *Geschichte des arabischen Schrifttums*, Vol. 2, 1975; Abū al-Faraj al-Iṣfahānī, *Kitāb al-Aghānī*, Beirut: Dar Sader Publishers, 2004, Vols. 25.

43 Denis Genequand and Christian Julien Robin, *Les Jafnides. Des Rois Arabes au service de Byzance,* Paris: Ed. de Boccard, 2015; Dietmar W. Winkler (ed.), *Syriac Churches Encountering Islam. Past Experiences and Future Perspectives,* Piscataway, NJ: Gorgias Press, 2010; Najib George Awad, *Umayyad Christianity. John of Damascus as a Contextual Example of Identity Formation in Early Islam,* Piscataway, NJ: Gorgias Press, 2018.

44 H. Lammens, 'Djābiya', *E.I.,* 2nd ed., Leiden: Brill, 1991, Vol. 2, 360; Irfan Shahid, *Byzantium and the Arabs in the Sixth Century,* Washington: Dumbarton Oaks, 2002, Vol. 2, part 1, pp. 96ff.; Ibn Sa'd, *Kitāb Ṭabaqāt al-kabīr,* ed. Eduard Sachau, Brill: Leiden, 1904–1921, Vol. 4 p. 1, p. 124, Vol. 5, pp. 28–9.

45 Hoyland, 'New Documentary Texts and the Early Islamic State', pp. 395–416; Hugh Kennedy, 'Syrian Elites from Byzantium to Islam: Survival or Extinction', in J. Haldon (ed.), *Money, Power and Politics in Early Islamic Syria,* London: Routledge, 2010, pp. 181–200.

46 Grigory I. Benevich, 'Christological Polemics and Maximus the Confessor and the Emergence of Islam onto the World Stage', *Theological Studies,* 72 (2011), pp. 335–44; Sidney H. Griffith, 'Anastasios of Sinai, the *Hodegos,* and the Muslism', *Greek Orthodox Theological Review,* 32/4 (1987), pp. 341–58; Daniel J. Sahas, *John of Damascus and Islam; the 'Heresy of the Ishmaelites',* Leiden: Brill, 1972; D. Bryan Rhodes, 'John of Damascus in Context', *St. Francis Magazine,* 7/2 (2011), pp. 96–173; Leor Halevi, 'The Paradox of Islamization: Tombstone Inscriptions, Qur'anic Recitations and the Problem of Religious Change', *History of Religions,* 44/2 (2004), pp. 120–52; G.R.D. King, 'The Paintings of the pre-Islamic Ka'ba', *Muqarnas,* 21, Essays in Honor of J.M. Rogers (2004), pp. 219–29; Sulaiman Bashear, 'Qibla Musharriqa and the Early Muslim Prayer in Churches', *The Muslim World,* 81/3–4 (1991), pp. 267–82.

47 Al-Wāḥidī, *Asbāb an-Nuzūl,* pp. 26, 87–9, 93, 105, 127.

48 Hoyland, *Seeing Islam as Others Saw It*; Al-Balādhuri, *Kitāb al-Futūḥ al-Buldān,* trans. Philip Kh. Hitti, New York: Columbia University Press, 1916, 2 Vols.

49 K.A.C. Creswell, *A Short Account of Early Muslim Architecture,* Aldershot: Scolar Press, 1989; C. Foss, 'A Syrian Coinage of Muʿāwiya, *Revue Numismatique,* 158 (2002), pp. 353–65; Robert G. Hoyland, *Arabia and the Arabs, from the Bronze Age to the Coming of Islam,* London: Routledge, 2001, pp. 167ff.

50 Fuess and Hartung, *Court Cultures in the Muslim World. Seventh to Nineteenth century,* pp. 30–90.

51 'Umār ibn Shabba, *Taʾrīkh al-Madīnah al-Munawwarh,* ed. F. Shaltūt, Jeddah: 4 Vols., pp. 7–8.

52 Paul L. Heck, 'Jihad Revisited', *Journal of Religious Ethics,* 32/1 (2004), pp. 95–128; Christian Décobert, 'Ascétisme et Jihad', *Mélanges de l'Université St. Joseph,* Actes du Colloque International: La Guerre Juste dans le Proche Orient ancient Médiéval: approches historique, philosophique et juridique, Beirut: Vol. 62 (2009), pp. 253–82.

Chapter 1

1 A. Guillaume, *The Life of Muhammad. A Translation of Ishāq's Sīrat Rasūl Allāh,* Oxford: Oxford University Press, 1955; Al-Balādhuri, *Kitāb Futūḥ al-Buldān,* trans. Ph. Khūry Ḥitti, New York: Columbia University Press, 1916, 2 Vols.; Al-Ṭabarī, *Ta'rīkh*

al-Rasul al-Mulūk, ed. M.J. de Goeje, Leiden: Brill, 1879–1901, 15 Vols.; al-Mas'ūdī, *Murūj al-Dhahab*, ed. Yūsuf As'ad Dāghir, Beirut: Dār al-Ṣādir, 1965–1966, 4 Vols.; Hishām Ibn al-Kalbi, *Kitāb al-Aṣnān*, ed. and trans. Nabith Amin Faris, Princeton, NJ: Princeton University Press, 2016; Ibn Sa'd Muḥammad, *Kitāb al-Ṭabaqāt al-Kabīr*, ed. Ed. Sachau, Leiden: Brill, 1904–1940, 9 Vols.; Al-Wāqidī, Muḥammad ibn 'Umar, *Kitāb al-Maghāzī*, ed. Marsden Jones, Oxford: Oxford University Press, 1966, 3 Vols.; Al-Baṣrī, Muḥammad Ibn 'Abdullāh Abū Ismā'īl al-Azdī, *Ta'rīkh Futūḥ al-Shām*, ed. 'Abd al-Mun 'im Abdullah 'Āmir, Cairo: Mu'assasa Sijil al-'Arab, 1970; Al-Ya'qūbī, Aḥmad, *Ta'rīkh al-Ya'qūbī*, Beirut: Dār al-Ṣādir, 1960, 2 Vols.

2 Evagrius, *The Ecclesiastical History of Evagrius*, ed. J.M. Bidez and L. Parmentier, London: Methuen & Co, 1898; John Malalas, *Chronographia*, Eng. trans. E. Jeffreys, R. Jeffreys and R. Scott, Melbourne: Australian Association of Byzantine Studies, 1986; John Malalas, *Chronographia*, ed. Ludovici Dindorfii, Bonn: Impensis ed Weberi, 1881 (Latin version); Theophylact Simocatta, *Historiae*, Eng. trans. M. Whitby and M. Whitby, Oxford: Clarendon Press, 1986; Theophanes Confessor, *The Chronicle of Theophanes Confessor*, trans. and ed. Cyril Mango and Roger Scott, Oxford: Clarendon Press, 1997; Philip Wood, *The Chronicle of Seert*, Oxford: Oxford University Press, 2013; Irfan Shahīd, *Byzantium and the Arabs in the Sixth Century*, Washington, DC: Dumbarton Oaks, 1995, Vol. 1, I–II, 2002, Vol. 2, I, 2009, Vol. 2, II; A. Caussin de Percevel, *Essais sur l'Histoire des Arabs avant l'Islamisme*, Paris: Librairie de Firmin Didot Frères, 1847–1848, 3 Vols.; Th. Nöldeke, *Die Ghassānischen Fürsten aus dem Hause Gafna's*, Berlin: Abhandlungen der königlichen Akademie der Wissenschaften zu Berlin, 1887; Fisher G., *Between Empires. Arabs, Romans and Sasanians in Late Antiquity*, Oxford: Oxford University Press, 2011; M. Whittow, 'Rome and the Jafnides: Writing the History of a 6th century tribal dynasty', in J.H. Humphreys (ed.), *The Roman and Byzantine Near East 2: Some Recent Archaeological Research*, Portsmouth, RI: Journal of Roman Archaeology, 1999, pp. 207–24; Denis Genequand and Christian J. Robin, *Les Jafnides. Des rois Arabes au service de Byzance*, Paris: éditions de Boccard, 2015.

3 Robert G. Hoyland, *Seeing Islam as Others Saw It*, Princeton, NJ: The Darwin Press, 1997; Fred Donner, *Narratives of Islamic Origins. The Beginnings of Islamic Historical Writings*, Princeton, NJ: The Darwin Press, 1998.

4 Aghatias Scholasticus, *The Histories*, trans. Frendo Joseph D.C., Corpus Fontium Historiae Byzantinae, The Hague: De Gruyter, 2011; Aghatias, *Histories, guerres et malheurs du temps sous Justinien*, ed. Pierre Maraval, Paris: Les Belles Lettres, 2007.

5 Shahid, *Byzantium and the Arabs in the Sixth Century*, Vol. 2, p. II, pp. 4ff., 118ff., 277ff.; Greg Fisher (ed.), *Arabs and Empires before Islam*, Oxford: Oxford University Press, 2015, pp. 214ff., 276ff.

6 Ibid., Vol. 2, p. I, pp. 143ff.; Jonathan M. Bloom, *Early Islamic Art and Architecture*, London: Routledge, 2016, xvi, pp. 7–86; Richard Ettinghausen, Oleg Grabar and Marylin Jenkings-Madina, *Islamic Art and Architecture, 650–1250*, New Haven, CT: Yale University Press, 2001, pp. 4–5; D. Genequand, 'Some Thoughts on Qasr al-Hayr al-Gharbi, Its Dam, Its Monastery and the Ghassanids', *Levant*, 38 (2006), pp. 63–83; Pierre-Louis Gatier, 'Les Jafnides dans l'épigraphie grecque au VI siècle', in D. Genequand, and Ch. J. Robin (eds), *Les Jafinides. Des rois arabes au service de Byzance*, pp. 193–222.

7 M. Piccirillo, 'The Church of Saint Sergius at Nitl. A Centre of the Christian Arabs in the Steppe at the Gates of Madaba', *Liber Annus* 51 (2001), pp. 267–84;

Genequand, 'Some Thoughts on Qasr al-Hayr al-Gharbi, Its Dam, Its Monastery and the Ghassanids', p. 79; U. Avner, L. Nehmé, and C. Robin, 'A Rock Inscription Mentioning Tha'alaba, an Arab King from Ghassān', *Arabian Archaeology and Epigraphy*, 24/2 (2013), pp. 237–56.

8 Greg Fisher and Philip Wood, 'Writing the History of the Persian Arabs. The Pre-Islamic Perspective of the Naṣrids of al-Ḥīrah', *Iraninan Studies*, 49/2 (2016), pp. 247–90.

9 The Roman-Greek is more sceptical about the Arabs *Foederati*; the non-Greek is more benevolent towards the same (this is a clear generalization).

10 Al-Ṭabarī, *Ta'rīkh al-Rasul al-Mulūk*, ed. M.J. de Goeje, 1038–1039, trans. C.E. Bosworth, *The History of al- Ṭabarī*, New York: Suny Press, 1999, Vol. 5, pp. 370–3; al-Mas'ūdī, *Murūj al-Dhahab*, trans. C. Barbier de Meynard and Pavet de Couteille, Paris: Imprimerie Impériale, 1861, Vol. 3, pp. 181–213; Procopius, *History*, ed. A.G. Roos and G. Wirth, Bibliotheca Teubnriana, reprint, Leipzig, 1962, Vol. 1, XVIII, 40, Vol. 2, XX, p. 18; Cyril of Scythopolis in His Life of John Hesychastes, see *Kyrillos von Skythopolis*, ed. E. Schwartz, TU 49, Leipzig, 1939, p. 211.

11 Fisher and Wood, 'Writing the History of the Persian Arabs', pp. 250–4.

12 Carolus Mullerus, *Fragmenta Historicum Graecorum*, Paris: Editore Ambrosio Firmin Didot, 1851, Vol. 4, pp. 178–80; Christian J. Robin, 'Le royaume hujride, dit "royaume de Kinda", entre Himyar et Byzance', *Comptes rendus des séances de l'Académie des Inscriptions et Belles-Lettres*, 140/2 (1996), pp. 665–714.

13 Cécile Morrison (ed.), *Le Monde Byzantin. L'Empire Romain d'Orient (330–641)*, Paris: Puf, 2006, pp. 166–8.

14 M. Lecker, 'Kinda on the Eve of Islam and during the Ridda', *Journal of Royal Asiatic Society*, Third Series, 4/3 (1994), pp. 333–56.

15 Olinder, G., 'Al-Jaun of the Family of Ākil al-Murār', *Le Monde Orientale*, 25 (1931), pp. 208–29, 'The Kindites in Hajar and al-Mushaḳḳar must absolutely have been dependent on the Persians, who during the second half of the sixth century developed a strong disposition for political expansion exactly on the Persian bay. And when this expansion was extended to South Arabia, the Kindites, after their adversities in Najd and al-Yamāma, ought to have greeted with delight the possibility of returning as the confederates of the Persians to their old country', pp. 228ff.

16 Shahid, *Byzantium and the Arabs in the Fifth Century*, pp. 242ff.; Irfan Kawar (alias Shahid), 'The Last Days of Salīḥ', *Arabica*, 5/2 (1958), pp. 145–58.

17 Joshua the Stylite, *The Chronicle of Pseudo-Joshua the Stylite*, trans. Frank Trombley and J. Watt, Liverpool: Liverpool University Press, 2000, pp. 68–9.

18 Fisher and Wood, 'Writing the History of the Persian Arabs', p. 253.

19 Isabel Toral-Niehoff, 'Imperial Contests and the Arabs: The World of Late Antiquity on the Eve of Islam', in Aa. Vv. (ed.), *The Wiley Blackwell History of Islam*, London: Wiley Blackwell, 2018, pp. 66–7.

20 Irfan Shahid, *The Martyrs of Najran: New Documents*, Brussels: Société de Bollandistes, 1971, pp. 32–63.

21 The Banū Naṣr belong to the Jafnids, just as the confederation of the Lakhm belongs to the Ghassān. This prominent aspect will need to be better interpreted when we understand the complexity of the relationships of these confederations with the proto-Islamic clans of the Ḥijāz. M. Lecker, 'Were the Ghassānids and the Byzantines behind Muḥammad's Hijra?', in Denis Genequand and Christian J. Robin (eds), *Les Jafnides. Des rois Arabes au service de Byzance*, pp. 277–93.

22 Peter Eldwell, 'Arabs in the Conflict between Rome and Persia, AD 491–630', in G. Fisher (ed.), *Arabs and Empires before Islam,* Oxford: Oxford University Press, 2015, p. 221.
23 Robert Hoyland, *Arabia and the Arabs. From the Bronze Age to the Coming of Islam,* London/New York: Routledge, 2001, p. 82.
24 *Corpus Inscriptionum Semiticarum IV,* II: n. 541; J. Beaucamp, Briquel-Chatonnet, Ch. Robin, 'La persécution des chrétiens de Najrān et la chronologie hymarite', *Aram,* 11–12 (1999–2000), pp. 71–2.
25 Hoyland, *Arabia and the Arabs,* pp. 80–1; Irfan Kawar (Shahid), 'Arethas, Son of Jabalah', *Journal of the American Oriental Society,* 75/4 (1955), pp. 207–9.
26 Malchus, *Byzantine History,* ed. and trans. R.C. Blockey in *The Fragmentary Classicising Historians of the Late Roman Empire II,* Liverpool, UK: Francis Cairns, 1983, Frag. 1.
27 Theophylact Simocatta, *Historiae,* trans. Michael and Mary Whitby, Oxford: Clarendon Press, 1986, book 8, 1. 2–3.
28 Malalas, *Chronographia,* p. 464; Shahid, *Byzantium and the Arabs in the Sixth Century,* Vol 1. I, p. 136.
29 Shahid, *Byzantium and the Arabs in the Sixth Century,* Vol 1. I, p. 146.
30 Ariel S. Levin, 'Did the Roman Empire Have a Military Strategy and the Jafinids Were Part of It?', in Denis Genequand and Christian J. Robin (eds), *Les Jafnides. Des rois Arabes au service de Byzance,* pp. 169ff.; John Haldon, *The Byzantine Wars,* Gloucestershire, UK: The History Press, 2008, pp. 21–42.
31 S.T. Parker, *Romans and Saracens. A History of the Arabian Frontier,* Winona Lake (IN), Eisenbraun: American School of Oriental Research, 1986, p. 151; J.P. Casey, 'Justinian, the *limitanei,* and Arab-Byzantine Relations in the Sixth Century', *Journal of Roman Archaeology,* 9 (1996), p. 221; Ch. Robin, 'Les Arabes de Himyar, des Romains et des Perses (III–VI siècle de l'ère chrétienne)', *Semitica et Classica,* 1 (2008), pp. 178–81.
32 Al-Ṭabarī, *Ta'rīkh al-Rasul al-Mulūk,* ed. M.J. de Goeje, 2065–66, trans. Khalid Yahya Blankinship, *The History of al- Ṭabarī,* New York: Suny Press, 1993, Vol.11, pp. 57–9; Al-Balādhuri, *Kitāb Futūḥ al-Buldān,* pp. 95–7.
33 A.G. Grouchevoy, 'Trois niveaux des Phylarques. Étude terminologique sur les relations de Rome et de Byzance avec les Arabes avant l'Islam', *Syria,* 72 (1995), pp. 25–6; M.C.A. Macdonald, 'Nomads and the Hawran in the Late Hellenistic and Roman Periods. A Reassessment of the Epigraphic Evidence', *Syria,* 70 (1993), pp. 368–77.
34 Procopius, *The Wars of Justinian,* trans. H.B. Dewing, Indianapolis, IN: Hackett Publishing Co., 2014, II, 28, 12–14.
35 Michael the Syrian, *Chronique,* ed. and trans. J.H. Chabot, Paris: Ernest Leroux Ed., 1901, Vol. 2, L. 9, ch.33, p. 269; it is possible that Jabalah was the first son of al-Ḥārith in relation to the Arab custom of giving the eldest son the name of the grandfather. Shahid, *Byzantium and the Arabs in the Sixth Century,* Vol 1. I., p. 243.
36 Shahid, *Byzantium and the Arabs in the Sixth Century,* Vol 1. I, pp. 266–88.
37 R. Blockey, *The History of Menander, the Guardsman,* Liverpool, UK: Cairns Ed., 1985, p. 73.
38 Books and articles have tried to depict a clearer understanding of Meccan trade: Patricia Crone, *Meccan Trade and the Rise of Islam,* Piscataway, NJ: Gorgias Press, 2004, pp. 147ff.; M.J. Kister, 'Mecca and Tamīm', *Jesho,* 8 (1965), pp. 113–63; Gene

W. Heck, 'Arabia without Spices: An Alternative Hypothesis', *JAOS*, 123/3 (2003), pp. 547–76.

39 Letter 2, Shahīd, *The Martyrs of Najran. New Documents.*

40 John of Ephesus, *Lives of the Eastern Saints*, ed. and trans. E. Brooks, Paris: Firmin-Didot Ed., 1923–1925, 3 Vols., in R. Graffin-F. Nau, in *Patrologia Orientalis*, T. 17, pp. 139–40.

41 Michael the Syrian, *Chronique*, Vol. 2, L. 10, Ch. 22, pp. 364ff.; Shahid, *Byzantium and the Arabs in the Sixth Century*, Vol. 1, p. 1, pp. 554ff.

42 *Diwān al-Nābigha al-Dhubyānī*, ed. M. Ibrāhīm, Cairo, 1977, p. 47, v. 24; F. Nau, 'Un colloque du Patriarche Jean avec l'émir des Agaréens', *Journal Asiatique*, 11/5 (1915), pp. 257–79.

43 Michael the Syrian, *Chronique*, Vol. 2, L. 9, Ch. 29, pp. 246–7.

44 George Bevan, Greg Fisher and Denis Genequand, 'The Late Antique Church at Tall al-ʿUmayrī East: New Evidence for the Jafnid Family and the Cult of St. Sergius in Northern Jordan', *Basor*, 373 (2015), pp. 49–68.

45 Mariusz Pandura, 'Perceiving Otherness, Creating Resemblance – The Byzantinisation of Nomads in the Age of Justinian I: The Arabs', *Acta Euroasiatica*, 1 (2013), pp. 43–69.

46 Dianne Van de Zande, 'The Cult of Saint Sergius in Its Socio-Political Context', *Eastern Christian Art*, 1 (2004), pp. 141–52.

47 Ibn Qutayba, *Kitāb al-Maʿārif*, ed. Th.ʿUkāsha, Cairo, 1981, p. 642; Shahid, *Byzantium and the Arabs in the Sixth Century*, Vol 1. I, p. 324.

48 J. van Ginkel, *John of Ephesus. A Monophysite Historian in Sixth-Century Byzantium* (PhD Diss., Rijksuniversiteit, Groningen), 1995, pp. 12–19, 106–8, 119–22, 207–16.

49 Evagrius, *The Ecclesiastical History of Evagrius*, 5.20; Malalas, *Chronographia*, Eng. trans. E. Jeffreys, R. Jeffreys and R. Scott, p. 466; John of Ephesus, *Iohannis Ephesini Historiae ecclesiasticae pars tertia*, ed. and trans. E.W. Brooks, 2 Vols., 3.6.16–17; 3.3.41–43, 54–56.

50 John of Ephesus, *Iohannis Ephesini Historiae*, 3.3.41–42.

51 Contrary to what Greg Fisher maintains (2015), in Michael the Syrian, *Chronique*, Vol. 2, L. 10, Ch. 23, pp. 371ff., there is no concrete information on the relationship between Emperor Maurice and al-Nuʿmān, and Shahid's Appendix is also unable to clarify which sources state that al-Mundhir's son reached Constantinople and was imprisoned there. Shahid, *Byzantium and the Arabs in the Sixth Century*, Vol 1. I, pp. 529ff.

52 John Wood, *The Chronicle of Seert. Critical Historical Imagination in Late Antique Iraq*, Oxford: Oxford University Press, 2013, pp. 134, 178, 200.

53 Shahid, *Byzantium and the Arabs in the Sixth Century*, Vol 1. I, pp. 549ff.

54 Ibid., pp. 562ff.

55 Walter E. Kaegi, *Byzantium and the Early Islamic Conquests*, Cambridge: Cambridge University Press, 1992, p. 53.

56 Graffin and Nau, *Patrologia Orientalis*, Vol. 13, LXI, pp. 468–9; Wood, *The Chronicle of Seert*, p. 192ff.

57 Ibid., p. 469.

58 Greg Fisher and Philip Wood, 'Writing the History of Persian Arabs: The pre-Islamic Perspective of the Naṣrids of al-Ḥīra', *Iranian Studies*, 49/2, pp. 274–6; Wood, *The Chronicle of Seert*, pp. 185, 190, 192ff.

59 Parvaneh Pourshariati, *Decline and Fall of the Sasanian Empire*, London: I.B. Tauris, 2008, pp. 132ff.

60 Ignazio Guidi, *Chronicle of Khuzistan*, Leuven: Peeters, 1903, pp. 18–20; Fisher, *Arabs and Empires before Islam*, pp. 270–1.

61 Graffin and Nau, *Patrologia Orientalis*, p. 469.

62 Shahīd, *Byzantium and the Arabs in the Sixth Century*, Vol 1. I, pp. 626ff.

63 Simocatta, *Historiae*, Vol. 2, chp. 2, p. 5; 2, 10, pp. 6–7; *Chronicle of 1234, Chronicum anonymum ad annum Christi 1234 pertinens*, ed. and trans. Albir Abuna, Ighnatius Afram, J.B. Chabot, 2 Vols., Louvain: L. Durbecq, 1917, p. 215.

64 Al-Ṭabarī, *The History of al-Ṭabarī*, Vol. 5, pp. 358ff.; al-Mas'ūdī, *Murūj al-Dhahab*, Vol. 3, pp. 205–10; Ḥamzah al-Iṣfahānī, *Ta'rīkh*, pp. 94–5.

65 Al-Ṭabarī, *The History of al-Ṭabarī*, Vol. 30, pp. 201ff.

66 F. Donner, 'The Bakr Ibn Wā'il Tribes and Politics in North-eastern Arabia on the Eve of Islam', *Studia Islamica* 51 (1980), pp. 5–38; Lecker, 'Were the Ghassānids and the Byzantines behind Muḥammad's *Hijra*?', pp. 277–93.

67 'Abd al-Malik ibn Hishām, *Al-Sīra an-Nabawiyya*, ed. F. Wüstenfled, Göttingen: Dieterich, 1858–1860, pp. 401–3; Shahīd, *The Martyrs of Najrān*, p. 227.

68 Ibn Hazm, *Jamharat ansāb al-'arab*, ed. 'Abd al- Salām Muḥammad Hārūn, Cairo: Dār al-Ma'ārif, 1971, p. 314.

69 F. Donner, 'The Bakr Ibn Wā'il Tribes and Politics in North-eastern Arabia on the Eve of Islam', *Studia Islamica*, 51 (1980), pp. 5–38.

70 Al-Ṭabarī, *The History of al-Ṭabarī*, Vol. 5, pp. 338ff.; Al-Ya'qūbī, *Ta'rīkh*, ed. M.T. Houtsma, 2 Vols., Brill: Leiden, 1883, Vol. 1, pp. 246, Vol. 2, p. 47; Muḥammad ibn Ḥabīb, *Muḥabbar*, ed. Ilse Lichtenstädeter, Hyderabad: 1942, pp. 360–1; al-Mas'ūdī, *Murūj al-Dhahab*, Vol. 2, pp. 227–8; Vol. 3, pp. 205–9; Abū al-Faraj al-Iṣfahānī, *Kitāb al-Aghānī*, Cairo: Vol. 24, pp. 53–71.

71 Donner, 'The Bakr Ibn Wā'il Tribes and Politics in North-eastern Arabia on the Eve of Islam', p. 30.

72 Al-Ya'qūbī, *Ta'rīkh*, ed. M.T. Houtsma, 2 Vols., Brill: Leiden, 1883, Vol. 1, pp. 233–6; Ḥamza al-Iṣfahānī, *Ta'rīkh sinī mulūk al-arḍ wa-al-anbiyā'*, Leipzig: I.M.E. Gottwaldt, 1844, pp. 90ff, 118–21; Abū al-Faraj al-Iṣfahānī, *Kitāb al-Aghānī*, Cairo: 17 Vols., pp. 166–7; al-Ṭabarī, *The History of al-Ṭabarī*, Vol. 4, pp. 128ff.; Vol. 5, pp. 44ff., 74ff., 161–3.

73 Greg Fisher and Philip Wood, 'Arabs and Christianity', in G. Fisher (ed.), *Arabs and Empires before Islam*, pp. 276–372.

74 F.C. Conybeare, 'Antiochus Strategos – The Capture of Jerusalem by the Persians in 614 A.D.', *English Historical Review*, 25 (1910), pp. 502–17; Gideon Avni, 'The Persian Conquest of Jerusalem (614 CE), an archaeological assessment', 2010, online: www.bibleinterp.com/articles/pers357904.shtml

75 Fisher and Wood, 'Arabs and Christianity', pp. 313ff. (only in relation to the Jafnids).

76 Ibn Ḥabīb M., *Kitāb al-Muḥabbar*, ed. Ḥaydar Ābād al-Dakkan, Damascus: Maṭba'at Jam'īyat Dā'irat al-Ma'ārif al-Uthmānīyah, 1942, p. 162; *Al-Munaqqam fī akhbār Quraysh*, ed. Kurshīd Aḥmad Farīq, Beirut: 'Ālam al-Kutub, 1985, chp. Ḥadīth al-Īlāf; Ella Landau-Tasseron, 'The Status of Allies in pre-Islamic and Early Islamic Arabian Society', *Islamic Law and Society*, 13/1 (2006), pp. 6–32; 'Alliances among the Arabs', *Al-Qantara*, 26/1 (2005), pp. 141–73.

77 Kister, 'Mecca and Tamīm: Aspects of Their Relations', pp. 131–4.

78 Ḥabīb, *Al-Munaqqam fī akhbār Quraysh*, pp. 249–60; Al-Qurṭubī, Ibn 'Abd al-Barr al-Namarī, *Al-Istī'āb fī Ma'arifat al-Aṣḥāb*, Beirut: Dār al-Jīl, 1992, Vol. 3, p. 78, no. 71.

79 Ḥazm, *Jamharat Ansāb al-'Arab*, ed. 'A.S. Hārūn, Cairo: 1962, pp. 362–3, '*sārat 'Āmir ilā l-Shām ma'a Ghassān wa-sāra ayḍan 'ammuhā 'Adī ibn Ka'b ibn al-*

Khazraj ibn al-Ḥārith ibn al-Khazraj ilā l-Shām maʿa Ghassān fa-hum kulluhum hunālika illā anna rajulayni min banī ʿAdī kānā bi-l-Madīna wa-humā Abū l-Dardāʾ [...] *naqīb* [...] *wa-Subayʿ ibn Qays*'.

80 Lecker, 'Were the Ghassānids and the Byzantines behind Muḥammad's Hijra?', p. 287.

81 Said Amir Arjomand, 'The Constitution of Medina: A Sociolegal Interpretation of Muhammad's Acts of Foundation of the Umma', *International Journal of Middle Eastern Studies*, 41/4 (2009), pp. 555–75.

82 Consider this possibility in relation to Ella Landau-Tasseron's analysis of the *Nisba*, as shown by her article, 'The Status of Allies in pre-Islamic and Early Islamic Arabian Society', pp. 15–19.

83 Tommaso Tesei, '"The Romans Will Win!" Q. 30: 2–7 in the Light of the 7th C. Political Eschatology', *Der Islam* 95/1 (2018), pp. 1–29.

84 Lecker, 'Were the Ghassānids and the Byzantines behind Muḥammad's Hijra?', pp. 289–90.

85 Landau-Tasseron, 'The Status of Allies in pre-Islamic and Early Islamic Arabian Society', pp. 19–25; 'Alliances among the Arabs', pp. 153–64; Fred Donner, 'The Role of the Nomads in the Near East in Late Antiquity (400–800 C.E.)', in F.M. Clover and R.S. Humphreys (eds), *Tradition and Innovation in Late Antiquity*, Madison: The University of Wisconsin Press, 1989, pp. 73–85; Toral-Niehoff, 'Imperial Contests and the Arabs: The World of Late Antiquity on the Eve of Islam', pp. 59–75.

86 al-Ṭabarī, *The History of al- Ṭabarī*, Vol. 6, p. 16; Ibn Saʿd, *Kitāb al-Ṭabaqāt al-kabīr*, ed. Ed. Sachau, Vol. 1, pp. 43–6; Ibn Ḥabīb, *Al-Munaqqam fī akhbār Quraysh*, pp. 169–70.

87 Paul L. Heck, 'Jihad Revisited', *Journal of Religious Ethics*, 32/1 (2004), pp. 95–128; Christian Décobert, 'Ascétisme et Jihād', *Mélanges de l'Université St. Joseph*, 62 (2009), pp. 253–82.

88 Ammonius, *History and Historiography from the Late Antique Sinai*, trans. D.F. Caner, with S. Brock, M.R. Price and K.V. Bladel, Liverpool: Liverpool University Press, 2010, p. 151; probably the same history is narrated by Procopius and Evagrius in Shahid, *Byzantium and the Arabs in the Sixth Century*, Vol. 1, t. 1, p. 352.

89 Shahid, *Byzantium and the Arabs in the Sixth Century*, Vol. 2, t. 1, pp. 338; Vol. 1, t. 1, pp. 13–15, 18, 21, 27, 183, 220, 232, 352, 437.

90 Michael McCormick, *Eternal Victory: Triumphal Rulership in Late Antiquity, Byzantium and the Early Medieval West*, Cambridge: Cambridge University Press, 1986.

91 Ibid., pp. 100–11; Shahid, *Byzantium and the Arabs in the Sixth Century*, Vol. 2, t. 2, pp. 209–12.

92 Michael the Syrain, *Chronique*, Vol. 2, p. 269; P. Van den Ven, *La vie ancienne de Siméon stylite le jeune*, Subsidia Hagiographica 52, Brussels: 1962, Vol. 1, pp. 164–6, Vol. 2, pp. 188–90; Al-A'lam al-Shantamarī, *Diwan 'Alqama al-Faḥl*, ed. D. al-Khaṭīb and I. Ṣaqqāl, Aleppo: 1969, pp. 43–5.

93 P. Van den Ven, *La vie ancienne de Syméon stylite le jeune*, Vol. 1., p. 165; Shahid, *Byzantium and the Arabs in the Sixth Century*, Vol. 2, t. 2, pp. 214–17; Shahid, *Byzantium and the Arabs in the Sixth Century*, Vol. 1, t. 1, pp. 249–51.

94 *Diwān al-Nābigha al-Dhubyānī*, ed. M. Ibrāhīm, Cairo: 1977, 50 v. 4; Giorgio Levi Della Vida, *Versi Antichi di Arabia*, Milano: All'Insegna del Pesce d'Oro, 1967, pp. 53–5; Shahid, *Byzantium and the Arabs in the Sixth Century*, Vol. 2, t. 2., p. 215.

95 *Maurice's Strategikon. Handbook of Byzantine Military Strategy*, trans. George T. Dennis, Philadelphia: University of Pennsylvania Press, 1984, pp. 33, 65, 77, 89;

Shahid, *Byzantium and the Arabs in the Sixth Century,* Vol. 1, t. 1, pp. 243–4, 568–71; Nöldeke Th., 'Die Ghassānishen Fürsten aus dem Hause Gafna's', *Abhandlungen der königlichen Akademie der Wissenschaften zu Berlin,* 1887, Vol. 2, pp. 38–9.

96 Van den Ven, *La vie ancienne de Siméon stylite le jeune,* p. 164; Al-A'lam al-Shantamarī, *Diwan 'Alqama al-Faḥl,* pp. 43–4, v. 25–28.

97 *Diwān al-Nābigha al-Dhubyānī,* pp. 46–8, trans. R. Nicholson, *A Literary History of the Arabs,* New York: Charles Scribner's Sons, 1907, p. 54.

98 *Chronicum Maroniticum,* trans. J.B. Chabot, *Chronica Minora, pars secunda,* Vol. 4, p. 111, lines 14–15.

99 Muḥammad al-Marzubāni, *Mu'jam al-Shu'arā',* ed. 'A al-Sattār Farrāj, Cairo: Dār Iḥya al-Kutub al-'Arabiyyah, 1960, p. 86; G. Rothstein, *Die Dynastie der Lahmiden in al-Ḥira,* Berlin: Verlag Von Reuther & Reichard, 1899, p. 85.

100 The Christian pre-Islamic poet Abū Du'ād al-Iyādī seems to be particularly appreciated by al-Mundhir, king of al-Ḥīra (d. 554) for his ability in describing the horses. C.A. Nallino, *La Letterature Araba dagli inizi all'epoca della dinastia Umayyade,* Roma: Instituto per l'Oriente, 1948, p. 36.

101 Shahid, *Byzantium and the Arabs in the Sixth Century,* Vol. 1, t.1, pp. 379ff.

102 John of Ephesus, *Iohannis Ephesini Historiae ecclesiasticae pars tertia,* 2 Vols., 3.6.4, pp. 284–7; *Ecclesiastical History, third part,* trans. R. Payne Smith, Oxford: Oxford University Press, 1860, pp. 244–9.

103 John of Ephesus, *Iohannis Ephesini Historiae ecclesiasticae pars tertia,* p. 217, lines 20–26.

104 Shahid, *Byzantium and the Arabs in the Sixth Century,* Vol. 1, t.1., p. 382; 'Adī ibn Zayd al-'Ibadī, *Diwān,* ed. al-Mu'aybid M. Jabbār, Baghdād: Sharikat Dār al-Jumhūriyya li-al-Nashr wa al-Tawz', 1965, pp. 114–15.

105 Robert G. Hoyland, 'Epigraphy and the Emergence of Arab Identity', in Petra Sijpesteijn (ed.), *From al-Andalus to Khurasan. Documents from Medieval Muslim World,* Leiden: Brill, 2006, pp. 219–42; 'Early Islam as a Late Antique Religion', in Scott Fitzgerald Johnson (ed.), *The Oxford Handbook of Late Antiquity,* Oxford: Oxford University Press, 2012, pp. 1053–77; Fischer, *Arabs and Empires before Islam,* pp. 172ff; D. Genequand and Christian J. Robin, *Les Jafnides. Des Rois Arabes au service de Byzance,* pp. 193ff., 259ff.

106 Theodoretus, *Ecclesiastical History. A History of the Church,* London: Samuel Bagster and Sons, 1843, Ch. XVIII, pp. 62–4.

107 Th. Sizgorich, *Violence and Belief in Late Antiquity,* pp. 81ff, pp. 109ff.

108 A.H. Drake, *Constantine and the Bishops: The Politics of Intolerance,* Baltimore, MD: Johns Hopkins University Press, 2000, pp. 409–10; Errington R. Malcolm, 'Christian Accounts of the Religious Legislations of Theodosius I', *Klio,* 79 (1997), pp. 398–443.

109 Procopius, *Opera,* ed. and trans. H.B. Dewing, Cambridge, MA: Harvard University Press, 7 Vols., 1961, VII, pp. 368–77.

110 D. Brakke, 'Outside the Places, within the Truth': Athanasius of Alexandria and the Localization of the Holy', in D. Frankfurter (ed.), *Pilgrimage and Holy Space in Late Antique Egypt, 445–481,* Leiden: Brill, 1998, pp. 446–81.

111 J. Goehring, 'The Dark Side of Landscape: Ideology and Power in the Christian Myth of the Desert', *JMEMS,* 33/3 (2003), pp. 437–51.

112 'Spurious Like of Jacob Baradeus', in *Patrologia Orientalis,* Paris: Firmin-Didot et Cie, Imprimeurs Editeur, 1926, Vol. 19, pp. 233–5 (trans. Brock), in G. Fisher (ed.), *Arabs and Empires before Islam,* pp. 316–17.

113 'The Baptism of al-Nu'mān, in *Chronicle of Seert*, PO, Vol. 13, pp. 468–9, in G. Fisher, *Arabs and Empires before Islam,* p. 359.

114 Hoyland, 'Epigraphy and the Emergence of Arab Identity', p. 230; Ch. Robin, 'Les Arabes de Himyar, des "Romains" et des Perses (III–VI siècles de l'ère Chrétienne)', pp. 178–80; F. Millar, 'Rome's Arab Allies in Late Antiquity. Conceptions and Representations from within the Frontiers of the Empires', in H. Börm and J. Wiesehöfer (eds), Commutatio et Contentio, *Studies in the Late Roman, Sasanian and Early Islamic Near East,* Düsseldorf: Wellem, 2010, pp. 210–19; Shahid, *Byzantium and the Arabs in the Sixth Century,* Vol. 1, t.1., pp. 258–61, 489–92; *Byzantium and the Arabs in the Sixth Century,* Vol. 2, t.1, pp. 153ff.; M. Sartre, 'Deux phylarques dans l'Arabie byzantine', *Le Muséon,* 106 (1993), pp. 145–55; 'L'armée romaine et la défense de la Syrie du Sud', in Lewin and Pellegrini (eds), *The Late Roman Army in the Near East from Diocletian to the Arab Conquest*, Oxford: Bar International Series 1717, 2007, pp. 263–73.

115 Sa'īd ibn Baṭrīq (Eutychios), *Annales,* ed. L. Cheicko, Lipsiae: Otto Harrassowitz, 1909, 51, 2–3.

116 Augustine of Hippo (d. 430), thinking about *Romans* 13, 4, argues in *Contra Faustum Manichaeum* (book 22, 69–76) that on specific occasions the governmental forces need to protect peace and punish wickedness using force, while in the *City of God,* he established that the wise man is able to to frame just wars. Ambrose of Milan (d. 397), although not approving war, was to justify it. Th. Sizgorich, *Violence and Beliefs in Late Antiquity,* pp. 34ff.; J. Johnson Turner, *The Holy War Idea in Western and Islamic Tradition,* University Park: The Pennsylvania State University, 1997, pp. 47ff.

117 Hoyland, *Arabia and the Arabs,* pp. 58, 100; J.M.B. Jones, 'The Maghāzī Literature', in A.F.L. Beeston, T.M. Johnstone, R.B. Serjeant and G.R. Smith (eds), *Arabic Literature to the End of the Umayyad Period,* Cambridge: Cambridge University Press, 2012, chp. 16; C. Alfonso Nallino, *La Letteratura Araba dagli inizi all'epoca della dinastia Umayyade,* Roma: Ipo, 1948, pp. 69ff.; Ibn Khadun, *The Muqaddimah. An Introduction to History,* ed. F. Rosenthal, Bollingen Series, Princeton, NJ: Princeton University Press, 1967, 223ff.

Chapter 2

1 A. Guillaume, *The Life of Muhammad,* p. 143ff.; Al-Ṭabarī, *The History of al-*98ff.; M. Watt, *Muhammad: Prophet and Statesman*, Oxford: Oxford University Press, 1961, pp. 66; *Muhammad at Mecca*, Oxford: Oxford University Press, pp. 110–11.

2 Hoyland, *In God's Path,* pp. 8–30; F. Donner, *Muhammad and the Believers,* trans. *Maometto e le Origini dell'Islam*, pp. 4–40; Th. Sizgorich, 'Narrative and Community in Islamic Late Antiquity', *Past & Present*, 185 (2004), pp. 9–42; 'Sanctified Violence: Monotheist Militancy as the Tie That Bound Christian Rome and Islam', *Journal of the American Academy of Religion*, 77/4 (2009), pp. 895–921.

3 Ibn Ishāq, *Sīra,* ed. M. Hamidullah, Rabat: 1976, fol. N. 282–284.

4 Guillaume, *The Life of Muhammad,* p.155.
5 Ibn 'Abd al-ḥakam, *Futūḥ Miṣr*, ed. C.C. Torrey, New Haven, CT: Yale University Press, 1922, pp. 252–3; Al-Ṭabarī, *The History of al- Ṭabarī,* Vol. 8, pp. 143–5.
6 Nadia Maria El-Cheick, 'Muhammad and Heraclius: A Study in Legitimacy', *Studia Islamica*, 89 (1999), pp. 5–21; Leah Kinberg, 'Literal Dreams and Prophetic Ḥadīths in Classical Islam. A Comparative of Two Ways of Legitimation', *Der Islam*, 70 (1993), pp. 279–300; Suliman Bashear, 'The Mission of Diḥyā al-Kalbī and the Situation in Syria', *Der Islam*, 74 (1997), pp. 64–91.
7 Donner, *Narratives of Islamic Origins*, pp. 112–22; Jonathan E. Brockopp, *Muhammad's Heirs. The Rise of Muslim Scholarly Communities, 622–950*, Cambridge: Cambridge University Press, 2017, pp. 18–23; M. Cooperson, *Classical Arabic Biography: The Heirs of the Prophets in the Age of al-Ma'mūn*, Cambridge: Cambridge University Press, 2000; R. Stephen Humphreys, *Islamic History: A Framework for Inquiry*, Princeton, NJ: Princeton University Press, 1991, pp. 187–207; Tarif Khalidi, *Arabic Historical Thought in the Classical Period*, Cambridge: Cambridge University Press, 1994, pp. 28ff.
8 Kh. 'Athamina, 'The Appointment and Dismissal of Khalīd ibn al-Walīd from the Supreme Command. A Study of the Political Strategy of the Early Muslim Caliphs in Syria', *Arabica*, 41 (1994), pp. 253–72.
9 F. Donner, "Umar ibn al-Khaṭṭāb, 'Amr ibn al- 'Āṣ and the Muslim Invasion of Egypt', in A.R. Sālimī, Brannon Wheeler et al. (eds), *Community, State, History and Changes: Festschrift for Prof. Riḍwān Al-Sayyid*, Beirut: Arab Network for Research and Publishing, 2011, pp. 67–84.
10 Al-Wāqidī, *The Life of Muḥammad. Al-Wāqidī's Kitāb al-Maghāzī*, ed. R. Faizer, trans. R. Faizer, Amal Ismail and Abdulkader Tayob, London: Routledge, 2013, p. 307.
11 There are no academic works on the evangelic origin of this sentence, thinking about Jesus's Sermon on the Mount. Guillaume, *The Life of Muhammad,* p. 596.
12 Ibid., pp. 596–7.
13 F. Buhl, 'Mu'tah', Encyclopaedia of Islam, Leiden: Brill, 1993, Vol. VII, pp. 756–7; Al-Ṭabarī, *The History of al- Ṭabarī*, Vol. 8, pp. 152–60; Muḥammad b. 'Abdullah al-Azdī al-Basrī, *Ta'rīkh futūḥ al-Shām*, ed. 'Abd al-Mun'im 'Abdullāh 'Amīr, Cairo: Mu'assasat Sijill al-'Arab, 1970, p. 29; Ibn Sa'd, *Kitāb Ṭabaqāt al-kabīr,* Vol. 3/1, p. 32; Guillaume, *The Life of Muhammad,* pp. 531–40; *Al-Wāqidī's Kitāb al-Maghāzī,* ed. Rizvi Faizer, pp. 372–8; L. Caetani, *Annales,* Vol. 2, t.1, pp. 80–9; F. Donner, *The Early Islamic Conquests,* pp. 101–10; Kaegi, *Byzantium and the Early Islamic conquests,* pp. 67ff.; Alfred-Louis de Prémare, *Les Fondations de l'Islam. Entre écriture et histoire*, Paris: Ed. du Seuil, 2002, pp. 138–40.
14 Al-Ṭabarī, *The History of al- Ṭabarī,* Vol. 39, pp. 6–9.
15 David S. Powers, *Zayd*, Philadelphia: Pennsylvania University Press, 2014; on this publication, I would like to suggest Prof. Fred Donner's review: https://journals.sagepub.com/doi/pdf/10.1177/2050303214567676
16 Lecker, 'Were the Ghassānids and the Byzantines behind Muḥammad's *Hijra*?', pp. 287–90.
17 Al-Wāqidī, *Kitāb al-Maghāzī*, ed. Mardsen Jones, Oxford: Oxford University Press, 1966, pp. 755ff.; Ibn Sa'd, *Kitāb Ṭabaqāt al-kabīr,* Vol. 2/1, pp. 92–4; Ibn 'Asākir, *Ta'rīkh Madīnat Dimashq*, Damascus: Ẓāhiriyya Library, 19 Vols., 1951, Vol. 1, pp. 402–7.
18 Donner, *The Early Islamic Conquests,* p. 104.

19 *The Chronicle of Theophanes,* trans. Cyril Mango, p. 36; *Chronique de Seert,* part. 2, in *Patrologia Orientalis,* Vol. 13, pp. 600ff.; Nicephoros, *Nicephori Archiepiscopi Constantinopolitani opuscula historica,* ed. C. de Boor, Leipzig: 1880, pp. 65–7.

20 In Hoyland, *Seeing Islam as Others Saw It,* there is no trace of a Chronicle which reports any Byzantine intention to conquer Medina or to organize a military expedition to the south. It is historically evident that during the Byzantine age, no emperor ever tried to reach the oasis of Ḥijāz. Hela Ouardi's analysis in *Les derniers jours de Muhammad,* Paris: Albin Michel, 2016, pp. 23–33, stressed the disaffection of the Prophet's companions in supporting Muḥammad's command in reaching Ṭābuk.

21 Al-Ṭabarī, *The History of al-Ṭabarī,* Vol. 9, pp. 47–81; however, Ṭabarī, unlike other sources, did not spend many words about the expedition to Dūmat al-Jandal, pp. 58–9, contrary to: Al-Balādhuri, *Kitāb Futūḥ al-Buldān,* pp. 95–7; *The Life of Muḥammad. Al-Wāqidī's Kitāb al-Maghāzī,* ed. Rizvi Faizer, pp. 502–27; Guillaume, *The Life of Muhammad,* pp. 607–9; Ibn Sa'd, *Kitāb Ṭabaqāt al-kabīr,* Vol. 1, pp. 396–7, 412; Ibn 'Asākir, *Ta'rīkh madīnat Dismashq,* ed. M. 'Amrāwī, Beirut: Dār al-Fikr, 1995, 80 Vols., 2, pp. 4–5, 31, 41; Abū Bakr Bayhaqī, *Dalā'il al-nubuwwa wa ma'rifat ahwāl sahib al-sharī'ah,* ed. A. Qal'aji, Beirut: Dār al-Kutub al- 'ilmiyya, 1984, 7 Vols., 5, pp. 20–231; Caetani, *Annales,* Vol. 2, t.1, pp. 262–8; F. Donner, *The Early Islamic Conquests,* pp. 101–10; Kaegi, *Byzantium and the Early Islamic Conquests,* p. 82.; Alfred-Louis de Prémare, *Les Fondations de l'Islam. Entre écriture et histoire,* pp. 135–6.

22 Donner, *Narrative of Islamic Origins,* pp. 174ff; L. Conrad, 'Al-Azdī's History of the Arab Conquests in Bilād al-Shām: Some Historiographical Observations', in M. 'Adnān al-Bakhīt (ed.), *Proceedings of the Second Symposium on the History of Bilād al-Shām during the Early Islamic Period Up to 40 AH/640 AD,* Amman: Jordanian University, 1987, pp. 28–62; R. Hoyland, 'History, Fiction and Authorship in the First Centuries of Islam', in J. Bray (ed.), *Writing and Representation in Medieval Islam: Muslim Horizons,* London: Routledge, pp. 16–46.

23 Chase F. Robinson, *Islamic Historiography,* Cambridge: Cambridge University Press, 2003, pp. 18ff.; Tarif Khalidi, *Islamic Historical Thought in the Classical Period,* pp. 30ff.; Nancy Khalek, *Damascus after the Muslim Conquests,* Oxford: Oxford University Press, 2011, pp. 9ff.; Donner, *Narrative of Islamic Origins,* pp. 174ff; Boaz Shoshan, *The Arabic Historical Tradition and the Early Islamic Conquests. Folklore, Tribal Lore, Holy War,* London: Routledge, 2016; Suleiman A. Mourad, 'On Early Islamic Historiography: Abū Ismā'īl Al-Azdī and His Futūḥ al-Shām', *Journal of American Oriental Society,* 120/4 (2000), pp. 577–93; Alfred-Louis de Prémare, *Les Fondations de l'Islam. Entre écriture et histoire,* pp. 343ff.

24 Muḥammad Ḥamidullah, 'Ḥadīth al-Īlāf, ou les rapports économico-diplomatiques de La Mecque pré-Islamique', in *Mélanges Louis Massignon,* Vol. 2 Damascus: Institut Français de Damas, 1957, pp. 293–311.

25 Irfan Shahid, *Byzantium and the Arabs in the Sixth Century,* Vol. 2, p. 2, pp. 10ff.; 'The Arabs and the Peace Treaty of A.D. 561', *Arabica,* 3/2 (1956), pp. 192–7.

26 M.J. Kister, 'Mecca and the Tribes of Arabia: Some Notes on Their Relations', in M. Sharon (ed.), *Studies in Islamic History and Civilization in Honour of Prof. David Ayalon,* Leiden: Brill, 1986, pp. 55–7.

27 G.R.D. King, 'The Paintings of the pre-Islamic Ka'ba', *Muqarnas,* 21 (2004), pp. 219–29.

28 Ibid., Ibn Qutayba, *Kitāb al-Ma'ārif*, ed. Thawrat 'Ukāsha, Cairo: 1969, p. 561.

29 Irfan Shahid, *Byzantium and the Arabs in the Sixth Century*, Vol. 1, p. 2, p. 948; Donner, *Muhammad and the Believers. At the Origin of Islam*, pp. 184–5; P.K. Hitti, *The History of Syria*, London: Macmillan, 1951, p. 431, 452, 581.

30 Dale F. Eickelman, 'Musaylima. An Approach to the Social Anthropology of Seventh Century Arabia', *Journal of the Economic and Social History of the Orient*, 10 (1967), pp. 2–52; Lecker, 'Kinda on the Eve of Islam and during the Ridda', pp. 333–56; S. Shoufani, *Al-Riddah and the Muslim Conquests of Arabia*, Toronto: University of Toronto Press, 1973; Qasim al-Samarrai (ed.), *'Umar al-Tamīmī: Kitāb al-Ridda wa'l-futūh and Kitāb al-Jamal wa masīr 'Ā'isha wa 'Alī*. A Facsimile Edition of the Fragments Preserved in the University Library of Imām Muḥammad Ibn Sa'ud Islamic University in Riyadh, Saudi Arabia, Leiden: Smitskamp Oriental Antiquarium, 1995; Ella Landau-Tasseron, *Aspects of the Ridda War*, PhD Diss., Jerusalem, 1981; 'Alliances among the Arabs', *Al-Qantara*, 26/1 (2005), pp. 141–73; 'On the Reconstruction of Lost Sources', *Al-Qantara*, 25/1 (2004), pp. 45–91.

31 Shoufani, *Al-Riddah and the Muslim Conquests of Arabia*, pp. 96ff.; Donner, *The Early Islamic Conquests*, pp. 85ff.

32 Ella Landau-Tasseron, 'On the Reconstruction of Lost Sources', *Al-Qantara* 25/1 (2004), pp. 45–91.

33 Shoufani, *Al-Riddah and the Muslim Conquests of Arabia*, p. 144; Donner, *The Early Islamic Conquests*, pp. 88–90.

34 Donner, *The Early Islamic Conquests*, pp. 89–90.

35 Hoyland, *Seeing Islam as Others Saw It*, pp. 44–9.

36 John Moschus, *Pratum Spirituale*, *PC* 87, 2852–3112; M. Rouet de Journel, trans. *John Moschus: le Pré Spirituel* (Sources chrétiennes 12; Paris, 1946); D.C. Hesseling, partial tr. *Marceaux choisis du Pré Spirituel de Jean Moschos* (Paris, 1931).

37 Herbert Busse, 'Die 'Umar-Moschee im östlichen Atrium der Grabeskirche', *Zeitschrift des deutschen Palästina-Vereins*, 109 (1993), pp. 73–82.

38 Sophronius, *Ep. synodica*, *PG* 87, 3197D-3200A. For an elucidation of the theological content of the letter see von Schonborn, *Sophrone*, 201–24. Olster, *Roman Defeat, Christian Response*, 99–115, discusses Sophronius's attitude towards the Byzantine empire and Arab victory; Daniel Sahas, 'Sophronius, patriarch of Jerusalem', in David Thomas and Barbara Roggema (eds), *Christian-Muslim Relations: A Biographical History*, Vol. 1 600–900, Leiden: Brill, 2009, pp. 120–7.

39 R. Hoyland, *Seeing Islam as Others Saw It*, p. 73.

40 Ibid., pp. 78ff.

41 Anastasius of Sinai, *Dialogue against the Jews*, *PG* 89, 1221C-D: *Dialogue of Papiscus and Philo* IX, pp. 60–1. Thiimmel, *Friihgeschichte der ostkirchlichen Bilderlehre*, pp. 260–1, argues convincingly that the former text is by Anastasius; on the latter text see McGiffert, *Dialogue between a Christian and a Jew*, pp. 28–47; John Haldon, 'The Works of Anastasius of Sinai: A Key Source for the History of Seventh-Century East Mediterranean Society and Belief', in A. Cameron and L. Conrad (eds), *The Byzantine and Early Islamic Near East, Volume I: Problems in the Literary Source Material*, Princeton, NJ: Darwin Press, 1992, pp. 107–47.

42 Warren Treadgold, *A History of the Byzantine State and Society*, Stanford, CA: Stanford University Press, 1997, pp. 701ff.

43 Monoenergism as Monothelitism (Christ has two natures but only one will) were condemned by the Sixth Ecumenical Council of Constantinople in 680. John

Meyendorff, *Byzantine Theology: Historical Trends and Doctrinal Themes*, New York: Fordham University, 1983, pp. 32ff, 151ff.

44 Dragon, and Déroche, *Doctrina Jacobi nuper Baptizati*, in 'Juifs et chrétiens dans l'Orient du VIIe siècle', *Travaux et Mémoires*, 11 (1991), pp. 17–248; Hoyland, *Seeing Islam as Others Saw It*, pp. 55–61; Alfred-Louis de Prémare, *Les Fondations de l'Islam. Entre écriture et histoire*, pp. 148–60; Brockopp, *Muhammad's Heirs*, pp. 14–24.

45 G. Bardy (ed.), *Les Trophées de Damas. Controverse Judéo-Chrétienne du VII siècle*, Paris: Firmin-Didot & Co., 1920.

46 Al-Balādhuri, *Kitāb Futūḥ al-Buldān*, pp. 191–3.

47 Bardy (ed.), *Les Trophées de Damas*, pp. 233–4.

48 Anastasius of Sinai, *Viae dux*, ed. J.-P. Migne, PC 89, Paris: Biblitecae Cleri Universae, 1865, p. 41; K.H. Uthemann, *Viae Dux*, CCSG 8, Turnhout: Brepols, 1981, p. 9.

49 S. Griffith, 'Anastasios of Sinai, the Hodegos and the Muslim', *Greek Orthodox Theological Review*, 32/4 (1987), p. 16; *The Church in the Shadow of the Mosque*, Princeton, NJ: Princeton University Press, 2008, pp. 28–32.

50 George Awad, *Umayyad Christianity. John of Damascus as a Contextual Example of Identity Formation in Early Islam*, pp. 190ff; Griffith, *The Church in the Shadow of the Mosque*, pp. 30–1.

51 Hoyland, *Seeing Islam as Others Saw It*, pp. 162–3.

52 Ibid., p. 166; F. Nau, 'Traduction des lettres XII et XIII de Jacques d'Edesse', *Revue de l'Orient Chrétien* 10 (1905), pp. 197–208, 258–82; F. Nau, 'Cinq Lettres de Jacques d'Edesse à Jean le Stylite (traduction et analyse)', *Revue de l'Orient Chrétien*, 14 (1909), pp. 427–40.

53 Thomas the Presbyter, *Chronicle*, E.W. Brooks, ed. J.B. Chabot, trans. *Chronicon miscellaneum ad annum domini 724 pertinens* (*CSCO* 3–4 *scr. syri* 3–4; Paris, 1904), pp. 77–154/63–119.

54 Ibid., pp. 147–8.

55 Robert W. Thomson, 'Muhammad and the Origin of Islam in Armenian Literary Tradition', in Thomson, *Studies in Armenian Literature and Christianity*, Aldershot: Variorum Collected Studies series 451, 1994, pp. 829–85.

56 Sabeos, *The Armenian History Attributed to Sabeos*, trans. R.W. Thomson, J.H. Johnston and Ass. T. Greenwood, Liverpool: Liverpool University Press, 2000, III, pp. 134–77.

57 Ibid., pp. 134–5.

58 Ibid.

59 Al-Ṭabarī, *The History of al-Ṭabarī*, Vol. 11–13; Al-Balādhuri, *Kitāb Futūḥ al-Buldān*, Vol. 1, pp. 207–12; Ibn 'Asākir, *Ta'rīkh Madīnat Dimashq*, ed. Munajjid, Vol. 1, pp. 527–8, 535–45; Khalīfa ibn Khayyāṭ al-'Uṣfūrī, *Ta'rīkh*, ed. Akram Ḍiyā' al-'Umarī, 2 Vols., Najaf: 1967, 1, pp. 87–100.

60 *Chronicon ad Annum 724*, Ed. J.P.N. Land, *Symbolae Syriacae*, 4 Vols., Leiden: Brill, 1867, 1, pp. 18–19; Dionysius of Tel Mahre, *Historia ecclesiastica Zachariae rhetori vulgo adscripta*, ed. E.W. Brock, 2 Vols., Louvain: L. Durbecq, 1919–1924, pp. 144–50, 154–65; Ignazio Guidi, *Chronicle of Khuzistan*, Leuven: Peeters, 1903, p. 45; John of Nikiu, *The Chronicle of John (d. 690 ca) Bishop of Nikiu: Being a History of Egypt before and during the Arab Conquest*, ed. R.H. Charles, trans. H. Zotenberg's edition of the Ethiopic Version, London: Williams & Northgate, 1916, pp. 178–201.

61 Hoyland, *Seeing Islam as Others Saw It*, p. 128.

62 *The Armenian History Attributed to Sabeos*, p. 147.

63 Dionysius of Tel Mahre, *Historia ecclesiastica Zachariae rhetori vulgo adscripta*, pp. 173–80; Theophanes the Confessor, *The Chronicle of Theophanes*, pp. 43ff.; *Theophilus of Edessa's Chronicle*, trans. and intro. by Robert G. Hoyland, Liverpool: Liverpool University Press, 2011.

64 Hoyland, *Seeing Islam as Others Saw It*, p. 156. At the same time, one of the early Papyri which bears an Arabic-Greek protocol comprising a Muslim profession of faith is dated between 698 and 733 and, as we will see, is close to the early archaeological sources which, discovered in the last decades, show a complete Islamic *shahāda*, p. 112.

65 Isho'yahb III, *Liber epistularum*, ed. and trans. Rubens Duval, *CSCO* 11–12 *scr. Syri* 11–12, Paris, 1904–1905; Philip Scott-Montcrief, *The Book of Consolations, or the Pastoral Epistles of Mār Ishō'yahbh of Kuphlana in Adiabene*, London: Luzac & Co, 1904, 14C, p. 251.

66 John bar Penkaye, *Sources Syriaques*, Vol. 1, ed. A. Mingana, Leipzig: Otto Harrassowitz, 1908; Brock, *North Mesopotamia in the Late 7th Century: Book 15 of John Bar Penkaye's 'Ris Melle'*, *Jerusalem Studies in Arabic and Islam*, 9: 1987, reprinted in *Studies in Syriac Christianity*, 1992, chp. 2, pp. 57–61.

67 Hoyland, *Seeing Islam as Others Saw It*, p. 182.

68 Brock, *North Mesopotamia in the Late 7th Century: Book 15 of John Bar Penkaye's 'Ris Melle'*, pp. 66–7.

69 Ibid., p. 72.

70 *The Chronicle of Zuqnin, Parts III and IV*, trans. Amir Harrak, Toronto: Pontifical Institute of Medieval Studies, 1999, p. 147.

71 Adomnan, *De Locis Sanctis*, ed. L. Bieler, *Itinera et alia geographica*, Corpus Christianorum series latina 175, Turnhout: Brepols, 1965, pp. 177–234; Tober and Molinier (eds), *Itinera Hierosolymitana et descriptiones terrae sanctae*, Geneva, 1879, pp. 141–210; T. Wright, partial tr. *Early Travels in Palestine*, London, 1848, pp. 1–12; Wilkinson, tr. *Jerusalem Pilgrims*, pp. 93–116.

72 F. Donner, 'Visions of the Early Islamic Expansion: Between the Heroic and the Horrific', in *Byzantiums in Early Islamic Syria*, ed. Nadia M. El Cheikh and Shaun O'Sullivan, Proceedings of a Conference Organized by the American University of Beirut and the University of Balamand, Beirut: 2011, p. 22.

73 A. Palmer, S. Brock and R. Hoyland, *The Seventh Century in the West-Syrian Chronicles*, Liverpool: Liverpool University Press, 1993, pp. 145–55; F. Donner, 'Visions of the Early Islamic Expansion: Between the Heroic and the Horrific', pp. 24–5.

74 Palmer, *The Seventh Century in the West-Syrian Chronicles*, pp. 202–5.

75 Jacob of Edessa, *Replies to Addai*, nos. 56–7, De Lagarde (ed.), *Reliquiae iuris*, pp. 139–40/Lamy, ed./trans. *Dissedatio de Syrorum fide*, pp. 154–7; Hoyland, *Seeing Islam as Others Saw It*, p. 162.

76 Ibid., pp. 58–9, De Lagarde, p. 140/Lamy Ed., pp. 158–9.

77 H. Munt, 'No Two Religions: Non-Muslims in the Early Islamic Ḥijāz', *Bulletin of SOAS*, 78/2 (2015), p. 267.

78 Tor Andrae, *Die Person Muhammeds in Lehre und Glauben seiner Gemeinde*, Stockholm: Norstedt, 1918, p. 245.

79 Contrary to F. Donner, I do not think that early Believers were more Messianically or Apocalyptically associated than Christians or Jews in different historical phases, as both aspects had a huge impact on identifying a more Islamic religious consciousness. I will discuss this later.

80 F. Donner, 'From Believers to Muslims: Confessional Self-Identity in the Early Islamic Community', *Al-Abhath, Journal of the Faculty of Arts and Sciences*, American University of Beirut, Vol. 50–51, 2002–2003, p. 12; *Muhammad and the Believers. At the Origin of Islam*, tr. It. pp. 59ff., 139ff., 204ff.
81 S. Griffith, 'The Prophet Muhammad. His Scripture and His Message According to the Christian Apologies in Arabic and Syriac from the first 'Abbasid Century', in Toufic Fahd (ed.), *La Vie du Prophète Mahomet*, Colloque de Strasbourg, 1980, Paris: Puf, 1983, pp. 118–21; U. Rubin, 'Ḥanīfiyya and Ka'ba. An Inquiry into the Arabian pre-Islamic Background of *dīn Ibrāhīm*', *Jerusalem Studies in Arabic and Islam*, 13 (1990), pp. 85–112.
82 Ibid., p. 87. This is probably one of the reasons why few Banū Aws initially attended the second pledge of 'Aqaba.
83 M. Gil, 'The Medinan Opposition to the Prophet', *Jerusalem Studies in Arabic and Islam*, 10 (1987), pp. 65–96.
84 Ibn Sa'd, *Al-Ṭabaqāt al-Kubrā*, Vol. 4, pp. 383–4.
85 Ibid., Vol. 3, p. 289.
86 W. Madelung, *The Succession to Muhammad. A Study of the Early Caliphate*, Oxford: Oxford University Press, 1997, pp. 6, 16–18, 31–2; M.A. Shaban, *Islamic History. A New Interpretation*, Cambridge: Cambridge University Press, 1983, pp. 26–7.
87 Al-Ṭabarī, *The History of al-Ṭabarī*, Vol. 9, pp. 189–206; 'Abd al-Razzāq al-Ṣan'ānī, *Al-Muṣannaf*, ed. Ḥabīb al-Raḥman al-'A'ẓamī, Beirut: 1970–1972, Vol. 2, p. 443; Aḥmad ibn Ḥanbal, *Musnad*, Beirut, Vol. 3, p. 129; Al-Suyūṭi, *Ta'rīkh al-Khulafā'*, ed. M.M. 'Abd al-Ḥamīd, Cairo: 1964, p. 9; Donner, *The Early Islamic Conquests*, pp. 82–3.
88 Khalil 'Athamina, 'The Pre-Islamic Roots of Early Muslim Caliphate: The Emergence of Abū Bakr', *Der Islam*, 76 (1999), pp. 1–32.
89 Al-Ṭabarī, *The History of al-Ṭabarī*, Vol. 10, pp. 1ff.; W. Madelung, *The Succession to Muhammad*, p. 37.
90 Ibn Khaldūn, *The Muqaddimah*, pp. 120ff. In other words, after the Prophet's death, the Arabs were once again fragmented on a clan-confederation basis. This division continued with a policy of alliances that the Umayyad perfectly incarnate. In the following century, as well as after the 'Abbāsid's 'revolution', the clan's inner relations led to a predominant political outcome, even if the canonization of Islam was making them more equally affiliated with a new religious dogma.
91 M.J. Kister, 'The Struggle against Musaylima and the Conquest of Yamāma', *Jerusalem Studies in Arabic and Islam*, 27 (2002), pp. 23ff.; R. Hoyland, 'Reflections on the Identity of the Arabian Conquerors', *Al-'Uṣūr al-Wusṭā* 25 (2017), pp. 132–4.
92 Ibn 'Asākir, *Ta'rīkh Madināt Dimashq*, ed. Munajjid, Vol. 1, pp. 159–76; Azdī, Abū Ismā'īl, *Ta'rīkh Futūḥ al-Shām*, ed. 'Āmir, pp. 215–45; Al-Ṭabarī, *The History of al-Ṭabarī*, Vol. 11, pp. 58–9, 87–122; Al-Balādhuri, *Kitāb Futūḥ al-Buldān*, Vol. 1, pp. 207–12; F. Donner, *The Early Islamic Conquests*, pp. 128–48; Hoyland, *In God's Path*, pp. 56–65.
93 Donner, *The Early Islamic Conquests*, pp. 148, 186–9; Hoyland, *In God's Path*, p. 58; W. al-Qadi, 'Non-Muslims in the Muslim Conquest Army', in Borrut A. and F. Donner (eds), Chicago, IL: University of Chicago Press, 2016, pp. 83–127; Mohsen Zakeri, *Sasanid Soldier in the Early Muslim Society. The Origins of 'Ayyārān and Futuwwa*, Wiesbaden: Harrassowitz Verlag, 1995, pp. 95ff; Kh. Athamina, 'Non-Arab Regiments and Private Militias during the Umayyad Period', *Arabica*, 45/3 (1998), pp. 347–78.

94 Azdī, Abū Ismā'īl, *Ta'rīkh Futūḥ al-Shām*, pp. 219, 234; Ibn 'Asākir, *Ta'rīkh Madināt Dimashq*, pp. 163, 174; Al-Balādhuri, *Kitāb Futūḥ al-Buldān*, Vol. 1, pp. 208–9; Al-Ya'qūbī, Aḥmad, *Ta'rīkh*, ed. M.Th. Houtsma, 2, pp. 160–8; Pseudo-Wāqidī, *Futūḥ al-Shām*, Beirut: 1972, 2, pp. 155–64.

95 It would be even harder to understand why Jabala ibn al-Ayham was not in his capital.

96 Hoyland, *Seeing Islam as Others Saw It*, pp. 284, 412–13, 418 n. 104, 589; Arietta Papaconstantinou, 'Administering the Early Islamic Empire: Insights from the Papyri', in John Haldon (ed.), *Money, Power and Politics in Early Islamic Syria: A Review of Current Debates*, London: Routledge, 2010, pp. 62–4; Clive Foss, 'Mu'āwiya's State', in John Haldon (ed.), *Money, Power and Politics in Early Islamic Syria*, pp. 84–5; Michael G. Morony, 'The Age of Conversions: A Reassessment', in M. Gervers and Ramzi J. Bikhazi (eds), *Conversion and Continuity. Indigenous Christian Communities in Islamic Lands*, Toronto: Pontifical Institute of Medieval Studies, 1990, pp. 135–50; Donner, *Muhammad and the Believers. At the Origins of Islam*, pp. 139ff.

97 F. Donner, *Muhammad and the Believers. At the Origins of Islam*, pp. 156–62.

98 Kh. Athamina, 'The Appointment and Dismissal of Khālib ibn al-Walīd', pp. 253–72; 'A'rab and Muhajirūn in the Environment of Amṣār', *Studia Islamica*, 66 (1987), pp. 5–25; F. Donner, 'Umar ibn al-Khaṭṭāb, 'Amr ibn al- 'Āṣ, and the Muslim Invasion of Egypt', in *Community, State, History and Changes*, in honour of Ridwan al-Sayyid for his Sixtieth Birthday, pp. 67–84.

99 Arietta Papaconstantinou, 'Administering the Early Islamic Empire: Insights from the Papyri', pp. 62ff.; 'Between Umma and Dhimma. The Christians of the Middle East under the Umayyads', *Annales Islamologiques*, 42 (2008), pp. 127–56; M.G. Morony, 'Religious Communities in Late Sasanian and Early Muslim Iraq', *Jesho*, 17/2 (1974), pp. 113–35; M. Levy-Rubin, 'Shurūṭ 'Umar and Its Alternatives: The Legal Debate on the Status of the Dhimmīs', *Jerusalem Studies in Arabic and Islam*, 30 (2005), pp. 170–206; Kennedy, 'Syrian Elites from Byzantium to Islam: Survival or Extinction', pp. 181–200.

100 Arietta Papaconstantinou, 'Between Umma and Dhimma. The Christians of the Middle East under the Umayyads', p. 132.

101 Isabel Toral-Niehoff, 'The 'Ibād of al-Ḥira: An Arab Christian Community in Late Antique Iraq', in A. Neuwirth, N. Sinai and M. Marx (eds), *The Qur'an in Context*, Leiden: Brill, 2010, pp. 323–47.

102 Brock, *North Mesopotamia in the Late 7th Century: Book 15 of John Bar Penkaye's 'Ris Melle'*, pp. 61–2; Palmer, *The Seventh Century in the West-Syrian Chronicles*, pp. 29–35; J.B. Chabot, *Synadicom Orientale*, Paris: Imprimerie Nationale, 1902, pp. 219–20, 225–6.

103 If al-Jāḥiẓ, in the ninth century, was still complaining that many urban Christians did not accept paying the *Jizya*, the recognition of being part of a sort of *Dhimma* was quite problematic. *Radd 'alā al-Naṣārā*, ed. J. Finkel, Cairo: 1926, vv. 158ff.

104 Arietta Papaconstantinou, 'Between Umma and Dhimma. The Christians of the Middle East under the Umayyads', p. 137.

105 Ibn 'Asākir, *Ta'rīkh Madināt Dimashq*, ed. Munajjid, Vol. 1, pp. 553–9; Ibn Sa'd, *Al-Ṭabaqāt al-Kubrā*, Vol. 4, p. 124, Vol. 5, pp. 28–9; Al-Ṭabarī, *The History of al-Ṭabarī*, Vol. 18, p. 216; Ṣalāḥ al-Dīn al-Munajjid, *Madināt Dimashq 'ind al-Jughrāfiyyīn wa-l Rāḥilīn*, Beirut: Dār al-Kitāb al-Jadīd, 1967, pp. 19–21; I. Shahid, *Byzantium and the Arabs in the Sixth Century*, Vol. 1, t. 1, pp. 648–9; Khalek, *Damascus after the Muslim Conquests*, p. 44.

106 Ibn 'Asākir, *Ta'rīkh Madināt Dimashq*, pp. 554–5; Hishām ibn al-Kalbī, *Jahamarat al-Nasab*, Beirut: 'Ālam al-Kutub, 1986, pp. 179–81.
107 Nehemia Levtzion, 'The Conversion to Islam in Syria and Palestine and the Survival of Christians Communities', in M. Gervers and Ramzi J. Bikhazi (eds), *Indigeneous Christian Communities in Islamic Lands Eight to Eighteenth Centuries*, Toronto (Canada): Pontificial Institute of Medieval Studies, 1990, pp. 229–331.
108 Harry Munt, 'What Did Conversion to Islam Mean in the Seventh-Century Arabia?', in A.C.S. Peacock (ed.), *Islamisation. Comparative Perspectives from History*, Edinburgh: Edinburgh University Press, 2017, pp. 84–101.
109 Isho'yahb III, *Liber Epistularum*, ed. and trans. R. Duval, Leipzig-Paris: Harrassowitz, Typographeo Republicae, 1905, p. 251/p. 182, quoted from Harry Munt, 'What Did Conversion to Islam Mean in the Seventh-Century Arabia?', p. 89.
110 Tayeb el-Hibri, *Parable and Politica in Early Islamic History*, pp. 174–5.
111 Al-Ṭabarī, *The History of al-Ṭabarī*, Vol. 15, pp. 254–5; M. Watt, *Muhammad. Prophet and Statesman*, London: Oxford University Press, 1961, pp. 131–2.
112 Guillaume, *The Life of the Prophet*, pp. 503–4; M. Watt, *Muhammad at Medina*, Oxford: Oxford University Press, 1956, p. 50.
113 I. Shahid, *Byzantium and the Arabs in the Sixth Century*, Vol. 2, t. 2, p. 310 n. 19; Ibn 'Abd Rabbih, *The Unique Necklace, al-'Iqd al-Farīd*, trans. Issa J. Boullata, London: Garnet Publishing, 2012, Vol. 3, pp. 294–5.
114 Abān ibn 'Uthmān, one of their sons, became governor of Medina under 'Abd al-Malik and he probably died around 723. Al-Ṭabarī, *The History of al-Ṭabarī*, Vol. 39, p. 59.
115 Al-Balādhurī, *Ansāb al-ashrāf*, ed. Muḥammad Ḥamīdullah, Cairo: 1959, Vol. I, p. 378; Ibn Ḥazm, *Jamharat ansāb al- 'arab*, ed. 'Abd al-Salām Hārūn, Cairo: 1962, p. 456; Ḥassān Ibn Thābit, *Diwān*, ed. Arafat, London: 1971, Vol. 1, p. 298; Sh. Guthrie, *Arab Women in the Middle Ages: Private Lives and Public Roles*, London: Saqi Books, 2013, p. 90; M.J. Kister, 'The Crowns of This Community. Some Notes on the Turban in the Muslim Tradition', *Jerusalem Studies in Arabic and Islam*, 24 (2000), p. 236; 'On the Wife of the Goldsmith from Fadak to Her Progenity. A Study in Jāhilī Genealogical Traditions', *Le Museon* 92 (1979), pp. 326–8.
116 It would be not useful here to open the debate on the Fadak oasis and the inheritance dispute between Fāṭimah and Abū Bakr, after the Prophet's death.
117 Al-Ṭabarī, *The History of al-Ṭabarī*, Vol. 18, p. 215.
118 Al-Ṭabarī (Vol. 19, p. 226) did not quote any Kalbite wife for Yazīd I, neither did Balādhurī. Ibn 'Asākir, *Ta'rīkh Madināt Dimashq*, ed. Munajjid, Vol. 1, pp. 575–6; and Ibn Sa'd, *Al-Ṭabaqāt al-Kubrā*, Vol. 5, pp. 64–72, did not give any exhaustive information either. However, different studies have stressed that the alliance between the Umayyads and the Kalbites continued: Philip Khuri Hitti, *History of the Arabs*, p. 281; H. Lammens, 'Le Califat de Yazid Ier', *Mélanges de la faculté orientale de l'Université Saint Joseph de Beirut*, Vol. 4, 1910, pp. 233–312; 'Études sur le règne du calife omaiyade Mo'āwia Ie (troisième série: la Jeunesse du Calife Yazid Ier)', *Mélanges de la faculté orientale de l'Université Saint Joseph de Beirut*, Vol. 3, 1908, pp. 143–312; Borrut and Donner, *Christians and Others in the Umayyad State*, pp. 42, 100–1, 109, 113 n. 254, 132, 181; Donner, *Muhammad and the Believers. At the Origin of Islam*, p. 189; Koser Parveen, Muhammad Sultan Shah, 'Interfaith Marriages in Islam: A Case Study of Christian Wives of Muslim Rulers', *Al-Ilm*, 1/1 2017, pp. 5–9; Joshua Mabra, *Princely Authority in the Early Marwānid State*, Piscataway, NJ: Gorgias Press, 2017, pp. 6ff.

119 Al-Kindī, M. ibn Yūsuf, *Wulāt Miṣr,* ed. Ḥusayn Nassār, Beirut: 1959, pp. 41ff.

120 Al-Ṭabarī, *The History of al-Ṭabarī,* Vol. 20, pp. 56ff; Al-Balādhurī, *Ansāb al-ashrāf,* Vol. 5, pp. 128ff.; Al-Ya'qūbī, *Ta'rīkh ibn Wāḍih,* Vol. 2, pp. 304ff.

121 P. Crone, 'Were the Qays and Yemen of the Umayyad Period Political Parties?', *Der Islam,* 71/1 (1994), pp. 44ff.

122 The mother of the caliph 'Abd al-Malik was a maternal aunt of Marwān ibn al-Ḥakam, whose father Ṣafwān was, as reported by M. Lecker, brother of Waraqa ibn Nafwal, the paternal Christian cousin of Khadīja bint Khuwaylid, the first wife of the Prophet. It is again historically and anthropologically important to emphasize that military alliance and internal fights often linked to purely economic and strategic reasons could also consider the complexity of a matrimonial policy that was not easily discernable. M. Lecker, 'The Monotheistic Cousins of Muḥammad's Wife Khadīja', *Der Islam,* 94/2 (2017), p. 366.

123 Al-Ṭabarī, *The History of al-Ṭabarī,* Vol. 20, pp. 56–71; 52; Al-Ṭabarī, *The History of al-Ṭabarī,* Vol. 21, pp. 156–7; Al-Balādhurī, *Ansāb al-ashrāf,* Vol. 5, pp. 159–60.

124 Ibid., Vol. 20, pp. 49–50, 56, 59.

125 Borrut, 'Al-Aṣamm, Sufyān ibn Abrad al-Kalbī', *EI.* 3rd ed., Leiden: Brill, 2014, pp. 7–9; H. Kennedy, *The Armies of the Caliph. Military and Society in the Early Islamic State*, London: Routledge, 2001, pp. 33–4, 99.

126 F. Donner, in *Muhammad and the Believers* (Tr. it. version), reports that the Taghlib went into battle on the Umayyad side with the Cross and some images of St Sergius, their patron saint, p. 189.

127 Al-Balādhurī, *Ansāb al-ashrāf* (2), 1, p. 530; Joshua Mabra, *Princely Authority in the Early Marwānid State,* p. 25.

128 I. Shahid, *Byzantium and the Arabs in the Sixth Century,* Vol. 2, t. 2, p. 35 n.8.

Chapter 3

1 Cicero, *De Inventione,* II, p. 161.

2 Kung, *Cristianesimo,* pp. 38ff.

3 Ibid., pp. 32–5; Th. Nöeldeke and A. Mueller, *Delectus Veterum Carminum Arabicorum,* Berlin: H. Reuther's Verlagsbuchhandlung: 1890, pp. 64ff.

4 Hishām ibn al-Kalbī, *Kitāb al-Aṣnām,* trans. Nabith Amin Faris, Princeton, NJ: Princeton University Press, 1952, pp. 9ff.

5 David Thomas and Barbara Roggema (eds), *Christian-Muslim Relations. A Biographical History,* Vol. 1 (600–900), Leiden: Brill, 2009, pp. 115ff.; E. Grypeou, Mark N. Swanson and D. Thomas, *The Encounter of Eastern Christianity with Early Islam,* Leiden: Brill, 2006, pp. 153ff., 171ff., 185ff., 237ff.

6 Donner, *Narratives of Islamic Origins: The Beginning of Islamic Historical Writings,* pp. 184ff.; *Muhammad and the Believers. At the Origin of Islam,* pp. 212ff.; Reynold A. Nicholson, *A Literary History of the Arabs,* pp. 193ff.; Jonathan E. Brockopp, *Muḥammad's Heirs. The Rise of Muslim Scholarly Communities, 622–950,* pp. 31ff.; Steven C. Judd, *Religious Scholars and the Umayyads,* London: Routledge, pp. 41ff.

7 M. Hinds, 'The Murder of the Caliph 'Uthman', *International Journal of Middle Eastern Studies,* 3 (1972), pp. 450–69; Al-Ṭabarī, *The History of al-Ṭabarī,* Vol. 15, pp. 181ff.; L. Caetani, *Annales,* Vol. 8, pp. 141ff.

8 Saīd ʿAbd al-ʿAzīz Salām, *Dirāsāt fī Taʾrīkh al-ʿArab*, Ta'īf: Dār al-Maʿārif, 1976, pp. 30ff.; Madelung, *The Succession to Muhammad*, pp. 25–35.

9 L.I. Conrad (ed.), *History and Historiography in Early Islamic Times: Studies and Perspectives*, Princeton, NJ: Darwin Press, 2006; Robinson, *Islamic Historiography*, pp. 20ff.

10 Donner, *Narratives of Islamic Origins: The Beginning of Islamic Historical Writings*, pp. 187–8.

11 Aḥmad Ibn A'tham al-Kūfī, *Kitāb al-Futūḥ*, ed. M. ʿAbd al-Mu'īd Khān, 8 Vols., Hyderabad: Dā'irat al-Maʿārif al-ʿUthmānīyya, 1968–1975, 8, pp. 195–6; Al-Balādhurī, *Ansāb al-ashrāf*, 3, pp. 159–60; Moshe Sharon, 'The Umayyads as Ahl al-Bayt', *Jerusalem Studies in Arabic and Islam*, 14 (1991), p. 120.

12 H. Ibn al-Kalbī, *Jamharat an-Nasab. Das Genealogische Werks des Hisham ibn Muhammad al-Kalbi*, ed. W. Caskel, 2 Vols., Leiden: Brill, 1966, pp. 259–61.

13 Abū Dāwūd, *Sunān*, ed. M.M. ʿAbd al-Ḥamīd, Beirut: Maktabat al-ʿAsriyyah, Vol. 4, pp. 107–8, ref. num. 4286, declared *Da'īf* (weak) by M. Nasiruddīn Albāni.

14 Attema, *De Mohammedaansche Opvattingen omtrent het Tijdstip van den Jongsten Dag en zijn Voorteekenen*, Amsterdam: Noord-Hollandsche Uitgevers, 1942, pp. 25ff.; Wilferd Madelung, ʿAbd Allāh b. al-Zubayr and the Mahdī', *Journal of Near Eastern Studies*, 40 (1981), pp. 291–305; Gerald R. Hawting, *The First Dynasty of Islam: The Umayyad Caliphate AD 661–750*, London: Routledge, 2000, pp. 46–50; Julius Wellhausen, *Das arabische Reich und sein Sturz*, Berlin: Georg Reimer, 1960, pp. 71–125; Henri Lammens, *Le Califat de Yazīd Ier*, Beirut, 1921; Buthayna Ibn-Ḥusayn, *al-Fitna al-thāniyya fī ʿahd al-khalīfa Yazīd ibn Muʿāwiya, 60–64 H./680–684* M., Beirut, 2013, pp. 125ff.; Meir J. Kister, 'The Battle of the Ḥarra: Some Socio-economic Aspects', in M. Rosen-Ayalon (ed.), *Studies in Memory of Gaston Wiet*, Jerusalem: The Hebrew University, 1977, pp. 33–49.

15 Mehdy Shaddel, ʿAbd Allāh ibn al-Zubayr and the Mahdī: Between Propaganda and Historical Memory in the Second Civil War', *Bulletin of SOAS*, 80/1 (2017), pp. 1–19.

16 Al-Ṭabarī, *The History of al-Ṭabarī*, Vol. 20, pp. 47ff.; Al-Balādhurī, *Ansāb al-ashrāf*, 5, pp. 230ff.; Ibn al-Athīr, *al-Kāmil fi'l-taʾrīkh*, ed. Abi'l-Fidāʾ ʿAbd Allāh al-Qāḍī, Beirut, 1987, 3, p. 377ff.; Ibn Kathīr, *al-Bidāya wa'l-nihāya*, ed. Muhyīm al-Dīn Mastū, Beirut and Damascus, 2010, 8, p. 213ff.; Ibn al-Jawzī, *al-Muntaz am fī taʾrīkh al-mulūk wa'l-umam*, ed. Muḥammad ʿAbd al-Qādir ʿAṭā and Muṣṭafā ʿAbd al-Qādir ʿAṭā, Beirut, 1995, 5, pp. 322ff.; Donner, *Muhammad and the Believers. At the Origins of Islam*, pp. 185ff.

17 Michael Cook, 'Eschatology and the Dating of Traditions', in H. Motzki (ed.), *Ḥadīth: Origins and Developments*, Aldershot: Ashgate, 2004, pp. 217–41.

18 Shaddel, "Abd Allāh ibn al-Zubayr and the Mahdī: Between Propaganda and Historical Memory in the Second Civil War', pp. 6ff.

19 Donner, *Muhammad and the Believers. At the Origins of Islam*, p. 189.

20 Ibid., pp. 197ff; Donner, 'From Believers to Muslims: Confessional Self-identity in the Early Islamic Community', pp. 9–53; Shoemaker, *The Death of the Prophet*, pp. 210ff.; Papaconstantinou, 'Between Ummah and Dhimma', pp. 139ff.

21 Hoyland, *Seeing Islam as Others Saw It*, pp. 545ff; 'New Documentary Text and the Early Islamic State', pp. 397, 409–10; Donner, *Muhammad and the Believers. At the Origins of Islam*, pp. 194–224; Alfred-Louis de Prémare, *Les Fondations de l'Islam*, pp. 193–4, 278ff.

22 Brockopp, *Muhammad's Heirs*, pp. 31ff.

23 Ibid., pp. 18–19 n. 40; Judd, *Religious Scholars and the Umayyads,* pp. 25–34; Nallino, *La Letteratura Araba, agli inizi all'epoca della dinastia Umayyade,* pp. 69–110.

24 Suleiman Mourad, *Early Islam between Myth and History: al-Ḥasan al-Baṣrī (d. 110H/728 CE) and the Formation of His Legacy in Classical Islamic Scholarship,* Leiden: Brill, 2006, pp. 121ff.

25 Donner, *Muhammad and the Believers. At the Origins of Islam,* pp. 197–202; W. al-Qadi, 'Non-Muslims in the Muslim Conquest Army', pp. 121–3; Al-Awzā'ī and al-Zuhrī, who, as reported above, lived under Umayyad rule as well as under the 'Abbāsids, allowed the payment of non-Muslims in the 'Islamic' army, with the exception that a Christian could become Caliph, Imām or Military Commander. David Grafton, *The Christians of Lebanon: Political Rights in Islamic Law,* London: Tauris Academic Studies, 2003, pp. 45–6.

26 Herbert Berg (ed.), *Method and Theory in the Study of Islamic Origins,* Leiden and Boston, MA: Brill, 2003, Vol. 49; Sheila Blair, 'What Is the Date of the Dome of the Rock?', in Julian Raby and Jeremy Johns (eds), *Bayt al-Maqdis. 'Abd al- Malik's Jerusalem,* Oxford: Oxford University Press, pp. 59–87; J. Johns, 'Archaeology and the History of Early Islam: The First Seventy Years', *Jesho* 46/4 (2003), pp. 411–36; Oleg Grabar, *The Shape of the Holy. Early Islamic Jerusalem,* Princeton, NJ: Princeton University Press, 1996; Josef Van Ess, "Abd al-Malik and the Dome of the Rock. An Analysis of Some Texts', in Julian Raby and Jeremy Johns (eds), *Bayt al-Maqdis. 'Abd al-Malik's Jerusalem,* Oxford: Oxford University Press, 1992, pp. 33–58; Nevo Y.D., 'Towards a Pre-History of Islam', *Jerusalem Studies in Arabic and Islam,* 17 (1994), pp. 108–41.

27 Hoyland, *Seeing Islam as Others Saw It,* pp. 124ff, 403ff.; Donner, *Muhammad and the Believers. At the Origins of Islam,* pp. 203ff.

28 Michael the Syrian, *Chronique,* Vol. 2, p. 450.

29 S. Heidemann, 'The Merger of Two Currency Zones in Early Islam. The Byzantine and Sasanian Impact on the Circulation in Former Byzantine Syria and Northern Mesopotamia', *Iran,* 38 (1998), p. 107.

30 M. Bates, 'The 'Arab Byzantine Bronze Coinage of Syria: An Innovation by 'Abd al-Malik', in *Colloquium in Memory of George Carpenter Miles,* New York: 1976, pp. 16–27, esp. 9.

31 Caspar J. Kraemer, *Excavations at Nessana. Volume 3: Non-Literary Papyri,* Princeton, NJ: Princeton University Press, 1958, p. 178.

32 Johns, 'Archaeology and the History of Early Islam: The First Seventy Years', p. 421.

33 *Chronicle Maronite,* E.D. Brooks ed./J.B. Chabot, tr. *Chronicon Maroniticum,* CSCO 3–4, Paris: 1904, pp. 37–57; the above translation is that appeared in R. Hoyland, *Seeing Islam as Others Saw It,* p. 135; Clive Foss, 'A Syrian Coinage of Mu'āwiya?', *Revue Numismatique* 158 (2002), pp. 360–1.

34 Julia Bailey, Gürlu Necipoglu (eds), 'Frontiers of Islamic Art and Architecture: Essays in Celebration of Oleg Grabar's Eightieth Birthday', *Muqarnas,* Vol. 25, Leiden: Brill, 2008, p. 82 n. 4.

35 Andrew Marsham, 'The Architecture of Allegiance in Early Islamic Late Antiquity: The Accession of Mu'āwiya in Jerusalem, CA. 661 CE', in A. Beihammer, S. Constantinou and Maria Parani (eds), *Court Ceremonies and Rituals of Power in Byzantium and the Medieval Mediterranean,* Leiden: Brill, 2013, pp. 87–112,

36 Theophanes the Confessor, *The Chronicle of Theophanes,* trans. Cyril Mango, pp. 48–58; Al-Ṭabarī, *The History of al-Ṭabarī,* Vol. 18, p. 32, 172; Agapius of Manbij (Hierapolis), *Histoire Universelle,* ed. A. Vasiliev, PO, Vol. 8, réunies en un seul

volume par Albocicade, 2017, pp. 491ff.; M. Canard, 'Les Expéditions des Arabes contre Constantinople', *Journal Asiatique*, Vol. 208, Paris: Impriméric Nationale, 1926, pp. 63ff.

37 Foss, 'A Syrian Coinage of Muʿāwiya?', pp. 362ff.; 'Muʿāwiya's State', in *Money, Power and Politics in Early Islamic Syria*, p. 86; J. Johns, 'Archaeology and the History of Early Islam: The First Seventy Years', pp. 423ff.; Robinson, *Empire and Elites after the Muslim Conquest. The Transformation of Northern Mesopotamia*, p. 41 n. 47.

38 Album St and Tony Goodwin, *The Pre-Reform Coinage of the Early Islamic Period*, Sylloge of Islamic Coins in the Ashmolean 1, Oxford: Ashmolean Museum, 2002, p. 27; Treadwell W. Luke, 'The "Orans" Drachms of Bishr ibn Marwān and the Figural Coinage of the Early Marwānids', in *Bayt al-Maqdis. Jerusalem and early Islam*, ed. Jeremy Johns, Oxford: Oxford University Press, 1991, p. 266 B1.

39 Al-Ṭabarī, *The History of al-Ṭabarī*, Vol. 18, pp. 210–11; Kh. Ibn Khayyāt al-ʿUṣfurī, *Taʾrīkh*, ed. S. Zakkār, 2 Vols., Damascus: 1968, 1, p. 234; Abū al-Ḥasan A. al-Masʿūdī, *Murūj adh-Dhahab wa-maʿādin al-Jawhar*, 5, p. 14 (*wa-būyiʿa Muʿāwiya fī Shawwāl sana iḥdā wa-arbaʿīn bi bayt al-Maqdis*).

40 Al-Ṭabarī, *The History of al-Ṭabarī*, Vol. 18, pp. 169–70; Ibn Saʿd, *al-Tabaqāt al-Kubrā*, 4, p. 254; Ibn Kathīr, *al-Bidāya wa al-Nihāya*, 8, p. 16; Keppel A.C. Creswell, *Early Muslim Architecture*, 2 Vols., Oxford: Oxford University Press, 1969, p. 35, Goiten, 'Jerusalem during the Arab Period', in *Jerusalem Research in Eretz Israel*, 1953, pp. 82–103.

41 S. Bashear, 'Qibla Musharriqa and Early Muslim Prayer in Churches', *The Muslim World*, 31/3–4 (1991), pp. 267–82; M. Guidetti, *In the Shadow of the Church. The building of Mosques in Early Medieval Syria*, Leiden: Brill, 2017, pp. 36ff.; contrarily to Keppel A.C. Creswell, *Early Muslim Architecture* and Ocana Jimenez, 'La Basilica de San Vicente y la Gran Mezquita de Cordoba', *Al- Andalus*, 7/2 (1942), pp. 347–66.

42 Bingelli, 'Foires et Pèlerinage sur la route du Hajj. A propos de quelques sanctuaries chrétiens et musulmans dans le sud du Bilad ash-Sham d'aprés le *Kitab al-azmina* d'Ibn Masawayh (9e s.)', *Aram*, Vol. 18–19 (2006), pp. 559–82.

43 Guidetti, *In the Shadow of the Church*, p. 67.

44 Bashear, 'Qibla Musharriqa and Early Muslim Prayer in Churches', pp. 277ff.

45 Hoyland, *Seeing Islam as Others Saw It*, p. 221, on Arculf's journey to Jerusalem, probably around 680–683 AD.

46 Oleg Grabar, 'The Umayyad Dome of the Rock in Jerusalem', in *Jerusalem*, Vol. 4, Constructing the Study of Islamic Art, Hampshire, UK: Ashgate Publishing Limited, 2005, pp. 1–45; Rina Avner, 'The Dome of the Rock in the Light of the Development of Concentric Martyria in Jerusalem: Architecture and Architectural Iconography', *Muqarnas*, 28 (2010), pp. 31–49.

47 St. Shoemaker, 'Christmas in the Qurʾān: the Qurʾanic Accounts of Jesus' Nativity and Palestinian Local Traditions', *Jerusalem Studies in Arabic and Islam*, 28 (2003), p. 35; Guidetti, *In the Shadow of the Church*, p. 69.

48 Oleg Grabar, *The Dome of the Rock*, Cambridge, MA: Harvard University Press, 2006, p. 148.

49 Bashear, 'Qibla Musharriqa and Early Muslim prayer in Churches', pp. 281–2.

50 Moshe Sharon, 'The Birth of Islam in the Holy Land', in M. Sharon (ed.), *The Holy Land in History and Thought*, Leiden: Brill, 1988, pp. 230ff.

51 Y. al-Shdaifat, A. al-Jallad, Zeyad al-Salameen and Rafe Harahsheh, 'An Early Christian Arabic Graffito mentioning "Yazīd the King"', *Arabian Archeology and Epigraphy*, 28 (2017), pp. 315–24.

52 Ibid., p. 319; Ch. J. Robin, 'Ghassān en Arabie', in D. Genequand and Ch. J. Robin (eds), *Les Jafnides. Des Rois Arabes au service de Byzance*, Paris: Ed. de Boccard, 2015, pp. 79–81.
53 Hoyland, *Seeing the Arabs as Others Saw Them*, p. 620, n. 28.
54 S. Anthony, 'Fixing John Damascene's Biography: Historical Notes on His Family Background', *Journal of Early Christian Studies*, 23/4 (2015), pp. 614–15.
55 al-Shdaifat, al-Jallad, al-Salameen, Harahsheh, 'An Early Christian Arabic Graffito mentioning "Yazīd the King"', p. 322.
56 Ch. Kessler, "Abd al-Malik's Inscription in the Dome of the Rock: A Reconsideration', *The Journal of the Royal Asiatic Society of Great Britain and Ireland*, 1 (1970), p. 4.
57 Nuha N.N. Khoury, 'The Dome of the Rock, the Ka'ba and Ghumdam: Arab Myths and Umayyad Monuments', in *Muqarnas*, Vol. 10, Leiden: Brill, 1993, p. 58.
58 Jean-Mohammed 'Abd al-Jalil, *Marie et l'Islam*, Paris: Beauchsne, 1950.
59 David Thomas, Barbara Roggema, *Christian-Muslim Relations. A Bibliographical History*, Leiden: Brill, 2009, 1, pp. 203ff.
60 Johns, 'Archaeology and the History of Early Islam: The First Seventy Years', pp. 411–35; S. Heidemann, 'The Representation of the Early Islamic Empire and Its Religion on Coin Imagery', in A. Fuess and J.P. Hartung (eds), *Court Cultures in the Muslim World*, London: Routledge, 2011, pp. 30–53; Adam R. Gaiser, 'What Do We Learn about the Early Khārijites and Ibāḍiyya from Their Coins?', *Journal of American Oriental Society*, 130/2 (2010), pp. 167–87.
61 P. Crone and M. Hinds, *God's Caliph. Religious Authority in the First Century of Islam*, Cambridge: Cambridge University Press, 1986, pp. 24ff.
62 Ibn Ḥajar al-'Asqalānī, *Bulūgh al-Marām min 'Adla al-Aḥkām*, Vol. 13, n. 22.
63 ibn Yazīd ibn Mājah, *Sunan ibn Mājah*, Vol. 5, n. 1478.
64 Ya'qūbī, *Ta'rīkh ibn Wāḍih*, ed. Dār Sādir, Beirut: 1960, 2, p. 261.
65 Rabbat, 'The Dome of the Rock Revisited: Some Remarks on al-Wasiti's Accounts', *Muqarnas*, Volume in Honor of O. Grabar, 10 (1993), pp. 66–75.
66 O. Grabar, 'The Umayyad Dome of the Rock in Jerusalem', *Ars Orientalis* 3 (1959), pp. 47–52, plate 3.
67 Eva Baer, 'The Mihrab in the Cave of the Dome of the Rock', *Muqarnas*, 3 (1985), p. 17–18.
68 Both dynasties lived in a historical period in which the Byzantine 'Macedonian' emperors (867–1056) were assuming on the northern border a more offensive position reconquering some areas at the Syrian *limes* as well as inflicting important defeats on Islamic forces. John Haldon, *The Byzantine Wars*, Brimscombe Port Stroud: The History Press, 2009, pp. 94ff.
69 Hayrettin Yücesoy, *Messianic Beliefs & Imperial Politics in Medieval Islam*, Columbia: South Carolina University Press, 2009, pp. 18ff.; F. Donner, 'La question du messianisme dans l'Islam Primitif', in *Mahdisme et Millénarisme en Islam*, Aix En Provence: Edisud Ed., 2000, pp. 17–27; Stephen J. Shoemaker, *The Death of a Prophet*, Philadelphia: University of Pennsylvania Press, 2012; *The Apocalypse of Empire. Imperial Eschatology in Late Antiquity and Early Islam*, Philadelphia: University of Pennsylvania Press, 2018, pp. 146ff.
70 Shoemaker, *The Death of a Prophet*, p. 123.
71 D. Cook, *Studies in Muslim Apocalyptic*, Princeton, NJ: Darwin Press, 2002.
72 Shoemaker, *The Death of a Prophet*, pp. 18ff.
73 Ibid., pp. 126ff.; F. Donner, 'La question du messianisme dans l'Islam Primitif', p. 21; Donner, *Narratives of Islamic Origins*, p. 30 n. 78, 46.

74 Shoemaker, *The Death of a Prophet*, p. 24; Suliman Bashear, 'The Title of Fārūq and Its Association with 'Umar II', in *Studies in Early Islamic Tradition*, Jerusalem: The Max Schloessinger Memorial Foundation, 2004, pp. 47–70.
75 The debate among the Christian exegetes on whether these verses were elaborated *post-eventum*, the destruction of the Temple by the Romans of Titus in 70 AD and attributed to Jesus to stress his prophetic figure, is not a topic covered by this essay.
76 Al-Tirmidhī, *Al-Jāmi'al-ṣaḥīḥ*, ed. I. 'Awaḍ, 5 Vols., Cairo: 1965, 5, p. 3192; M. Tesei, '"The Romans Will Win!" Q. 30: 2–7 in Light of the 7th C. Political Eschatology', *Der Islam*, 95/1 (2018), pp. 1–29.
77 Shoemaker, *The Apocalypse of Empire*, pp. 151–3.
78 Lecker, 'Were the Ghassānids and the Byzantines behind Muḥammad's Hijra?', pp. 275–93; M. Ibrahim, 'Social and Economic Conditions in Pre-Islamic Mecca', *Ijmes*, 14/3 (1982), pp. 350ff.; Gene W. Heck, 'Arabia without Spices: A Alternate Hypothesis', *Journal of American Oriental Society*, 123/3 (2003), pp. 547–76; R.B. Serjeant, 'Meccan Trade and the Rise of Islam: Misconception and Flawed Polemics', *Journal of American Oriental Society*, 110/3 (1990), pp. 475–6, 480.
79 David S. Powers, *Muhammad Is Not the Father of Any of Your Men*, Philadelphia: Pennsylvania University Press, 2009, p. 225.
80 Guillaume, *The Life of the Prophet*, pp. 682–3; Ibn Sa'd, *al-Tabaqāt al-Kubrā*, 2, p. 262, about 'Umar's affliction reports: 'But I had hoped that the Messenger of God would live [as] he had said, and that he would be the last of us [alive]. God chose for His messenger that which was with Him rather than that which was with you. Hold fast to this book, by which God guided your messenger, and you will be guided as the Messenger of God was guided'; Ibn Kathīr, *al-Bidāya wa al-Nihāya*, 5, p. 262; Balādhurī, *Ansāb al-Ashraf*, 2, pp. 236–7; Al-Ṭabarī, *The History of al-Ṭabarī*, 9, pp. 183–9.
81 Guillaume, *The Life of the Prophet*, pp. 682–3.
82 Powers, *Muhammad Is Not the Father of Any of Your Men*, p. 226.
83 Uri Rubin, 'Muḥammad's Night Journey (Isrā') to al-Masjid al-Aqṣā. Aspects of the Early Origin of the Islamic Sanctity of Jerusalem', *Al-Qanṭara*, 29/1 (2008), pp. 147–641.
84 Flavius, *The Jewish War*, 6, 2.6–5.3.
85 Y. Friedmann, 'Finality of Prophethood in Sunni Islam', *Jerusalem Studies in Arabic and Islam*, 7 (1986), pp. 178–215; T. Fahd, *La Divination Arabe. Etudes religieuses, sociologiques et folkloriques sur le milieu natif de l'Islam*, Paris: Sindbad, 1987, pp. 25ff.
86 Shoemaker, *The Death of a Prophet*, pp. 20ff.; Hoyland, *Seeing Islam as the Others Saw It*, ch. 8, pp. 257ff.
87 Hoyland, *Seeing Islam as the Others Saw It*, pp. 67ff.; Meyendorff, *Imperial Unity and Christian Divisions: The Church 450–680 A.D.*, St Vladimir's Seminary Press, 1989.
88 Yücesoy, *Messianic Beliefs & Imperial Politics in Medieval Islam*, p. 19.
89 P.M. Holt, 'Islamic Millenarianism and the Fulfillment of Prophecy: A Case Study', in *Prophecy and Millenarianism: Essays in Honour of Majorie Reeves*, Ann Williams (ed.), Essex: Logman, 1980, pp. 337ff.
90 W. Madelung, "Abd Allah ibn al-Zubayr and the Mahdi', *Journal of Near Eastern Studies*, 40/4 (1981), pp. 291–305; 'Mahdī', in *EI*. 2nd ed. 1986, 5, pp. 1230–8.
91 Al-Ṣan'ānī, *Al-Muṣannaf*, ed. Ḥabīb al-Raḥman al-A'zamī, Beirut: al-Majlis al-'Ilmī, 1970, 11, p. 375; Nu'aym al-Khuzā'ī, *Kitāb al-Fitan*, ed. Zakkār, Beirut: Dār al-Fikr, 1993, pp. 390, 421; Ḥanbal, *Musnad*, ed. Aḥmad M. Shākir, Cairo: Dār al-Ma'ārif, 1955, n. 3523, 3570, 4088, 7969, 9407; Dāwūd, *Kitāb al-Sunan*, ed. M. 'Awwāma, Jeddah: Dār al-Qibla, 1998, n. 3712.

92 Geddes, 'The Messiah in South Arabia', *The Muslim World*, 1967, pp. 311–20.
93 Al-Ṣanʿānī, *Al-Muṣannaf*, 11: p. 388; Nuʿaym al-Khuzāʿī, *Kitāb al-Fitan*, pp. 66–7.
94 Balādhurī, *Ansāb al-Ashraf*, 2, p. 22; Ibn Qutayba, *Kitāb al-Maʿārif*, p. 385; Geddes, 'The Messiah in South Arabia', pp. 315–16.
95 Ibn Saʿd, *Tabaqāt*, 5, p. 333; Nuʿaym al-Khuzāʿī, *Kitāb al-Fitan*, pp. 57–8, 67–8.
96 W. Madelung, 'The Sufyānī between Tradition and History', *Studia Islamica*, 63 (1986), pp. 5–48; H. Lammens, 'Le "Sofiani": Héros National des Arabes Syriens', in *études sur les siècles des Omeyyades*, Beirut: Imprimerie Catholique, 1930, pp. 391ff.
97 Brockopp, *Muhammad's Heirs. The Rise of Muslim Scholarly Communities, 622–950*, pp. 83ff.; Donner, *Narratives of Islamic Origins*, pp. 297–306; Rudd, *Religious Scholars and the Umayyad*, pp. 40ff.
98 Georges Khoury, *Wahb Ibn Munabbih*, 2 Vols., Wiesbaden: Harrassowitz, 1972, 1, pp. 16, 52; Gordon Newby, *The Making of the Last Prophet. A Reconstruction of the Earliest Biography of Muhammad*, Columbia: University of South Carolina Press, 1989, pp. IX, 157–8.
99 Shoemaker, *The Apocalypse of Empire*, p. 146.
100 Ibid., p. 147.
101 Ibid., pp. 146ff; Cook, *Understanding Jihad*, pp. 5ff; *Studies in Muslim Apocalyptic*, pp. 14, 165–6, 268, 329, 374–5.
102 Ibid., p. 148.
103 Dennet, *Conversion and Poll Tax in Early Islam*, Delhi: 1950, pp. 3ff.; M. Shaban, 'Conversion to Early Islam', in N. Levtzion (ed.), *Conversion to Islam*, New York: NH publishers, 1979, pp. 24–9; Steven M. Wasserstrom, *Between Muslim and Jew. The Problem of Symbiosis under Early Islam*, Princeton, NJ: Princeton University Press, 1995, pp. 17ff.; Yohanan Friedmann, 'Conditions of Conversion in Early Islam', in A. Destro, M. Pesce (eds) *Rituals and Ethics. Patterns of Repentance, Judaism, Christianity and Islam*, Louvain: Peeters Ed., 2004, pp. 95–106; *Tolerance and Coercion in Islam. Interfaith Relation in Muslim Tradition*, Cambridge: Cambridge University Press, 2003, pp. 13ff.
104 Shoemaker, *The Apocalypse of Empire*, p. 148.
105 Hoyland, 'Reflections on the Identity of the Arabian Conquerors', pp. 114–34; *God's Path*, pp. 56–61; 'Muslims and Others', in R. Hoyland (ed.), *Muslims and Others in Early Islamic Society*, Aldershot: Ashgate Variorum, 2004, pp. xiii–xxx.
106 Donner, *Muhammad and the Believers*, pp. xii; 'Review of God's Path', *Al-ʿUṣūr al-Wusṭā*, 23 (2015), pp. 134–40; Peter Webb, 'Identity and Social Formation in the Early Caliphate', in H. Berg (ed.), *Routledge Handbook on Early Islam*, London: Routledge, 2017, pp. 129–58; *Imaging the Arabs: Arab Identity and the Rise of Islam*, Edinburgh: Edinburgh University Press, 2016.
107 M. Lombard, *The Golden Age of Islam*, Princeton, NJ: Markus Wiener Publishers, 2004, chapters 5 and 6.
108 H. Kennedy, 'Military Pay and the Economy of the Early Islamic State', *Historical Research*, 75/188 (2002), pp. 155–69; *The Armies of the Caliphs: Military and Society in the Early Islamic State*, London: Routledge, 2001, pp. 59–95; R. Bulliet, *Islam: The View from the Edge*, New York: Columbia University Press, 1994, pp. 67–79; S. Heidemann, 'The Merger of Two Currency Zones in Early Islam', *Iran*, 26 (1998), pp. 95–112.
109 Kennedy, 'Military Pay and the Economy of the Early Islamic State', p. 162; *The Armies of the Caliphs: Military and Society in the Early Islamic State*, chapters 2 and 3.

110 Khuri Hitti, *History of the Arabs,* p. 281; Claudio Lo Jacono, *Storia del Mondo Islamico. Il Vicino Oriente*, Torino: Einaudi, 2003, pp. 113ff.

111 D. Cook, 'Muslim Apocalyptic and Jihad', *Jerusalem Studies in Arabic and Islam,* 20 (1996), p. 71.

Chapter 4

1 Th. Sizgorich, *Violence and Belief in Late Antiquity,* Introduction, pp. 5–20; 'Sanctified Violence: Monotheist Militancy as the Tie That Bound Christian Rome and Islam', pp. 895–921.

2 *Chronique de Michel le Syrien,* ed. J.B. Chabot, 2, pp. 484–5; R. Guilland, 'L'Expedition de Maslama contre Constantinople (717–718)', *al-Mashriq,* 1955, pp. 89–112.

3 *Bar Hebraeus's Chronography,* ed. and trans. E.A. Wallis Budge, London: Oxford University Press, 1932, p. 10: 'And there went with them also thirty thousand warriors who of their own proper motion and at their own expense set out to fight, that is to say on "the road of God"; and they were called in their own language, Mutaṭawwia'ah'.

4 Theophanes, *The Chronicle of Theophanes the Confessor,* ed. Cyril Mango, pp. 80ff.; trans. Cyril Mango, R. Scott, pp. 538ff; Agapius of Hierapolis, *Kitāb al-'Unwan (Histoire Universelle),* ed. E.A. Vasiliev, pp. 240ff.; *The Chronicle of Zuqnin, Parts III and IV,* pp. 150ff.

5 Al-Ṭabarī, *History of al-Ṭabarī,* Vol. 24, pp. 35ff.; al-Ya'qūbī, *Ta'rīkh ibn Wāḍih,* 2, p. 299; Ibn Qutayba, *Kitāb al- 'Uyūn,* 1, p. 25.

6 Al-Tirmidhī, *Al-Jāmi'al-ṣaḥīḥ,* 4, n. 2238; Abū Dāwūd, *Sunān,* n. 4295; Yazīd ibn Mājah, *Sunan ibn Mājah,* Vol. 5, n. 4092.

7 Ibid., 4, n. 2239, – فَتْحُ الْقُسْطُنْطِينِيَّةِ مَعَ قِيَامِ السَّاعَةِ- which can be also interpreted as 'until the day of the resurrection, Constantinople will not be conquered'.

8 Yazīd ibn Mājah, *Sunan ibn Mājah,* Vol. 4, n. 2779.

9 Abū Dāwūd, *Sunān,* n. 4294.

10 H. Kennedy, 'Military Pay and the Economy of the Early Islamic State', p. 161; M.J. Kister, 'Do Not Assimilate Yourselves ... lā tashabbahū', in R. Hoyland (ed.), *Muslims and Others in the Early Islamic Society,* Aldershot, UK: Ashgate Variorum, 2004, pp. 125ff.

11 Th. Sizgorich, 'Sanctified Violence: Monotheistic Militancy as the Tie that Bound Christian Rome and Islam', p. 903; L. Conrad, 'Heraclius in Early Islamic Kerygma', in Gerrit J. Reinink, Bernard H. Stolte (eds), *The Reign of Heraclius (610–641): Crisis and Confrontation,* Leuven: Peeters, 2002, pp. 113–56.

12 Nadia Maria El-Cheick, 'Muhammad and Heraclius: A Study in Legitimacy', pp. 5–21.

13 Michael the Syrian, *Chronique,* Vol. 2, Book 11, chp. 19, pp. 488–91; Agapius of Hierapolis, *Kitāb al-'Unwan (Histoire Universelle),* Book 8, chp. 3, p. 503; The *Kitāb al-Aghānī* and Balādhurī admit a correspondence between the Caliph and the Muslim prisoners of Constantinople and those of Latikieh after a Roman incursion on the Syrian coast (718).

14 Arthur Jeffery, 'Ghevond's Text of the Correspondence between Umar II and Leo III', *Harvard Theological Review,* 37/4 (1944), pp. 269–332; R. Hoyland,

'The Correspondence of Leo III (717–741) and 'Umar II (717–720)', pp. 165–77; J.M. Gaudeul, 'The Correspondence between Leo and 'Umar. 'Umar's Letter Rediscovered', *Islamochristiana*, 10 (1984), pp. 116–57; D. Sourdel, 'Un pamphlet musulman anonyme d'époque abbaside contre les Chrétiens', *Revue des études Islamiques*, 34 (1966), pp. 27–33/13–26; Tim Greenwood, 'The Letter of Leo III of Ghewond', in *Christian Muslim Relations: A Biographical History*, Leiden: Brill, 2009, Vol. 1, pp. 203–8.

15 Arthur Jeffery, 'Ghevond's Text of the Correspondence between Umar II and Leo III', p. 298.

16 Ibid., pp. 309–32.

17 Muḥammad ibn al-Ḥasan al-Shaybānī, *Kitāb al-Siyat al-Ṣaghīr*, trans. Majid Khadduri, Baltimore, MD: Johns Hopkins University, 1966; Abū Isḥāq al-Fazārī, *Kitāb al-Siyar*, ed. Fārūk Ḥamād, Beirut: 1987; Anas ibn Mālik, *Al-Muwatta'*, ed. Y. Ibn al-Laithī, Beirut: Dār al-Kutub al-'Ilmiyyah, 2005, chp. 21.

18 Abdallāh Ibn al-Mubārak, *Kitāb al-Jihād*, ed. Nazīh Ḥammād, Cairo: Mujamma' al-Buḥūth al-Islāmiyya, 1978.

19 Calasso Giovanna and Lancioni Giuliano, *Dār al-Islām/Dār al-Ḥarb. Territories, People, Identities*, pp. 9–11, 21–47.

20 M. Bonner, *Aristocratic Violence and Holy War*, pp. 11–42; Michael Bonner, 'Some Observations Concerning the Early Development of Jihad on the Arab Byzantine Frontier', *Studia Islamica*, 75 (1992), pp. 5–31; Michael Bonner, 'Ja'ā'il and Holy War in Early Islam', *Der Islam*, 68/1 (1991), pp. 45–64; Michael Bonner, 'The Naming of the Frontier: Awāṣim, Thughūr and the Arab Geographers', *BSOAS*, 57/1 (1994), pp. 17–24; Michael Bonner, 'Ibn Ṭulūn's Jihad: the Damascus' Assembly of 269/883', *Journal of American Oriental Society*, 130/4 (2010), pp. 573–605.

21 Theophylact Simocatta, *Historiae*, trans. Michael and Mary Whitby, 5.1ff.

22 Theodoret, *Historia Religiosa*, ed. and trans. Pierre Canivet and A. Leroy Molinghen, 2 Vols., Paris: 1977–1979, 2, pp. 190–7.

23 Irfan Shahid, *Byzantium and the Arabs in the Sixth Century*, 2 t.2, pp. 291ff., 220–8,

24 Michael Bonner, 'Ja'ā'il and Holy War in Early Islam', p. 51, n. 36.

25 'Abd al-Razzāq, *al-Muṣannaf*, ed. H.R. al-A'ẓamī, Beirut: Dār al-Kutub al-'Ilmiyyah, 1970–1972, n. 9459.

26 Al-Shāfi'ī, *Kitāb al-Umm*, Al-Manṣūra: Dār al-Wafā', 2001, 4: 87. 19–20; 90.9ff.

27 Al-Ṭabarī, *History of al-Ṭabarī*, Vol. 27, pp. 168ff.; Al-Azdī Yazīd ibn Muḥammad, *Ta'rīkh al-Mawṣil*, ed. 'Alī Ḥabība, Cairo: 1967, pp. 126–7.

28 Al-Ṭabarī, *History of al-Ṭabarī*, Vol. 28, pp. 252ff.

29 Al-Azdī Yazīd ibn Muḥammad, *Ta'rīkh al-Mawṣil*, pp. 194–5.

30 H. Kennedy, *The Armies of the Caliphs*, tr. it., *Gli Eserciti dei Califfi*, pp. 92ff.

31 Al-Ṭabarī, *History of al-Ṭabarī*, Vol. 27, pp. 162ff.; Al-Azdī Yazīd ibn Muḥammad, *Ta'rīkh al-Mawṣil*, ed. 'Alī Ḥabība, Cairo: 1967, p. 129.

32 Ibn Isḥāq, *Sirāt Rasūl Allah*, trans. A. Guillaume, pp. 14–15, 79–82, 119–20, 136–44; Ibn Manẓur, *Mukhtaṣar ta'rīkh Dimashq li ibn 'Asākir*, ed. R. al-Khās, M.M. al-Ḥāfiẓ, 29 Vols., Damascus, 1984–1991, 5, pp. 154–5.

33 Al-Ṭabarī, *History of al-Ṭabarī*, Vol. 4, pp. 171ff.; Sozomenos, *Historia Ecclesistica*, ed. J. Bidez and G.C. Hansen, Berlin: De Gruyter, 1960, 8.11; Theodoret, *Historia Religiosa*, 5.29; Ambrose, *Epistulae*, ed. M. Zelzer, *Santi Ambrosi Opera. Pars X: Epistulae et Acta*, CSEL 82, Wien, ep. 40–41, pp. 145–77; M. Gaddis, *There Is No Crime for Those Who Have Christ*, Berkeley: University of California Press, 2005, chp. 5, pp. 92–5.

34 Many of them are quoted in S.A. Mourad's article, 'Christian Monks in Islamic Literature: A Preliminary Report on Some Arabic *Apophthegmata Patrum*', pp. 5ff.; other important sources are also cited in Ignazio di Francesco, *Il Lato Segreto delle Azioni*, Studi Arabo-Islamici del Pisai no. 19, Roma: PISAI, 2014.
35 Ibn Ḥanbal, *Kitāb al-Zuhd*, ed. M. 'Abd al-Salam Shāhīn, Beirut: Dār al-Kutub al-'Ilmiyya, 1999, pp. 95–6, no. 314.
36 Abū Bakr al-Dīnawarī, *Kitāb al-Mujālasa*, 1, pp. 141–2; Ibn Qutayba, *'Uyūn al-Akhbār*, 2, p. 368.
37 Ibn Qutayba, *'Uyūn al-Akhbār*, 4, p. 297; al-Azdī al-Basrī, *Ta'rīkh futūḥ al-Shām*, pp. 115–16.
38 Georg Ostrogorsky, *Geschichte des Byzantinischen Staates*, München, 1963, tr. it., P. Leone, *Storia dell'Impero Bizantino*, Torino: Einaudi, 1968, p. 145.
39 Feryal Salem, *The Emergence of Early Sufi Piety and Sunnī Scholasticism*, Leiden: Brill, 2016, p. 79.
40 Crone, 'Were the Qays and Yemen of the Umayyad Period Political Parties?', pp. 44ff.
41 P. Crone, *Slaves and Horses. The Evolution of Islamic Polity*, pp. 34–5, 99–100.
42 Y. Frenkel, *Ḍaw' al-sārī li-ma'rifat khabar Tamīm al-Dārī (On Tamīm al-Dārī and His Waqf in Hebron)*, Leiden: Brill, 2014,
43 Feryal Salem, *The Emergence of Early Sufi Piety and Sunnī Scholasticism*, p. 81.
44 Lyall R. Armstrong, *The Quṣṣāṣ of Early Islam*, Leiden: Brill, 2017, pp. 49ff.
45 Ibn al-Mubārak, *Kitāb al-Zuhd al-raqā'iq*, ed. Ḥabīb al-A'ẓamī, Beirut: Dār al-Kutub al- 'ilmiyyah, 2004, n. 142.
46 Ibn al-Mubārak, *Kitāb al-Jihād*, p. 34.
47 Ibid., pp. 36–7, as translated in Feryal Salem, *The Emergence of Early Sufi Piety*, p. 96–7.
48 Al-Bukhārī, *Ṣaḥīḥ*, Book 64, n. 265.
49 Ibn al-Mubārak, *Kitāb al-Jihād*, p. 100.
50 Ibn Ḥanbal, *Musnad*, Vol. 3, p. 266; Ibn al-Mubārak, *Kitāb al-Jihād*, n. 15.
51 Al-Bukhārī, *Ṣaḥīḥ*, Book 8, n. 6491.
52 Ibn al-Mubārak, *Kitāb al-Jihād*, n. 17; Ibn al-Mubārak, *Kitāb al-Zuhd al-raqā'iq*, n. 840.
53 Ch. Melchert, 'Ibn al-Mubārak's *Kitāb al-Jihād* and Early Renunciant Literature', in R. Gleave, Istvan T. Kristò-Nagy (eds), *Violence in Islamic Thought*, Edinburgh: Edinburgh University Press, pp. 65ff.
54 Anas ibn Ḥanbal, *Kitāb al-Zuhd*, ed. M. 'Abd al-Salam Shāhīn, Beirut: Dār al-Kutub al- 'ilmiyya, 1999, p. 151.
55 Mālik ibn Anas, *al-Muwaṭṭā*, p. 482.
56 Abū Nu'aym al-Iṣfahānī, *Ḥilyat al-awliyā' wa-ṭabaqāt al-aṣfiyā'*, Cairo: Maktabat al-Khānjī, 10 Vols., 1967, 7, p. 368.
57 Ignazio de Francesco, *Il Lato Segreto delle Azioni*, p. 151, this tradition passed from Ḥumayd ibn Hānī' al-Khawlāni and 'Amr ibn Mālik al-Jambī to the Medinese companion Faḍāla ibn Ubays (n. 120).
58 Ibn al-Nadīm, *Al-Fihrist*, ed. and trans. Bayard Dodge, New York: Columbia University Press, 2 Vols., 1970, 2, pp. 737ff.
59 Al-Jāḥiz, '*Manāqib al-Turk*', in G. Van Vloten (ed.), *Tria Opuscula Auctore Abu Othman Amr ibn Bahr al-Djahiz Basrensi*, Leiden: Brill, 2nd ed. 1968, pp. 1–56.
60 Khalīl Ibn al-Haythām al-Hartamī, *Mukhtaṣar Sīyāsāt al-Ḥurūb lil-Ḥarthamī Ṣaḥīb al-Ma'mūm*, ed. 'Abd al-Ra'uf 'Awn, Cairo: Maktabat al-'Ilmiyya, 1964. This source, probably written by someone directly affiliated to Harthama ibn A'yan, a famous

'Abbāsid general, in power from al-Hādī (d. 786) until al-Ma'mūn, is lost: however, a manuscript which seems to be a resume of this text is in the Köprulü Library of Istanbul.

61 W. Treadgold, *The Byzantine Revival 780–842*, Stanford, CA: Stanford University Press, 1988, pp. 280–3.

62 Al-Jāḥiz, *Manāqib al-Turk*, pp. 4–5.

63 Ibid., pp. 11–17.

64 Al-Ṭabarī, *The History of al-Tabari*, Vol. 29, pp. 196ff., 206, 210ff., 220–1; Vol. 30, pp. 167–8, 238–40, 257, 261–4, 267–8, 306–7; Vol. 32, pp. 55, 184–8, 194–9; Vol. 33, pp. 93–121; *The Chronicle of Zuqnin, Parts III and IV*, pp. 206–16, 222–6, 233–4; H. Kennedy, *The Armies of the Caliphs*, pp. 175–8.

65 Al-Ṭabarī, *The History of al-Tabari*, Vol. 30, pp. 261–8.

66 Baghdād deeply resisted al-Ma'mūn's siege and as long as the caliph decided to reside there, it remained in quite an anarchic state; al-Ṭabarī, assuming a pro-caliphate position, argues that the 'volunteer fighters *al-Muṭṭawwai'ah*' rid the capital of evildoers, but more specifically, it is hard to understand what the real meaning was. *The History of al-Tabari*, Vol. 32, pp. 55ff.

67 Khalīl Ibn al-Haythām al-Hartamī, *Mukhtaṣar Sīyāsāt al-Ḥurūb lil-Ḥarthamī Ṣaḥīb al-Ma'mūm*, pp. 23, 26–7.

68 Ibid., pp. 8–10.

69 Ibid., pp. 65–71; H. Kennedy, *The Armies of the Caliphs*, pp. 203, 297–304.

70 Khalīl Ibn al-Haythām al-Hartamī, *Mukhtaṣar Sīyāsāt al-Ḥurūb lil-Ḥarthamī Ṣaḥīb al-Ma'mūm*, pp. 2.

71 Malik Mufti, 'The Art of Jihad', *History of Political Thought*, 28/2 (2007), p. 206.

72 Feryal Salem, *The Emergence of Early Sufi Piety and Sunnī Scholasticism*, p. 141; Sulamī, *Ṭabaqāt al-Ṣūfīyah*, ed. J. Pedersen, Leiden: Brill, 1960; Kalābādhī, *Kitāb al-ta'arruf li-madhhab ahl al-Taṣawwuf*, trans. Roger Deladriere, *Traité de Soufisme, les maîtres et les étapes*, Paris: Babel, 2005; Al-Sarrāj, *Kitāb al-luma' fī-l-Taṣawwuf*, Cairo: Maktabat al-'Ilmiyyah, 1960; Ignazio de Francesco, *Il lato segreto delle azioni*, pp. 114ff., 121ff.

73 Paul L. Heck, 'Jihad Revisited', *Journal of Revised Ethics*,32/1 (2004), pp. 95–128; Ch. Décobert, 'Ascétisme et Jihād', pp. 268–80.

74 Th. Sizgorich, *Violence and Belief in Late Antiquity*, chp. 6–8; 'Sanctified Violence: Monotheist Militancy as the Tie that Bound Christian Rome and Islam', pp. 895–914; J. Wansbrough, *The Sectarian Milieu*, Oxford: Oxford University Press, 1978, pp. 71–87; P. Brown, 'The Saint as Exemplar in Late Antiquity', in J.S. Hawley (ed.), *Saints and Virtues*, Berkeley: California University Press, 1987, pp. 6–7.

75 Abū Bakr al-Khallāl, *Ahl al-milal wa-'radda wa-'l-zanādiqa*, ed. Ibrāhīm Ibn M. al-Sulṭān, 2 Vols., Riyad, 1996, pp. 55–7, 120–1.

76 Al- Jāḥiẓ, *Al-Radd 'alā al-Naṣārā*, trans. Jim Colville, London: Routledge, 2002, pp. 71–94.

77 Abū Bakr al-Khallāl, *Ahl al-milal*, p. 317.

78 Ibid., p. 317.

79 Ibid., pp. 71–85.

80 Th. Sizgorich, *Violence and Belief in Late Antiquity*, pp. 268–70.

81 Abū Dāwūd al-Sijistānī, *Sunan*, Book 39, n. 54.

Chapter 5

1 Mark Juergensmeyer, *Terror in the Mind of God. The Global Rise of Religious Violence*, 3rd ed., Berkeley: University of California Press, 2003; *The New Cold War? Religious Nationalism Confronts the Secular State*, 1993; S.P. Huntington, *The Clash of Civilizations and the Remaking of World Order*, New York: Simon and Schuster, 1996; 'The Clash of Civilizations', *Foreign Affairs*, 72/3 (1993), pp. 22–49; René Girard, *Violence et le Sacré*, Eng. *Violence and the Sacred*, Baltimore, MD: Johns Hopkins University, 1977; C. Crocket, *Religion and Violence in a Secular World: Toward a New Political Theology*, Charlottesville: University of Virginia Press, 2006; Cowdell, Fleming, Hodge and Osborn (eds), *Does Religion Cause Violence? Multidisciplinary perspectives on Violence and Religion in the Modern World*, 2018; *Religious Violence, Political Ends. Nationalism, Citizenship and Radicalizations in the Middle East and Europe*, Demichelis Marco (ed.), Hildesheim: Goerg Olms Verlag, Religion and Civil Sociey Series, 2018.

2 W.M. Watt, *Muḥammad at Mecca*, Oxford: Oxford University Press, 1953; *Muḥammad at Medina*, Oxford: Oxford University Press, 1956; *Muḥammad, Prophet and Statesman*, Oxford: Clarendon Press, 1961; F.E. Peters, *Muḥammad and the Origins of Islam*, Albany: Suny Press, 1994.

3 Nöldeke Th., Schwally Fr., Bergsträßer G. and Preztl O., *The History of the Qur'an*, ed. and trans. Wolfgang H. Behn, Leiden: Brill, 2013; Watt M. and Bell R., *Introduction to the Qur'an*, Edinburgh: Edinburgh University Press, 1970; R. Blachère, *Introduction au Coran*, Paris: G.P. Maisonneuve, 1947.

4 Nöldeke Th., Schwally Fr., Bergsträßer G. and Preztl O., *The History of the Qur'an*, pp. 48–9; Ya'qūbi, *Ta'rīkh*, Vol. 2., 33ff., pp. 43ff.; Dodge, *The Fihrst of al-Nadīm*, Vol. 1, pp. 49–52.

5 J. Wansbrough, *Quranic Studies*, pp. 85ff, 119ff.; *The Sectarian Milieu: Content and Composition of Islamic Salvation History*, Oxford: Oxford University Press, 1978; contrarily, F. Donner, in *Narratives of Islamic Origins*, ch. 1, argues differently, assuming that an early preliminary and partial crystallization is probably datable before the first *Fitna* (656–661), even though we need to wait longer for its real canonization.

6 G. Hawting, *The Idea of Idolatry and the Emergence of Islam. From Polemic to History*, Cambridge: Cambridge University Press, 1999, pp. 111ff.

7 A. Neuwirth, N. Sinai and M. Marx, *The Qur'ān in Context. Historical and Literary Investigation in the Qur'ānic Milieu*, Leiden: Brill, 2011; in particular, it would be relevant to consider the contributions of F. De Blois, 'Islam in Its Arabian context', pp. 615–24; Gregor Scholer, 'The Codification of the Qur'ān: A Comment on the Hypothesis of Burton and Wansbrough', pp. 779–84; and Omar Hamdan, 'The Second Maṣāḥif Project: A Step towards the Canonisation of the Qur'anic Text', pp. 795–835.

8 M.A.S. Abdel Haleem, 'Qur'anic Jihād: A Linguistic and Contextual Analysis', *Journal of Qur'anic Studies*, 12 (2010), pp. 147–66; Reuven Firestone, *Jihād. The Origin of Holy War in Islam*, Oxford: Oxford University Press, 1999, pp. 13ff, *Jihad*, in A. Rippin (ed.), *The Blackwell Companion to the Qur'ān*, Oxford: Blackwell Publishing, 2006, pp. 308–20.

9 A. Afsaruddin, *Striving in the Path of God*, p. 4.

10 Ibid., pp. 35–6.

11 Ibid., pp. 37–8.
12 A. Guillaume, *The Life of Muhammad,* pp. 212–13.
13 Abdel Haleem, *Understanding the Qur'ān. Themes and Style,* London: I.B. Tauris, 1999, p. 63.
14 A. Afsaruddin, *Striving in the Path of God,* pp. 41–2; Reuven Firestone, *Jihād. The Origin of Holy War in Islam,* pp. 53–6.
15 This author was adopted by Osama bin Laden in his speeches since the 1990s in developing a more aggressive interpretation of some Qur'anic verses. B. Lawrence, *Messages to the World – The Statements of Osama bin Laden,* New York: Verso, 2005, trans. *Messaggi al Mondo,* Roma: Fandango Libri, 2007, pp. 113, 115, 190, 205.
16 J. Burton, '*Naskh*', *EI.* 2nd ed., Vol. 7, pp. 1010–15; *Encyclopaedia of the Qur'ān,* ed. J.D. McAuliffe, Vol. 1, pp. 11–19.
17 Al-Rāzī, *Al-Tafsīr al-Kabīr,* 16 Vols., Beirut: Dār al-Iḥyā' al-Turāth al-'Arabī, Vol. 5, p. 132.
18 M. Watt and R. Bell, *Introduction to the Qur'ān,* Edinburgh: Edinburgh University Press, 1990, p. 120; G.R. Hawting, 'The Significance of the Slogan: lā hukma illā lillāh, and the References to the Hudūd in the Traditions about the Fitna and the Murder of 'Uthmān', *BSOAS,* 41/3 (1978), pp. 453–63; Badawi, Haleem, *Arabic-English Dictionary of Qur'anic Usage,* p. 692.
19 G.R. Hawting, *The Idea of Idolatry and the Emergence of Islam,* pp. 67ff.; T. Izutsu, *Ethico Religious Concepts in the Qur'ān,* Montreal&Kingston: McGill-Queen's University Press, 2002, pp. 119ff.; M. Robinson Waldman, 'The Development of the Concept of Kufr in the Qur'ān', *JAOS,* 88/3 (1968), pp. 453–5; Anne-Sylvie Boisliveau, 'Présentations coraniques des messages prophétiques anciens. L'attitude de Kufr dénoncée', in C. Gilliot, R. Tottoli, A. Rippin (eds) *Books and Written Culture of Islamic World. Studies Presented to Claude Gilliot on the Occasion of His 75th Birthday,* Leiden: Brill, 2014, pp. 144–58.
20 About whom, we need to consider *fakhr:* being proud of himself and of his genealogy, *ḥamāsa:* courage and contempt for danger, *karam:* generosity and hospitality, *'irḍ:* high sense of honour, *ṣabr*: patience in adversities and finally *ḥilm*: self-control. S. Natij, 'Murū'a. Soucis et interrogations éthiques dans la culture arabe Classique (1ère partie)', *Studia Islamica,* 112 (2017), pp. 216ff.
21 F. Donner, *Narratives of Islamic Origins,* pp. 174ff.
22 Elsaid M. Badawi and M. Abdel Haleem, *Arabic-English Dictionary of Qur'anic Usage,* pp. 471–2; the term *Siyar* and its derivatives appear twenty-seven times in the Islamic revelation.
23 W. Ende, *Arabische Nation und Islamische Geschichte,* Beirut: Orient-Institut, Beirut Texte und Studien, 1977, ch. 5.
24 N. Sinai, *The Qur'an. A Historical-Critical Introduction,* Edinburgh: Edinburgh University Press, 2017, p. 191.
25 Reuven Firestone, *Jihād. The Origin of Holy War in Islam,* p. 39.
26 Ibid., p. 132; N. Sinai, *The Qur'an,* p. 192.
27 N. Sinai, *The Qur'an,* p. 102; Maysam J. al-Faruqi, 'Umma: The Orientalists and the Qur'ānic Concept of Identity', *Journal of Islamic Studies,* 16/1 (2005), pp. 1–34; F. Mathewson Denny, 'The Meaning of Ummah in the Qur'ān', *History of Religions,* 15/1 (1975), pp. 34–70; Papacostantinou, 'Between Umma and Dhimma. The Christians of the Middle East under the Umayyads', pp. 127–56; D. Marshall, *God, Muhammad and the Unbelievers,* London: Routledge, 2013, pp. 118ff.
28 M. Watt and R. Bell, *Introduction to the Qur'ān,* p.120.

29 Hishām Ibn al-Kalbi, *Kitāb al-Aṣnān*, pp. 8ff.
30 R. Hawting, *The Idea of Idolatry and the Emergence of Islam*, pp. 112–13; P. Crone, 'Religion and the Qur'anic Pagans', *Arabica*, 57/2010, pp. 154–6, 162–3; Ch. Robin, 'Filles de Dieu de Saba à la Mecque: Reflexions sur l'engagement des panthéons dans l'Arabie ancienne', *Semitica*, 50 (2001), pp. 113–92; 'A propos des "Filles de Dieu": Complément à l'article publié dans *Semitica*', *Semitica*, 52–3 (2002–07), pp. 139–48.
31 H. Gätje, *The Qur'an and Its Exegesis*, Oxford: Oneworld, 2008, pp. 141–3.
32 A pagan Arab custom of using Arrows to take decisions, in drawing lots as to determine the idols' will is reported in the Qur'ān itself (5: 3, 90).
33 Al-Azraqī, *Kitāb Akhbār Makkah*, pp. 110–11, trans. from Peters F., *Muhammad and the Origins of Islam*, Albany: Suny Press, 1994, p. 141; Uri Rubin, 'Ḥanifiyya and Ka'ba', p. 102.
34 Greg Fisher and Philip Wood, 'Arabs and Christianity', pp. 370–1, where Sozomen, *Ecclesistical History*, 6: 38, is cited; I. Shahīd, *Byzantium and the Arabs in the Fifth Century*, pp. 154–6, 167–80. Even if Genesis argues that Abraham let Hagar and Ishmael go into the desert of Paran which has been usually identified with the Negev and not with the Ḥījāz.
35 'Alī Aḥmad al-Wāhidī, *Asbāb al-Nuzūl*, pp. 168–70; Al-Zamakhsharī, *Tafsīr al-Kashshāf 'an ḥaqā'iq ghawāmiḍ at-tanzīl wa-uyūn al-'aqāwīl fī wujūh at-ta'wīl*, Calcutta: Ṭabi' fī maṭba'al-laysī al-wāqia' fī Dār al-'Imāra, 1379 (A.H.), pp. 1644ff.; Fleischer H.O., *Behidhawii commentarius in Coranum*, 2 Vols., Leipzig: 1846–1849, 2, pp. 858ff.
36 H. Ibn al-Kalbi, *Kitāb al-Aṣnān*, pp. 27–31, 36, 38, 46.
37 Ibid., pp. 8–13, all of those cited in the Qur'anic verse are quoted by al-Kalbi in his eighth-century pamphlet.
38 *Tanwīr al-Miqbās min Tafsīr Ibn 'Abbās*, pp. 27–8.
39 Al-Ṭabarī, *Jāmi' al-bayān fī Tafsīr al-Qur'ān*, Vol. 2, pp. 4ff.; *Tanwīr al-Miqbās min Tafsīr Ibn 'Abbās*, p. 90; Alī Aḥmad al-Wāhidī, *Asbāb al-Nuzūl*, p. 6; *Tafsīr al-Jalālayn*, p. 19, 92.
40 A. Guillaume, *The Life of Muhammad*, pp. 239ff., 242ff., 277ff.
41 H. Yaman, 'The Criticism of the People of the Book (*Ahl al-Kitāb*) in the Qur'ān: Essentialist or Contextual?' *Gregorianum*, 92/1 (2011), p. 185.
42 Aḥmad al-Wāhidī, *Asbāb al-Nuzūl*, p. 47; *Tafsīr al-Jalālayn*, pp. 83.
43 N. Sinai, *The Qur'an*, p. 125.
44 S.H. Griffith, 'The Melkites and the Muslims: The Qur'ān, Christology and Arab Orthodoxy', *al-Qantara*, 33/2 (2012), pp. 413–43; '*Answers for the Shaykh*: A "Melkite" Arabic Text from Sinai and the Doctrines of the Trinity and the Incarnation in "Arab Orthodox" Apologetics', in E. Grypeou, M. Swanson and D. Thomas (eds), *The Encounter of Eastern Christianity with Early Islam*, Leiden, Brill, 2006, pp. 277–309, The History of Christian-Muslim Relations, Vol. 5; Roggema, Barbara, 'A Christian Reading of the Qur'ān: The Legend of Sergius- Bahīrā and Its Use of Qur'ān and Sīra', in David Thomas (ed.), *Syrian Christians under Islam: The First Thousand Years*, Leiden, Brill, 2001, pp. 57–73; Samir, Samir Khalil, 'The Earliest Arab Apology for Christianity (c.750)', in Samir, Samir Khalil and Nielsen, Jøgen S. (eds), *Christian Arabic Apologetics during the Abbasid Period (750–1258)*, Leiden, Brill, 1994, pp. 57–114, Studies in the History of Religions, Vol. 63.
45 Demichelis Marco, *Salvation and Hell in Classical Islamic Thought*, London: Bloomsbury Academic, 2018, p. 19.

46 A. Neuwirth, 'Meccan Text- Medinan Addition? Politics and the Re-reading of Liturgical Communication', in Arnzen R. and Thielmann J. (eds), Orientalia Lovaniensia Analecta 139, *Words, Texts and Concepts Cruising the Mediterranean Sea: Studies on the Sources, Contents and Influences of Islamic Civilizations and Arabic Philosophy and Science, Dedicated to G. Endress on His Sixty-Fifth Birthday,* Leuven: Peeters, 2004, pp. 80–5.

47 Al-Ṭabarī, *Jāmi' al-bayān fī Tafsīr al-Qur'ān,* Vol. 9, pp. 196–9; *Tanwīr al-Miqbās min Tafsīr Ibn 'Abbās,* p. 101.

48 A. Guillaume, *The Life of Muhammad,* pp. 437ff, 461ff.

49 D. Marshall, *God, Muhammad and the Unbelievers,* pp. 164–75; H. Yaman, 'The Criticism of the People of the Book (*Ahl al-Kitāb*) in the Qur'ān: Essentialist or Contextual?', pp. 196–7.

Chapter 6

1 Nöldeke Th., Schwally Fr., Bergsträßer G. and Preztl O., *The History of the Qur'an,* pp. 47ff.; M. Watt and R. Bell, *Introduction to the Qur'ān,* pp. 108ff; R. Blachère, *Introduction au Coran,* pp. 64ff; W. Muir, *The Life of Mohamet and History of Islam to the Era of Hegira, with Introductory Chapters on the Orginal Sources for the Biography of Mohamet and on the pre-Islamic History of Arabia,* London: Smith, Elder & Co, 3ed. 1894; H. Grimme, *Mohammed. Das Leben den Quellen. Einleitung in den Koran; system der* koranisschen *Theologie,* Münster: 1892–1895; N. Sinai, *The Qur'an,* pp. 122–32; F. Donner, 'The Qur'ān in Recent Scholarship. Challenges and Desiderata', in G. Said Reynolds (ed.), *The Qur'ān in Its Historical Context,* London: Routledge, 2008, pp. 29ff; C. Gilliot, 'Reconsidering the Authorship of the Qur'ān: Is the Qur'ān Partly the Fruit of a Progressive and Collective Work?', in G. Said Reynolds (ed.), *The Qur'ān in Its Historical Context,* pp. 88ff.; G. Said Reynolds, 'Le problème de la Chronologie du Qur'ān', *Arabica,* 58 (2011), pp. 477–502; H. Motzki, *Reconstruction of a Source of Ibn Isḥāq's Life of the Prophet and Early Qur'ān Exegesis,* Piscataway, NJ: Gorgias Press, 2017.

2 M. Watt and R. Bell, *Introduction to the Qur'ān,* p. 207.

3 N. Robinson, *Discovering the Qur'ān,* pp. 37–44; B. Sadeghi, 'The Chronology of the Qur'ān: A Stylometric Research Programme', *Arabica,* 58 (2011), pp. 282ff.

4 N. Sinai, *The Qur'ān,* p. 122; N. Sinai, 'The Unknown-Known: Some Groundwork for Interpreting the Medinan Qur'ān', *Mélanges de l'Université Saint Joseph,* 66 (2015–2016), pp. 47–96.

5 Nöldeke Th., Schwally Fr., Bergsträßer G. and Preztl O., *The History of the Qur'an,* pp. 172–4.

6 Ibid., pp. 141ff.

7 Fleischer H.O., *Behidhawii commentarius in Coranum,* 1, pp. 154ff.; Al-Ṭabarī, *Jāmi' al-bayān fī Tafsīr al-Qur'ān,* Vol. 5, pp. 234ff.; Aḥmad al-Wāhidī, *Asbāb al-Nuzūl,* pp. 18–19; *Tanwīr al-Miqbās min Tafsīr Ibn 'Abbās,* p. 37; *Tafsīr al-Jalālayn,* p. 39; A. Guillaume, *The Life of the Prophet,* pp. 286ff.

8 Nöldeke Th., Schwally Fr., Bergsträßer G. and Preztl O., *The History of the Qur'an,* p. 151; N. Sinai, *The Qur'an,* pp. 198–9.

9 N. Robinson, *Discovering the Qur'ān,* pp. 40–1; al-Ṭabarī, *Jāmi' al-bayān fī Tafsīr al-Qur'ān,* Vol. 8, pp. 170ff.; Ibn Khatīr, *Tafsīr,* Vol. 4, pp. 332ff.; Aḥmad al-Wāhidī,

Asbāb al-Nuzūl, pp. 81ff; *Tanwīr al-Miqbās min Tafsīr Ibn 'Abbās,* p. 182ff; *Tafsīr al-Jalālayn,* pp. 183ff; *Tafsīr al-Tustarī,* pp. 81–2.

10 *Tafsīr al-Tustarī,* p. 82.

11 Ibn Khatīr, *Tafsir,* Vol. 4, pp. 368ff.

12 al-Ṭabarī, *Jāmi' al-bayān fī Tafsīr al-Qur'ān,* Vol. 8, pp. 175.; Aḥmad al-Wāhidī, *Asbāb al-Nuzūl,* pp. 81ff; *Tanwīr al-Miqbās min Tafsīr Ibn 'Abbās,* p. 192; *Tafsīr al-Jalālayn,* pp. 193.

13 M. Bonner, *Jihad in Islamic History,* pp. 72–83; A. Afsaruddin, *Striving in the Path of God,* pp. 150ff.; A. Morabia, *Le Ğihād dans l'Islam medieval,* pp. 251ff.; M. Canard, 'La guerre sainte dans le monde Islamique et dans le monde chrétien', *Revue Africaine* (1936), pp. 605–23; J. Flori, *Guerre Sainte, Jihad, Croisade: violence et religion dans le christianisme et l'Islam,* Paris: Le Seuil, 2002.

14 Ibn Khatīr, *Tafsir,* Vol. 9., pp. 107ff. In this commentary Ibn Khatīr seems to suggest that *qitāl* and *jihad* have become synonyms in his time; at the same time, he also argues that 'a general prohibition of severing the ties of kinship. In fact, Allah, has ordained to people to establish righteousness on earth, as well as to join the ties of kinship by treating the relative s well in speech, actions and spending wealth in charity'. The hermeneutical understanding of Ibn Khatīr seems to emphasize how one of the main reasons for the spread of corruption all over the land (*'an tufsidū fī al-'arḍi*) during the pre-Islamic age was the breaking of the ties of kinship, a topic that the Qur'an stressed as greatly in contrast with the proto-Islamic message in the clear attempt to increase the union among believers. However, this argument is also complex in relation to the same fragmentation that the emigration of the Believers had brought to the Meccan community. In this phase, Ibn Khatīr seems to emphasize that the clan ties are still parithetically important for every kind of religious affiliation, which is an aspect that will never change, concretely and continuously emerging as a problem in the early Islamic age.

15 Al-Zamakhsharī, *Tafsīr al-Kashshāf,* ed. Muṣṭafā Ḥusain Aḥmad, 4 Vols., Cairo: 1953–1955, 2, pp. 25ff; *Tanwīr al-Miqbās min Tafsīr Ibn 'Abbās,* p. 52; *Tafsīr al-Jalālayn,* p. 54.

16 Mark Beaumont, *Christology in Dialogue with Muslims,* Eugene, OR: Wipf and Stock Publishers, 2005, pp. 1–11.

17 A. Guillaume, *The Life of Muhammad,* pp. 363–4; M. Lings, *Muhammad: His Life Based on the Earliest Sources,* trad. Ita, *Il Profeta Muhammad,* Torino: Leone Verde Ed. 2004, pp. 164–6.

18 Ibn Khatīr, *Tafsir,* Vol. 2., pp. 243ff.; *Tanwīr al-Miqbās min Tafsīr Ibn 'Abbās,* p. 68.

19 Nöldeke Th., Schwally Fr., Bergsträßer G. and Preztl O., *The History of the Qur'an,* pp. 157–7.

20 M. Watt, 'Abd-Allah ibn Ubayy', in *EI.* 2nd ed. Leiden: Brill, 1986, Vol. 1, p. 53; L. Caetani, *Annales,* Vol. 1, pp. 418, 548, 602; M. Lings, *Muhammad,* pp. 182, 200, 242–4.

21 Al-Ṭabarī, *The History of al-Tabari,* Vol. 7, p. 108.

22 Ibid.

23 Ibid., p. 110.

24 Ibid., pp. 134–8.

25 Al-Ṭabarī, *The History of al-Tabari,* Vol. 7, pp. 85–7; 156–61; Vol. 8, pp. 27–41; Ibn al-Wāqīdī, *Kitāb al-Maghāzī,* ed. R. Faizer, London: Routledge, 2011, pp. 87–90; 177–87; 244–57; A. Guillaume, *The Life of Muhammad,* pp. 363–4; 437–9; 461–70; M. Lings, *Muhammad,* pp. 164–6; 207–9; 234ff.

26 Ibn al-Wāqīdī, *Kitāb al-Maghāzī*, pp. 260–1.
27 *Tanwīr al-Miqbās min Tafsīr Ibn 'Abbās*, p. 662; M. Lings, *Muhammad*, p. 221.
28 Ibn Khatīr, *Tafsir*, Vol. 2, pp. 514–17; *Tanwīr al-Miqbās min Tafsīr Ibn 'Abbās*, pp. 94–5; *Tafsir al-Jalalayn*, p. 97.
29 Ibn Khatīr, *Tafsir*, Vol. 2, pp. 555–8; Firestone, *Jihad. The Origin of Holy War in Islam*, p. 81.
30 N. Sinai, *The Qur'an*, p. 191; Firestone, *Jihad. The Origin of Holy War in Islam*, pp. 32ff.
31 Ibn Khatīr, *Tafsir*, Vol. 2., pp. 559–63.
32 Ibn Khatīr, *Tafsir*, Vol. 9, pp. 542ff.; *Tanwīr al-Miqbās min Tafsīr Ibn 'Abbās*, pp. 657ff.; M. Lings, *Muhammad*, pp. 207–9; Ibn al-Wāqīdī, *Kitāb al-Maghāzī*, pp. 186–8.
33 S. Natij, 'Murū'a. Soucis et Interrogations éthiques dans la culture arabe Classique (1ère partie)', *Studia Islamica*, 112 (2017), pp. 216ff.
34 Ibn Khatīr, *Tafsir*, Vol. 6, pp. 621ff.; Nöldeke argues, in fact, in his comment that 22 is 'commonly regarded as Meccan but occasionally also as Medinan', but it becomes 'primarily important for the Medinan parts which it contains, despite that it was largely revealed during the third Meccan period before the *Hijra*'. Nöldeke Th., Schwally Fr., Bergsträßer G. and Preztl O., *The History of the Qur'an*, pp. 172ff.
35 A. Guillaume, *The Life of Muhammad*, pp. 490–9; M. Lings, *Muhammad*, p. 247;
36 M. Lings, *Muhammad*, p. 259.
37 Ibn Khatīr, *Tafsir*, Vol. 9, pp. 144–5; *Tanwīr al-Miqbās min Tafsīr Ibn 'Abbās*, p. 598; Al-Ṭabarī, *The History of al-Tabari*, Vol. 8, pp. 115ff.; Ibn al-Wāqīdī, *Kitāb al-Maghāzī*, pp. 311; M. Lings, *Muhammad*, pp. 268–75; A. Guillaume, *The Life of Muhammad*, pp. 510ff.
38 Ibn al-Wāqīdī, *Kitāb al-Maghāzī*, pp. 311ff., 355–65, 369–84; Al-Ṭabarī, *The History of al-Tabari*, Vol. 7, pp. 10ff; Vol. 8, pp. 4ff.; A. Guillaume, *The Life of Muhammad*, pp. 281ff.; M. Lings, *Muhammad*, pp. 139ff.; Talal Asad, 'The Bedouin as a Military Force: Notes of Some Aspects of Power Relations between Nomads and Sedentaries in Historical Perspectives', in Cynthia Nelson (ed.), *The Desert and the Sown-Nomads in the Wider Society*, Berkeley, CA: Institute of International Studies, 1973, pp. 66ff.; J.W. Jandora, 'Developments in Islamic Warfare: The Early Conquests', *Studia Islamica*, 64 (1986), pp. 101–13; Donald Routledge Hill, 'The Role of the Camel and the Horse in the Early Arabs Conquests', in V.J. Parry and M.E. Yapp (eds), *War, Technology and Society in the Middle East*, London: Oxford University Press, 1975, pp. 39ff.
39 Nöldeke Th., Schwally Fr., Bergsträßer G. and Preztl O., *The History of the Qur'an*, p. 178.
40 A. Guillaume, *The Life of Muhammad*, pp. 592–7; M. Lings, *Muhammad*, pp. 316–20.
41 Wāḥidī, *Asbāb al-Nuzūl*, p. 167.
42 Bukhārī/Muslim, *Riyāḍ Al-Ṣāliḥīn*, Vol. 1, n, 114.
43 Ibn Khatīr, *Tafsīr*, Vol. 4, pp. 369ff.; Al-Ṭabarī, *Jāmi' al-Bayān 'an al-Ta'wil 'Āy al-Qur'ān*, Vol. 10., pp. 77–9; *Tanwīr al-Miqbās min Tafsīr Ibn 'Abbās*, pp. 192–3; *Tafsīr al-Jalālayn*, pp. 194–5; A. Guillaume, *The Life of Muhammad*, pp. 617ff; M. Lings, *Muhammad*, pp. 332–3.
44 The Sanaa Palimpsest, on the contrary, at least in relation to the manuscripts 1–27.1 of the *Dār al-Mukhṭūṭāt* in fol. 5a, notes the Basmala presence in 8:75 and 9:1 arguing that if the Cairo edition does not have it, some non-'Uthmānic *muṣḥafs* such as that of Ibn Mas'ūdm, al-Rabī' Ibn Khuthaym and Ṭalḥa note it. Asma Hilali, *The Sanaan Palimpsest. The transmission of the Qur'an in the first century AH*, Oxford: Oxford University Press, 2017, p. 102.

45 Abdel Haleem, 'Qur'anic *Jihād:* A Linguistic and Contextual Analysis', *Journal of Qur'anic Studies,* 12 (2010), p. 152.
46 R. Firestone, *Jihād. The Origin of Holy War,* pp. 88–9; 'Disparity and Resolution in the Qur'ānic Teaching on War: A Reevaluation of a Traditional Problem', *JNES,* 56/1 (1997), pp. 14–16.
47 Al-Ṭabarī, *The History of al-Tabari,* Vol. 8, p. 182.
48 R. Blachère, *Le Coran,* p. 216 n. 29; At the same time, the Sanaa Palimpsest in relation to Folio 6a–6b is unable to consider the verse 29 as it is non-existent and due to the impossibility of reading the manuscript. Asma Hilali, *The Sanaan Palimpsest,* p. 106.
49 *Tanwīr al-Miqbās min Tafsīr Ibn 'Abbās,* p. 197; Abdel Haleem, 'The Jizya Verse (9:29): Tax Enforcement on Non-Muslims in the First Muslim State', *Journal of Qur'anic Studies,* 14/2 (2012), p.74.
50 Ibid., p. 75.
51 M. 'Imāra, *Al-Islām wa-l-'aqalliyyāt,* Cairo: Maktabat al-Shurūk al-dawliyya, 2003, p. 15; Abdel Haleem, 'The Jizya Verse (9:29)', pp. 75–6; Abdel Haleem, ElSaid M. Badawi, *Arabic-English Dictionary of Quranic Usage,* Leiden: Brill, 2008, pp. 163–4.
52 Rubin, Uri, 'Quran and Tafsīr. The Case of 'an yadin', *Der Islam,* Vol. 70 (1993), pp. 134ff; Abdel Haleem and ElSaid M. Badawi, *Arabic-English Dictionary of Quranic Usage,* p. 1055.
53 Al-Ṭabarī, *The History of al-Tabari,* Vol. 11, pp. 34ff.
54 Anas ibn Mālik, *Al-Muwaṭṭa',* pp. 484–7; Uri Rubin, 'Quran and Tafsīr. The Case of 'an yadin', p. 141 n. 53.
55 I.S. Allouche, Un traité de polémique christiano-musulmane au IXe siècle, *Hespéris,* 26 (1939), 123–55; J. Finkel, 'A Risāla of Al-Jāḥiz', *Journal of the American Oriental Society,* 47 (1927), 311–34. Partial reprinted with helpful notes in N.A. Newman (ed.), *The Early Christian-Muslim Dialogue: A Collection of Documents from the First Three Islamic Centuries, 632–900 A.D,* Hatfield, PA: Interdisciplinary Biblical Research Institute, 1993, pp. 685–717; Jim Colville, 'Contra Christianorum', in *Sobriety and Mirth: A Selection of the Shorter Writings of Al-Jahiz,* London: Kegan Paul, 2002, pp. 70–93.
56 Bausani and Blachère, for example, usually translate *Kaffātan,* with *totalmente, totalement,* which is quite problematic because it cannot give the hermeneutical perception of a reaction. Arberry A.J., on the contrary, used the term *continuously,* while Abdel Haleem, *at any time.*
57 Ibn Khatīr, *Tafsīr,* Vol. 4, pp. 421–5; Al-Zamakhsharī, *Kashshāf,* Vol. 1, pp. 395–7.
58 Al-Qurṭubī, *Al-Jāmi'li-aḥkām al-Qur'ān,* ed. 'Abd al-Razzāq al-Mahdī, Beirut, 2001, Vol.2, pp. 347–8.
59 Ibn Khatīr, *Tafsīr,* Vol. 4, pp. 427ff.; *Tanwīr al-Miqbās min Tafsīr Ibn 'Abbās,* pp. 198–9; Wāḥidī, *Asbāb al-Nuzūl,* p. 87; M. Lings, *Muhammad,* pp. 325–8.
60 Ibn Khatīr, *Tafsīr,* Vol. 4, pp. 489ff.; *Tanwīr al-Miqbās min Tafsīr Ibn 'Abbās,* pp. 204–5; *Tafsīr al-Jalālayn,* pp. 205–6.
61 N. Sinai, *The Qur'an,* p. 191; N. Reda, *The al-Baqara crescendo: Understanding the Qur'an's style, Narrative Structure and Running Themes,* Montreal: McGill-Queen's University Press, 2017, p. 88; Ch. Torrey, *The Commercial-Theological Terms in the Koran,* Leiden: Brill, 1892, pp. 25ff.
62 Wāḥidī, *Asbāb al-Nuzūl,* pp. 94–5; Ibn Khatīr, *Tafsīr,* Vol. 4, pp. 523–4; *Tafsīr al-Jalālayn,* p. 210.

63 Ṭabarī, *The History of al-Tabari,* Vol. 9, p. 73, n. 500; A. Guillaume, *The Life of Muhammad,* pp. 623–4; M. Lings, *Muhammad,* p. 331; Mirkhond, *Rawḍat aṣ-Ṣafā',* ed. Abbad Parviz, Tehran, 1959, Vol. 2, pp. 671–2.
64 Abū Dāwud, *Sunan,* Book 21, *Kitāb al-Janā'iz,* n. 6.
65 Al-Nasā'i, *Sunan al-Sughrā,* Book 21, *Kitāb al-Janā'iz,* n. 83, n. 150; Ibn Mājah, *Sunan,* Book 6, n. 1590; al-Tirmidhī, *Jāmi' al-Mukhtaṣar min al-Sunan,* Book 47, n. 3380; Muslim, *Ṣaḥīḥ,* Book 51, *Kitāb Ṣifāt al-Munāfiqīn wa 'aḥkhāmihim,* n. 4.
66 Nöldeke Th., Schwally Fr., Bergsträßer G. and Preztl O., *The History of the Qur'an,* p. 183, n. 272–3.
67 Ibid., pp. 183–4; A. Guillaume, *The Life of Muhammad,* pp. 649ff; M. Lings, *Muhammad,* pp. 343ff.
68 M. Cuypers, *Le Festin. Une lecture de la sourate al-Mā'ida,* Paris: Lethielleux, Rethorique Semitique, 2007; Nöldeke Th., Schwally Fr., Bergsträßer G., Preztl O., *The History of the Qur'an,* pp. 184ff.; V. Comerro, 'La nouvelle alliance dans la sourate al-Mā'ida', *Arabica,* 3 (2001), pp. 285–314; G. Said Reynolds, 'The Quran and the Apostle Jesus', *BSOAS,* 76/2 (2013), pp. 209–27.
69 Ibn Khatīr, *Tafsīr,* Vol. 3, pp. 179ff.; *Tanwīr al-Miqbās min Tafsīr Ibn 'Abbās,* pp. 117–18; *Tafsīr al-Jalālayn,* p. 120; *Asbāb al-Nuzūl,* p. 68.
70 Ibn Khatīr, *Tafsīr,* Vol. 3, pp. 211ff.; *Tanwīr al-Miqbās min Tafsīr Ibn 'Abbās,* pp. 120–1; *Tafsīr al-Jalālayn,* pp. 122–3; *Asbāb al-Nuzūl,* pp. 69–70.
71 *Tanwīr al-Miqbās min Tafsīr Ibn 'Abbās,* pp. 124–5; *Asbāb al-Nuzūl,* p. 71.
72 A. Guillaume, *The Life of Muhammad,* pp. 634ff.; M. Holger Zellettin, '*Aḥbār* and *Ruhbān*: Religious Leaders in the Qur'ān in Dialogue with Christian and Rabbinic Literature', in A. Neuwirth and M. Sells (eds), *Qur'anic Studies Today,* Abingdon: Routledge, 2016, pp. 262–3.

Chapter 7

1 Uri Rubin, 'Prophets and Caliphs: The Biblical Foundation of the Umayyad Authority', in Herbert Berg (ed.), *Method and Theory in the Study of Islamic Origin,* Leiden: Brill, 2003, pp. 78ff.; 'Prophets and Prophethood', in Andrew Rippin (ed.), *Blackwell Companions to Religion: The Blackwell Companion to the Qur'an,* London: Blackwell Publishing, 2006, pp. 234–47; A.J. Wensinck, 'Muḥammad and the Prophets', in U. Rubin (ed.), *The Life of Muḥammad,* Aldershot: Ashgate, 1998: pp. 319–43; Rahman, 'Prophethood and Revelation', in *Major Themes of the Qur'an,* pp. 56–73.
2 Haleem and Badawi, *Arabic-English Dictionary of Quranic Usage,* pp. 1024–25.
3 Afsaruddin, *Striving in the Path of God: Jihad and Martyrdom in Islamic Thought,* p. 35.
4 Ibid., pp. 150ff.; Haleem and Badawi, *Arabic-English Dictionary of Quranic Usage,* pp. 497ff.; Anas ibn Mālik, *Al-Muwatta',* pp. 228–9; Peters, *Jihad. A History in Documents,* pp. 21–4; Bonner, *Jihad in Islamic History,* pp. 72ff., *Aristocratic Violence and Holy War,* pp. 34–6.
5 Khalek, *Damascus after the Muslim Conquest,* Chapters 2 and 3; Mabra, *Princely Authority in the Early Marwanid State,* pp. 13–32; 'Abdulwāḥid Dhanūn Ṭāḥa, *The Muslim Conquest and the Settlement of North Africa and Spain,* pp. 142–5, 201ff.
6 Ṭabarī, *The History of al-Tabari,* Vol. 15, pp. 181ff.; Balādhurī, *Ansāb al-Ashrāf,* Vol. 5, pp. 37ff.; Ibn Sa'd, *Kitāb Ṭabaqāt al-Kubra,* Vol. IV, pp. 108ff.; As-Suyūṭī, *Ta'rīkh*

al-Khulafā' al-Rāshidūn, pp. 157ff; Madelung, *The Succession to Muhammad. A Study of the Early Caliphate*, pp. 78ff.; Djait, *La Grande Discorde*, pp. 117ff.; Ouardi, *Les Derniers Jours de Muhammad*, pp. 94ff.

7 Ibn al-Mubārak, *Kitāb al-Jihād*, pp. 34ff.

8 Tirmidhī, *Sunan*, Vol. 4, n. 541; Vol. 37, n. 2622.

9 Abī Dawud, *Sunan*, n. 5132; Muslim, *Saḥīḥ*, n. 947; Bukhārī, *Saḥīḥ*, n. 6566.

10 Donner, *Narratives of Islamic Origins*, pp. 47–9.

11 Wensinck, *The Muslim Creed*, p. 104.

12 Ibid., p. 124.

13 Anas ibn Mālik, *Muwatta'*, Vol. 1, n. 973, p. 228.

14 Ibid., Vol. 1, n. 978, p. 229.

15 Ibid., no. 976, pp. 228–9.

16 Wensinck, *The Muslim Creed*, pp. 26–7.

17 Bukhārī, *Saḥīḥ*, ed. L. Krehl and Th. W. Juynboll, 4 Vols., Leiden: Brill, 1908, Book 56, no. 1.

18 Ibid., Book 56, no. 8.

19 Ibid., Book 56, no. 26.

20 Muslim, *Saḥīḥ*, Book 32, no. 3.

21 Abū Isḥāq al-Fazārī, *Kitāb al-Siyar*, ed. F. Ḥammada, Beirut: Mu'assasāt al-Risāla, 1987; Majid Khadduri, *The Islamic Law of Nations: Shaybāni's Siyar*, Baltimore, MD: Johns Hopkins University Press, 1966; 'Abd al-Salām ibn Sa'īd al-Tanūkhī, Saḥnūn, *Al_Mudawwana al-Kubra*, ed. Ḥamdī al-Damardash, Beirut: al-Maktaba al-'Aṣriyya, 1999; Al-Sarakhsī, *Kitāb al-Mabsūt*, ed. Muḥammad H. al-Shāfi'ī, Beirut: Dār al-Kutub al-'Ilmiiyya, 1976, Vol. 10; Abū Yūsuf, *Al-Radd 'alā Siyar al-Awzā'ī*, ed. Abū al-Wafā' al-Afghāni, Cairo: Lajnat Iḥyā' al-Ma'ārif al-Nu'māniyya, 1938; Al-Māwardī, *al-Ḥāwī al-kabīr fī fiqh madhhab al-imām al-Shāfi'ī raḍī allāhu 'anhu wa-huwa sharḥ mukhtaṣar al-muzānī*, ed. 'Alī Muḥammad Mu'awwad and 'Ādil Aḥmad 'Abd al-Mawjūd, Beirut: Dār al-Kutub al-'Arabiyya, 1994.

22 Unfortunately, the *Fitnas* revealed a different narrative about the inner conflicts among the Believers after Muḥammad's death.

23 Abū Isḥāq al-Fazārī, *Kitāb al-Siyar*, p. 298, n. 549.

24 M. Muranyi, 'Das Kitāb al- Siyar von Abū Isḥāq al-Fazārī', *JSAI*, 6 (1985), pp. 67–70.

25 Abū Isḥāq al-Fazārī, *Kitāb al-Siyar*, p. 193, n. 274.

26 Khadduri, *The Islamic Law of Nations: Shaybāni's Siyar*, pp. 250–1; Al-Sarakhsī, *Kitāb al-Mabsūt*, pp. 135–6.

27 Ibid., p. 133.

28 Ibid., p. 145.

29 Saḥnūn, *Al-Mudawwana al-Kubra*, 2, pp. 584–7.

30 H. Kennedy, *The Armies of the Caliphs: Military and Society in the Early Islamic State*, London: Routledge, 2001, chp. 5; D. Ayalon, 'The Military Reform of Caliph al-Mu'taṣim', in *Islam and the Abode of War*, London: Routledge, 1994.

31 Saḥnūn, *Al-Mudawwana al-Kubra*, 2, p. 617.

32 Al-Māwardī, *al-Ḥāwī al-kabīr*, 14, pp. 110–13, 140–51.

33 Abū Yūsuf, *Kitāb al-Kharāj li l-Qāḍī Yūsuf Ya'qūb ibn Ibrāhīm ṣāḥib al-Imām Abī Ḥanīfa*, Beirut: Dār al-Ma'rifa, 1985; *Abū Yūsuf's Kitāb al-Kharāj*, part. trans. A.B. Shemesh, Leiden: Brill, 1969.

34 Ibid., pp. 95–101.

35 Al-Shāfi'ī, *al-Risāla al-Uṣūl al-Fiqh*, trans. M. Khaddury, Baltimore, MD: Johns Hopkins University Press, 1961, pp. 82–7.

36 Ibid., pp. 82–3.
37 Ibid., p. 83, but this is a tradition of Abū Dāwūd, *Sunan*.
38 Ibid., pp. 219–22.
39 Ibid., p. 222.
40 Ibid., pp. 85–6.
41 Ibid., pp. 86–7.
42 Al-Māwardī, *al-Aḥkām al-Sulṭāniyya wa al-wilāyat al-dīniyya – The Ordinances of Government*, London: Garnet Publishing, 2000, pp. 57ff., 83ff.
43 Ibid., p. 58.
44 Al-Māwardī, *al-Aḥkām al-Sulṭāniyya wa al-wilāyat al-dīniyya*, p. 72.
45 Ibid., p. 73.
46 Ibid., p. 65.
47 Ibid., p. 60.
48 Ibid., pp. 83–97.
49 Athamina, 'A'rab and Muhajirūn in the Environment of the Amṣār', pp. 5–25; Donner, 'The Development of the Concept of *Dār al-Islām* and *Dār al-Ḥarb*', p. 7, unpublished, I am really grateful to Fred Donner for having provided a copy of this draft paper; G. Calasso/G. Lancioni, *Dār al-Islām/Dār al-Ḥarb. Territories, People, Identities*, Leiden: Brill, 2017, pp. 93ff, 108ff, 125ff.
50 Y. Friedmann, *Tolerance and Coercion in Islam: Interfaith Relations in the Muslim Tradition*, Cambridge: Cambridge University Press, 2003; Donner, *Muhammad and the Believers*, pp. 45-6
51 G. Vercellin, *Istituzioni del Mondo Musulmano*, Torino: Einaudi, 2002, p. 22; Villano, 'The Qur'anic Foundations of the dar al-Islam/dar al-Harb dichotomy. An Unusual Hypothesis', in Giovanna Calasso and Giuliano Lancioni (eds), *Dar al-Islam/Dar al-Harb. Territories, People, Identities*, Leiden: Brill, 2017, pp. 142–3.
52 It is clear that the Quranic moral-ethical dichotomy in making the *Hijra* is prominent, even when only considering the 'narrative' that Muḥammad, after the conquest of Mecca, decided to return to Medina, to be buried there in the 'city of the Prophet'. So, it is evident that the paradigmatic role of the *Hijra* started to play a significant goal really early in the Islamic age, but at the same time, we also need to consider that until the 690s Prophet Muḥammad rarely appears in any kind of source, including archaeological-epigraphic, and his emigration even less so.
53 Donner, 'The Development of the concept of *Dār al-Islām* and *Dār al-Ḥarb*', p. 2.
54 Anas ibn Mālik, *Muwatta'*, pp. 141–2, 198–213.
55 Khadduri, *The Islamic Law of Nations: Shaybānī's Siyar*, p. 91.
56 Ibid., p. 80.
57 Ibid., p. 90.
58 Ibid., p. 109; Abū Yūsuf, *Kitāb al-Radd*, pp. 39–40; Sarakhsī, *Mabsūṭ*, Vol. 10, p. 45.
59 Al-Shāfi'ī, *al-Risāla al-Uṣūl al-Fiqh*, pp. 58–60.
60 Bonner M., *Jihad in Islamic History. Doctrines and Practises*, pp. 43ff; 'Some Observations Concerning the Early Development of Jihad on the Arab Byzantine Frontier', *Studia Islamica*, 75 (1992), pp. 5–31; Michael Bonner, 'The Naming of the Frontier: Awāṣim, Thughūr and the Arab Geographers', *BSOAS*, 57/1 (1994), pp. 17–24; Gleave R. and Kristò-Nagy Istvàn T., *Violence in Islamic Thought from the Qur'ān to the Mongols*, pp. 49ff.; R. Haug, 'Frontiers and the State in Early Islamic History: *Jihād* between Caliphs and Volunteers', *History Compass* 9/8 (2011), pp. 634–43.
61 C.E. Bosworth, 'Mutaṭawwi'a', in *EI*. 2nd ed., Leiden: Brill, 1993, Vol. 7, pp. 776–7.

62 *Chronicle of 1234, Chronicum anonymum ad annum Christi 1234 pertinens,* Versio CSCO 109 OCR, p. 234.
63 Michael the Syrian, *Chronique,* Vol. 2, pp. 483–4.
64 Bar Hebraeus, *Chronographie,* ed. and trans. E.W. Budge, Oxford: Oxford University Press, 1932, 1, p. 107.
65 Ya'qūbī, *Ta'rīkh,* ed. M. Ṣādiq, 3 Vols., Najaf: al-Maktaba al-Ḥaydariyy, 1964, 3, p. 44; Al-Kūfī, Abū M. Aḥmad Ibn A'tham, *Kitāb al-Futūḥ,* 8 Vols., Hyderabad: Maṭba'at Majlis Dā'irat al-Ma'ārif al-'Uthmāniyya, 1968–1975, 7, pp. 298–306; al-Ṭabarī, *The History of al-Tabari,* Vol. 24, pp. 39–42; Ibn Khatīr, *Al-Bidāya wa-l-Nihāyah,* Vol. 9, pp. 174–5.
66 al-Ṭabarī, *The History of al-Tabari,* p. 43.
67 Ibid., Vol. 22, p. 184; Balādhurī, *Ansāb al-ashrāf,* 11, p. 313.
68 C. Edmund Bosworth, 'The City of Tarsus and the Arab-Byzantine Frontiers in the Early and Middle 'Abbāsid Times', *Oriens,* 33 (1992), p. 270; Nasser Rabbat, 'Ribāṭ', in *EI.* 2nd ed., Vol. 8, 1995, pp. 495ff.
69 Al-Sam'ānī, *Kitāb al-Ansāb,* Hyderabad: Maṭba'at Majlis Dā'irat al-Ma'ārif al-'Uthmāniyya, 1962–1982, 12, p. 317.
70 Al-Ṭabarī, *The History of al-Tabari,* Vol. 11, pp. 77–8; Balādhurī, *Ansāb al-ashrāf,* 4b, pp. 24.14; Al-Kūfī, Abū M. Aḥmad Ibn A'tham, *Kitāb al-Futūḥ,* 7, pp. 11–12.
71 Bonner, *Aristocratic Violence and Holy War,* pp. 20ff.
72 Sizgorich, *Violence and Belief in Late Antiquity,* pp. 144ff.; Wadād al-Qāḍī, 'Non-Muslims in the Muslim Conquest Army in Early Islam', pp. 88ff.; Mabra, *Princely Authority in the Early Marwānid State,* pp. 13ff.; Ch. Décobert, 'Ascetisme et Jihād', pp. 258ff.; Bonner, 'Some Observations Concerning the Early Development of Jihād on the Arab-Byzantine Frontier', pp. 19ff.; Suleiman 'Ali Mourad, 'Christian Monks in Islamic Literature: A Preliminary Report on Some Arabic Apophthegmata Patrum', pp. 90ff.
73 Ibn Mubārak, *Kitāb al-Jihād,* pp. 30ff.; *Kitāb al-Zuhd,* pp. 83ff.; Al-Azdī, *Ta'rīkh futūḥ al-Shām,* pp. 115–16; Ibn 'Asākir, *Ta'rīkh madīnat Dimashq,* 1, pp. 474–7; Aḥmad Ibn Ḥanbal, *Kitāb al-Zuhd,* pp. 114ff, 180ff.; Ibn Qutayba, *'Uyūn al-Akhbāb,* 4, pp. 290ff.; Abū Nu'aym al-Iṣfaḥānī, *Ḥilyat al-awliyā' wa-ṭabaqāt al-aṣfiyā',* 8, p. 29 cited by Bonner, *Aristocratic Violence and Jihād,* pp. 128–9; al-Dhahabī, *Siyar a'lām al-nubalā',* 8, pp. 474–5.
74 Shahid, *Byzantium and the Arabs in the Sixth Century,* Vol. 1, t. 2, pp. 949ff.
75 Feryal Salem, *The Emergence of Early Sufi Piety and Sunnī Scholasticism,* Leiden: Brill, 2016, p. 79.
76 Ibn Mubārak, *Kitāb al-Jihād,* p. 34.
77 Ibid., pp. 32–4, 50–1, 124–5.
78 Ibid., pp. 32–4; Ibn Abī Shayba, *Muṣannaf,* Riyad: Maktabat al-Rushd Nāshirūn, 2004, 7, pp. 5–70.
79 Ibid., p. 110.
80 Ibn Mubārak, *Kitāb al-Zuhd,* pp. 140–1; Th. Sizgorich, *Violence and Belief in Late Antiquity,* pp. 85.
81 Ibn Mubārak, *Kitāb al-Jihād,* pp. 35–6.
82 Ibid.
83 S. Sivri, 'Wa-Rahbānīyatan ibtada'ūhā. An Analysis of Traditions Concerning the Origin and Evolution of Christian Monasticism', *JSAI,* 13 (1990), p. 201.

84 Salem, *The Emergence of Early Sufi Piety and Sunnī Scholasticism*, pp. 34, 77, 81, 105ff.
85 Y. al-Shdaifat, A. al-Jallad, Zeyad al-Salameen, Rafe Harahsheh, 'An Early Christian Arabic Graffito Mentioning 'Yazīd the King', p. 322; Zeyad al-Salameen, Hani Falahat, Salameh Naimat and Fawzi Abudanh, 'New Arabic-Christian Inscription from Udhruḥ, Southern Jordan', *Arabian Archaeology and Epigraphy*, Vol. 22 (2011), pp. 232–42; Langfeldt, 'Recently Discovered Early Christian Monuments in Northern Arabia', pp. 32–60; Hoyland, 'Epigraphy and the Emergence of Arab Identity', pp. 219–42; M. Guidetti, *In the Shadow of the Church. The Building of Mosques in Early Medieval Syria*, Leiden: Brill, 2017.
86 Shahid, *Byzantium and the Arabs in the Sixth Century*, Vol. 1, t. 2, pp. 949ff.
87 Melchert, 'Ibn al-Mubārak's *Kitāb al-Jihād* and Early Renunciant Literature', pp. 64ff.
88 Hūd Ibn Muḥakkam, *Tafsīr Kitāb Allah al 'azīz*, ed. Balḥajj Ibn Sa'īd Sharīfī, Beirut: Dār al-Gharb al-Islāmī (4 Vols.), 1990, II, p. 32; Al-Munāwī, *'Abd al-Ra'ūf, Al-Kawākib al-durriyya fī al-tarādjim al-sādāt al-sūfiyya*, Cairo: 1938; Allāma Quṭb al-Dīn al-Ḥanafī, *Prayers for Forgiveness: Al-Istighfārāt al-Munqidha min al-Nār*, London: White Thread Press, 2004; Suleiman Ali Mourad, *Early Islam between Myth and History: Hasan al-Basri (d. 110/728) and the Formation of His Legacy in Classical Islamic Scholarship*, Leiden: Brill, 2005, pp. 33ff.
89 Bonner, *Aristocratic Violence and Holy War*, pp. 113ff.

Conclusions

1 Ibn Mubārak, *Kitāb al-Jihād*, p. 100.
2 Ibid., pp. 110ff.
3 L. Bonanate, *La Guerra*, Bari: Ed. Laterza, 1998.
4 F. Donner, *Narratives of Islamic Origin*, pp. 174ff.; Chase F. Robinson, *Islamic Historiography*, pp. 18ff.; Sarah Bowen Savant, 'Shaping Memory of the Conquests: The Case of Tustar', in R. Gleave and Istvan T. Kristo-Nagy (eds), *Violence in Islamic Thought, from the Qur'ān to the Mongols*, Edinburgh: Edinburgh University Press, 2015, pp. 70–89; Sarah Bowen Savant, *The New Muslims of Post-Conquest Iran: Tradition, Memory and Conversion*, Cambridge: Cambridge University Press, 2013, pp. 90ff.
5 Daniel J. Sahas, *John of Damascus on Islam. The Heresy of the Ishmaelites*, pp. 99ff.; Najib George Awad, *Umayyad Christianity*, pp. 153ff.; D. Bryan Rhodes, 'John Damascene in Context', pp. 96–173.
6 Walter Pohl (ed.), *Kingdoms of the Empire. The Integration of Barbarians in Late Antiquity*, Leiden: Brill, 1997; Danuta Shanzer and Ralph W. Mathisen (eds), *Romans, Barbarians, and the Transformation of the Roman World: Cultural Interaction and the Creation of Identity in Late Antiquity*, London & New York: Routledge, 2016.
7 John Moschus, *Pratum Spirituale, PC* 87, 2852–3112; M. Rouet de Journel, tr. *John Moschus: le Pré Spirituel* (Sources chrétiennes 12; Paris, 1946); D.C. Hesseling, partial tr. *Marceaux choisis du Pré Spirituel de Jean Moschos* (Paris, 1931); Sophronius, *Ep. synodica, PG* 87, 3197D-3200A. For an elucidation of the theological content of the letter see von Schonborn, *Sophrone*, 201–24. Olster *Roman Defeat, Christian Response*, 99–115, discusses Sophronius' attitude towards the Byzantine empire and Arab victory; Daniel Sahas, 'Sophronius, Patriarch of Jerusalem', in David Thomas and Barbara Roggema (eds), *Christian-Muslim Relations: A Biographical History*,

Vol. 1 600–900, Leiden: Brill, 2009, pp. 120–7; Anastasius of Sinai, *Dialogue against the Jews, PG* 89, 1221C-D: *Dialogue of Papiscus and Philo* IX, 60–1. Thiimmel, *Friihgeschichte der ostkirchlichen Bilderlehre,* 260–1, argues convincingly that the former text is by Anastasius; on the latter text see McGiffert, *Dialogue between a Christian and a Jew,* 28–47; Haldon, John, 'The Works of Anastasius of Sinai: A Key Source for the History of Seventh-Century East Mediterranean Society and Belief', in A. Cameron and L. Conrad (eds.), *The Byzantine and Early Islamic Near East, Volume I: Problems in the Literary Source Material*, Princeton: Darwin Press, 1992, pp. 107–47.

8 Ehsan Roohi, 'The Murder of the Jewish Chieftain Ka'b b. al-Ashraf: A re-Examination', *Journal of Royal Asiatic Society,* series 3 (2020), pp. 1–22; Richard W. Bulliet, 'Islamo-Christian Civilization', in Moshe Bildstein, Adam Silverstein, Guy Stroumsa (eds), *The Oxford Handbook of the Abrahamic Religions,* Oxford: Oxford University Press, 2015, pp. 67ff.

Bibliography

Primary sources

1. 'Abd al-'Azīz Salām, Saīd, *Dirāsāt fī Ta'rīkh al-'Arab*, Ta'īf: Dār al-Ma'ārif, 1976.
2. 'Abduh, M. and Riḍā R., *Tafsīr al-Qur'ān al-ḥakīm al-mashhūr bi-Tafsīr al-Manār*, Beirut: Dār al-Kutub al-'Ilmiyya, 1999.
3. Abū Bakr Bayhaqī, *Dalā'il al-nubuwwa wa ma'rifat ahwāl sahib al-sharī'ah*, ed. A. Qal'aji, 7 Vols., Beirut: Dār al-Kutub al- 'ilmiyya, 1984.
4. Abū Dāwūd, *Sunān*, ed. M.M. 'Abd al-Ḥamīd, Beirut: Maktabat al-'Asriyyah, 1974.
5. Abū Ḥanīfa, *Al-Fiqh al-Akhbar Explained*, ed. Abu 'l-Muntaha al-Maghnisawi, London: White Thread Press, 2007.
6. Abū Isḥāq al-Fazārī, *Kitāb al-Siyar*, ed. Fārūk Ḥamād, Beirut: Mu'assasat al-Risāla, 1987.
7. Abū l-A'lā al-Mawdūdī, *Jihād in Islām*, Beirut: The Holy Koran Publishing House, 1980.
8. Abū l-A'lā al-Mawdūdī, *Towards Understanding the Qur'an*, Markfield, UK: The Islamic Foundation, 1994, Vol. 7.
9. Abū Yūsuf, *Kitāb al-Kharāj li l-Qāḍī Yūsuf Ya'qūb ibn Ibrāhīm ṣāḥib al-Imām Abī Ḥanīfa*, Beirut: Dār al-Ma'rifa, 1985.
10. Adomnan, *De Locis Sanctis*, ed. L. Bieler, *Itinera et alia geographica*, Corpus Christianorum series latina 175, Turnhout: Brepols, 1965, pp. 177–234; T. Tober and A. Molinier (eds), *Itinera Hierosolymitana et descriptiones terrae sanctae*, Geneva, 1879, pp. 141–210; T. Wright, partial tr. *Early Travels in Palestine*, London, 1848, pp. 1–12; Wilkinson tr. *Jerusalem Pilgrims*, pp. 93–116.
11. Agapius de Hierapolis (Mahbūb ibn Qūsṭānṭīn), *Histoire Universelle. Depuis la Création du Monde justq'à l'an 777*, ed. Alexander Vasiliev, réunies en un seul volume par Albocicade, 2017.
12. Aghatias Scholasticus, *Histories, guerres et malheurs du temps sous Justinien*, ed. Pierre Maraval, Paris: Les Belles Lettres, 2007.
13. Agathias Scholasticus, *The Histories*, ed. and trans. Joseph D.C. Frendo, Corpus Fontium Historiae Byzantinae, The Hague: De Gruyter, 2011.
14. Akram Ḍiyā' al-'Umarī, al-*Ta'rīkh* Khalīfa ibn Khayyāṭ, Najaf: Maṭba'at al-Adāb, 1967, 2 Vol.
15. Ammonious, *History and Historiography from the Late Antique Sinai*, trans. D.F. Caner, with S. Brock, M.R. Price and K.V. Bladel, Liverpool: Liverpool University Press, 2010.
16. Anastasius of Sinai, *Viae dux*, ed. J.-P. Migne, PC 89, Paris: Biblitecae Cleri Universae, 1865.
17. *Armenian History Attributed to Sabeos*, trans. R.W. Thomson, J.H. Johnston and Ass. T. Greenwood, Liverpool: Liverpool University Press, 2000.
18. A'ẓami, Muḥammad M., *The History of Quranic Text. From Revelation to Compilation*, Leicester: Uk Islamic Academy, 2nd ed., 2011.

19. Azdī, Muḥammad Ibn ʿAbdullāh Abū Ismāʿīl, *Taʾrīkh Futūḥ al-Shām*, ed. ʿAbd al-Munʿim Abdullah ʿĀmir, Cairo: Muʾassasa Sijil al- ʿArab, 1970.
20. Azdī, Yazīd ibn Muḥammad al-, *Taʾrīkh al-Mawṣil*, ed. ʿAlī Ḥabība, Cairo: Dār al-Taḥrīr li-l-Ṭabʿ wa-l-Nashr, 1967.
21. Balādhuri, *Kitāb al-Futūḥ al-Buldān*, trans. Philip Kh. Hitti, 2 Vols., New York: Columbia University Press, 1916.
22. Balādhurī, *Ansāb al-ashrāf*, ed. Muḥammad Ḥamīdullah, Cairo: Dār al-Māʿārif, 1959.
23. Bar Hebraeus, *Extraits de Bar Hebraeus III*, ed. and trans F. Nau in *Patrologia Orientalis*, 1919, Vol. 13.
24. *Bar Hebraeus's Chronography*, ed. and trans. E.A. Wallis Budge, Oxford: Oxford University Press, 1932.
25. Blockey R., *The History of Menander, the Guardsman*, Liverpool, UK: Cairns Ed., 1985.
26. Bukhārī, *Saḥīḥ*, ed. L. Krehl and Th. W. Juynboll, 4 Vols., Leiden: Brill, 1908.
27. Cyril of Scythopolis in His Life of John Hesychastes, see *Kyrillos von Skythopolis*, ed. E. Schwartz, TU 49, Leipzig, 1939.
28. *Chronicle of Zuqnin*, parts III and IV, trans. Amir Harrak: AD 488–775, Toronto: Pontifical Institute of Medieval Studies, 1999.
29. *Chronicon ad Annum 724*, ed. J.P.N. Land, *Symbolae Syriacae*, 4 Vols., Leiden: Brill, 1867.
30. *Chronicum Maroniticum*, trans. J.B. Chabot, *Chronica Minora, pars secunda*, CSCO, Scriptores Syri, ser 3, Vol. 4, Paris: 1904.
31. *Chronicle of 1234, Chronicum anonymum ad annum Christi 1234 pertinens*, Versio CSCO 109 OCR.
32. *Nābighah al-Dhubyānī, Dīwān*, ed. Muḥammad Abū al-Faḍl Ibrāhīm. al-Qāhirah: Dār al-Maʿārif, 1977.
33. Dionysios of Tell Mahre, *Historia ecclesiastica Zachariae rhetori vulgo adscripta*, ed. E. W. Brock, 2 Vols., Louvain: L. Durbecq, 1919–1924.
34. Evagrius, *The Ecclesiastical History of Evagrius*, ed. J.M. Bidez and L. Parmentier, London: Methuen & Co, 1898.
35. Fazārī, Abū Isḥāq al-, *Kitāb al-Siyar*, ed. Fārūk Ḥamād, Beirut: Muʾassasat al-Risālah, 1987.
36. Fleischer H.O., *Behidhawii commentarius in Coranum*, 2 Vols., Leipzig: Sumtibus F.C.G. Vogelii, 1846–1849.
37. Guidi I., *Chronicle of Khuzistan*, Leuven: Peeters, 1903.
38. Hartamī, Khalīl Ibn al-Haythām al-, *Mukhtaṣar Sīyāsāt al-Ḥurūb lil-Ḥarthamī Ṣaḥīb al-Maʾmūm*, ed. ʿAbd al-Raʾuf ʿAwn, Cairo: Maktabat al-ʿIlmiyya, 1964.
39. ʿIbadī, ʿAdī ibn Zayd al-, *Dīwān*, ed. al-Muʿaybid M. Jabbār, Baghdād: Sharikat Dār al-Jumhūriyya li-al-Nashr wa al-Tawzʿ, 1965.
40. Ibn ʿAbbās/ al-Firūzabādī, *Tanwīr al-Miqbās min Tafsīr Ibn ʿAbbās*, trans. M. Guezzou, Amman: Royal Institute of Islamic Thought, 2007.
41. Ibn ʿAbd al-Ḥakam, *Futūḥ Miṣr*, ed. C.C. Torrey, New Haven, CT: Yale University Press, 1922.
42. Anas ibn, Mālik, *al-Muwaṭṭā*, ed. Bashār ʿAwwād Maʿrūf, Beirut: Dār al-Gharb al-Islāmī, 1997, Vols. 2.
43. Ibn ʿAsākir ʿAlī b. al-Ḥasan, *Taʾrīkh madīnat Dimashq*, ed. Salah al-Din al-Munajjid, Damascus: al-Majma 'al-'Ilmī al-ʿArabī, 1951.
44. Ibn al-Athīr, *al-Kāmil fiʾl-taʾrīkh*, ed. Abiʾl-Fidāʾ ʿAbd Allāh al-Qāḍī, Beirut, 1987, Vol. 3.

45. Ibn Baṭrīq, Sa'īd (Eutychios), *Annales*, ed. L. Cheicko, Lipsiae: Otto Harrassowitz, 1909.
46. Ibn Ḥabīb M., *Kitāb al-Muḥabbar*, ed. Ḥaydar Ābād al-Dakkan, Damascus: Maṭba'at Jam'īyat Dā'irat al-Ma'ārif al-Uthmānīyah, 1942.
47. Ibn Ḥabīb M., *Al-Munaqqam fī akhbār Quraysh*, ed. Kurshīd Aḥmad Farīq, Beirut: 'Ālam al-Kutub, 1985, chp. *Ḥadīth al-Īlāf.*
48. Ibn Ḥanbal Aḥmad, *Musnad*, ed. Aḥmad M. Shākir, Cairo: Dār al-Ma'ārif, 1955.
49. Ibn Ḥanbal Aḥmad, *Kitāb al-Zuhd*, ed. M. 'Abd al-Salam Shāhīn, Beirut: Dār al-Kutub al-'Ilmiyya, 1999.
50. Ibn Ḥazm, *Jamharat ansāb al-'arab*, ed. 'Abd al- Salām Muḥammad Hārūn, Cairo: Dār al-Ma'ārif, 1962, 1971.
51. Ibn Hishām, 'Abd al-Malik, *Al-Sīra an-Nabawiyya*, ed. F. Wüstenfled, Göttingen: Dieterich, 1858–1860.
52. Ibn-Ḥusayn, Buthayna, *al-Fitna al-thāniyya fī 'ahd al-khalīfa Yazīd ibn Mu'āwiya, 60–64 H./680–684*, Beirut, 2013.
53. Ibn Isḥāq, *Sirāt Rasūl Allah*, trans. A. Guillaume, Oxford: Oxford University Press, 1955.
54 Ibn Kathīr, Ismā'īl ibn 'Umar, *Al-Bidāya wa'l-nihāyah fī al-ta'rīkh*. 14 Vols. Cairo: Maṭba'at al-Sa'ādath, 1932–1939.
55. Ibn Kathīr, *Tafsīr ibn Khatir*, Vols. 10, Riyadh: Darussalam ed., 2000.
56. Ibn al-Kalbi, H., *Kitāb al-Aṣnān*, ed. and trans. Nabith Amin Faris, Princeton, NJ: Princeton University Press, 2016.
57. Ibn Mājah, M. ibn Yazīd, *Sunan ibn Mājah*, Cairo: Dār al-Ḥadīth, 1998.
58. Ibn al-Mubārak, A., *Kitāb al-Jihād*, ed. Nazīh Ḥammād, Cairo: Mujamma' al-Buḥūth al-Islāmiyya, 1978.
59. Ibn Mubārak, *Kitāb al-Zuhd al-raqā'iq*, ed. Ḥabīb al-A'ẓamī, Beirut: Dār al-Kutub al-'ilmiyyah, 2004.
60. Ibn Nadīm, *Al-Fihrist*, ed. and trans. Bayard Dodge, New York: Columbia University Press, 2 Vols., 1970
61. Ibn Qutayba, *Kitāb al-Ma'ārif*, ed. Th.'Ukāsha, Cairo: Dār al-Ma'ārif, 1981.
62. Ibn Sa'd, *Kitāb Ṭabaqāt al-kabīr*, ed. Eduard Sachau, 8 Vols., Brill: Leiden, 1904–1921.
63. Ibn Thābit, Ḥassān, *Diwān*, ed. Arafat, London: 1971.
64. Iṣfahānī, Abū al-Faraj, *Kitāb al-Aghānī*, Beirut: Dar Sader Publishers, 2004, Vols. 25.
65. Iṣfahānī, Abū Nu'aym al-, *Ḥilyat al-awliyā' wa-ṭabaqāt al-aṣfiyā'*, Cairo: Maktabat al-Khānjī, 10 Vols., 1967.
66. Iṣfahānī, Ḥamza, *Ta'rīkh sinī mulūk al-arḍ wa-al-anbiyā'*, Leipzig: I.M.E. Gottwaldt, 1844.
67. Jāḥiẓ al-, *Radd 'alā al-Naṣārā*, ed. J. Finkel in *Thalāth Rasā'il li Abī Uthmān al-Jāḥiẓ*, Cairo: 1926.
68. Jāḥiz al-, *Manāqib al-Turk*, in G. Van Vloten, *Tria Opuscula Auctore Abu Othman Amr ibn Bahr al-Djahiz Basrensi*, Leiden: Brill, 2nd ed., 1968, pp. 1–56.
69. John of Damascus, *John of Damascus on Islam: The Heresy of the Ishmaelites*, trans. D. Sahas, Leiden: Brill, 1972.
70. John of Ephesus, *Lives of the Eastern Saints*, ed. and trans. E. Brooks, Paris: Firmin-Didot Ed., 1923–1925, 3 Vols., in R. Graffin-F. Nau, in *Patrologia Orientalis*, T. 17.
71. John of Ephesus, *Iohannis Ephesini Historiae ecclesiasticae pars tertia*, ed. and trans. E.W. Brooks, 2 Vols., Louvain: Peeters, 1935–1936.
72. John Malalas, *Chronographia*, ed. Ludovici Dindorfii, Bonn: Impensis ed Weberi, 1881.
73. John Malalas, *Chronographia*, English translation by E. Jeffreys, R. Jeffreys and R. Scott, Melbourne: Australian Association of Byzantine Studies, 1986.

74. John Moschus, *Pratum Spirituale, PC* 87, 2852–3112, trans. M. Rouet de Journel, *John Moschus: le Pre Spirituel*, Sources chretiennes 12, Paris, 1946; D.C. Hesseling, partial tr. *Morceaux choisis du Pre Spirituel de Jean Moschos*, Paris, 1931.
75. John of Nikiu, *The Chronicle of John (d. 690 ca) Bishop of Nikiu: Being a History of Egypt before and during the Arab Conquest*, ed. R.H. Charles, trans. H. Zotenberg's edition of the Ethiopic Version, London: Williams & Northgate, 1916.
76. Joshua the Stylite, *The Chronicle of Pseudo-Joshua the Stylite*, trans. Frank Trombley and J. Watt, Liverpool: Liverpool University Press, 2000.
77. Kaegi W., 'Initial Byzantine Reactions to the Arabs Conquests', *Church History*, Vol. 38, no. 2 (1969), pp. 139–49.
78. Kalbī, Hishām ibn al-, *Jahamarat al-Nasab*, Beirut: 'Ālam al-Kutub, 1986.
79. Kalbī, Hishām ibn al-, *Jamharat an-Nasab. Das Genealogische Werks des Hisham ibn Muhammad al-Kalbi*, ed. W. Caskel, 2 Vols., Leiden: Brill, 1966.
80. Khalidi S.D., *Amrika min al-dakhil bi-minzar Sayyid Qutb*, Jeddah: Dar al-Manara, 1986.
81. Khallāl, Abū Bakr al-, *Ahl al-milal wa-'radda wa-'l-zanādiqa*, ed. Ibrāhīm Ibn M. al-Sulṭān, 2 Vols., Riyad, 1996.
82. Khuzā'ī, Nu'aym al-, *Kitāb al-Fitan*, ed. Zakkār, Beirut: Dār al-Fikr, 1993.
83. Kūfī, Aḥmad Ibn A'tham al-, *Kitāb al-Futūḥ*, ed. M. 'Abd al-Mu'īd Khān, 8 Vols., Hyderabad: Dā'irat al-Ma'ārif al-'Uthmānīyya, 1968–1975.
84. Malchus, *Byzantine History*, ed. and trans. R.C. Blockey in *The Fragmentary Classicising Historians of the Late Roman Empire II*, Liverpool, UK: Francis Cairns, 1983.
85. Munajjid, Ṣalāḥ al-Dīn al-, *Madināt Dimashq 'ind al-Jughrāfiyyīn wa-l Rāḥilīn*, Beirut: Dār al-Kitāb al-Jadīd, 1967.
86. Mas'ūdī, *Murūj al-Dhahab*, trans. C. Barbier de Meynard and Pavet de Couteille, 5 Vols., Paris: Imprimerie Impériale, 1861.
87. Mas'ūdī, *Murūj al-Dhahab*, ed. Yūsuf As'ad Dāghir, 4 Vols., Beirut: Dār al-Ṣādir, 1965–1966.
88. *Maurice's Strategikon. Handbook of Byzantine Military Strategy*, trans. George T. Dennis, Philadelphia: University of Pennsylvania Press, 1984.
89. Māwardī al-, *al-Aḥkām al-Sulṭāniyya wa al-wilāyat al-dīniyya – The Ordinances of Government*, London: Garnet Publishing, 2000.
90. Michael the Syrian, *Chronique*, ed. and trans. J.H. Chabot, Paris: Ernest Leroux Ed., 1901.
91. Mullerus Carolus, *Fragmenta Historicum Graecorum*, Paris: Editore Ambrosio Firmin Didot, 1851, Vol. 4.
92. Nicephoros, *Nicephori Archiepiscopi Constantinopolitani opuscula historica*, ed. C. de Boor, Leipzig: Typis B.G. Tevbneri, 1880.
93. Pseudo-Wāqidī, *Futūḥ al-Shām*, Beirut: Dār al-Kutub al-'ilmiyya, 1972.
94. Procopius, *Opera*, ed. and trans. H.B. Dewing, Cambridge, MA: Harvard University Press, 7 Vols., 1961.
95. Procopius, *History*, ed. A.G. Roos and G. Wirth, Bibliotheca Teubnriana, reprint, Leipzig: Bibliotheca Teubnriana, reprint, London: W. Heinemann, Cambridge, MA: Harvard University Press, 1962.
96. Procopius, *The Wars of Justinian*, trans. H.B. Dewing, Indianapolis, IN: Hackett Publishing Co., 2014.
97. Qurṭubī, Ibn 'Abd al-Barr al-Namarī, *Al-Istī'āb fī Ma'arifat al-Aṣḥāb*, Beirut: Dār al-Jīl, 1992, Vol. 3.

98. Al-Qurṭubī, *Al-Jāmi'li-aḥkām al-Qur'ān*, ed. 'Abd al-Razzāq al-Mahdī, Beirut: Dār al-Kutub al- 'ilmiyya, 21 Vols, 2001.
99. Qutb S., *Fa Zilal al-Qur'an*, Vols. 6, Beirut: Dar al-Shuruq, 1974.
100. Rāzī al-, *Al-Tafsīr al-Kabīr*, 16 Vols, Beirut: Dār al-Iḥyā' al-Turāth al-'Arabī, 1991.
101. Sam'ānī al-, *Kitāb al-Ansāb*, Hyderabad: Maṭba'at Majlis Dā'irat al-Ma'ārif al-'Uthmāniyya, 1962–1982.
102. Ṣan'ānī, 'Abd al-Razzāq al-, *Al-Muṣannaf*, ed. Ḥabīb al-Raḥman al-'A'ẓamī, Beirut: Al-Maktab al-Islāmī, 1970–1972.
103. Shāfi'ī al-, *Kitāb al-Umm*, Al-Manṣūra: Dār al-Wafā', 2001.
104. Shāfi'ī al-, *al-Risāla al-Uṣūl al-Fiqh*, trans. M. Khaddury, Baltimore, MD: Johns Hopkins University Press, 1961.
105. Shaltūt, Maḥmūd, *Al-Qur'ān wa al-Qitāl*, ed. Maṭba'at al-Naṣr, Cairo: Dār al-Kitāb al-'Arabī, 1951, trans. R. Peters, in *Jihad and Medieval Modern Islam*, Leiden: Brill, Vol. 5, 1977.
106. Shantamarī, Al-A'lam, *Diwan 'Alqama al-Faḥl*, ed. D. al-Khaṭīb and I. Ṣaqqāl, Aleppo: Dār al-Kitāb al-'Arabī, 1969.
107. Shaybānī, Muḥammad ibn al-Ḥasan, *Kitāb al-Siyat al-Ṣaghīr*, trans. Majid Khadduri, Baltimore, MD: Johns Hopkins University, 1966.
108. Simocatta T., *Historiae*, English translation by M. Whitby and M. Whitby, Oxford: Clarendon Press, 1986.
109. *Sophronius of Jerusalem and the Seventh Century Heresy. The Synodical Letter and Other Documents*, ed. and trans. Pauline Allen, Oxford: Oxford University Press, 2009.
110. Sozomenos, *Historia Ecclesistica*, ed. J. Bidez and G.C. Hansen, Berlin: Akademie Verlag, 1960.
111. Suyūṭī al-, Jalāl ad-Dīn 'Abd al-Raḥmān, *Al-Itqān fī 'Ulūm al-Qur'ān, The Perfect Guide to the Sciences of Quran*, ed. Osman A. Al-Bili, Reading: Garnet Publishing, 2011.
112. Suyūṭī al-, Jalāl ad-Dīn 'Abd al-Raḥmān, *Ta'rīkh al-Khulafā'*, ed. Abdassamad Clarke, London: Ta-Ha Publishers, 1995.
113. Suyūṭī Jalāl ad-Dīn al-, Maḥallī J. ad-Dīn, *Tafsīr al-Jalālayn*, trans. Feras Hamza, Amman: Royal Institute for Islamic Thought, 2007.
114. Ṭabarī, *Ta'rīkh al-Rasul al-Mulūk*, ed. M.J. de Goeje, 15 Vols., Leiden: Brill, 1879–1901.
115. Ṭabarī, *History of al- Ṭabarī*, 40 Vols., Albany, NY: Suny Press, 1987–2007.
116. Ṭabarī, *Jāmi' al-bayān fī Tafsīr al-Qur'ān*, ed. M. Muḥammad Shākir, Cairo: Dār al-Ma'ārif, 1954.
117. Tha'labī, Aḥmad Ibn Muḥammad, *'Arā'is al-Majālis fī Qiṣaṣ al-Anbiyā, or: Lives of the Prophets*, ed. William M. Brinner, Leiden: Brill, 2002.
118. Theodoretus, *Ecclesistical History. A History of the Church*, London: Samuel Bagster and Sons, 1843, chp. XVIII.
119. Theophanes the Confessor, *The Chronicle of Theophanes the Confessor*, trans. Cyril Mango and Roger Scott, Oxford: Clarendon Press, 1997.
120. *Theophilus of Edessa's Chronicle*, trans. and intro. by Robert G. Hoyland, Liverpool: Liverpool University Press, 2011.
121. Thomas the Presbyter, *Chronicle*, E.W. Brooks, ed. J.B. Chabot, tr. *Chronicon miscellaneum ad annum domini 724 pertinens, CSCO* 3–4 *scr. syri* 3–4, Paris: Librairie de Firmin Didot Frères, 1904.

122. Tirmidhī, *Al-Jāmi'al-ṣaḥīḥ*, ed. I. 'Awad, 5 Vols., Cairo: Dār al-Kutub, 1965.
123. Tustarī, Sahl b. 'Abd Allāh al-, *Tafsīr al-Tustarī*, trans. A. Keeler and Ali Keeler, Amman: Royal Institute of Islamic Thought, 2011.
124. Wāhidī, 'Alī Ibn Ahmad, *Asbāb an-Nuzūl*, trans. Mokrane Guezzou, Amman: Royal Institute of Islamic Thought, 2008.
125. Wāqidī, Muḥammad ibn 'Umar, *Kitāb al-Maghāzī*, ed. Marsden Jones, 3 Vols., Oxford: Oxford University Press, 1966.
126. Wood Ph., *The Chronicle of Seert*, Oxford: Oxford University Press, 2013.
127. Ya'qūbī, Aḥmad, *Ta'rīkh al-Ya'qūbī*, 2 Vols., Beirut: Dār al-Ṣādir, 1960.
128. Zamakhsharī al-, *Tafsīr al-Kashshāf*, ed. Khalīl Ma'mūn Shīḥā, Beirut: Dār al-Ma'rifa, 2002.

Critical studies

1. Abu-Rabi Ibrahim, *Intellectual Origins of Islamic Resurgence in the Modern Arab World*, Albany, NY: Suny Press, 1995.
2. Abdul-Raof, Hussein, *Schools of Qur'anic Exegesis*, London: Routledge, 2010.
3. Asfaruddin Asma, *Islam, the State of Political Authority*, New York: Palgrave Macmillan, 2011.
4. Afsaruddin, Asma, *Striving in the Path of God: Jihad and Martyrdom in Islamic Thought*, New York: Oxford University Press, 2013.
5. Album St., Goodwin T., *The Pre-Reform Coinage of the Early Islamic Period*, Sylloge of Islamic Coins in the Ashmolean 1, Oxford: Ashmolean Museum, 2002.
6. Algar Hamid, *Wahhabism: A Critical Essay*, Oneonta, NY: Islamic Publications International, 2002.
7. Ali Mourad S., *Early Islam between Myth and History: al-Ḥasan al-Baṣrī (d. 110H/728 CE) and the Formation of His Legacy in Classical Islamic Scholarship*, Leiden: Brill, 2006.
8. Awad, N. George, *Umayyad Christianity. John of Damascus as a Contextual Example of Identity Formation in Early Islam*, Piscataway, NJ: Gorgias Press, 2018.
9. Badawi Elsaid M. and M. Abdel Haleem, *Arabic-English Dictionary of Qur'anic Usage*, Leiden: Brill, 2008.
10. Bardy G. (ed.), *Les Trophées de Damas. Controverse judéo-chrétienne du VII siécle*, Paris: Firmin-Didot & Co., 1920.
11. Buruma I. and A. Margalit, *Occidentalism: The West in the Eyes of Its Enemies*, London: Atlantic Books, trans. Nina Isola, Torino: Giulio Einaudi Editore, 2004.
12. Bat Ye'or, *Islam and Dhimmitude. Where Civilizations Collide*, Hackensack: Fairleigh Dickinson Press, 2001.
13. Bell R., *The Origins of Islam in Its Christian Environment*, Edinburgh: Edinburgh University Press, 1925.
14. Berg H. (ed.), *Method and Theory in the Study of Islamic Origins*, Leiden and Boston, MA: Brill, 2003, Vol. 49.
15. Bin Laden, Osama, *Messages to the World: The Statements of Osama Bin Laden*, ed. Bruce Lawrence, New York: Verso, 2005.
16. Bloom M., *Early Islamic Art and Architecture*, London: Routledge, 2016.
17. Boaz Shoshan, *The Arabic Historical Tradition and the Early Islamic Conquests. Folklore, Tribal Lore, Holy War*, London: Routledge, 2016.

18. Bonner M., *Jihad in Islamic History. Doctrines and Practises*, Princeton, NJ: Princeton University Press, 2006.
19. Bostom, A., *The Legacy of Jihad*, Amherst, NY: Prometheus Books, 2005.
20. Bostom, A., *The Legacy of Islamic Anti-Semitism: From Sacred Text to Solemn History*, Amherst, NY: Prometheus Books, 2008.
21. Brockopp J. E., *Muḥammad's Heirs. The Rise of Muslim Scholarly Communities*, Cambridge: Cambridge University Press, 2017.
22. Bulliet R., *Islam: The View from the Edge*, New York: Columbia University Press, 1994.
23. Burton, John, *The Collection of the Qur'an*, Cambridge: Cambridge University Press, 1977.
24. Caetani, L., *Annali dell'Islam*, Milano: Ulrico Hoepli Ed., 1907, Vol. 2, t. 1.
25. Calasso Giovanna and Lancioni Giuliano, *Dār al-Islām/Dār al-Ḥarb. Territories, People, Identities*, Leiden: Brill, 2017.
26. Calvert, J., *Sayyid Qutb and the Origin of Islamic Radicalism*, New York: Columbia University Press, 2010.
27. Caskel, W., *Jamharat an-Nasab: das genealogische Werk des Hisham ibn Muḥammad al-Kalbī*, Leiden: Brill, 1966, Vol. 1.
28. Cole Juan, *Muhammad. Prophet of Peace amid the Clash of Empires*, New York: Nations Books, 2018.
29. Conrad Lawrence I., John Haldon, *The Byzantine and Early Islamic Near East*, Princeton, NJ: Darwin Press, 2004, Vol. VI.
30. Cook David, *Understanding Jihad*, The Regents of the University of California: California University Press, 2005, tr. (Italian), Torino: Giulio Einaudi Editore, 2007.
31. Cragg Kenneth, *The Event of the Qur'ān. Islam in Its Scripture*, Oxford: Oneworld, 1994.
32. Creswell K.A.C., *A Short Account of Early Muslim Achitecture*, Aldershot: Scolar Press, 1989.
33. Crone Patricia, *Slaves on Horses. The Evolution of Islamic Polity*, London: Cambridge University Press, 1980.
34. Crone Patricia, *Meccan Trade and the Rise of Islam*, Piscataway, NJ: Gorgias Press, 2004.
35. Crone P., M. Cook, *Hagarism. The Making of the Islamic World*, Cambridge: Cambridge University Press, 1977.
36. Crone P., Martin Hinds, *God's Caliph. Religious Authority in the First Centuries of Islam*, Cambridge: Cambridge University Press, 1986.
37. Cupyers M., *Le Festin. Une Lecture de la Sourate al-Mā'ida*, Paris: Lethielleux, Rhétorique Sémitique, 2007.
38. Cuypers M., *The Composition of the Qur'an*, London: Bloomsbury Academic, 2015.
39. Della Vida, Giorgio Levi, *Versi Antichi di Arabia*, Milano: All'Insegna del Pesce d'Oro, 1967.
40. Dennet C. Daniel, *Conversion and Poll Tax in Early Islam*, Cambridge MA: Harvard University Press, 1950.
41. Caussin de Percevel, *Essais sur l'Histoire des Arabes avant l'Islamisme*, 3 Vols., Paris: 1847–1848.
42. De Premare Alfred Louis, *Les Fondations de l'Islam. Entre Ecriture et historie*, Paris: Edition du Seuil, 2002.
43. De Premare Alfred Louis, *Aux origines du Coran, questions d'hier, approches d'aujourd'hui*, Paris: Téraèdre, 2016.

44. Déroche Francois, *Qurans of the Umayyads: A First Overview*, Leiden: Brill, 2014.
45. Di Francesco Ignazio, *Il Lato Segreto delle Azioni*, Studi Arabo-Islamici del Pisai n. 19, Roma: PISAI, 2014.
46. Donner Fred, *The Early Islamic Conquests*, Princeton, NJ: Princeton University Press, 1981.
47. Donner Fred, *Narratives of Islamic Origins. The Beginning of Islamic Historical Writing*, Princeton, NJ: Darwin Press, 1998.
48. Donner Fred, *Muhammad and the Believers. At the Origin of Islam*, tr. Italian, *Maometto e le origini dell'Islam*, Torino: Giulio Einaudi Editore, 2011.
49. Ettinghausen R., Oleg Grabar, Marylin Jenkings-Madina, *Islamic Art and Architecture, 650–1250*, New Haven, CT: Yale University Press, 2001.
50. ElSayed Amin M.A., *Reclaming Jihad. A Qur'anic Critique of Terrorism*, Markfield: The Islamic Foundation, 2014.
51. Finazzo Giancarlo, *I Musulmani e il Cristianesimo. Alle origini del pensiero Islamico (sec. VII-X)*, Roma: Studium ed., 2005.
52. Firestone Reuven, *Jihād. The Origin of Holy War in Islam*, Oxford: Oxford University Press, 1999.
53. Fisher G., *Between Empires. Arabs, Romans and Sasanians in Late Antiquity*, Oxford: Oxford University Press, 2011.
54. Franklin A., Margarit Roxane E., Rustow M., Simonsohn U., *Jews, Christians and Muslims in Medieval and Early Modern Times*, A Festschrift in Honor of Mark R. Cohen, Leiden: Brill, 2014.
55. Friedmann Y., *Tolerance and Coercion in Islam. Interfaith Relations in the Muslim Tradition*, Cambridge: Cambridge University Press, 2003.
56. Gaddis M., *There Is No Crime for Those Who Have Christ*, Berkeley: University of California Press, 2005.
57. Gambetta D., S. Hertog, *Engineers of Jihad. The Curious Connection between Violent Extremism and Education*, Princeton, NJ: Princeton University Press, 2016, tr. it. *Gli Ingegneri della Jihad. I sorprendenti legami tra istruzione ed estremismo*, Milano: Bocconi University Press, 2017.
58. Gätje H., *The Qur'an and Its Exegesis*, Oxford: Oneworld, 2008.
59. Genequand D., Christian Julien Robin, *Les Jafnides. Des Rois Arabes au service de Byzance*, Paris: Ed. de Boccard, 2015.
60. Girard René, *Battling the End: Conversations with Benoît Chantre*, East Lansing: Michigan State University Press, 2010.
61. Gleave R., Kristò-Nagy Istvàn T., *Violence in Islamic Thought from the Qur'ān to the Mongols*, Edinburgh: Edinburgh University Press, 2015.
62. Grabar O., *The Shape of the Holy. Early Islamic Jerusalem*, Priceton, NJ: Princeton University Press, 1996.
63. Griffith S., *The Church in the Shadow of the Mosque*, Princeton, NJ: Princeton University Press, 2008.
64. Grypeou E., Mark N. Swanson, D. Thomas, *The Encounter of Eastern Christianity with Early Islam*, Leiden: Brill, 2006.
65. Guidetti M., *In the Shadow of the Church. The Building of Mosques in Early Medieval Syria*, Leiden: Brill, 2017.
66. Guillaume A., *The Life of Muhammad*, Oxford: Oxford University Press, 1955.
67. Haldon J., *The Byzantine Wars*, Gloucestershire, UK: The History Press, 2008.
68. Haleem A., *Understunding the Qur'ān. Themes and Style*, London: I.B. Tauris, 1999.

69. Hartung J.-Peter, *A System of Life. Maududi and the Ideologization of Islam*, London: Hurst, 2013.
70. Hashmi, H. Sohail, *Interpretating the Islamic Ethics of War and Peace*, in *Islamic Political Ethics. Civil Society, Pluralism and Conflict*, ed. Sohail H. Hashmi, Princeton, NJ: Princeton University Press, 2002.
71. Hawting R. Gerard., *The Idea of Idolatry and the Emergence of Islam. From Polemic to History*, Cambridge: Cambridge University Press, 1999.
72. Hawting R. Gerard, *The First Dynasty of Islam: The Umayyad Caliphate AD 661–750*, London: Routledge, 2000.
73. Hilali Asma, *The Sanaa Palimpsest. The Trasmission of the Qur'an in the First Centuries A.H.*, Oxford: Oxford University Press, 2017.
74. Hoyland, Robert G., *Arabia and the Arabs. From the Bronze Age to the Coming of Islam*, London: Routledge, 2001.
75. Hoyland, Robert G., *In God's Path. The Arab Conquests and the Creation of an Islamic Empire*, New York: Oxford University Press, 2015.
76. Hoyland, Robert G., *Seeing Islam as Others Saw It. A Survey and Evaluation of Christian, Jewish and Zoroastrian Writings on Early Islam*, Princeton, NJ: Darwin Press, 1997.
77. Hoyland Robert G., *Muslims and Others in Early Islamic Society*, Aldershot: Ashgate Variorum, 2004.
78. Humphreys R. Stephen., *Islamic History: A Framework for Inquiry*, Princeton, NJ: Princeton University Press, 1991.
79. Hussein Abdul-Raof, *Schools of Quranic Exegesis: Genesis and Dvelopment*, London: Routledge, 2013.
80. Izutzu, T., *Ethnico-Religious Concepts in the Qur'an*, Montreal: McGill's University Press, 2002.
81. Janses, J.J.G., *The Interpretation of the Quran in Modern Egypt*, Leiden: Brill, 1974.
82. Johnson Turner, J., *The Holy War Idea in Western and Islamic Tradition*, University Park: The Pennsylvania State University, 1997.
83. Judd Steven C., *Religious Scholars and the Umayyads*, London: Routledge, 2013.
84. Kaegi Walter E., *Byzantium and the Early Islamic Conquests*, Cambridge: Cambridge University Press, 1992.
85. Kennedy H., *The Armies of the Caliph. Military and Society in the Early Islamic State*, London: Routledge, 2001.
86. Kennedy H., *The Great Arab Conquests*, London: Phoenix Paperback, 2007.
87. Khadduri, Majid, *War and Peace in the Law of Islam*, New Jersey: The Lawbook Exchange Ltd., 2006.
88. Khalek Nancy, *Damascus after the Muslim Conquests*, Oxford: Oxford University Press, 2011.
89. Khalil M. Hassan, *Jihad, Radicalism and the New Atheism*, Cambridge: Cambridge University Press, 2017.
90. Kostiner, Joseph, 'On Instruments and Their Designers: The Ikhwan of Najd and the Emergence of the Saudi State', *Middle Easten Studies*, Vol. 21, no. 3 (1985), pp. 298–323.
91. Lauzière H., *The Making of Salafism. Islamic Reform in the Twentieth Century*, New York: Columbia University Press, 2015.
92. Lings M., *Muhammad: His Life Based on the Earliest Sources*, trad. Ita, *Il Profeta Muhammad*, Torino: Leone Verde Ed. 2004.

93. Luxemburg Chr., *The Syro-Aramaic Reading of the Koran*, Berlin: Verlag Hans Schiler, 2007.
94. Mabra J., *Princely Authority in the Early Marwānid State*, Piscataway, NJ: Gorgias Press, 2017.
95. Madelung W., *The Succession to Muhammad. A Study of the Early Caliphate*, Oxford: Oxford University Press, 1997, pp. 6, 16–18, 31–2.
96. Marshall David, *God, Muhammad and the Unbelievers*, London: Routledge, 2013.
97. Philip Scott-Montcrief, *The Book of Consolations, or the Pastoral Epistles of Mār Ishō'yahbh of Kuphlana in Adiabene*, London: Luzac &Co, 1904.
98. Morabia A., *Le Ǧihād dans l'Islam medieval*, Paris: Albin Michel, 1993.
99. Morrison C. (ed.), *Le Monde Byzantin. L'Empire Romain d'Orient (330–641)*, Paris: Puf, 2006.
100. Motzki H., *Reconstruction of a Source of Ibn Isḥāq's Life of the Prophet and Early Qur'ān Exegesis*, Piscataway, NJ: Gorgias Press, 2017.
101. Nallino C. Alfonso, *La Letteratura Araba, dagli inizi all'epoca della dinastia Umayyade*, Roma: Instituto per l'Oriente, 1948.
102. Neuwirth A., N. Sinai, M. Marx, *The Qur'ān in Context. Historical and Literary Investigation in the Qur'ānic Milieu*, Leiden: Brill, 2011.
103. Nevo Y., Judith Koren, *Crossroads to Islam. The Origins of the Arab Region and the Arab State*, Amherst, NY: Prometheus Books, 2003.
104. Newby Gordon, D., *A History of Jews of Arabia: from Ancient Times to Their Eclipse under Islam*, Columbia: University of South Carolina Press, 2009.
105. Nöldeke, Th., *The Qur'an: An Introductory Essay*, ed. N.A. Newman, Haytfield: Interdisciplinary Biblical Research Institute, 1992.
106. Nöeldeke Th., A. Mueller, *Delectus Veterum Carminum Arabicorum*, London, New York: 1890.
107. Nöldeke, Th., Schwally F., Bergsträßer G. and Pretzel O., *The History of the Qur'an*, Leiden: Brill, 2013.
108. Nöldeke, *Die Ghassānischen Fürsten aus dem Hause Gafna's*, Berlin: Abhandlungen der königlichen Akademie der Wissenschaften zu Berlin, 1887.
109. Ostrogorsky G., *Geschichte des Byzantinischen Staates*, München, 1963, trad. it., *Storia dell'Impero Bizantino*, Torino: Einaudi, 1968.
110. Ouardi H., *Les derniers jours de Muhammad*, Paris: Albin Michel, 2016.
111. Palmer A., Brock S., Hoyland R., *The Seventh Century in the West-Syrian Chronicles*, Liverpool: Liverpool University Press, 1993.
112. Pentz, Peter, *The Invisible Conquest. The Ontogenesis of Sixth and Seventh Century Syria*, Copenhagen: The National Museum of Denmark, 1992.
113. Peters R., *Islam and Colonialism*, The Hague: Mouton Publishers, 1979.
114. Peters R., *Jihad. A History in Documents*, Princeton, NJ: Markus Wiener Publishers, 2016.
115. Petra M. Sijpesteinijn, Lennart Sundelin, *Papyrology and the History of Early Islamic Egypt*, Leiden: Brill, 2004.
116. Pourshariati, P., *Decline and Fall of the Sasanian Empire*, London: I.B. Tauris, 2008.
117. Rahman, Fazlur, *Major Themes of the Qur'an*, Chicago, IL: University of Chicago Press, 1980.
118. Rippin, Andrew, *The Formation of Classical Islamic World. The Qur'an Formative Interpretation*, Aldershot: Ashgate Publishing, Vol. 25, 1999.
119. Rippin, Andrew, *The Formation of Classical Islamic World. The Qur'an, Style and Contents*, Adershot: Ashgate Publishing, Vol. 24, 2001.
120. Rippin, Andrew, *The Blackwell Companion to the Qur'ān*, Oxford: Blackwell Publishing, 2006.

121. Robinson N., *Discovering the Qur'an*, London: SCM press, 2003.
122. Robinson, F. Chase, *Empire and Elites after the Muslim Conquest. The Transformation of Northern Mesopotamia*, Cambridge: Cambridge University Press, 2000.
123. Robinson, F. Chase, *Islamic Historiography*, Cambridge: Cambridge University Press, 2003.
124. Roy O., *The Sainte Ignorance. Les temps de la Religion sans Culture*, tr. it. *La Santa Ignoranza. Religioni senza Cultura*, Milano: Feltrinelli, 2009.
125. Rothstein G., *Die Dynastie der Lahmiden in al-Ḥira*, Berlin: Verlag Von Reuther & Reichard, 1899.
126. Rubin, Uri, *Muhammad the Prophet and Arabia*, London: Routledge, 2011.
127. Rudolph, Peter, *Islam and Colonialism: The Doctrine of Jihad in Modern History*, New York: De Gruyter Mouton, 2015.
128. Rudolph, Peter, *Jihad. A History in Documents*, Princeton, NJ: Markus Wiener Publishers, 2016.
129. Daniel J. Sahas, *John of Damascus and Islam; the 'Heresy of the Ishmaelites'*, Leiden: Brill, 1972.
130. Salem F., *The Emergence of Early Sufi Piety and Sunnī Scholasticism*, Leiden: Brill, 2016.
131. Salihi, Zahida, *The Career of 'Abdallah ibn az-Zubayr, with Special Reference to the Period 61–73/680–692*, PhD Diss., University of Edinburgh.
132. Sezgin F., *Geschichte des arabischen Schrifttums*, Leiden: Brill, 1975.
133. Shaban M.A., *Islamic History. A New Interpretation*, Cambridge: Cambridge University Press, 1983.
134. Shah, Niaz A., *Self-defence in Islamic and International Law. Assessing al-Qaeda and the Invasion of Iraq*, New York: Palgrave Macmillan, 2008.
135. Shahid Irfan, *Byzantium and the Arabs in the IV Century*, Washington, DC: Dumbarton Oaks, 1984.
136. Shahid Irfan, *Byzantium and the Arabs in the V Century*, Washington, DC: Dumbarton Oaks, 1989.
137. Shahid Irfan, *Byzantium and the Arabs in the VI century*, Vols. 1–2, t. 1–2, Washington: Dumbarton Oaks, 1995–2009.
138. Shoemaker Stephen J., *The Death of a Prophet. The End of Muhammad's Life and the Beginnings of Islam*, Philadelphia: University of Pennsylvania Press, 2012.
139. Shoemaker Stephen J., *The Apocalypse of Empire. Imperial Eschatology in Late Antiquity and Early Islam*, Philadelphia: University of Pennsylvania Press, 2018.
140. Shoufani S., *Al-Riddah and the Muslim Conquests of Arabia*, Toronto: University of Toronto Press, 1973.
141. Sinai N., *The Qur'an. A Historical-Critical Introduction*, Edinburgh: Edinburgh University Press, 2017.
142. Sizgorich, Thomas, *Violence and Beliefs in Late Antiquity*, Philadelphia: University of Pennsylvania Press, 2009.
143. Thomas D. and Barbara Roggema (eds), *Christian-Muslim Relations. A Biographical History*, Vol. 1, pp. 600–900, Leiden: Brill, 2009.
144. Tibi, Bassam, *War and Peace in Islam*, in *Islamic Political Ethics. Civil Society, Pluralism and Conflict*, ed. Sohail H. Hashmi, Princeton, NJ: Princeton University Press, 2002.
145. Treadgold, Warren, *The Byzantine Revival 780–842*, Stanford, CA: Stanford University Press, 1988.
146. Treadgold, Warren, *A History of the Byzantine State and Society*, Stanford, CA: Stanford University Press, 1997.

147. Turner, J., *The Holy War Idea in Western and Islamic Tradition*, University Park: The Pennsylvania State University, 1997.
148. Van den Ven P., *La vie ancienne de Siméon stylite le jeune*, Subsidia Hagiographica 52, Brussels: 1962, Vol. 1.
149. Vercellin G., *Istituzioni del Mondo Musulmano*, Torino: Einaudi, 2002.
150. Wansbrough, John, *The Sectarian Milieu*, Oxford: Oxford University Press, 1978.
151. Wansbrough, John, *Quranic Studies: Sources and Methods of Scriptural Interpretation*, Oxford: Oxford University Press, 1977.
152. Watt M. and Bell R., *Introduction to the Qur'an*, Edinburgh: Edinburgh University Press, 1970.
153. Watt M., *Muhammad at Mecca*, Oxford: Oxford University Press, 1952.
154. Watt M., *Muhammad at Medina*, Oxford: Oxford University Press, 1956.
155. Watt M., *Muhammad: Prophet and Statesman*, Oxford: Oxford University Press, 1961.
156. Webb P., *Imaging the Arabs: Arab Identity and the Rise of Islam*, Edinburgh: Edinburgh University Press, 2016.
157. Wensinck, A.J., *The Muslim Creed*, New York: Barnes & Noble, 1932.
158. Yucevoy, H., *Messianic Beliefs & Imperial Politics in Medieval Islam*, Columbia: South Carolina University Press, 2009.
159. Zakeri M., *Sasanid Soldier in the Early Muslim Society. The Origins of 'Ayyārān and Futuwwa*, Wiesbaden: Harrassowitz Verlag, 1995.

Academic articles

1. Asani, Ali S., 'Pluralism, Intolerance and the Qur'an', *The American Scholar*, Vol. 71, no. 1 (2002), pp. 52–60.
2. Ali Mourad S., 'On Early Islamic Historiography: Abū Ismā'īl Al-Azdī and His Futūḥ al-Shām', *Journal of American Oriental Society*, Vol. 120, no. 4 (2000), pp. 577–93.
3. Allouche I.S., 'Un traité de polémique christiano-musulmane au IXe siècle', *Hespéris*, Vol. 26 (1939), 123–55.
4. Afsaruddin, Asma, 'The Islamic State: Genealogy, Facts and Myths', *Journal of Church and State*, Vol. 48, no. 1 (2006), pp. 153–73.
5. Asfaruddin Asma, 'Mawdūdī's Theo-Democracy: How Islamic Is It Really?', *Oriente Moderno*, Anno Vol. 87, no. 2 (2007), pp. 301–25.
6. Arjomand Said Amir, 'The Constitution of Medina: A Sociolegal Interpretation of Muhammad's Acts of Foundation of the Umma', *International Journal of Middle Eastern Studies*, Vol. 41, no.4 (2009), pp. 555–75.
7. Asad T., 'The Bedouin as a Military Force: Notes of Some Aspects of Power Relations between Nomads and Sedentaries in Historical Perspectivies', in *The Desert and the Sown-Nomads in the Wider Society*, ed. Cynthia Nelson, Berkeley, CA: Institute of International Studies, 1973, pp. 61–73.
8. Athamina, Kh., 'A'rāb and Muhājirūn in the Environment of Amṣār', *Studia Islamica*, Vol. 66 (1987), pp. 5–25.
9. Athamina, Kh., 'The Appointment and Dismissal of Khālib ibn al-Walīd', *Arabica*, Vol. 41 (1994), pp. 253–72.
10. Athamina, Kh., 'Non-Arab Regiments and Private Militias during the Umayyād Period', *Arabica*, Vol. 45, no. 3 (1998), pp. 347–78.

11. Athamina, Kh., 'The Pre-Islamic Roots of the Early Muslim Caliphate: The Emergence of Abū Bakr', *Der Islam*, Vol. 76 (1999), pp. 1–32.
12. Athamina, Kh., 'Abraham in Islamic Perspective. Reflections on the Development of Monotheism in Pre-Islamic Arabia', *Der Islam*, Vol. 81 (2004), pp. 184–205.
13. Avner Rina, 'The Dome of the Rock in the Light of the Development of Concentric Martyria in Jerusalem: Architecture and Architectural Iconography', *Muqarnas*, Vol. 28 (2010), pp. 31–49.
14. Ayalon D., 'The Military Reform of Caliph al-Mu'taṣim. Their Background and Consequences', in *Islam and the Abode of War*, London: Routledge, 1994, pp. 1–39.
15. Bacharach Jere L., Anwar Sherif, 'Early Versions of the *shahada*: Tombstone from Aswan of 71 A.H., the Dome of the Rock and Contemporary Coinage', *Der Islam*, Vol. 89, no. 2 (2012), pp. 60–9.
16. Baer E., 'The Mihrab in the Cave of the Dome of the Rock', *Muqarnas*, Vol. 3 (1985), pp. 8–19.
17. Bailey J. and Gürlu Necipoglu (eds), 'Frontiers of Islamic Art and Architecture: Essays in Celebration of Oleg Grabar's Eightieth Birthday', *Muqarnas*, Vol. 25, Leiden: Brill, 2008.
18. Bashear S., 'The Title of Fārūq and its Association with 'Umar I', *Studia Islamica*, Vol. 90 (1972), pp. 47–70.
19. Bashear S., 'Qibla Musharriqa and the Early Muslims Prayer in Churches', *The Muslim World*, Vol. 81 no. 3–4 (1991), pp. 267–82.
20. Bashear S., 'The Mission of Diḥyā al-Kalbī and the Situation in Syria', *Der Islam*, Vol. 74 (1997), pp. 64–91.
21. Bates M., 'The "Arab Byzantine" Bronze Coinage of Syria: An Innovation by 'Abd al-Malik', in *Colloquium in Memory of George Carpenter Miles*, New York: The American Numismatic Society Press, 1976, pp. 16–27, esp. 9.
22. Benevich Grigory I., 'Christological Polemics and Maximus the Confessor and the Emergence of Islam onto the World Stage', *Theological Studies*, Vol. 72 (2011), pp. 335–44.
23. Bingelli A., 'Foires et Pélerinage sur la route du Hajj. A propos de quelques sanctuaires chrétiens et musulmans dans le sud du Bilad ash-Sham d'après le *Kitab al-azmina* d'Ibn Masawayh (9e s.)', *Aram*, Vol. 18–19 (2006), pp. 559–82.
24. Blair, Sheila, 'What Is the Date of the Dome of the Rock?', in *Bayt al-Maqdis. 'Abd al-Malik's Jerusalem*, ed. Julian Raby and Jeremy Johns, Oxford: Oxford University Press, 1992, pp. 59–87.
25. Blazej, Cecota, 'Islam, the Arabs and Umayyad Rulers According to Theophanes the Confessor's Chronography', *Studia Ceranea*, Vol. 2 (2012), pp. 97–111.
26. Bonner, Michael, 'Ja'ā'il and Holy War in early Islam', *Der Islam*, Vol. 68, no. 1 (1991), pp. 45–64.
27. Bonner, Michael, 'Some Observations Concerning the Early Development of Jihad on the Arab Byzantine Frontier', *Studia Islamica*, Vol. 75 (1992), pp. 5–31.
28. Bonner, Michael, 'The Naming of the Frontier: Awāṣim, Thughūr and the Arab Geographers', *BSOAS*, Vol. 57, no. 1 (1994), pp. 17–24.
29. Bori, Caterina, 'Il Pensiero radicale islamico da Ibn 'Abd al-Wahhāb a Mawdūdī e Sayyid Quṭb: tradizione o modernità?' in *Le Religioni e il Mondo Moderno. L'Islam*, ed. G. Filoramo and R. Tottoli, Vol. 3, Torino: Einaudi, 2009, pp. 69–113.
30. Brakke D., '"Outside the Places, within the Truth": Athanasius of Alexandria and the Localization of the Holy', in *Pilgrimage and Holy Space in Late Antique Egypt*, ed. D. Frankfurter, Leiden: Brill, 1998, pp. 445–81.

31. Brock S., 'Syriac Views of Emergent Islam', in *Studies in the First Century Islamic Society*, ed. G.H.A. Juynboll, Carbondale Edwardsville: Southern Illinois University Press, 1982, pp. 9–21.
32. Brock S., *North Mesopotamia in the Late 7th Century: Book 15 of John Bar Penkaye's 'Ris Melle'*, Jerusalem Studies in Arabic and Islam, 9: 1987, reprinted in *Studies in Syriac Christianity*, 1992, chp. 2, pp. 57–61.
33. Busse, Heribert, 'Die 'Umar-Moschee im östlichen Atrium der Grabeskirche', *Zeitschrift des deutschen Palästina-Vereins*, Vol. 109 (1993), pp. 73–82.
34. Canard Marius, 'Les Expéditions des Arabes contre Costantinople dans l'Histoire et dans la Légende', *Journal Asiatique*, Paris: Imprimerie Nationale, T. 108 (1926), pp. 61–121.
35. Canard Marius, 'La guerre sainte dans le monde jslamique et dans le monde chrétien', *Revue Africaine*, Alger: Revue Africaine, Deuxième Congrès de la Federación des Societes Savantes de l'Afrique du Nord, 1936, pp. 605–23.
36. Cohen, Mark R., 'What Was the Pact of 'Umar? A Literary Historical Study', *Jerusalem Study in Arabic and Islam*, Vol. 23 (1999), pp. 100–31.
37. Colville J., 'Contra Christianorum', in *Sobriety and Mirth: A Selection of the Shorter Writings of Al-Jahiz*, London: Routledge, 2002, pp. 70–93.
38. Comerro V., 'La nouvelle alliance dans la sourate al-Mā'ida', *Arabica* 48/3 (2001), pp. 285–314.
39. Conrad L., 'Al-Azdī's History of the Arab Conquests in Bilād al-Shām: Some Historiographical Observations', in *Proceedings of the Second Symposium on the History of Bilād al-Shām during the Early Islamic Period Up to 40 AH/640 AD*, ed. M. 'Adnān al-Bakhīt, Amman: Jordanian University, 1987, pp. 28–62.
40. Conrad L., 'Heraclius in Early Islamic Kerygma', in *The Reign of Heraclius (610–641): Crisis and Confrontation*, ed. Gerrit J. Reinink, Bernard H. Stolte, Leuven: Peeters, 2002, pp. 113–56.
41. Conybeare F.C., 'Antiochus Strategos – The Capture of Jerusalem by the Persians in 614 A.D.', *English Historical Review*, Vol. 25 (1910), pp. 502–17.
42. Cook D., 'Muslim Apocalyptic and Jihad', *Jerusalem Studies in Arabic and Islam*, Vol. 20 (1996), pp. 66–120.
43. Cook M., 'Eschatology and the Dating of Traditions', in *Ḥadīth: Origins and Developments*, ed. H. Motzki, Aldershot: Ashgate, 2004, pp. 217–41.
44. Cowdell S., C. Fleming, J. Hodge and C. Osborn (eds), *Does Region Cause Violence? Multidisciplinary Perspectives on Violence and Religion in the Modern World*, New York: Bloomsbury Academic, 2018.
45. Crone, Patricia, 'The First Century Concept of "Hijra"', *Arabica*, Vol. 41, no. 3 (1994), pp. 352–87.
46. Crone, Patricia, 'Were the Qays and Yemen of the Umayyad Period Political Parties?', *Der Islam*, Vol. 71 (1994), pp. 1–56.
47. Dale F. Eickelman, 'Musaylima. An Approach to the Social Anthropology of Seventh Century Arabia', *Journal of the Economic and Social History of the Orient*, Vol. 10 (1967), pp. 17–52.
48. Décobert Christian, 'Ascétisme et Jihād', *Mélanges de l'Université Saint Joseph*, Vol. 62 (2009), pp. 253–82.
49. De Zande D. Van, 'The Cult of Saint Sergius in Its Socio-Political Context', *Eastern Christian Art*, Vol. 1 (2004), pp. 141–52.
50. Donner Fred, 'The Bakr Ibn Wā'il Tribes and Politics in North-Eastern Arabia on the Eve of Islam', *Studia Islamica*, Vol. 51 (1980), pp. 5–38.

51. Donner Fred, 'The Formation of the Islamic State', *Journal of the American Oriental Society*, Vol. 106, no. 2 (1986), pp. 283–96.
52. Donner Fred, 'The Role of the Nomads in the Near East in Late Antiquity (400–800 C.E.)', in *Tradition and Innovation in Late Antiquity*, ed. F.M. Clover, R.S. Humphreys, Madison: The University of Wisconsin Press, 1989, pp. 21–33.
53. Donner Fred, 'The Sources of Islamic Conception of War', in *Just War and Jihad. Historical and Theoretical Perspectives on War and Peace in Western and Islamic Traditions*, ed. J. Kelsay and James Turner Johnson, New York: Greenwood Press, 1991, pp. 32–69.
54. Donner Fred, 'The Growth of Military Institutions in Early Caliphate and Their Relation with Civilian Authority', *Al-Qantara, Revistas de Estudios Arabos*, Vol. 14, no. 2 (1993), pp. 312–26.
55. Donner Fred, 'Centralized Authority and Military Autonomy in the Early Islamic Conquests', in *The Byzantine and Early Islamic Near East*, ed. Averil Cameron, New York: Darwin Press, Vol. 3 (1995), pp. 337–60.
56. Donner Fred, 'La question du Messianisme dans l'Islam primitive', in *Mahdisme et millénarisme en Islam*, Revue des Mondes Musulmanes et de la Méditerranée, Aix en Provence: Edisud ed., 2000, pp. 17–28.
57. Donner Fred, 'Uthmān and the Rāshidūn Caliphs in Ibn 'Asākir's Ta'rīkh madīnat Dimashq: A Study in Strategies of Compilations', in *Ibn 'Asākir and Early Islamic History*, ed. James E. Lindsay, New York: Darwin Press, 2001, pp. 44–61.
58. Donner Fred, 'From Believers to Muslims: Confessional Self-identity in the Early Islamic Community', *Al-Abhath*, American University of Beirut, Vol. 50–51 (2002–2003), pp. 9–53.
59. Donner Fred, 'The Islamic Conquests', in *A ompanion to the History of Middle East*, ed. Youssef M. Choueiri, London: Blackwell Publishing, 2005, pp. 28–50.
60. Donner Fred, 'The Qur'an in Recent Scholarship: Challenges and Desiderata', in *The Qur'ān in Its Historical Context*, ed. Gabriel Said Reynolds, London: Routledge, 2008, pp. 29–51.
61. Donner Fred, 'The Historian, the Believer and the Qur'an', in *New Perspectives on the Qur'ān. The Qur'ān in Its Historical Context 2*, ed. Gabriel Said Reynolds, London: Routledge, 2011, pp. 25–37.
62. Donner Fred, 'Umar ibn al-Khaṭṭāb, 'Amr ibn al- 'Āṣ, and the Muslim Invasion of Egypt', in *Community, State, History and Changes: Festschrift for Prof. Riḍwān Al-Sayyid*, ed. A.R. Sālimī, Brannon Wheeler et al., Beirut: Arab Network for Research and Publishing, 2011, pp. 67–84.
63. Donner Fred, 'Visions of the Early Islamic Expansion: Between the Heroic and the Horrific', in *Byzantium in Early Islamic Age*, ed. Nadia Maria El Cheikh, Shau O'Sullivan, Beirut: American University Press, 2011, pp. 9–29.
64. Dragon G., Déroche V., *Doctrina Jacobi nuper Baptizati*, in 'Juifs et chrétiens dans l'Orient du VIIe siècle', *Travaux et Mémoires*, Vol. 11 (1991), pp. 17–248.
65. El-Cheick Nadia Maria, 'Muhammad and Heraclius: A Study in Legitimacy', *Studia Islamica*, Vol. 89 (1999), pp. 5–21.
66. Eickelman Dale F., 'Musaylima. An Approach to the Social Anthropology of the Seventh Century Arabia', *Journal of the Economic and Social History of the Orient*, Vol. 10 (1967), pp. 2–52.
67. Euben L., Roxanne, 'Killing for Politics: Jihad, Martyrdom and Political Action', *Politica Theory*, Vol. 3, no. 1 (2002), pp. 4–35.

68. Fares S., 'Christian Monasticism on the Eve of Islam: Kilwa (Saudi Arabia) - New Evidence', *Arabian Archaeology and Epigraphy*, Vol. 22 (2011), pp. 243–52.
69. Faruqi Maysam J. al-, 'Umma: The Orientalists and the Qur'ānic Concept of Identity', *Journal of Islamic Studies*, Vol. 16, no. 1 (2005), pp. 1–34.
70. Finkel J., A Risāla of Al-Jāḥiz, *Journal of the American Oriental Society*, 47 (1927), 311–34. Partially reprinted with helpful notes in N.A. Newman (ed.), *The Early Christian-Muslim Dialogue: A Collection of Documents from the First Three Islamic Centuries, 632–900 A.D.*, Hatfield, PA: Interdisciplinary Biblical Research Institute, 1993, pp. 685–717.
71. Firestone R., 'Disparity and Resolution in the Qur'ānic Teaching on War: A Reevaluation of a Traditional Problem', *Jnes*, Vol. 56, no. 1 (1997), pp. 1–19.
72. Firestone R., '*Jihad*', in *The Blackwell Companion to the Qur'ān*, ed. A. Rippin, Oxford: Blackwell Publishing, 2006, pp. 308–20.
73. Fisher G., Philip Wood, 'Writing the History of the Persian Arabs. The Pre-Islamic Perspective of the Naṣrids of al-Ḥīrah', *Iraninan Studies*, Vol. 49, no. 2 (2016), pp. 247–90.
74. Foss C., 'A Syrian Coinage of Mu'awiya', *Revue Numismatique*, Vol. 158 (2002), pp. 353–65.
75. Foss C., 'Mu'āwiya's State', in *Money, Power and Politics in Early Islamic Syria*, ed. John Haldon, 2010, pp. 75–96.
76. Fox J., 'The Rise of Religious Nationalism and Conflict: Ethnic Conflict and Revolutionary Wars, 1945–2001', *Journal of Peace Research* Vol. 41, no. 6 (2004), 715–31.
77. Friedmann Y., 'Finality of Prophethood in Sunni Islam', *Jerusalem Studies in Arabic and Islam*, Vol. 7 (1986), pp. 178–215.
78. Friedmann Y., 'Conditions of Conversion in Early Islam', in *Rituals and Ethics. Patterns of Repentance, Judaism, Christianity and Islam*, ed. A. Destro, M. Pesce, Louvain: Peeters Ed., 2004, pp. 95–106.
79. Gaiser, Adam R., 'What Do We Learn about the Early Khārijites and Ibāḍiyya from Their Coins?', *Journal of American Oriental Society*, Vol. 130, no. 2 (2010), pp. 167–87.
80. Gatier P-Louis, 'Les Jafnides dans l'épigraphie grecque au VI siècle', in *Les Jafinides. Des rois arabes en service de Byzance*, ed. D. Genequand and Ch. J. Robin, Paris: Editions de Boccard, 2015, pp. 193–222.
81. Gaudeul J.M., 'The Correspondance between Leo and 'Umar. 'Umar's Letter Rediscovered', *Islamochristiana*, Vol. 10 (1984), pp. 116–57.
82. Geddes C.L., 'The Messiah in South Arabia', *The Muslim World*, Vol. 57, no. 4 (1967), pp. 311–20.
83. Genequand D., 'Some Thoughts on Qasr al-Hayr al-Gharbi, Its Dam, Its Monastery and the Ghassanids', *Levant*, Vol. 38 (2006), pp. 63–83.
84. Gilliot C., 'Reconsidering the Authorship of the Qur'ān: Is the Qur'ān Partly the Fruit of a Progressive and Collective Work?', in *The Qur'ān in Its Historical Context*, ed. G. Said Reynolds, London: Routledge, 2008, pp. 88–108.
85. Grabar O., 'The Umayyad Dome of the Rock in Jerusalem', *Ars Orientalis*, Vol. 3 (1959), pp. 47–52, plate 3.
86. Grabar O., 'The Umayyad Dome of the Rock in Jerusalem', in *Jerusalem*, Vol. 4, Constructing the Study of Islamic Art, Hampshire, UK: Ashgate Publishing Limited, 2005, pp. 1–45.

87. Greenwood T., 'The Letter of Leo III of Ghewond', in *Christian Muslim Relations: A Biographical History*, ed. David Thomas and Barbara Roggema, Leiden: Brill, 2009, Vol. 1, pp. 203–8.
88. Griffith H. Sydney, 'The Prophet Muhammad. His Scripture and His Message According to the Christians Apologies in Arabic and Syriac from the First 'Abbasid Century', in *La Vie du Prophete Mahomet*, ed. Toufic Fahd, Colloque de Strasbourg, 1980, Paris: Puf, 1983, pp. 118–21.
89. Griffith H. Sydney, 'The Arabic Account of 'Abd al-Masīh an-Najrānī al-Ghassānī', *Le Museon*, Vol. 98, 1985, pp. 331–74.
90. Griffith H. Sydney, 'Anastasios of Sinai, the *Hodegos*, and the Muslism', *Greek Orthodox Theological Review*, Vol. 32, no. 4 (1987), pp. 341–58.
91. Goehring J., 'The Dark Side of Landscape: Ideology and Power in the Christian Myth of the Desert', *JMEMS*, Vol. 33, no.3 (2003), pp. 437–51.
92. Guilland R., 'L'Expedition de Maslama contre Constantinople (717–718)', *al-Mashriq*, 1955, pp. 89–112.
93. Haldon, John, 'The Works of Anastasius of Sinai: A Key Source for the History of Seventh-Century East Mediterranean Society and Belief', in *The Byzantine and Early Islamic Near East, Volume I: Problems in the Literary Source Material*, ed. A. Cameron and L. Conrad, Princeton, NJ: Darwin Press, 1992, pp. 323–64.
94. Haleem Abdel, M.A.S., 'Qur'anic '*Jihād*: A Linguistic and Contextual Analysis', *Journal of Qur'anic Studies*, Vol. 12 (2010), pp. 147–66.
95. Haleem Abdel, M.A.S., 'The jizya verse (Q. 9:29): Tax Enforcement on non-Muslims in the First Muslim State', *Journal of Qur'anic Studies*, Vol. 14, no. 2 (2012), pp. 72–89.
96. Halevi L., 'The Paradox of Islamization: Tombstone Inscriptions, Qur'anic Recitations and the Problem of Religious Change', *History of Religions*, Vol. 44 no. 2 (2004), pp. 120–52.
97. Haug R., 'Frontiers and the State in Early Islamic History: *Jihād* between Caliphs and Volunteers', *History Compass*, Vol. 9, no. 8 (2011), pp. 634–43.
98. Heck, Paul, 'Jihad Revisited', *Journal of Revised Ethics*, Vol. 32, no. 1 (2004), pp. 95–128.
99. Heck Gene W., 'Arabia without Spices: An Alternative Hypothesis', *JAOS*, Vol. 123, no. 3 (2003), pp. 547–76.
100. Heidemann S., 'The Merger of Two Currency Zones in Early Islam. The Byzantine and Sasanian Impact on the Circulation in Former Byzantine Syria and Northern Mesopotamia', *Iran*, Vol. 38 (1998), pp. 95–112.
101. Hewer, Chris, 'Theological Issues in Christian-Muslim Dialogue', *New Blackfriars*, Vol. 89, no. 1021 (2008), pp. 311–23.
102. Hikmet, Yaman, 'The Criticism of the People of the Book (*Ahl al-Kitāb*) in the Qur'an: Essentialist or Contextual?', *Gregorianum*, Vol. 92, no. 1 (2011), pp. 183–98.
103. Hoyland G. Robert, 'The Correspondance of Leo III (717–741) and 'Umar II (717–720)', *Aram* 6 (1994), pp. 165–77.
104. Hoyland, G. Robert, 'The Early Christian Writings on Muhammad: An Appraisal', in *Muhammad. The Issue of the Sources*, ed. Harald Motzki, Leiden: Brill, 2000, pp. 276–97.
105. Hoyland, G. Robert, 'New Documentary Texts and the Early Islamic State', *Bullettin of the School of Oriental and African Studies*, Vol. 69, no. 3 (2006), pp. 395–416.
106. Hoyland, G. Robert, 'Epigraphy and the Emergence of Arab Identity', in *From al-Andalus to Khurasan. Documents from the Medieval Muslim World*, ed. Petran M. Sijpesteijn, Lennart Sundelin, Sofia Torallas Tovar and Amalia Zomeno, Leiden: Brill, 2007, pp. 219–42.

107. Hoyland, G. Robert, 'Early Islam as a Late Antique Religion', in *The Oxford Handbook of Late Antiquity*, ed. Scott Fitzgerald Johnson, Oxford: Oxford University Press, 2012, pp. 1053–77.
108. Hoyland, G. Robert, 'The Earliest Attestation of the Dhimma of God and His Messenger and the Rediscovert of P. Nessana 77 (60s AH/680 CE)', in *Islamic Cultures, Islamic Contexts. Essays in Honor of Professor Patricia Crone*, eds. Asad Q. Ahmed, Behnam Sadeghi, Robert G. Hoyland and Adam Silverstein, Leiden: Brill, 2014, pp. 51–71.
109. Hoyland, G. Robert, 'Reflections on the Identity of the Arabian Conquerors', *Al-'Uṣūr al-Wusṭā* Vol. 25 (2017), pp. 132–4.
110. Irfan, A. Omar, 'Islam and the Other: The Ideal vision of Mawlana Wahiduddin Khan', *Journal of Ecumenical Studies*, Vol. 36, no. 3–4 (1999), pp. 423–38.
111. Irfan, A. Omar, 'Genealogy of the Islamic State: Reflections on Maududi's Political Thought and Islamism', *The Journal of Royal Anthropological Institute*, Vol. 15 (2009), pp. 145–62.
112. Isma'il R. Khalidi, 'The Arab Kingdom of Ghassan: Its Origins, Rise and Fall', *The Muslim World*, Vol. 46, no. 3 (1956), pp. 193–206.
113. Jansen Johannes J.G., *The Neglected Duty. The Creed of Sadat's Assassins*, New York: Rvp Publishers, 1986.
114. Jeffery A., 'Ghevond's Text of the Correspondence between Umar II and Leo III', *Harvard Theological Review*, Vol. 37, no. 4 (1944), pp. 269–332.
115. Jeremy Johns, 'Archaeology and the History of Early Islam: The First Seventy Years', *Jesho*, Vol. 46, no. 4 (2003), pp. 411–36.
116. Jones J.M.B., 'The Maghāzī Literature', in *Arabic Literature to the End of the Umayyad Period*, ed. A.F.L. Beeston, T.M. Johnstone, R.B. Serjeant and G.R. Smith, Cambridge: Cambridge University Press, 2012, chp. 16.
117. Juergensmeyer M., *The New Cold War? Religious Nationalism Confronts the Secular State*, Berkeley: University of California Press, 1993.
118. Juergensmeyer M., *Global Rebellion: Religious Challenges to the Secular State, from Christians Militias to al-Qaeda*, Berkeley: University of California Press, 2009.
119. Kawar, Irfan, 'The Arabs in the Peace Treaty of A.D. 561', *Arabica*, Vol. 3, no. 2 (1956), pp. 181–213.
120. Kawar, Irfan, 'Procopious and the Ghassanids', *JAOS*, Vol. 77, no. 2 (1957), pp. 79–87.
121. Kawar, Irfan, 'Arethas, Son of Jabalah', *JAOS*, Vol. 75, no. 5 (1955), pp. 206–16.
122. Kawar, Irfan, 'The Last Days of Salīḥ', *Arabica*, Vol. 5, no. 2 (1958), pp. 145–58.
123. H. Kennedy, 'Military Pay and the Economy of the Early Islamic State', *Historical Research*, Vol. 75, no. 188 (2002), pp. 155–69.
124. Kerr, David, 'Christianity of Islam: Clash of Civilization or Community of Reconciliation? Questions for Christian – Muslim Studies', *Studies in World Christianity*, Vol. 8, no. 1 (2002), pp. 81–98.
125. Keshk, Khaled, 'When Did Mu'āwiya Become Caliph?', *Journal of Near Eastern Studies*, Vol. 69, no.1 (2010), pp. 31–42.
126. Kessler Ch., 'Abd al-Malik's Inscription in the Dome of the Rock: A Reconsideration', *The Journal of Royal Asiatic Society of Great Britain and Ireland*, Vol. 1 (1970), pp. 2–14.
127. Khalil Samir S. 'The Earliest Arab Apology for Christianity (c.750)', in *Christian Arabic Apologetics during the Abbasid Period (750–1258)*, ed. Samir Khalil Samir, Jørgen S. Nielsen, Leiden, Brill, 1994, pp. 57–114.

128. Khatab, Seyed, 'Hakimiyya and Jahiliyya in the Thought of Sayyid Qutb', *Middle Eastern Studies*, Vol. 38, no. 3 (2002), pp. 145–70.
129. King, Goeffrey R.D., 'A Mosque Attributed to 'Umar ibn al-Khaṭṭāb in Dūmat al-Jandal in al-Jawf, Saudi Arabia', *The Journal of Royal Asiatic Society of Great Britain and Ireland*, Vol. 2 (1978), pp. 109–23.
130. King, Goeffrey R.D., 'The Paintings of the Pre-Islamic Ka'ba', *Muqarnas*, Vol. 21, volume in Honor of J.M. Rogers (2004), pp. 219–29.
131. Kinberg Leah, 'Literal Dreams and Prophetic Ḥadīths in Classical Islam. A Comparative of Two Ways of Legitimation', *Der Islam*, Vol. 70 (1993), pp. 279–300.
132. Kister, M.J., 'Mecca and Tamīm', *Jesho*, Vol. 8 (1965), pp. 113–63.
133. Kister, M.J., 'On the Wife of the Goldsmith from Fadak to Her Progenity. A Study in Jāhilī Genealogical Traditions', *Le Museon*, Vol. 92 (1979), pp. 321–30.
134. Kister, M.J., 'Mecca and the Tribes of Arabia: Some Notes on Their Relations', in *Studies in Islamic History of Civilization in Honour of Professor David Ayalon*, ed. M. Sharon, Leiden: Brill, 1986, pp. 33–57.
135. Kister, M.J., 'The Crowns of This Community. Some Notes on the Turban in the Muslim Tradition', *Jerusalem Studies in Arabic and Islam*, Vol. 24 (2000), pp. 217–45.
136. Kister, M.J., 'The Struggle against Musaylima and the Conquest of Yamāma', *Jerusalem Studies in Arabic and Islam*, Vol. 27 (2002), pp. 1–56.
137. Kister, M.J., 'Do Not Assimilate Yourselves … lā tashabbahū', in *Muslims and Others in the Early Islamic Society*, ed. R. Hoyland, Aldershot, UK: Ashgate Variourum, 2004, pp. 321–71.
138. Khodr, Georges, 'Christianity in a Pluralistic World – The Economy of the Holy Spirit', *The Ecumenical Review*, Vol. 23, no. 2 (1971), pp. 118–28.
139. Khoury Nuha N.N., 'The Dome of the Rock, the Ka'ba and Ghumdam: Arab Myths and Umayyad Monuments', *Muqarnas*, Vol. 10, Leiden: Brill, 1993, pp. 51–65.
140. Lammens H., 'Études sur le règne du calife omaiyade Mo'āwia Ie (troisième série: la Jeunesse du Calife Yazid Ier)', *Mélanges de la faculté orientale de l'Université Saint Joseph de Beirut*, Vol. 3 (1908), pp. 143–312.
141. Lammens H., 'Le Califat de Yazid Ier', *Melanges de la faculte orientale de l'Universite Saint Joseph de Beirut*, Vol. 4 (1910), pp. 233–312.
142. Lecker M., 'Where the Ghassānids and the Byzantine behind the Muḥammad's Hijra?', in *Les Jafnides. Des Rois Arabes au service de Byzance*, ed. Denis Genequand, Christian J. Robin, Paris: Editions de Boccard, 2015, pp. 277–94.
143. Lecker M., 'Kinda on the Eve of Islam and during the Ridda', *Journal of Royal Asiatic Society*, Third Series, Vol. 4, no. 3 (1994), pp. 333–56.
144. Lecker M., 'Glimpses of Muḥammad's Medinan Decade', in *The Cambridge Companion to Muhammad*, ed. Jonathan E. Brockopp, Cambridge: Cambridge University Press, 2009, pp. 61–79.
145. Lecker M., 'The Monotheistic Cousins of Muḥammad's Wife Khadīja', *Der Islam*, Vol. 94, no. 2 (2017), pp. 363–84.
146. Ariel S. Levin, 'Did the Roman Empire Have a Military Strategy and the Jafinids Were Part of It?', in *Les Jafnides. Des rois Arabes au service de Byzance*, ed. Denis Genequand, Christian J. Robin, Paris: Editiond de Boccard, 2015, pp. 155–92.
147. Levtzion N., 'The Conversion to Islam in Syria and Palestine and the Survival of Christians Communities', in *Indigeneous Christian Communities in Islamic Lands Eight to Eighteenth Centuries*, ed. M. Gervers and Ramzi J. Bikhazi, Convesion and Continuity: Indigenous Christian, 1990, pp. 229–331.

148. Levy-Rubin M., 'Shurūṭ 'Umar and Its Alternatives: The Legal Debate on the Status of the Dhimmīs', *Jerusalem Studies in Arabic and Islam*, Vol. 30 (2005), pp. 170–206.
149. Madelung W., 'Abd Allāh b. al-Zubayr and the Mahdī', *Journal of Near Eastern Studies*, Vol. 40 (1981), pp. 291–305.
150. Madelung W., 'The Sufyānī between Tradition and History', *Studia Islamica*, Vol. 63 (1986), pp. 5–48.
151. Marsham A., 'The Architecture of Allegiance in Early Islamic Late Antiquity: The Accession of Mu'āwiya in Jerusalem, CA. 661 CE', in *Court Ceremonies and Rituals of Power in Byzantium and the Medieval Mediterranean*, ed. A. Beihammer, S. Constantinou and Maria Parani, Leiden: Brill, 2013, pp. 87–112.
152. Mathewson Denny F., 'The Meaning of Ummah in the Qur'ān', *History of Religions*, Vol. 15, no. 1 (1975), pp. 34–70.
153. Melchert Ch., 'Ibn al-Mubārak's *Kitāb al-Jihād* and Early Renunciant Literature', in *Violence in Islamic Thought*, ed. R. Gleave and Istvan T. Kristò-Nagy, Edinburgh: Edinburgh University Press, 2015–2016, pp. 49–69.
154. Millar F., 'Rome's Arab Allies in Late Antiquity. Conceptions and Representations from within the Frontiers of the Empires', in *Studies in the Late Roman, Sasanian and Early Islamic Near East*, Commutatio et Contentio, ed. H. Börm, J. Wiesehöfer, Düsseldorf: Wellem, 2010, pp. 210–19.
155. Morony Michael G., 'Religious Communities in Late Sasanian and Early Muslim Iraq', *Jesho*, Vol. 17, no. 2 (1974), pp. 113–35.
156. Morony Michael G., 'The Age of Conversions: A Reassessment', in *Conversion and Continuity. Indigenous Christian Communities in Islamic Lands*, ed. M. Gervers, Ramzi J. Bikhazi, Toronto: Pontifical Institute of Medieval Studies, 1990, pp. 135–50.
157. Munt H., 'No Two Religions: Non-Muslims in the Early Islamic Ḥijāz', *Bulletin of Soas*, Vol. 78, no. 2 (2015), pp. 249–69.
158. Munt H., 'What Did Conversion to Islam Mean in Seventh-century Arabia?', in *Islamisation. Comparative Perspectives from History*, ed. A.C.S. Peacock, Edinburgh: Edinburgh University Press, 2017, pp. 84–101.
159. Muranyi M., 'Das Kitāb al- Siyar von Abū Isḥāq al-Fazārī', *JSAI*, Vol. 6 (1985), pp. 63–97.
160. Natij S., 'Murū'a. Soucis et interrogations éthique dans la culture arabe classique (1ère partie)', *Studia Islamica*, Vol. 112 (2017), pp. 1–59.
161. Nau F., 'Traduction des lettres XII et XIII de Jacques d'Edesse', *Revue de l'Orient Chrétien*, Vol. 10 (1905), pp. 197–208, 258–82.
162. Nau F., 'Cinq Lettres de Jacques d'Edesse à Jean le Stylite (traduction et analyse)', *Revue de l'Orient Chrétien*, Vol. 14 (1909), pp. 427–40.
163. Nevo Y. and J. Koren, 'Towards a Prehistory of Islam', *JSAI*, Vol. 17 (1994), pp. 108–41.
164. O'Sullivan, Declan, 'The Interpretation of the Qur'anic Text to Promote or Negate the Death Penalty for Apostates and Blasphemers', *Journal of Qur'anic Studies*, Vol. 3, no. 2 (2001), pp. 63–93.
165. Pandura M., 'Perceiving Otherness, Creating Resemblance – The Byzantinization of Nomads in the Age of Justinian I: The Arabs', *Acta Euroasiatica*, Vol. 1 (2013), pp. 43–69.
166. Papaconstantinou, Arietta, 'Between Umma and Dhimma. The Christians of the Middle East under the Umayyads', *Annales Islamologiques*, Vol. 42 (2008), pp. 127–56.

167. Papaconstantinou, Arietta, 'Administering the Early Islamic Empire: Insights from the Papyri', in *Money, Power and Politics in Early Islamic Syria: A Review of Current Debates*, ed. John Haldon, London: Routledge, 2010, pp. 62–4.
168. Parveen K., Muhammad Sultan Shah, 'Interfaith Marriages in Islam: A Case Study of Christian Wives of Muslim Rulers', *Al-Ilm*, Vol. 1, no. 1 (2017).
169. Piccirillo M., 'The Church of Saint Sergius at Nitl. A Centre of the Christians Arabs in the Steppe at the Gates of Madaba', *Liber Annus*, Vol. 51 (2001), pp. 267–84.
170. Qadi W. al-, 'Non-Muslims in the Muslim Conquest Army', in *Christians and Others in the Umayyad State*, ed. A. Borrut and F. Donner, Chicago, IL: University of Chicago Press, 2016, pp. 83–127.
171. Rabbat N., 'The Dome of the Rock Revisited: Some Remarks on al-Wasiti's Accounts', *Muqarnas*, Volume in Honor of O. Grabar, Vol. 10 (1993), pp. 66–75.
172. Rahman F., 'Prophetood and Revelation', in *Major Themes of the Qu'an*, Chicago, IL: Chicago University Press, 1980, pp. 80–105.
173. Reynolds, Gabriel Said, 'Le Problème de la Chronologie du Coran', *Arabica*, Vol. 58 (2011), pp. 477–502.
174. Reynolds, Gabriel Said, 'The Quran and the Apostles Jesus', *BSOAS*, Vol. 76, no. 2 (2013), pp. 209–27.
175. Rhodes D. Bryan, 'John of Damascus in Context', *St. Francis Magazine*, Vol. 7, no. 2 (2011), pp. 96–173.
176. Robin Christian J., 'Le royaume hujride, dit "royaume de Kinda," entre Himyar et Byzance', *Comptes rendus des séances de l'Académie des Inscriptions et Belles-Lettres*, Vol. 140, no. 2 (1996), pp. 665–714.
177. Robin Christian J., 'Les Arabes de Himyar, des Romains et des Perses (III-VI siècle de l'ère chrétienne)', *Semitica et Classica*, Vol. 1 (2008), pp. 178–81.
178. Rogan E., 'Sectarianism and Social Conflict in Damascus: The 1860 Events Reconsidered', *Arabica*, Vol. 51, no. 4 (2004), pp. 493–511.
179. Rubin, Uri, '*Al-Ṣamad and the High God. An Interpretation of Sūra CXII*', *Der Islam*, Vol. 61, no. 2 (1984), pp. 197–217.
180. Rubin, Uri, 'Ḥanīfiyya and Ka'ba. An Inquiry into the Arabian Pre-Islamic Background of *dīn Ibrāhīm*', *Jerusalem Studies in Arabic and Islam*, Vol. 13 (1990), pp. 85–112.
181. Rubin, Uri, 'Quran and Tafsīr. The case of "an yadin"', *Der Islam*, Vol. 70 (1993), pp. 133–44.
182. Rubin, Uri, 'Prophets and Caliphs: The Biblical Foundation of the Umayyad Authority', in *Method and Theory in the Study of Islamic Origin*, ed. Herbert Berg, Leiden: Brill, 2003, pp. 73–99.
183. Rubin, Uri, 'Prophets and Prophethood', in *Blackwell Companions to Religion: The Blackwell Companion to the Qur'an*, ed. Andrew Rippin, London: Blackwell Publishing, 2006, pp. 234–47.
184. Rubin, Uri, 'Muḥammad's Night Journey (Isrā') to al-Masjid al-Aqṣā. Aspects of the Early Origin of the Islamic Sanctity of Jerusalem', *Al-Qanṭara*, Vol. 29, no. 1 (2008), pp. 147–64.
185. Sahas D., 'Sophronius, Patriarch of Jerusalem', in *Christian-Muslim Relations: A Biographical History*, Vol. 1 600–900, ed. David Thomas, Barbara Roggema, Leiden: Brill, 2009, pp. 120–7.
186. Said Reynolds G., 'Le problème de la Chronologie du Qur'ān', *Arabica*, Vol. 58 (2011), pp. 477–502.

187. Sartre M., 'Deux phylarques dans l'Arabie byzantine', *Le Muséon*, Vol. 106 (1993), pp. 145–55.
188. Serjeant R.B., 'Meccan Trade and the Rise of Islam: Misconception and Flawed Polemics', *Journal of American Oriental Society*, Vol. 110, no. 3 (1990), pp. 472–86.
189. Shaban M., 'Conversion to Early Islam', in *Conversion to Islam*, ed. N. Levtzion, New York: NH Publishers, 1979, pp. 24–9.
190. Shaddel M., 'Abd Allāh ibn al-Zubayr and the Mahdī: Between Propaganda and Historical Memory in the Second Civil War', *Bulletin of SOAS*, Vol. 80, no. 1 (2017), pp. 1–19.
191. Shahid Irfan, 'Arab Christianity before the Rise of Islam', in *Christianity. A History of Middle East*, ed. Habib Badr, Beirut: Middle East Council of Churches, Studies & Research Programme, 2001, pp. 435–51.
192. Sharon M., 'The Birth of Islam in the Holy Land', in *The Expansion of the Early Islamic State*, ed. F. Donner, London: Routledge, 2016, pp. 229–40.
193. Shdaifat al- Y., A. al-Jallad, Zeyad al-Salameen, Rafe Harahsheh, 'An Early Christian Arabic Graffito Mentioning 'Yazīd the King', *Arabian Archeology and Epigrahy*, Vol. 28 (2017), pp. 315–24.
194. Shepard E. William, 'The Development of the Thought of Sayyid Qutb as Reflected in Earlier and Later Editions of Social Justice in Islam', *Die Welt des Islams*, New Series, Vol. 32, no. 2 (1992), pp. 196–236.
195. Shepard E. William, 'Muhammad Said al- Ashmawi and the Application of the Sharia in Egypt', *International Journal of Middle Eastern Studies*, Vol. 28, no. 1 (1996), pp. 39–58.
196. Shepard E. William, 'Sayyid Qutb's Doctrine of Jahiliyya', *International Journal of Middle Eastern Studies*, Vol. 35, no. 4 (2003), pp. 521–45.
197. Sinai N., 'The Unknown-Known: Some Groundwork for Interpreting the Medinian Qur'ān', *Mélanges de l'Université Saint Joseph*, Vol. 66 (2015–2016), pp. 47–96.
198. Sivan, E., 'Ibn Taymiyya: Father of Islamic Revolution', *Encounter*, Vol. 60, no. 5 (1983), pp. 41–50.
199. Sizgorich, Thomas, 'Narrative and Community in Islamic Late Antiquity', *Past & Present*, Vol. 185 (2004), pp. 9–42.
200. Sizgorich, Thomas, 'Sanctified Violence: Monotheist Militancy as the Tie that Bound Christian Rome and Islam', *Journal of America Academy of Religion*, Vol. 77, no. 4 (2009), pp. 895–921.
201. Syed Ali Ashraf, 'The Qur'ānic Concept of History', London: The Islamic Foundation, Seminar papers 4, 1980.
202. Streusand, Douglas E., 'What Does Jihad Mean?', *Middle East Quarterly*, September (1997), pp. 9–17.
203. Tampio, N., 'Costructing the Space of Testimony: Tariq Ramadan's Copernican Revolution', *Political Theory*, Vol. 39 (2011), pp. 600–29.
204. Tasseron Ella Landau, 'On the Reconstruction of Lost Sources', *Al-Qantara*, Vol. 25, no. 1 (2004), pp. 45–91.
205. Tasseron Ella Landau, 'Alliances among the Arabs', *Al-Qantara*, Vol. 26, no. 1 (2005), pp. 141–73.
206. Tasseron Ella Landau, 'The Status of Allies in Pre-Islamic and Early Islamic Arabian Society', *Islamic Law and Society*, Vol. 13, no. 1 (2006), pp. 6–32.
207. Tesei, T. Heraclius 'War Propaganda and the Qur'ān'sPromise of Reward for Dying in Battle', *Studia Islamica*, Vol. 114 (2019), pp. 219–47.

208. Tommaso Tesei, '"The Romans Will Win!" Q. 30: 2-7 in the Light of the 7th C. Political Eschatology', *Der Islam*, Vol. 95, no. 1 (2018), pp. 1–29.
209. Isabel Toral-Niehoff, 'Imperial Contests and the Arabs: The World of Late Antiquity on the Eve of Islam', in *The Wiley Blackwell History of Islam*, ed. Aa.Vv., London: Wiley Blackwell, 2018, pp. 61–76.
210. Isabel Toral-Niehoff, 'The 'Ibād of al-Ḥira: An Arab Christian Community in Late Antique Iraq', in *The Qur'an in Context*, ed. A. Neuwirth, N. Sinai and M. Marx, Leiden: Brill, 2010, pp. 323–47.
211. Treadwell W. Luke, 'The 'Orans' Drachms of Bishr ibn Marwān and the Figural Coinage of the Early Marwānids', in *Bayt al-Maqdis. Jerusalem and Early Islam*, ed. Jeremy Johns, Oxford: Oxford University Press, 1999, pp. 223–69.
212. Van Ess, Josef, 'Abd al-Malik and the Dome of the Rock. An Analysis of Some Texts', in *Bayt al-Maqdis. 'Abd al-Malik'ss Jerusalem*, ed. Julian Raby and Jeremy Johns, Oxford: Oxford University Press, 1992, pp. 33–58.
213. Villano R., 'The Qur'anic Foundations of the dar al-Islam/ dar al-Harb Dichotomy. An Unusual Hypothesis', in *Dar al-Islam/Dar al-Harb. Territories, People, Identities*, ed. Giovanna Calasso and Giuliano Lancioni, Leiden: Brill, 2017, pp. 125–45.
214. Waldman M. Robinson, 'The Development of the Concept of Kufr in the Qur'ān', *Journal of American Oriental Society*, Vol. 88, no. 3 (1968), pp. 442–55.
215. Ward, Seth, 'A Fragment from an Unknown Work by al-Ṭabarī on the Tradtion "Expel the Jews and Christians from the Arabian Peninsula (And the Lands of Islam)"', *Bulletin of the School of Oriental and African Studies*, Vol. 53, no. 3 (1990), pp. 407–20.
216. Webb P., 'Identity and Social Formation in the Early Caliphate', in *Routledge Handbook on Early Islam*, ed. H. Berg, London: Routledge, 2017, pp. 129–58.
217. Wensinck, A.J., 'Muḥammad and the Prophets', in *The Life of Muḥammad*, ed. U. Rubin, Aldershot: Ashgate, 1998, pp. 319–43.
218. Whittow M., 'Rome and the Jafnides: Writing the History of a 6th Century Tribal Dynasty', in *The Roman and Byzantine Near East 2: Some Recent Archaeological Research*, ed. J.H. Humphreys, Portsmouth, RI: Journal of Roman Archaeology, 1999, pp. 207–24.
219. Yaman H., 'The Criticism of the People of the Book (*Ahl al-Kitāb*) in the Qur'ān: Essentialist or Contextual?', *Gregorianum*, Vol. 92, no. 1 (2011), pp. 183–98.
220. Zeyad al-Salameen, Hani Falahat, Salameh Naimat, Fawzi Abudanh, 'New Arabic-Christian Inscription from Udhruḥ, Southern Jordan', *Arabian Archeology and Epigraphy*, Vol. 22 (2011), pp. 232–42.

Appendix

Jafnids (Ghassānid Confederation), sixth century

1. Jabalah ibn al-Ḥārith (d. 528)
2. Al-Ḥārith V ibn Jabalah (d. 569, *phylarch Phoenice, Syrian and Euphratensis*) __________ (brother) Abū Karib ibn Jabalah (*phylarch, Palestina Tertia, Arabia Deserta*)
3. Al-Mundhir III ibn al-Ḥārith, (d. *c.* 602, reign until 581, in exile in Sicily from 581)
4. Al-Nuʿmān VI ibn al-Mundhir (reign 581–583, d. unknown, in exile in Sicily too)

Naṣrids (Lakhmīds Confederation), sixth century

1. Abū Yaʿfur ibn ʿAlqamā (d. unknown, not mentioned in the book)
2. Al-Mundhir III ibn Nuʿmān (d. 554) during the battle of Chalcis
3. ʿAmr III ibn al-Mundhir (d. *c.* 569–570) __________ (brother) Qābūs ibn al-Mundhir (reign from *c.* 569–570 to 573) __________ (brother) Al-Mundhir IV ibn al-Mundhit (reign 574–580)
4. Al-Nuʿmān III ibn al-Mundhir (d. 602, converted to Christianity *c.* 594)
5. Ḥasan ibn al-Mundhir (d. unknown) __________ (brother) al-Nuʿmān IV ibn al-Mundhir (d. unknown) both converted to Christianity (*c.* 594)

Index

'Abbāsid (Caliphate) xi, 4, 5, 7, 10, 15, 28, 61, 68, 69, 88, 90, 94, 95, 97, 98, 100, 104, 105, 106, 133, 155, 157, 160, 161, 167, 168, 169, 189, 194, 202
'Abdallāh ibn 'Abbās (d. ca. 688) 88
'Abdallāh ibn 'Āmir (d. 678) 90
'Abdallāh ibn 'Awn al-Arṭubān (d. ca. 768) 72
'Abdallah ibn Jaḥsh al-Asadī 115
'Abdallāh ibn Muslim ibn Qutayba (d. 889) 93, 100
'Abdallāh ibn Rawāḥā (d. 629) 44, 45
'Abdallāh ibn Ubayy (d. 631) 135, 136, 147, 148
'Abdallāh ibn 'Uthmān 61
'Abd al-Azīz ibn Marwān (d. 705) 54, 64
'Abd al-Kāfī 111
'Abd al-Malik ibn 'Abd Allāh 76
'Abd al-Malik ibn Marwān (d. 705) 3, 10, 54, 58, 63, 64
'Abd al-Muṭṭalib (Prophet's grandfather) 30, 62
'Abd al-Raḥmān al-Awzā'ī (d. 774) 103, 156
  Kitāb al-Siyar 103
'Abd al-Raḥmān ibn 'Awf (d. 652) 64
'Abd al-Wāḥid ibn Zayd (d. ca. 750) 99
Abyssinia 32, 41, 42, 44, 61, 98, 121, 122, 164
Abnā' 105
Abraha (ca. 553) 18
Abraham/Abrahamic x, 1, 3, 9, 32, 51, 56, 67, 69, 72, 73, 81, 84, 88, 91, 93, 95, 98, 100, 107, 108, 111, 115, 118, 121, 125, 134, 136, 139, 148, 169
Abraham's ram 81
Abū 'Āmir 'Abd 'Amr ibn Ṣayfī 55, 56
Abū Ayyūb al-Anṣārī (d. 674) 75
Abū Bakr (d. 632) 47, 54, 56, 57, 82, 142, 153
Abū Dhu'ayb Khuwaylid ibn Khālid (ca. d. 649) 7
Abū Ḥanīfa, al-Nu' mān (d. 767) 97, 153
  Fiqh Akbar 153, 154
Abū al-Hudhayl, al-Allāf (d. 840) 99
Abū Isḥāq al-Fazārī (d. 804) 7, 101, 102, 103, 107, 156, 157
Abū Karib ibn Jabalah 19, 20, 239
Abū Mikhnaf (d. 774) x, 46, 100
  Futūḥ al-'Irāq 46
  Futūḥ al-Shām 46, 100
Abū al-Qāsim al-Junayd (d. 910) 99, 106
Abū Qays Ṣirma ibn Abī Anas 55
Abū Sulaymān al-Dārānī (d. 830) 99
Abū Ṭālib (d. 619) 41, 44, 52, 75, 98, 147, 158
Abū Yūsuf al-Anṣārī (d. 798) 157
  Kitāb al-Kharāf 157
Adulis (seaport) 41
Aetius, Flavius (d. 454) 17
Afsaruddin, A. 112
Agapius of Manbij (Hierapolis) (d. 942) 16, 93
Aghatias Scholasticus (d. 582) 16
Ahl al-Baghy 103
Ahl al-Bayt 10, 69
Ahl al-Kitāb 68, 118, 119, 121, 129, 156, 160, 169
Ahl al-Ridda 103
Aḥmad ibn Ḥanbal (d. 855) 101, 103, 154
  Musnad 154, 189, 197
Aḥūdemmeh (d. 575) 38
'Ā'isha (Prophet's wife) 52, 186
'Ā'isha bint Mu'āwiya ibn al-Mughīra 63
Akhbār (information) 7, 30, 41, 42, 46, 95, 101, 154
Akroinos (battle 740) 100
Aksum/Aksumite 17, 42
Al-'Ākhirah 120
Al-Akhtāb, Ghiyāt al-Taghlibī (d. 710) 79
Al-Aqṣā (mosque) 54, 80, 81, 197

Al-Aṣbagh ibn ʿAmr (Kalbite) 63, 64, 71
Al-Azdī al-Baṣrī (d. ca. 825) 46, 100, 176, 184, 185, 200, 201, 213
Al-Baiḍāwī, Nāṣir ad-Dīn ibn ʿUmar (d. 1286) 119
Al-Balādhurī, Aḥmad Ibn (d. 892) x, 46, 51, 175, 178, 185, 187, 189, 190, 191, 192, 193
al-Baydā/ al-Kashf bi l-Baydā 70
Al-Bukhārī, Abū ʿAbd ʿAllāh M. (d. 870) 155, 201
Al-Fazārī, Isḥāq (d. 777) 7, 101, 102, 103, 107, 156, 157, 174, 200, 211
Kitāb al-Siyar 7, 102, 174, 200, 211
Al-Furāfiṣa, Nāʾila, b. al-Aḥwaṣ b. ʿAmr b. ʿAdiyy b. Jandal 62
Al-Gharnāṭī, Abū Ḥayyān (d. 1344) 144
Al-Ḥīra (city) 18, 19, 21, 22, 25, 26, 27, 34, 35, 36, 59, 177, 179, 182, 190
Al-Iṣfahānī, Ḥamzah (d. ca. 961) 28, 180
Al- Iṣfahānī, Abū Faraj (d. 967) 174, 180
Al-Iṣfahānī, Abū Nuʿaym (d. 1038) 201, 213
Al-Khallāl, Abū Bakr (d. 923) 107, 202
Ahl al-milal 107, 202
Al-Jābiyah, al-Jabala (camp) 8, 18, 19, 22, 23, 24, 34, 50, 55, 58, 60, 62, 63
Al-Jāḥiz, Abū ʿUthmān (d. 868) 104, 105, 107, 108, 144, 190, 201, 202, 209
Manāqib al-Turk 104, 201, 202
Al-Radd ʿalā al-Naṣārā 107, 202
Al-Lāt (divinity) 119
Al-Masʿūdī, Abū al-Ḥasan (d. 956) 195
Al-Manṣūr, Abū Jaʿfar (caliph, d. 775) 97
Al-Mawardī, Abū al-Ḥasan (d. 1058) 158, 159, 211, 212
Al-Aḥkām al-Sulṭāniyya 158, 212, 219
Al-Mukhtār al-Thaqafī (d. 687) 53, 63, 73
Al-Muzanī (d. 878) 103
al-Mukhtaṣar 103, 105
Al-Nābighah al-Dhubyānī 34
Al-Naṣārā 122
Al-Qaraḍāwī, Yūsuf x
Al-Qayrawānī, Ibn Abī Zayd (d. ca. 996–997) 103
Al-Qurṭubī, M. ibn Aḥmad (d. 1273) 114, 180, 209
Al-Rāzī, Fakhr ad-Dīn x, 114, 115, 204
Al-Shāfiʿī, Ibn Idris M. (d. 820) 97, 103, 157, 158, 160, 211, 212
Kitāb al-Umm 97, 103, 200
Risāla fī ʿUṣūl al-Fiqh 103
Al-Ṣanʿānī, ʿAbd al-Razzāq (d. 827) 97, 103, 197, 198
Al-Sijistānī, Abū Dāwūd (d. 889) 70, 202
Kitāb al-Sunan 70, 197
Al-Ṭabarī, Abū Jaʿfar Muḥammad ix, x, 20, 26, 28, 32, 42, 46, 93, 97, 98, 105, 114, 121, 135, 144, 161, 175, 177, 178, 180, 181, 183, 184, 185, 187, 189, 190, 191, 192, 193, 194, 195, 197, 199, 200, 202, 205, 206, 207, 208, 209, 210, 213
Al-Tirmidhī, al-Ḥākim (d. 892) 83, 94, 106, 153, 197, 199, 210
Jāmiʿ, 94, 197, 199, 210
al-Tustarī, ʿAbd Allah (d. 896) 106, 131, 207
al-ʿUzzah (divinity) 119
Al-Wāhidī, ʿAlī ibn Ahmad (d. 1075) 119, 141, 149, 174, 175, 205, 206, 207
Asbāb an-Nuzūl 7, 9, 174, 175, 221
Al-Wāqidi, Abūʿ Abd Allāh (d. 823) x, 46, 47, 136, 176, 184, 185, 207, 208
Kitāb al-Ridda 47
Kitāb al- Maghāzī xi, 176, 184, 185, 207, 208, 221
Al-Wāsitī, Yaḥyā Ibn Maḥmūd (d. unknown) 81, 196
Faḍāʾil al-Bayt al-Muqaddas 81
Al-Yahūd 122
Al-Yaʿqūbī, Aḥmad, Wahn ibn Waḍīḥ (d. 898) 93, 111, 190
Al-Zamakhsharī, Abū al-Qāsim (d. 1144) 119, 205, 207, 209
Alexandria 3, 22, 23, 33, 37, 39, 49, 53, 182, 228
Ambrose of Milan, St. 37, 183, 200
Amin, El Sayed, M.A. viii
ʿAmmān 16, 57
Ammonius 33, 181
Amorioum 105
ʿAmr ibn ʿAbd ʿAllāh al-Ḥaḍramī (d. 624) 115, 129
Anastasius of Sinai/Sinaita (d. ca. 701) 49, 186, 187, 215
Hodegos/Via Dux 50, 175, 187
Ancyra 105

Anṣār 43, 56, 57, 58, 116, 131, 133, 135, 136
Antioch 3, 22, 25, 34, 49, 90
'Aqabah 19, 30
'Aqīdah 151, 154
Arabia 6, 8, 15, 18, 19, 21, 29, 30, 34, 44, 46, 48, 52, 60, 61, 62, 63, 68, 78, 88, 117, 177, 180, 185
Arabia Deserta 20, 239
Arabia (Palestina) Tertia 20, 239
Arab Christians 8, 9, 60, 64, 65, 88, 95, 118
Arab conquests x, 3, 7, 11, 15, 28, 46, 48, 51, 74, 83, 86, 87, 88, 90, 93, 156, 172, 185
Arculf 54, 195
Ardashir, Rev. 60
Arianism 37
Arjomand, S.A. 31, 181
Ark of Covenant 81
Armah (Negus, d. ca. 631) 121
Ash-Shammākh adh-Dhubyānī (d. 656) 7
'aṭā' (pension system) 90, 158, 163
'Athamina, Khalil 6, 43, 174, 184, 189
Athanasius Bar Gumoye 54
Attila (d. 453) 2, 17
Augsburg (peace treaty, 1555) 1
Augustine St. 183
  City of God 183
'Ayn Ubāgh (battle, 570) 35
Azdī al-Baṣrī, Abū Ismā'īl 46, 57, 100, 184, 201

Babylonian/s 85, 86
Badr (battle, 624) 8, 115, 129, 130, 132, 133, 134, 135, 136, 141, 159, 167
Baghdād 28, 90, 104, 105, 202
Baḥira (alias Sergius) monk 86, 98, 149, 164, 205
Bahrām Chobin 27
Banū 'Abd-Shams 62
Banū 'Adī ibn Janāb (Kalbite branch) 64
Banū 'Āmila 21
Banū Aslam 47
Banū Aws 55, 189
Banū Bakr ibn Wā'il 28
Banū Bakrī 28
Banū Balī 21, 45, 48, 57, 65
Banū Fazāra 62
Banū Ghassān/Ghassānids 8, 15, 18, 24, 25, 31, 32, 33, 34, 35, 44, 50, 64, 152, 172, 176, 177, 180, 181, 184, 197
Banū Ghaṭafān 48, 62
Banū Ghifār 47
Banū Hammām ibn Murra 29
Banū Ḥārith ibn al-Khawraj 30
Banū Hāshim 32, 41, 44, 61, 69
Banū Hawāzin 43, 141, 143
Banū 'Ibād 59, 190
Banū Iyād 21
Banū Jadīla 62
Banū Judhām 21, 57, 63, 64, 100, 101, 152, 163
Banū Juhayna 47
Banū Jundūb 62
Banū Jusham 43
Banū Kalb/Kalbite 20, 21, 44, 45, 46, 47, 48, 57, 62, 63, 64, 65, 70, 71, 72, 73, 78, 79, 90, 98, 100, 101, 152, 163, 169, 191
Banū Khazraj 30, 31, 44, 135, 181
Banū Kinānah 137, 142
Banū Kinda 17, 18, 63, 177, 186
Banū Lakhm 17, 19, 21, 25, 26, 30, 57, 152, 177
Banū Makhzūm 62
Banū Naḍīr 138
Banū Najjār 30, 31
Banū Naṣr/Naṣrid 20, 21, 26, 27, 28, 29, 35, 37, 60, 106, 177
Banū Qaynuqā 134, 160
Banū Qays 19, 28, 43, 63, 192
Banū Qurayẓa 136, 137, 160
Banū Salīḥ/Salīḥids 18, 24, 33, 70
Banū Sulaym 47
Banū Taghlib 21, 192
Banū Tanūkh/Tanūkhids 18, 20, 33, 57, 152
Banū Tamīm 47, 57, 178, 180, 201
Banū Taym 41, 69
Banū Thaqīf 43, 84, 116, 141, 143
Banū 'Udhra 44, 48
Banū Zurayq 30
Baradeus, Jacob (d. 578) 38, 183
Bar Kokhba's revolt (135 AD) 94
Bar Hebraeus 53, 93, 161, 199, 213
Barmakīds 28
Bashear S. 76, 77, 82, 175, 184, 195, 197

Basmala 130, 142, 148, 208
Baṣra 4, 90
Bates, Michael 74, 194
Battle of the Trench (ca. 626–627) 135, 136, 137, 138
bay'ah 100
bayt al-maqdis 80, 194, 195
Bedouins 90, 140
Belisarius (general) 20
Bell, Richard 83, 118, 127, 203, 204, 206
Benjamin I Patriarch of Alexandria (d. 665) 53
Bethlehem 77
Bible (Old Testament) 4, 34, 113
Bin Laden, Osama 204
Bīshāpūr 76
Blachère, R. 111, 127, 141, 143, 203, 206, 209
Bonner, M. x, 97, 100, 165, 173, 200, 207, 210, 212, 213, 214
Borrut, A. 64, 189, 191, 192
Bostra 25
Bosworth, C.E. 162, 172, 177, 212, 213
Brockopp, J.E. 72, 88, 101, 184, 187, 192, 193, 198
Brown, Peter 202
Bu'ath (battle, 617) 30
Busse, Herbert 48, 186

Caesarea Maritima 23, 41, 49
Callinicum (battle, 531) 20
Camel (battle, 656) 52
Casanova, Paul 82
Catalaunian Plains (battle) 17
Catherine St. (monastery) 23, 50
Chalcis (battle, 554) 20, 33, 34, 239
Chalcedonian 21, 22, 25, 26, 29, 37, 38, 49, 59, 163, 165
Children of Israel 55, 83, 85, 86, 117, 129, 149
Chronicle of 741 78
Chronicle of 1234 161, 180, 213
Chronicle of Seert (Siirt) 16, 25, 26, 176, 179, 183
Chosroes II (emperor, d. 628) 26, 27, 97
Cicero 67, 192
Clash of Civilizations (theory) 203
Cold War ix, xi
Colonialism ix, xi, 2, 107
confederations 6, 8, 9, 10, 16, 21, 22, 28, 29, 30, 32, 37, 44, 45, 46, 47, 57, 61, 65, 83, 97, 152, 164, 168, 177
Conrad, Lawrence I. 45, 95, 173, 174, 185, 186, 193, 199, 215
Constantine, the Great (d. 337) 15, 52, 182
"Constitution of Medina" 132, 136, 141, 181
Cook, D. 82, 91, 196, 198, 199
Cook, M. 4, 5, 71, 82, 172, 193
Crone, P. 2, 4, 5, 63, 82, 162, 172, 178, 192, 196, 201, 205
Crown of Kisra 81
Ctesiphon 3, 5, 16, 20, 21, 28, 29, 31, 59
cuius regio, eius religio 1
Cyprus 52, 75
Cyril of Alexandria (Patriarch) 37

Daesh/Isis xi
Ḍa'īf (weak) 94
Dajjāl 85, 94
Damascus 3, 4, 15, 23, 24, 50, 52, 57, 58, 59, 60, 63, 64, 71, 72, 73, 75, 76, 81, 90
Damian of Alexandria (d. 605) 22
Dār al-Islām/Dār al-Ḥarb/Dār al-Kufr 158, 159, 160, 162, 200, 212
Dāthin (battle, 634) 52
Dayr al-Jamājim (battle, 702) 64
Dayr Dāwūd 23
Décobert, Ch. 10, 175, 181, 202, 213
De Prémare, Alfred-Louis 6, 174, 184, 185, 187, 193
Dhimmi 59, 157, 160
Dhi Qār (battle) 27, 28, 29
Docetism/Docetist 85, 122
Doctrina Iacobi nuper Baptizati 5, 86
Dome of the Rock 77, 79, 80, 81, 173, 194, 195, 196
Donner, Fred x, xii, 2, 5, 6, 7, 15, 28, 45, 48, 54, 55, 57, 71, 79, 82, 90, 159, 172, 173, 176, 180, 181, 183, 184, 185, 186, 188, 189, 190, 191, 192, 193, 194, 196, 198, 203, 204, 206, 211, 212, 214
    Narratives of Islamic Origins 7, 15, 172, 176, 184, 192, 193, 196, 198, 203, 204, 211
    Muhammad and the Believers. At the Origins of Islam 9, 172, 173, 183,

186, 189, 190, 191, 192, 193, 194, 198, 212
Dūmat al-Jandal 20, 23, 45, 46, 47, 57, 64, 65, 163, 185
Durra al-Yatīma's pearl 81

Ecbatana 3
Edessa 3, 5, 51, 54, 76
Egypt x, xi, 3, 37, 41, 43, 50, 52, 54, 58, 59, 63, 68, 76, 77, 80, 88, 91, 111, 168, 184, 190
Ella Asbeha (Negus) 41
Euphratensis 20, 239
Eutychios (Melike Bishop of Alexandria) 39, 173, 183
Evagrius Scholasticus (d. 594) 18

Fadak (oasis) 21, 62, 191
Fākhitah bint Ghazwān 62
Fākhitah bint Qaraẓah ibn ʻAbd Manāf 62
Fars 60, 80
Fasād 115, 131
Fāṭima bint al-Walīd 62
Fāṭimīd (dynasty) 82
Feryal Salem 100, 106, 164, 201, 202, 213
Fiqh Akhbar 7, 154
Firestone R. 117, 142, 203, 204, 208, 209
Fitna/Fitnas 6, 9, 10, 32, 47, 51, 52, 53, 54, 55, 58, 60, 62, 63, 64, 65, 68, 69, 70, 72, 73, 75, 76, 81, 85, 86, 87, 91, 94, 95, 100, 114, 115, 118, 129, 130, 131, 144, 151, 152, 153, 162, 167, 193, 203, 204, 211, 218
Foederati 8, 16, 18, 21, 26, 27, 28, 29, 30, 31, 33, 35, 39, 41, 48, 49, 57, 63, 95, 96, 100, 102, 107, 164, 168, 177
Foss, Clive 74, 175, 190, 194, 195
Fuṣṭāṭ-al 78
Futūḥ (conquests) vii, 3, 4, 41, 46, 93, 100, 116, 156, 175, 176, 178, 184, 185, 186, 187, 189, 190, 193, 201, 213

Gabriel of Qartmin (d. ca. 648) 53
Gaza 41, 52, 75
George, St. 24
Germans/Germanic (population) ix, 16, 17, 168
Ghāzī 10, 104, 107, 117, 161
Ghazwa/ghazawāt (raid/raids/pillage) vii, ix, 3, 10, 17, 26, 32, 41, 45, 46, 52, 56, 65, 105, 112, 129, 139
Girard, René 171, 203
Global Jihadism ix
Goehring, J. 37, 182
Gospels (New Testament) 4, 8, 80, 82, 118
Graffito 78, 79, 195, 196, 214
Griffith S. 50, 51, 172, 175, 187, 189, 205
Guidetti M. 76, 195, 214

Ḥadīth/aḥādīth 7, 9, 70, 71, 72, 80, 88, 94, 102, 153, 154, 155, 156, 180, 184, 185, 193
Haleem Abdel M.A.S. 111, 123, 143, 144, 172, 174, 203, 204, 209, 210
Ḥamās ix
Ḥanīfiyya/Ḥanīf 55, 56, 57, 68, 72, 81, 118, 119, 189, 205, 211
Ḥaram al-Sharīf 77
Ḥarb 106, 111, 112, 159, 160, 200, 212
Ḥarrah (battle, 683) 63, 71, 73
Ḥarrān al-Lajā 24
Ḥārūm al-Rashīd (caliph, d. 809) 105
Hassān el-Ḥawāry 79
Ḥawrān (region) 57, 178
Hawting, G.R. 2, 112, 193, 203, 204, 205
Heck, Paul L. 10, 175, 179, 181, 197, 202
Heidemann, S. 74, 194, 196, 198
Hephthalite 2
Heraclius (emperor, d. 641) 25, 26, 39, 42, 45, 46, 52, 74, 95, 96, 98, 164, 184, 199
Ḥijāz 6, 20, 21, 29, 30, 31, 32, 41, 43, 45, 47, 48, 57, 68, 69, 96, 142, 143, 146, 148, 149, 153, 177, 185, 188, 205
Hijā' 7
Hijra 31, 32, 41, 44, 68, 117, 120, 140, 141, 151, 159, 160, 161, 163, 172, 177, 180, 181, 184, 197, 208, 212
Ḥilf/aḥlāf (allegiance) 48, 59
Ḥimyarite (kingdom) 17
Hitti, Ph. Kh. 91, 175, 186, 191, 199
Ḥnanishoʻ the exegete (d. 700) 79
Ḥirābah (Terrorism) viii
Holt, P.M. 87, 197
Holy Land 5, 34, 52, 104, 195
Holy War viii, 116, 154, 155, 171, 183, 185, 200, 203, 204, 208, 209, 210, 213, 214

Hoyland, R. ix, x, 5, 6, 15, 16, 41, 45, 52, 79, 96, 101, 159, 172, 173, 174, 175, 176, 178, 182, 183, 185, 186, 187, 188, 189, 190, 193, 194, 195, 196, 197, 198, 199, 214
Holy Land 5, 34, 52, 104, 195
Hubal (divinity) 119
Ḥudaybiyyah (treaty, 628) 61
Ḥunayn (battle, 630) 8, 43, 45, 84, 141, 143, 158, 159, 167
Huns x, 2, 17
Ḥuwwārīn 24

Ibn ʿAbd al-Azīz, ʿUmar (caliph, d. 720) 88
Ibn ʿAbd al-Ḥakam (d. 871) 41, 42, 184
Ibn ʿAbd al-Malik al-Kindī, Ukaydir 45
Ibn ʿAbd al-Malik, Sulaymān (caliph d. 717) 90, 161
Ibn ʿAbd al-Malik Yazīd II (caliph, d. 724) 90
Ibn ʿAbd al-Malik, Walīd I (caliph d. 715) 90
Ibn ʿAbd al-Manāf, Hāshim (d. ca. 497) 32
Ibn ʿAbdullāh, Jarīr 57
Ibn Abī l-Ṣalt, Umayya 55
Ibn Abī Sufyān, Muʿāwiya (d. 680) 6, 9, 47, 75, 77, 153, 195
Ibn Abī Ṭālib, Jaʿfar (d. 629) 44, 45
Ibn Adham, Ibrāhīm (d. 777) 99, 104, 107
Ibn ʿAffan, ʿUthman (d. 656) 4, 52, 58, 61, 68, 72, 169
Ibn ʿAlī, Ḥusayn (d. 680) 70, 71
Ibn al-ʾAbrad al-Kalbī, Sufyān (general, d. 701) 63, 64
Ibn al-Aiham, Jabalah (d. ca. 645) 29, 58
Ibn al-ʿĀṣ, ʿAmr (d. 664) 41, 42, 43, 45, 58, 59, 64, 76, 78, 167
Ibn al-Ashʿath, Abd al-Raḥmān (d. 704) 64
Ibn al-ʾAswad, Yazīd 78
Ibn al-ʿAwwām, az-Zubayr (d. 656) 58
Ibn al-Ḥakam, Marwān (caliph, 685) 63, 192
Ibn al-Ḥanifiyya, Muḥammad (d. 700) 72
Ibn al-Ḥārith, Arethas 16
Ibn al-Ḥārith, Jabalah IV (d. 528) 18
Ibn al-Ḥārith, Mundhir III (d. 602) 22, 24, 25, 35, 36, 38, 239
Ibn al-Ḥasan al-Shaybānī, M. (d. 803 or 805) 7, 103, 156, 174, 200
Ibn al-Haythām al-Hartami, Khalīl 104, 201, 202
Mukhtaṣar Sīyāsāt al-Ḥurūb 104, 201, 202
Ibn al-Kalbī, H. (d. 819) x, 32, 46, 47, 60, 62, 68, 120, 176, 191, 192, 193, 205
Kitāb al-Aṣnām 68, 120, 192
Ibn al-Khaṭṭāb, ʿUmār (d. 642) 8, 43, 52, 56, 57, 58, 59, 60, 61, 76, 84, 95, 139, 142, 147, 157, 184, 190
Ibn al-Mubārak, A. (d. 797) 7, 100, 101, 102, 103, 104, 106, 107, 153, 163, 164, 165, 167, 170, 174, 200, 201, 211, 214
Kitāb al-Jihād xi, 7, 102, 103, 106, 156, 160, 167, 174, 200, 201, 211, 213, 214
Kitāb al-Zuhd 102, 103, 106, 201, 213
Ibn al-Mundhir, al-Mundhir IV (d. 580) 34, 239
Ibn al-Mundhir, al-Nuʿmān III (d. 602) 21, 26, 37, 38, 239
Ibn al-Mundhir, al-Nuʿmān IV (d. unknown) 26, 239
Ibn al-Mundhir, al-Nuʿmān VI (d. unknown) 25, 38, 239
Ibn al-Nadīm (d. 995 or 998) 104, 111, 201
Ibn al-Nuʿmān, Mundhir III (d. 554) 20, 33, 34, 37, 239
Ibn al-Qaʿṭal, al-Jawwās 47
Ibn al-Walīd, Khālid (d. 642) 20, 29, 43, 44, 45, 46, 47, 59, 62, 144, 184, 190
Ibn al-Zubayr, ʿAbd Allāh (d. 692) 53, 63, 64, 68, 71, 72, 73, 76, 80, 81, 87, 88, 193, 197
Ibn al-Zubayr, ʿUrwah (d. 713) 88
Ibn ʿAmr ibn al-Muzayqiyāʾ, Kaʿb 78
Ibn ʿAsākir (d. 1175) 57, 60, 184, 185, 187, 189, 190, 191, 200, 213
Taʾrīkh Madināt Dimashq 60, 184, 187, 189, 190, 191, 213
Ibn Bashīr al-Ansārī, al-Nuʿmān (d. 684) 71
Ibn Fiḍḍa, Maṭar 57
Ibn Ghanm, ʿIyād (d. 641) 51
Ibn Ḥabīb, Musaylima (d. 632) 57
Ibn Ḥabīb (historian d. 859) 30
Ibn Ḥāritha, Zayd (d. 629) 44, 45
Ibn Hārūn al-Rashīd, al-Amīn (caliph, d. 813) 105

Ibn Hārūn al-Rashīd, al-Ma'mūn (caliph, d. 833) 104, 105
Ibn Hārūn al-Rashīd, al-Mu'taṣim (caliph, d. 842) 104, 105, 157
Ibn Ḥassān ibn Ḍirar, al-Mundhir 57
Ibn Hishām (d. 835) 46, 180
Ibn Ḥurayth ibn Baḥdal al-Kalbī, Ḥumayd (general d. 693) 63
Ibn ʿIḍāh al-Ashʿarī, ʿAbd Allāh 71
Ibn Isḥāq (ca. d. 761/767) x, 46, 88, 114, 147, 174, 183, 200, 206
Sīra an-Nabawiyya 7, 41, 147, 180
Ibn Jabalah, al-Ḥārith V (d. 569) 18, 19, 20, 21, 22, 25, 33, 34, 37, 38, 239
Ibn Kabasat, Yazīd 78
Ibn Khalīfa, Diḥya 57
Ibn Khatīr, Al-Qurashī al-Damishqī viii, 142, 206, 207, 208, 209, 210, 213
Ibn Khūwaylid, Ṭulayḥa (d. 642) 57
Ibn Mālik ibn Baḥdal al-Kalbī, Ḥassān (d. ca. 688–89) 60, 63
Ibn Manṣūr al-Rūmī al-Naṣrānī, Sarjūn 79
Ibn Maẓ'ūn, 'Uthmān 56
Ibn Mu'āwiya, Yazīd (caliph, d. 683) 62, 63, 68, 69, 70, 71, 72, 75, 78, 79, 100, 191, 193, 196, 214
Ibn Munabbih, Wahb (d. ca. 725–737) 88, 99, 198
Ibn Nu'mān ibn Bashīr, Muḥammad (d. 684) 111
Ibn Numayr al-Sakūnī, al-Hụsạyn (d. 686) 71
Ibn Qays al-Ḥujrid, Yazīd 78
Ibn Sa'd, Muḥammad (d. 845) 46, 176, 181, 198
Ibn Sālim al-Kalbī, Ubayy 46, 47
Ibn Sarjūn, Manṣūr 59
Ibn 'Ubayd Allāh, Ṭalḥa (d. 656) 58
Ibn Unayf ibn al-Kalbī, Baḥdal (d. ca. 650) 62
Ibn ʿUqba al-Murrī, Muslim (d. 683) 71
Ibn Yūsuf, al-Ḥajjāj (d. 714) 64, 80, 96
Ibrāhīm Ḥammād ibn Isḥāq (d. 935) 103
Ikhshīdīyūn (dyansty) 82
'Imām 'ādil 61
Imām al-Mālik (d. 795) 7
Al-Muwaṭṭā 7, 174, 200, 201, 209, 210
Imru' al-Qays (Amorkesus, d. 544) 19
Iran/Iranian 58, 68, 90, 98, 105, 157, 172
Isho'yahb III of Adiabene (d. 659) 53, 60, 61, 188, 191
Isho'zkha (bishop of Lashom) 26
'Isrā' and *Mi'rāj* 85

ja'ā'il (soldier substitution) 97, 162
Jabalah, son of Ibn al- Ḥārith, Mundhir III (d. 554, battle of Chalcis) 34
Jābiyah 8, 18, 19, 22, 23, 24, 34, 50, 55, 58, 60, 62, 63
Jacob of Edessa (d. 708) 50, 51, 53, 54, 55, 188
Jafnid/Jafnids 18, 20, 21, 22, 24, 25, 26, 29, 30, 31, 33, 34, 35, 38, 39, 46, 49, 64, 65, 177, 180
Jāhilī/Jāhilīyya 145
Jalliq (Dayr Kiswa monastery) 23, 24
Jazīra (region) 8, 37, 41, 57, 65, 163
Jericho 52, 75
Jerusalem x, 3, 5, 23, 29, 48, 49, 51, 52, 54, 59, 60, 64, 75, 76, 77, 78, 79, 80, 81, 85, 87, 94, 167, 180, 186
Jesus, 'Īsā Ibn Maryam 46, 50, 52, 67, 80, 82, 85, 98, 120
Jihadism ix, xi, 89, 106, 167
Jizya 45, 58, 143, 144, 160, 161, 190, 209
Johannes St. 76
John bar Penkaye (d. 687) 53, 79, 188, 190
John Chrysostom, St. 33, 37
John Malalas (d. 578) 18, 20, 176
John Moschus (d. 619) 52, 186, 214
John of Ephesus (d. 588) 16, 18, 22, 35, 36, 179, 182
John of Damascus (d. 749) 50, 52, 59, 172, 175, 187, 214
John the Baptist 24
John the Stylite (of Litarab, d. ca. 737–738) 51
Josephus, Titus F. 86
Joshua the Stylite 18, 177
Judaism/Jews/Jewish x, 3, 5, 9, 18, 29, 31, 32, 37, 49, 50, 51, 54, 67, 68, 86, 91, 94, 98, 101, 107, 112, 114, 117, 118, 119, 120, 121, 122, 123, 124, 127, 128, 129, 130, 133, 134, 135, 136, 140, 143, 144, 145, 147, 148, 149, 156, 157, 160
Judd, St. x, 88, 101, 192, 194
Juergensmeyer, M. 1, 171, 203

Julian, St. 24, 165, 194
Just War (warrior) viii, ix, 35, 39, 65, 67, 91, 107, 152, 155, 156, 163, 171, 183
Justin I (emperor, d. 532) 17
Justin II (emperar, d. 578) 24
Justinian I (emperor, d. 562) 17, 19, 20, 21, 22, 24, 33, 36, 37, 152, 178, 179
Juwayriya bint al-Ḥārith (d. 676) 139

Ka'bah 119, 139
Kaegi, Walter E. 25, 172, 174, 179, 184, 185
Kāfir/Kāfirūn/ Kuffār 118
Kāhin 86
Kathisma Church 77
Kennedy, H. 2, 64, 90, 98, 105, 172, 175, 190, 192, 198, 200, 202, 211
Kerbalā 71, 95
Khadīja bint Khuwaylid (d. 619) 41, 44, 192
Khaybar (oasis) 21, 25, 139, 140, 149
Khalīfa Allāh 80
Khalīfa/Khulafā' al-Rashidīn/Rashidūn 47, 56, 60, 62, 69, 133, 211
Kharāj (poll tax system) 90, 211
Khawārij/Khārijītes 64, 153, 162, 196
Khāzir (battle, 686) 64
Khurāsāniyya (army) 105, 106
Khātam al-nabiyyīn (Seal of Prophets/ Prophecy) 84
Khwārazm 3
Khorāsān 3, 157
Kister, M.J. 2, 46, 62, 178, 180, 185, 189, 191, 193, 199
Kūfā 4, 28
Kufr 115, 159, 160, 204
Kung H. 67, 192

Landau-Tasseron, Ella 6, 47, 174, 180, 181, 186
Las Navas de Tolosa (battle, 1212) 114
Layla bint Zabbān ibn al-Aṣbagh al-Kalbī 63
Laylā bint Zabān ibn al-Aṣbagh ibn 'Amr ibn Tha'laba 64, 71
Lecker, M. 2, 28, 30, 31, 44, 172, 177, 180, 181, 184, 186, 192, 197
Leo III the Isaurian (emperor, d. 741) 95
Logos 49
Louis-Gatier, Pierre 16
Lüling, Günter 4
Luke, St. 82, 99

Ma'arrat al-Nu'mān 24
Mabra J. 191, 192, 210, 213
Mādabā region (Jordan) 16
Madelung W. 71, 87, 189, 193, 197, 198, 211
Maghāzī (lit.) xi, 47, 116, 117, 140, 161, 165, 176, 183, 184, 185, 207, 208
Maḥajja 24
Mahdī 70, 72, 83, 85, 87, 88, 105, 193, 197, 209
Malik (King) 79
Mālik Ibn Dīnār (d. 744) 106
Manāt (divinity) 119
Manicheans 22, 37
Mardin 51
Margiana 3
Marj Rāhiṭ (battle, 684) 60, 63, 71
Mark, St. 80, 82
Maronite Chronicle 53, 75, 76, 79, 194
Marsham, A. 76, 194
Martyrdom 22, 24, 39, 96, 98, 132, 160, 162, 164, 210
Martyria 77, 80, 195
Marwānid 62, 64, 72, 191, 193, 210
Mary/Maryam 77, 96, 122, 133
Maskin (battle, 703) 64
Matthew, St. 82, 99
Maurice (emperor, d. 602) 24, 25, 27, 38, 179
Mawlā/mawālī 90, 97, 162
Maximus the Confessor (d. 662) 50, 175
Maysūm bint Baḥdal 62, 71, 78
Mayṭūr, al- 24
Mecca 8, 16, 18, 31, 32, 36, 41, 42, 43, 44, 45, 46, 47, 61, 70, 71, 72, 73, 77, 78, 81, 84, 85, 98, 116, 120, 128, 129, 133, 136, 137, 139, 140, 141, 142, 143, 150, 151, 169, 178, 183, 185, 203, 212
Medina 4, 16, 18, 21, 28, 30, 31, 32, 44, 45, 47, 55, 56, 58, 61, 70, 72, 73, 78, 81, 102, 116, 120, 121, 122, 123, 128, 130, 132, 134, 135, 136, 137, 138, 139, 140, 141, 149, 151, 160, 181, 185, 191, 203, 212
Melchert, C. 102, 201, 214

Mesopotamia x, xi, 3, 17, 26, 27, 50, 58, 64, 65, 68, 74, 88, 91, 144, 163, 168, 188, 190, 194, 195
Miaphysite 22, 29
Michael the Syrian (d. 1199) 16, 22, 25, 33, 75, 93, 161, 178, 179, 184, 199, 213
Middle East/Levant ix, 2, 4, 8, 163
Miḥna 105, 107, 108
Miḥrāb 81
Milvian Bridge (battle) 15
Mithāq 124, 148
modernity 1, 2
modernism/modernist ix, 2, 81, 171
Mongols x, 2, 107, 114, 212, 214, 223
Monophysite/Non-Chalcedonians 22, 26, 28, 29, 35, 49, 50, 53, 79, 81, 179
Monothelitism 87, 186
Morony, M.G. 59, 190
Moses, Mūsā 57, 84, 90, 117, 134, 186, 189, 197, 198, 200, 219, 220, 229, 230, 234
Muʿāwiya in Abī Sufyān: 52, 53, 55, 58, 59, 60, 62, 63, 64, 70, 71, 74, 75, 76, 78, 79, 175, 190, 194, 195
Moṣul 90
muḥaddithūn 72, 88, 101, 179
mujāhid/mujāhidūn/mujāhidīn 10, 94, 102, 104, 105, 113, 138, 146, 151, 152, 154, 155, 156, 158, 161, 162, 163, 164, 165
Mujāhir Ibn Jabr (d. 722) 179
Muhājirūn 30, 43, 56, 57, 116, 129, 131, 133, 135, 136, 151, 174, 190, 212, 227
Muḥammad (Prophet, d. 632) ix, x, 2, 3, 4, 5, 6, 7, 8, 9, 10, 28, 30, 31, 32, 35, 36, 41, 42, 43, 44, 45, 46, 47, 50, 51, 52, 55, 56, 61, 62, 67, 68, 69, 72, 73, 75, 76, 79, 80, 82, 83, 84, 86, 87, 88, 89, 95, 96, 98, 100, 101, 103, 107, 111, 112, 115, 118, 119, 120, 121, 122, 123, 124, 125, 127, 128, 129, 130, 132, 133, 134, 135, 136, 137, 139, 140, 141, 142, 143, 145, 147, 148, 149, 151, 153, 160, 163, 169, 172, 173, 174, 175, 176, 177, 179, 180, 181, 182, 184, 185, 186, 187, 189, 190, 191, 192, 193, 194, 197, 198, 199, 200, 203, 204, 205, 206, 207, 208, 210, 211, 212, 217, 219, 220, 221, 222, 223, 224, 225, 226, 227, 230, 232, 234, 236, 237, 238
Mu'min/mu'minīn 31, 63, 69, 72, 80, 140, 148, 179
Munāfiq/munafiqūn 45, 63, 95, 118, 127, 132, 135, 139
Muqātil ibn Sulaymān (d. 767) 113
Muqātil/Muqātilīn 113, 138
murābiṭūn 161
muruwwa 116, 139
Mūsā ibn Nuṣayr (d. 716) 90
Mu'tah (battle) 9, 43, 45, 46, 57, 84, 102, 184
Mutaṭawwiʿa/mutaṭawwiʿūn (military volunteers) 93, 104, 105, 161, 162, 163, 212
Muttaqīn 115
Mazūnāyē 60, 61

Nabateans 16
Nadia Maria el-Cheick 95, 184, 199
Nā'ila bint al-Furāfiṣa 62
Nā'ila bint ʿUmārah al-Kalbī 62
Najd 44, 48, 57, 62, 177, 224
Najrān (oasis) 22, 24, 28, 64, 98, 143, 172, 177, 178, 179, 180, 232
Najrān, Martyrs of 22, 98, 177, 179, 180
Naqīb 30, 104, 181, 201, 202, 218
Nebuchadnezzar II 85
Negus 32, 41, 42, 121, 149, 164
Nessana papyri 75
Nestorians 6, 22, 53
Nilus of Sinai 33
9/11 (terrorist attack) 1, 171
Nitl (village) 16, 23, 24, 176, 236
Niyya 102, 103, 104, 105, 106, 107, 158, 163, 193, 211, 212, 213, 218,219
Noah 85, 120, 128
Nöldeke Th. 83, 182
Nonnosus 17, 18, 78

Occidentalism 221
Orientalism ix, xi

Palestina Tertia/Salutaris 19, 239
Palestine 5, 8, 17, 19, 24, 26, 27, 29, 31, 32, 41, 43, 49, 50, 51, 52, 57, 59, 60, 62, 63, 64, 65, 68, 75, 77, 88, 91, 100, 112, 159, 160, 163, 168, 188, 191, 216, 234
Palmyrene 20, 57

Patrikios 21
People of the Book 51, 117, 118, 119, 122, 123, 124, 129, 130, 133, 134, 136, 143, 144, 147, 148, 150, 156, 158, 159, 205, 206, 232, 238
Peter of Callinicum (d. 591) 22
Peters, R. 225
Pharaoh (generic) 42, 131, 132
Phoenice 20, 239
Phocas (emperor, d. 610) 27
Phylarch 20
Pseudo Ephrem's sermon on the End of Times 86
Pseudo Methodious Apocalypse 86

Qaṣr Hishām/Qaṣr Mshatta 78
Qaysite 90, 98
Qibla 77, 78, 175, 195, 197, 228
Qatala 112, 117, 177
quḍāt 88, 103
Qumrān 67
Quraysh 31, 32, 41, 42, 46, 47, 56, 57, 58, 62, 63, 69, 71, 95, 121, 129, 168, 180, 181, 218
Quwwah (power/strenght) i, viii
Quwwād (professional military commander) 64

Raghes (Ray) 3
Rahbāniyya (monasticism) 102
Rāhib (monk) 98
Ramlah bint Shaybah 62
Rawḥ ibn Zinbāʿ al- Judhāmī (d. ca. 702–703) 100, 101, 163
Red Sea 17, 41, 44, 139
Religio 1, 67
Renaissance/Humanism 2
Rénan, E. 171
Ridda 9, 18, 29, 43, 45, 46, 47, 48, 57, 103, 141, 153, 177, 186, 234
Rizq 186, 226
Robinson, Chase F. 6, 45, 173, 174, 185, 193, 195, 206, 214, 226
Roman-Persian war (602–628), 3, 8, 18, 26, 27, 29, 74, 167
Rubin, U. 2, 172, 189, 190, 197, 205, 209, 210, 226, 236, 238
Rudd, Steven C. 198
Ruqayyah bint Muḥmmad (d. 624) 61
Sabeos 51, 52, 187, 216
ṣabr 26, 111, 112, 117, 151, 204
ṣaḥāba 26, 69, 78
Said Reynolds, G. 206, 210, 230, 231
Sajāḥ bint al-Ḥārith ibn Suayd 57
Ṣalāt 149
Samaritan 19, 31, 49, 50, 51
Sammāʾ 24
Ṣanʿāʾ Quranic Palimsest 7
Saqīfah 47
Saracens 5, 18, 19, 22, 29, 33, 48, 49, 50, 52, 54, 169, 172, 178
Sasanid/Sasanians (empire) ix, 3, 16, 18, 21, 28, 41, 164, 168, 176, 189, 223, 227
sayyid al-Ḥarb 106
Serge/Sergius saint 16
Seriane 24
Sergiopolis (Reṣāfa or Ruṣāfa) 23, 24
Shaddel, Mehdy 71, 193, 237
Shahādah 7, 10, 72, 74, 76, 151
Shahanshah 26, 27
Shahid, I. (alias Kawar I.) 163
shāhid 2, 6, 15, 16, 18, 20, 21, 24, 27, 35, 36, 152, 163, 164, 172, 173, 174, 175, 176, 177, 178, 179, 180, 181, 182, 183, 185, 186, 190, 191, 192, 200, 205, 213, 214, 226, 237
Shakiriyya (army) 105
Shirk 115, 145
Shoemaker, Stephen J. 5, 6, 82, 83, 86, 88, 91, 173, 193, 195, 196, 197, 198, 226
Shūrā 56, 63
Ṣiffin (battle, 657) 52, 60, 75
Sijistān 70, 161, 202
Simeon bin Jabir (alias Sabrishoʿ) 26
Simeon of Beth Arsham (d. ca. 540) 18, 22
Simeon the Younger, St. (d. 592) 33, 34
Sinai, N. 10, 33, 122, 175, 181, 186, 187, 204, 205, 206, 208, 209, 215, 216, 225, 232
Sīra al-Nabawiyya 4
Siyar xi, 7, 102, 103, 111, 117, 155, 156, 160, 161, 165, 174, 200, 204, 211, 212, 213, 216, 217, 235
Sizgorich, Th. 6, 10, 95, 98, 162, 174, 182, 183, 199, 202, 213, 226, 237
Sogdiana 3
Solachon (battle) 25
Spīndārī, ʿAbd al-Raḥmān viii, 64, 220

Sprenger, Aloys 82
Stilicho, Flavius (d. 408) 17, 82
Strategikon 25, 181, 219
Subay' Ibn Qays 30
Sub-Saharan Africa 2
Sufyān al-Thawrī, Abū 'Abdullāh (d. 778) 72
Sufyānī 62, 63, 64, 70, 88, 198, 235
Sunna 70, 72, 159
Sunnite 61
Susa 3
Syria x, xi, 3, 6, 8, 15, 16, 17, 18, 20, 21, 22, 24, 25, 26, 27, 29, 32, 33, 35, 37, 41, 43, 46, 47, 48, 49, 50, 51, 52, 54, 57, 58, 59, 60, 62, 63, 64, 65, 67, 69, 74, 75, 76, 77, 78, 81, 83, 88, 91, 93, 96, 97, 98, 101, 104, 156, 159, 160, 161, 163, 168, 172, 173, 175, 178, 179, 184, 186, 187, 188, 190, 194, 195, 196, 199, 205, 213, 214, 217, 219, 223, 225, 228, 229, 231, 232, 234, 236, 239
Sultans 2

Tabūk (expedition) 9, 43, 44, 45, 46, 57, 95, 141, 146, 158, 185
Taḥāluf (Arab Confederation) 7
taḥrīf (alteration) 99
Ṭā'if 45, 47, 55, 84, 116, 141, 193, 216
takbīr 103, 164
Ṭalās (battle) x
Tall al-'Umayrī 16, 179
Tarahhub 55
Tawbā 147, 164
Tawḥīd 120
Tayeb el-Hibri 61, 191
Ṭayyāyē (Aramaic) 18, 38, 61, 93
Thalatha (Trinity) 80
Theodora, Justinian's wife 22, 37
Theodosious I (emperor, d. 395) 49, 169
Theophanes the Confessor (d. 817) 52, 75, 93, 172, 188, 194, 199, 220, 228
Theophilus of Edessa (d. 785) 52, 161, 188, 220
Theopilos (emperor, d. 842) 105
Thirty Years' War (1618–1648) 1
Thomas the Presbyter (d. ca. 640) 50, 51, 52, 187, 220
threskeia/threskos 67
Thughūr/'Awāṣīm 10, 96, 97, 100, 102, 161, 162, 200, 212, 228
Tiberius II (emperor, d. 582) 24, 25
Tor Andrae 77, 188
Torah 117, 118, 147
Tours/Poitier (battle) x
Transjordan 57
Tumāḍir bint al-Aṣbagh ibn 'Amr 64

'Ubaydallāh al-Zuhrī (b. ca. 670–678) 72
'Ubaydallāh ibn Abī Bakrah 161
Uḥud (battle, ca. 625) 135, 136, 137, 138, 150
Umayyad (Caliphate) xi, 3, 6, 7, 8, 10, 15, 16, 47, 58, 59, 60, 61, 62, 63, 64, 68, 69, 71, 72, 73, 74, 75, 76, 78, 79, 81, 87, 88, 89, 90, 91, 95, 96, 97, 100, 101, 102, 105, 133, 144, 152, 156, 161, 162, 163, 167, 169, 174, 175, 182, 183, 187, 189, 190, 191, 192, 193, 194, 195, 196, 204, 210, 214, 223, 224, 227, 228, 229, 231, 233, 234, 235, 236
Umm al-Banīn bint Uyaynāh 62
Umm 'Amr Umm Najm bint Jundūb 62
Umm Ḥabība ibn Abū Sufyān (d. 665) 98
Umm Khālid bint Abī Hāshim 63
Umm Salama (Prophet's wife) 70
Ummah viii, 31, 137, 153, 193, 204, 235
Umm al-Raṣāṣ 24
'Uqba ibn Nāfi' (d. 683) 90
'Utba al-Ghulām (d. 784) 107

Vistāhm 27

Wahhābīsm/Wahhābī/Wahhabite viii, 221
Waḥy, awḥā (inspiration) 41
Waḥy, awḥā 41
Wansbrough, John 2, 172, 202, 203, 227
Warqa ibn Nawfal (d. ca. 610) 164, 192
Wāsiṭ 81, 90, 196, 236
Wensinck, J. 153, 154, 174, 210, 211, 227, 238
Westphalia (peace treaty, 1648) 1
Whittow, M. 15, 176, 238

Yarmuk (battle, 636) 52, 57, 58, 167
Yazīd III bin al-Walīd (caliph, d. 744) 90
Yemen 32, 41, 192, 201, 229
Yucevoy, H. 173, 227

Zāb (battle 750) 63, 64, 71, 97, 172, 217
Zakat 144, 154, 158
ẓālim, ẓālimūn 120, 137
Zamindawar 3
Zayd, Muṣṭafā (d. 1978) viii, 27, 36, 44, 45, 84, 99, 103, 124, 182, 184, 217
Zoroastrians 22
Zubayrid 63, 71, 72, 76
Zuckerman, Constantin 18
Zuhd 7, 9, 101, 102, 103, 106, 164, 165, 201, 213, 218
ẓulm 120

Index of Qur'anic Passages

Q. 2: 27 124
Q. 2: 45 151
Q. 2: 62 123, 129
Q. 2: 104 121
Q. 2: 111–121 118
Q. 2: 111–113 129
Q. 2: 125 118
Q. 2: 142–150 7
Q. 2: 143 152
Q.2: 154 112
Q. 2: 165–167 120, 134
Q. 2: 172 120
Q. 2: 173 119
Q. 2: 178 152
Q. 2: 190–191 128, 129
Q. 2: 190–195 7
Q. 2: 191 114, 151
Q. 2: 193 115
Q. 2: 194 145
Q. 2: 216 96, 102, 115, 152
Q. 2: 216–218 115
Q. 2: 218 116, 138
Q. 2: 245 117
Q. 2: 246 117, 147
Q. 2: 262 9

Q. 3: 7 133
Q. 3: 19 119, 121, 124, 133, 136
Q. 3: 28 133
Q. 3: 45 133
Q. 3: 52 133
Q. 3: 55 134
Q. 3: 58–61 134
Q. 3: 59 122
Q. 3: 67 118
Q. 3: 69 134
Q. 3: 75 121, 122
Q. 3: 75–76 121, 122
Q. 3: 84 134
Q. 3: 85 134
Q. 3: 104 118
Q. 3: 110 118, 134, 147
Q. 3: 110–112 134
Q. 3: 113–115 122, 124, 134
Q. 3: 142 112, 134
Q. 3: 146 117, 147, 151
Q. 3: 157–158 112
Q. 3: 165–167 134
Q. 3: 184 162
Q. 3: 199 121, 124, 136
Q. 3: 199–200 136

Q. 4: 44–46 121
Q. 4: 47–48 121
Q. 4: 51 121
Q. 4: 74 112, 152
Q. 4: 77 137
Q. 4: 88–91 137
Q. 4: 92–93 137
Q. 4: 95 137, 138, 152
Q. 4: 95–96 138
Q. 4: 97 138
Q. 4: 113 124
Q. 4: 124 113
Q. 4: 154–162 124
Q. 4: 157–158 122
Q. 4: 171 42, 51, 80, 122, 124

Q. 5: 3 119, 205
Q. 5: 4–5 148
Q. 5: 7 124
Q. 5: 8 148
Q. 5: 12 113, 122, 124, 169
Q. 5: 12–14 124
Q. 5: 12–19 122, 169
Q. 5: 17 122
Q. 5: 33 148
Q. 5: 48 7, 124
Q. 5: 65 113
Q. 5: 66 147
Q. 5: 69 123
Q. 5: 73–75 122, 124

Q. 5: 82 98, 123, 124, 145, 164
Q. 5: 82–83 98, 164
Q. 5: 87–88 152

Q. 6: 20 122
Q. 6: 82 120

Q. 7: 105 120
Q. 7: 157 123
Q. 7: 167–171 124

Q. 8: 1–5 130
Q. 8: 9–15 130
Q. 8: 28 152
Q. 8: 37 130
Q. 8: 38 130
Q. 8: 39 130
Q. 8: 41 130
Q. 8: 45 131
Q. 8: 46 131
Q. 8:49 151
Q. 8: 47–52 131
Q. 8: 55 131
Q. 8: 67 131
Q. 8: 72 114, 116, 131, 137, 151
Q. 8: 73 114, 116, 131, 137, 151
Q. 8: 75 131, 132, 133, 208

Q. 9: 5 7, 112, 124, 142
Q. 9: 24 152
Q. 9: 29 124, 143, 144, 148, 209, 232
Q. 9: 28–35 143
Q. 9: 30 123, 124, 125, 145, 147
Q. 9: 30–35 145
Q. 9: 31–34 164
Q. 9: 34–35 99, 111
Q. 9: 36 145, 157
Q. 9: 37 96, 102
Q. 9: 38 9, 145, 151
Q. 9: 38–42 145
Q. 9: 79 162
Q. 9: 81 146
Q. 9: 84 148
Q. 9: 88 152
Q. 9: 90 146
Q. 9: 98 146
Q. 9: 97–98 140
Q. 9: 99 147
Q. 9: 111 117
Q. 9: 113–114 123

Q. 10: 40 147
Q. 10: 46 118
Q. 10: 94 122, 130
Q. 10: 94–95 130

Q. 13: 40 118

Q. 14: 34 120

Q. 16: 78 56
Q. 16: 110 112
Q. 16: 115 119

Q. 17: 4–8 124
Q. 17: 76 9
Q. 17: 101 122

Q. 18: 35 120

Q. 19: 27 120
Q. 19: 34–40 122

Q. 20: 111 120

Q. 21: 8–21 119
Q. 21: 9 152

Q. 22: 17 122
Q. 22: 30 118
Q. 22: 38–48 128
Q. 22: 38–39 128, 129
Q. 22: 39–41 7
Q. 22: 40 114, 123

Q. 26: 197 122

Q. 29: 46 122, 169
Q. 29: 65 119

Q. 30: 2–7 3, 31, 172, 181, 197, 238
Q. 30: 21 56

Q. 31:31 151

Q. 32: 16 9

Q. 33: 6 132, 133
Q. 33: 40 84

Q. 36: 37 120

Q. 41: 86 122

Q. 42: 13 120

Q. 43: 57–61 120
Q. 43: 57–65 122

Q. 44: 30 152

Q. 46: 20 152

Q. 47: 4 132
Q. 47: 4–6 132

Q. 48: 15–20 139

Q. 49: 14–18 140

Q. 49: 14–15 140

Q. 53: 19–23 140

Q. 57: 11–18 117

Q. 59: 14 138

Q. 60: 8–9 137

Q. 61: 4 117

Q. 62: 9–11 7

Q. 64: 1 117
Q. 64: 17 117

Q. 96: 1–5 56

Q. 98: 6 129

Q. 105 42

Q. 113: 1–5 119

www.ingramcontent.com/pod-product-compliance
Lightning Source LLC
Chambersburg PA
CBHW052112010526
44111CB00036B/1891
* 9 7 8 0 7 5 5 6 3 8 0 3 1 *